ARCHAEOLOGY
OUTSIDE THE BOX

See page 233.

ARCHAEOLOGY
OUTSIDE THE BOX

EDITED BY
HANS BARNARD

UCLA COTSEN INSTITUTE OF ARCHAEOLOGY PRESS

Library of Congress Cataloging-in-Publication Data

Names: Society for American Archaeology. Annual Meeting (84th : 2019 : Albuquerque, N.M.) | Barnard, H., editor.
Title: Archaeology outside the box / edited by Hans Barnard.
Description: [Los Angeles, California] : Cotsen Institute of Archaeology Press, [2023] | Partial collection of papers presented during the Eighty-fourth Annual Meeting of the Society for American Archaeology held in Albuquerque, New Mexico in April 2019.
Identifiers: LCCN 2022056273 | ISBN 9781950446292 (hardback) | ISBN 9781950446322 (ebook)
Classification: LCC CC72.4 .S66 2023 | DDC 930.101--dc23/eng/20221129
LC record available at https://lccn.loc.gov/2022056273

CONTENTS

ILLUSTRATIONS

See page 45.

TABLES

See page 173.

CONTRIBUTORS

Emre Arolat
EAA–Emre Arolat Architecture

John Aycock
University of Calgary

Doug Bailey
San Francisco State University

Hans Barnard
University of California, Los Angeles

Valda Black
Washington State University

Reinhard Bernbeck
Free University of Berlin

Katie Biittner
MacEwan University

Gabriel Canter
Undocumented Migration Project

Bill Caraher
University of North Dakota

John F. Cherry
Brown University

Bonnie J. Clark
University of Denver

Filomena Cruz
Independent artist

Annie Danis
California Polytechnic University, Pomona

Jason De León
University of California, Los Angeles

Enrico Ferraris
Museo Egizio, Turin

David Fredrick
University of Arkansas

Jerzy Gawronski
Emeritus, University of Amsterdam

Cameron Gokee
Appalachian State University

Alfredo González-Ruibal
Institute of Heritage Sciences–Spanish National Research Council, Spain

Alice Gorman
Flinders University

Peter G. Gould
Indiana University Bloomington and DigVentures, Ltd.

Anthony P. Graesch
Connecticut College

Timothy Hartshorn
University of California, Irvine

Ian Kuijt
Notre Dame University

Danielle Kurin
Proyecto de Investigación Arqueológica Sondor

La Vergne Lehmann
University of Adelaide

Torill Christine Lindstrøm
University of Bergen

Beatriz Lizarraga
Universidad San Antonio Abad del Cusco

William Loder
University of Arkansas

Barra O'Donnabhain
University College Cork

Susan A. Phillips
Pitzer College

Ivanna Robledo
Texas State University, San Marcos

Gail Rothschild
Independent fine artist

Krysta Ryzewski
Wayne State University

Austin E. Shipman
Undocumented Migration Project

Robin Skeates
Durham University

Nicole Smith
University of California, Los Angeles

Haeden Stewart
University of Massachusetts Amherst

Ruth Tringham
University of California, Berkeley

Annelou van Gijn
Leiden University

Henk van Rensbergen
Airline pilot and photographer

Rhodora G. Vennarucci
University of Arkansas

Justin Walsh
Chapman University

Bret Weber
University of North Dakota

Willeke Wendrich
University of California, Los Angeles

Larry J. Zimmerman
Indiana University–Purdue University Indianapolis

Maite Zubiaurre
University of California, Los Angeles

ARCHAEOLOGY OUTSIDE THE BOX

AN INTRODUCTION

HANS BARNARD

The aim of this volume and all those who have contributed to it, in predictable as well as more unconventional ways, is to explore the edges of archaeology—and any *terra incognita* that may lie beyond—in an effort to make archaeology more germane, both inside and outside academia. Here I would first like to acknowledge archaeologist Ran Boytner PhD, without whom this chapter, or this volume, would ever have materialized. A cascade of events, which were and are interpreted differently by all involved, resulted in his absence from the final product, but that in no way diminishes his contribution in its creation. He conceived of the idea and organized the symposium that is at the basis of this volume during the Eighty-fourth Annual Meeting of the Society for American Archaeology, in Albuquerque, New Mexico, on 11 April 2019.

Our goal is to showcase projects and ideas that broaden the applicability of archaeology by either using innovative research avenues to reflect on archaeological remains in novel ways, or by using archaeological research methods and theory to address contemporary issues. By illustrating the fascinating and pertinent nature of archaeological research, we hope to take archaeology outside the box in which it seems too often placed by interested outsiders and at the same time investigate what constitutes that box and what we expect to gain from our exit. Many of the following chapters also provide arguments, albeit at times in lateral or whimsical ways, relevant to the soul-searching and existential discussions that are currently taking place within archaeology worldwide, further accelerated by the Black Lives Matter movement and the Covid-19 pandemic.[1]

Our primary intent is to address the interested general public, but we hope that our colleagues will also enjoy reading about projects and research that may be outside their usual fields of interest. We invite the former to feel free and ignore the references to the additional information and supporting literature provided in the endnotes and bibliography following each chapter.

THE STRATIGRAPHY OF THIS VOLUME

In archaeology, as in geology, history usually reveals itself in reverse order: the first layers exposed are the last to have been deposited, while the deepest layers are usually the oldest and encountered last. To reflect this phenomenon the alphabetical order in which the authors are listed below has been reversed in the table of contents. The chapters and pages are numbered as a stratigraphic sequence to emphasize the archaeological and at the same time unconventional character of this volume.[2] As each chapter stands on its own, it is eminently possible to pick and chose, and read them in any order.

This introduction is directly followed by a chapter by Willeke **Wendrich,** director of the Cotsen Institute of Archaeology at UCLA, in which she discusses the link between Lloyd Cotsen's last project and our efforts to free archaeology of some of its most pressing problems, including its historical connection to the European colonial enterprise and difficulties of being sufficiently inclusive. The remaining twenty-nine chapters in this volume cover a wide range of subjects and are arranged within the three broad themes. The eight chapters in the first part primarily discuss novel to outright unconventional approaches of ancient archaeological remains.

Emre **Arolat**, of EAA—Emre Arolat Architecture, discusses his work integrating a large building project in Antakya and the archaeological remains already present on the site. In his chapter he describes his personal journey into the field of archaeology and the resulting design and construction of a building seamlessly combining ancient and modern architectural elements.

David **Fredrick**, Rhodora G. **Vennarucci**, and William **Loder**, of the University of Arkansas, describe the various uses of a virtual reality model they created of Pompeii. Their model enables visitors to experience ancient Pompeii in ways that are not possible in modern times and at the same time allows scholars to study possible interactions between the city and its inhabitants.

Jerzy **Gawronski**, of the University of Amsterdam, discusses the narratives on the urban history of Amsterdam that can be extracted from material debris from the river Amstel found during the extension of the Amsterdam underground light railway system. The objects unearthed during this project range from ancient to modern. These were presented in a volume that received two awards and exhibited in unusual ways in order to reach a new and larger audience.

Peter G. **Gould**, of Indiana University (Bloomington) and DigVentures, Ltd., discusses the influence and possible benefits of contemporary capitalism on the field of archaeology. He proposes to engage the current turmoil in the world to bring archaeological ethics and practices together in new ways to facilitate archaeology making a real difference in the world.

Danielle **Kurin**, Valda **Black**, Beatriz **Lizarraga**, and Ivanna **Robledo**, of the University of California–Santa Barbara, Washington State University, Universidad San Antonio Abad del Cusco, and Texas State University–San Marcos, respectively, elaborate how the past and the present are intertwined in the Peruvian Andes. In their chapter they describe the Chanka people of south-central Peru who, far from being exterminated by the Inca or Colonial invaders, maintain a continuous cultural presence that permeates daily life in the region.

Torill Christine **Lindstrøm**, of the University of Bergen, uses research techniques from modern psychology to analyze Bronze Age wall paintings from Thera, Greece, exploring emotions, personalities, and values. Based on this, she explains the remarkable absence of large central administrative centers and the apt response to the Theran volcanic eruption during the Bronze Age, by the value placed on personal traits and responsibilities.

Robin **Skeates**, of Durham University, explores the sensory experience of ancient dwelling and landscapes, in particular the Su Cannisoni rock shelter on the island of Sardinia. He recognizes at least four benefits that sensory archaeology can bring to our understanding of the past: expanding the established scientific method, bringing together scholarly thought on memory and emotion, encouraging more full-bodied narratives of past people, and directing scholars to pay closer attention to the sensory experiences inherent to human behavior.

Finally, Annelou **van Gijn**, of the University of Leiden, describes the insights gained from the construction and destruction of dwellings that replicate those of the Neolithic Vlaardingen culture. In her chapter she presents her long-term experimental project to put human life into Neolithic houses and investigate in great detail domestic crafts and subsistence activities.

The fourteen chapters in the second part address the archaeology of the contemporary world and living memories.

John **Aycock** and Katie **Biittner**, of the University of Calgary and MacEwan University, respectively, introduce the archaeology of early video games. They argue that the inherent immateriality of these culturally increasingly important digital artifacts can make archaeogaming a bellwether for grappling with the current explosion of digital cultural artifacts.

Reinhard **Bernbeck**, of the Free University of Berlin, analyzes a single find from the excavations of a Nazi labor camp at Tempelhof Airfield in Berlin. The locket that is the focus of his chapter serves as a reminder of the separation of people by war and signals the pain at the loss of a memento. The object can bridge the time between deposit and excavation for us, but not for the former owner.

William **Caraher** and Bret **Weber**, of the University of North Dakota, provide an overview of their research of the temporary settlements of those working in the oil industry in the Bakken oil patch in North Dakota. Following the composition style of Lauren Berlant and Kathleen Stewart's book *The Hundreds* (2019) they combine hundred-word statements with images to reveal the material and social conditions of the Bakken oil patch in a dreamlike fashion.

Bonnie J. **Clark** and Ian **Kuijt**, of the University of Denver and Notre Dame University, respectively, narrate some of the stories of previous inhabitants of the Irish island of Inishark and the Second World War internment camp for Japanese Americans in Amache, Colorado. In their chapter they do not create a cautionary tale for archaeologists without access to the stories of things, but rather challenge all of us to imagine the importance and value of the mundane.

Alfredo **González-Ruibal**, of the Institute of Heritage Sciences at the Spanish National Research Council, analyzes a few of the objects found in the excavation of an archaeological site in Madrid dating to the Spanish Civil War (1936–39). He shows how this war radically altered the landscape, transforming an existing space of care and education into a machine for killing, modifications that last until today. At the same time he emphasizes the poetry of things.

Alice C. **Gorman** and Justin St. P. **Walsh**, of Flinders University and Chapman University, respectively, report on their necessarily mostly remote research of the objects that made their way onto the International Space Station and back. In their chapter they consider the space station as an example of human adaptation to gravity and the lack thereof. This may well be the beginning of a trajectory in which the social and material forms that appear to persist in radically different circumstances will reveal much about the nature of human existence.

Anthony P. **Graesch** and Timothy **Hartshorn**, of Connecticut College and the University of California–Irvine, respectively, describe what can be inferred from discarded cigarette ends, in particular those found in New London, Connecticut. They challenge the perceived triviality of discarded cigarettes by showcasing familiar analytic concepts that warrant an archaeological gaze and argue that cigarette discard is, as both a social practice and a material assemblage, culturally generative.

La Vergne **Lehmann**, of the University of Adelaide, analyzes modern kitchen waste in southeastern Australia. Unlike curbside garbage audits or studies of the secondhand market stream, she includes elements of behavioral science allowing for the methodologies of contemporary archaeology to be applied. While looking at what is coming out of the kitchen in this way it becomes possible to consider what is being consumed and which processes have occurred.

Barra **O'Donnabhain,** of University College Cork, confronts ideologies of whiteness in the discipline of archaeology through an examination of the origins of modern prison systems and the role that ideas of race played in that development. He suggests that individual archaeologists and the discipline as a whole need to examine hidden assumptions and unquestioned privileges that seep into narratives and frame research while creating and sustaining structural inequalities and rank injustice.

Susan A. **Phillips**, of Pitzer College, shows how place-based material expressions are layered in the past and the present through her research on graffiti in Los Angeles. In her chapter she describes graffiti as a massive global art movement, with an accompanying, powerful art market, but at the same time the center of citywide battles over spatial control. Combining cultural anthropological and archaeology she records often ignored images in their specific locations and social contexts to give a voice to those that created them.

Krysta **Ryzewski** and John F. **Cherry**, of Wayne State University and Brown University, respectively, report on their ongoing research on the volcanic island of Montserrat, mostly in the abandoned AIR Studios. They emphasize the role of archaeological research of these studies in examining the tensions between music as an ephemeral product and the desire of stakeholders to preserve the remains of the setting in which creative expressions were produced. At the same time, it is well suited to attract broad interest among non-professional audiences.

Nicole **Smith**, Gabriel **Canter**, Austin **Shipman**, Cameron **Gokee**, Haeden **Stewart**, and Jason **De León**, of Appalachian State University, the University of California–Los Angeles and the University of Massachusetts–Amherst, discuss their ongoing project to raise awareness about the death of migrants along the border between Mexico and the United States. In their chapter they demonstrate that explicating an archaeological sensibility in unexpected locations, such as a public exhibition, has the potential to introduce new audiences to the power of understanding ourselves and our shared human history.

Ruth **Tringham** and Annie **Danis**, of the University of California–Berkeley, describe their research and community interactions at Albany Bulb in the San Francisco Bay. They discuss the meaning of performances, the value of materials, and narratives of home to create a sustained, personal, and embodied reflection on what it means to throw things, histories, memories, or people away.

Larry J. **Zimmerman**, of Indiana University–Purdue University Indianapolis, reports on research of campsites of homeless people in Indianapolis and suggests how archaeology might change the negative narratives about homelessness and improve social services. He urges archaeologists to recognize a darker heritage, in which people are ignored or selectively edited out of narratives to make larger communities seem more palatable, challenge such existing narratives, and make useful recommendations to assist marginalized people.

The seven chapters in the third and final part of this volume address the intimate relation that humans have with the objects that they produce, use, and discard. A relationship that can span large expanses of time and space.

Doug **Bailey**, of San Francisco State University, discusses how the decommissioning and destruction of ancient and modern objects provoke questions about core tenets of archaeology. Merging archaeology with art, he does not call for more written treatises about what has come before, but instead calls to do, to make, to create, to explore, to experiment.

In the next two chapters I discuss my personal relationship with some of the objects around me. In my first exercise in autovocality I describe how at times narratives can lead to the creation of objects, rather than the more common reverse. In my second exercise in autovocality I describe how objects can fundamentally affect our being in the world, using my own collection and experience as a paradigm.

Enrico **Ferraris**, of Museo Egizio in Turin, discusses the temporary exhibition *Invisible Archaeology*, in particular the section in which contemporary objects present themselves in brief autobiographies. He shows how each object, whether ancient or contemporary, has its own unique and unrepeatable biography not ending with the age or civilization from which it originated. Objects connect those who produced them with those who observe them and museums continuously refine that contact.

Henk **van Rensbergen**, a Boeing 787 pilot and photographer, presents some of his photographs of deteriorating buildings, documenting the archaeology of our times in the making. Each of his photographs is accompanied by a brief written description.

Gail **Rothschild**, an independent fine artist, presents some of her large-scale paintings inspired by ancient textile fragments. Each of her paintings is accompanied by a brief written description.

Maite **Zubiaurre** and Filomena **Cruz**, of the University of California–Los Angeles and her alter ego, respectively, describe their ongoing community art project *The Wall that Gives/El muro que da* in Venice, California. They do not engage in archaeology *sensu strictu,* but the motivation behind creating *The Wall that Gives/El muro que da* was, and is, trash. It was born out of the imperious need to elevate and 'detrash' the discarded by making collages with *objets trouvés* and pictures of litter.

TRANSPARENT THINGS

The modern discipline of archaeology can be defined as the study of human development, relations, behavior, and history, as inferred from their material remains and those of the world around them (Figure 31.1). This is greatly facilitated by the fact that all objects created and used by humans intricately complement functionality with meaning.[3] This intimate relation between humans and the objects around them has considerable time-depth (Figure 31.2); it certainly also existed for Neanderthals *(Homo neanderthalensis* or *H. sapiens neanderthalensis),* the last of our close genetic relatives to go extinct.[4]

The careful study of objects can therefore reveal a wealth of information about their human owners, producers, and users. Such studies can focus on raw materials and production techniques, but also address function and use (wear and tear, molecular residues), taphonomy and diagenesis (processes affecting objects after they have been lost or discarded), and the inferred value and associated social status of the object to its maker or owner. The resulting data can be confronted with information about the context in which the object was found, as well as data on other objects from the same context and similar objects from different contexts. This often results in meaningful and reliable statements about the age of the object as well as the context in which it was found and, more broadly, about the cultural affiliation, social stratification, and stage of technological development of the associated human society at the time.

Well before archaeology was established as an academic discipline (Figure 31.2), ancient objects with a real or perceived intrinsic, aesthetic, or cultural value attracted attention and inspired later generations.[5] "The extraordinary stability of tools such as hand-axes over time (1.5 million years) and over space (Europe, Africa, Asia) could not have been an accident, nor due solely to inertia. . . . When manufacturing tools, the toolmaker would be making a sign as well as an instrument, and he would want his sign to say the same things as had the tools made by his predecessors."[6] The attachment of humans to objects without an immediately evident practical value seems demonstrated by the fossil of an *Aspa marginata* shell, the outside of which had been painted red with hematite. This was found in the Fumane Cave in northern Italy and brought there by a Neanderthal around 45,000 years ago, from at least 100 kilometers (60 miles) away. The pigment was collected at least 20 kilometers (12 miles) away and the painted shell likely served as personal adornment.[7]

A very similar, unequivocal example of the fundamental human connection with noticeable objects is the fossil of an Eocene sea urchin found between 1903 and 1906 in the Temple of Heliopolis in modern Cairo, Egypt. This object was inscribed with the text "Found to the south of Ik [an unidentified place south of Heliopolis] by the god's father [a priestly title] Tjanefer."[8] It was apparently collected during the Ramesside Period (1550–1350 BCE) and likely put on display in the temple as a meaningful object (Figure 31.3, top). Today, some 3,500 years later, it serves the same function in Museo Egizio in Turin, Italy. Greek and Roman temples likewise often contained exotic curiosities—which were usually retained when these temples were converted into Christian churches, such as at least six ancient Egyptian obelisks in Rome—while in early medieval cities like Baghdad and Cairo scientific instruments and manuscripts were collected, often as tribute or part of the spoils of war.

Among the earliest unambiguous evidence of inspiration taken from objects created by previous generations is a potsherd found in Tell Mozan, ancient Urkesh, in modern Syria.[9] This is a fragment of a bowl with a zig-zag decoration along its rim and the only example of this type dating to around 2100 BCE.

Figure 31.1. Human footprints preserved in a plaster layer in the foundation of the Great Aten Temple in Akhetaten (modern Tell al-Amarna), Egypt, provide a snapshot of a moment in time around 3,300 years ago (about 1350 BCE).

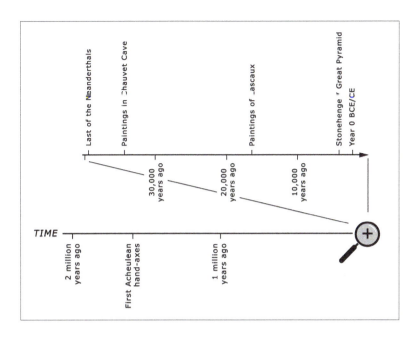

Figure 31.2. Timeline demonstrating the time-depth of human cultural history. Note that the Paleolithic paintings of Lascaux (southern France) are closer in time to the copies made in 1983 (Lascaux II), than they are to the paintings in Chauvet Cave (also in southern France). Similarly, the world today (at the tip of the arrow) is closer to Year 0 than either the monuments of Stonehenge or the Great Pyramid in Giza.

Figure 31.3. Fossil of a mid-Eocene sea urchin (*Echinolampas africanus*), likely collected and inscribed during the Ramesside Period (1550–1350 BCE), kept in Museo Egizio. Ninevite V bowl (left, around 2700 BCE) and a later bowl (right, around 2100 BCE) with imitated decoration. *Top: adapted from Karlshausen and De Putter 2017; bottom: courtesy of the International Institute for Mesopotamian Area Studies and the Mozan/Urkesh Archaeological Project, adapted from Kelly-Buccellati 2012, Figure 10.3.*

It appears that the potter at the time was inspired by potsherds with a similar decoration made about five hundred years earlier, during the Ninevite V period (around 2700 BCE), which can be found scattered across the site (Figure 31.3, bottom). Seen side by side, it is apparent that the clay and temper are different, but that the idea of the decoration was imitated from ancient artifacts and even executed with a similar toothed tool.

The pharaohs of the 25th Dynasty of ancient Egypt (750–650 BCE) entered and ruled Egypt from the Kingdom of Kush in modern Sudan. During their relatively short reign they revived old religious traditions and artistic styles, and restored many temples throughout Egypt. They also constructed a number of pyramids, most famously at Nuri in the upper Nile Valley (Figure 31.4, top). These were obviously inspired by the ancient Egyptian pyramids in Saqqara and Giza, built around 2550 BCE, about 1500 years earlier (Figure 31.2), and the small pyramids on some of the New Kingdom tombs on the west bank of the Nile near Luxor (approximately (1550–1050 BCE).

A few centuries later these new pyramids in turn inspired the kings of Meroë, farther south in Sudan, to construct their own pyramids in Meroë and Gebel Barkal (Figure 31.4, bottom).

Around the same time, King Nabonidus of Babylonia (556–539 BCE) reports on what can only be described as an archaeological excavation in the text on a clay cylinder found in Tell Abu Habbah, ancient Sippar, in modern Iraq (now kept in the British Museum, London).

> While I led [the god] Šamaš out of its midst [of his temple] and caused him to dwell in another sanctuary, I removed the debris of that temple, looked for its old foundation deposit, dug to a depth of eighteen cubits into the ground and then Šamaš, the great lord, revealed to me the original foundations of Ebabbar, the temple which is his favorite dwelling, by disclosing the foundation deposit of [King] Naram-Sin, son of Sargon, which no king among my predecessors had found in three thousand and two hundred years.

Princess Ennigaldi-Nanna, one of the daughters of Nabonidus, likely maintained a small museum in Ur, complete with clay labels for the objects on display.[10]

Similar proof of a deep interest in the material remains of the past is the evidence of tourists visiting the antiquities of Egypt in ancient times. Many of these left written testimony of their visit, such as Dadouchios, who around 250 CE wrote on one of the walls of the tomb of Pharaoh Ramses VI (KV9) in Luxor: "I, Dadouchios, scholar and physician, came and admired in silence bearing a torch." As the word for torch in the original Greek is *daidoukhos,* this graffito contains a pun on the name of its author. The most famous early tourist, however, may be Hadrian, who was emperor of the Roman Empire from 117 until 138 CE. In 130 CE he visited Egypt together with his lover Antinous, who died under mysterious circumstances during the trip. Following this dramatic event, Hadrian had Antinous deified and in his honor founded the city Antinoöpolis, modern Sheikh 'Abada, near the place of his death. Upon his return to Rome, Hadrian had a series of marble statues carved in a remarkable style which is a peculiar mix of Roman and Egyptian

elements. These are now on display in Room 3 (Villa Adriana) of Museo Gregoriano Egizio in the Vatican Museums in Rome.

The original Museum (House of the Muses) was founded around 280 BCE by Ptolemy I (Soter) and Ptolemy II (Philadelphus) in Alexandria, Egypt. It comprised the famous Library of Alexandria, lecture and banquet halls, living quarters for scholars, and gardens. This institution thus more resembled a university than a modern museum. In ancient Mesoamerica and China ancient manuscripts and objects likewise served as sources of inspiration for artisans and historians.[11] The famous Chinese historian Sima Qian, who wrote the monumental *Records of the Grand Historian*—a project initiated by his father Sima Tan—lived around 100 BCE during the Han Dynasty and used his collection of ancient objects, his visits to ancient sites, and his interviews with local elders to supplement his study of the written sources.[12]

However, throughout human history this interest in objects often deteriorated into their ethically questionable appropriation. In 1 Kings 14: 25–26, for instance, it is said that "it came to pass in the fifth year of king Rehoboam, that Shishak, king of Egypt [likely Shoshenq I, 940–925 BCE], came up against Jerusalem. And he took away the treasures of the house of the Lord, and the treasures of the king's house; he even took away all: and he took away all the shields of gold which Solomon had made" (translation from the King James Bible, repeated almost verbatim in 2 Chronicles 12: 9). A relief in the Arch of Titus, erected near the Roman Forum by Emperor Domitian, depicts the similar transport of valuable objects from Jerusalem to Rome in 70 CE by the victorious troops of Titus. The most important object in this collection, the gold lampstand from the temple (the Menorah), was not then melted down for its intrinsic value, but rather put on display in the Temple of Peace because of its cultural and symbolic meaning.

The Ottoman Empire likewise accumulated a vast collection of jewelry, works of art, and precious objects by transporting them from conquered regions to its capital Istanbul—the city previously known as Byzantium and Constantinople—which had been conquered by the Ottoman Sultanate in 1453. Six years later its conqueror, Sultan Mehmed II, started the

Figure 31.4. Some of the 25th Dynasty pyramids (750–650 BCE) at Nuri (top), and some of the Meroitic pyramids (250–0 BCE) at Gebel Barkal (bottom), both in modern Sudan.

construction of what is now known as Topkapi Palace, but originally called Yeni Saray (New Palace). One of the buildings of the palace complex is the Conqueror's Kiosk, designed to house the growing imperial treasury. After the dissolution of the Ottoman Empire in 1923, the palace was transformed into a public museum, of which the treasury in the Conqueror's Kiosk is one of the main attractions.

This often forceful collection of objects of archaeological, biological, ethnographic, geological, historical, paleontological, or religious interest by individuals or groups with the power to do so is described in almost all human societies. It did occur at an unprecedented scale, however, during the European colonization of large parts of the world between 1500 and 1950. Modern museums, whimsically and not entirely accurately named after the Ptolemaic institution in Alexandria, grew out of the *Wunderkammer*s and cabinets of curiosities established by the increasingly wealthy aristocrats and merchants of sixteenth- and seventeenth-century Europe.[13] Initially driven by Renaissance curiosity—ultimately resulting in severing the reliance on ancient written sources and instead stimulating personal observations and experiments—and the colonial enterprise—which provided increasing access to a plethora of rich, exotic, and fascinating sources—these collections were later arranged to create narratives and presented to the general public. This was mostly driven by the humanistic ideals of the Enlightenment to use the spread of knowledge and education to eliminate repression and superstition.[14] This made them prominent features in the development of the modern natural sciences—including anthropology, archaeology, biology, ethnography, geology, and paleontology—and indirectly also the Industrial Revolution.

During the nineteenth century, European museums developed into institutions primarily serving national interests. These celebrated the nation state, justified its colonial projects, and maintained a narrative of cultural and ethnic superiority. European practices were more or less replicated in North America and can in an amended form currently be seen in the Gulf states, several of which are housing expanding collections of precious foreign objects in impressive buildings such as the Louvre Abu Dhabi, the Museum of Islamic Art in Doha,

and the Sheikh Abdullah al-Salem Cultural Centre in Kuwait. Archaeology was perceived as another tool for the acquisition of objects of museum quality or ancient texts in the form of manuscripts or inscriptions.[15] It was often combined with the trade in antiquities, with objects moving from one domain into the other, often without sufficiently clear records being kept. Remnants of these early modern practices are still traceable within modern archaeology or influence the perception of the discipline, especially in the eyes of those not intimately familiar with the ongoing changes and developments of the field.

Others chose a more systematic approach, most notably Heinrich Schliemann (1822–90), August Lane-Fox Pitt-Rivers (1827–1900), W.M. Flinders Petrie (1853–1942), and R.E. Mortimer Wheeler (1890–1976). This nascent scholarly specialty also included relatively many women, among whom Sara Yorke Stevenson (1847–1921), Margaret Murray (1863–1963), Edith Hayward Hall Dohan (1877–1943), Gertrude Caton-Thompson (1888–1985), Dorothy Garrod (1892–1968), and Anna Osler Shepard (1903–71). With notable exceptions, the explanations and interpretations that they formulated for their observations were often based on the misinterpreted evolutionary theories and racially prejudiced views of the time, most recognizably by Karl R. Lepsius (1810–84) and George A. Reisner (1867–1942), albeit among many others.

Around the beginning of the twentieth century, practitioners aimed to place archaeology on a more theoretical foundation, a movement largely driven by Gustaf Kossinna (1858–1931), Franz U. Boas (1858–1942), and V. Gordon Childe (1892–1957). They set out to explain the past from its material remains by logical (inductive) reasoning, partly forced to do so because of a lack of methods to determine the age of objects, or even their exact material composition. The resulting field of culture-historical archaeology focused mostly on cultures and the main events in the history of humanity such as enduring cultures and empires, the Neolithic revolution, and early state development.

Some fifty years later, Philip Phillips (1900–94), Gordon R. Willey (1913–2002), and Lewis Binford (1931–2011) promoted a different approach, which they called New Archaeology, but was subsequently labeled processual archaeology by their academic opponents. They interpreted human culture and history as the result of sets of behavioral processes, which can be studied using anthropological methods, supplemented by techniques borrowed from the natural sciences, most importantly radio-carbon dating and material analysis, fields initiated by Willard F. Libby (1908–80) and Alfred Lucas (1867–1945), respectively. New Archaeology primarily focuses on daily life and the differences between ethnic groups. These developments rendered the information that can be inferred from objects more important than the objects themselves and made archaeology not about finding things, but rather about finding things out.[16]

Towards the end of the twentieth century it was pointed out that archaeology cannot be classified as a science, as it cannot have its foundation in controlled, repeatable experiments. It is obviously not possible to turn back time, change one or more parameters, and observe how events unfurl under these new conditions. Furthermore, as archaeologists necessarily destroy the evidence as they collect the data on which they base their inferences, the process of data collection cannot be replicated and tested as it would be in the natural sciences. The consequences of this realization were taken into account by Ian Hodder, Rosemary Joyce, Lynn Meskell, Bruce G. Trigger, Christopher Tilley, Ruth Tringham, and others, when they developed post-processual archaeology, a name reflecting the wider intellectual movement of postmodernism at the time. Among the main components of post-processual archaeology are multi-vocality—giving a voice to all individuals, past and present, who feel a connection with the ancient remains—and the ethics of archaeology.

The struggle between processual and post-processual archaeology was once fierce, but over time varying combinations of elements of the two schools of thought made twenty-first century archaeology into the most humanistic branch of the sciences and the most scientific branch of the humanities. This volume aims to add to this ongoing development by demonstrating the value of archaeological research, insights, and methods to address contemporary concerns.[17] At the same time, we hope to address some of the issues resulting from the checkered history of the field.

Like all other scholars, we do so standing on the shoulders of the giants who have deployed similar initiatives before us. These can roughly be divided into three groups, each with its own central focal point. First are those aiming to bridge the divide between processual and post-processual archaeology more formally or develop a new theoretical framework.[18] Second is the expansion of archaeology, its theories, and its methodologies into contemporary times.[19] Third and final are those addressing the problematic remnants from the history of archaeology itself and developing new attitudes and practices.[20]

The separation between these three groups is as imprecise as the references above and below are incomplete. Additional points of attention and references can be found throughout the chapters in this volume. Furthermore, specialists in other fields increasingly incorporate data or methods from archaeology into their own work, including artists, criminologists, geologists, historians, neuroscientists, philosophers, and sociologists.[21]

Recent developments within archaeology and society as a whole, briefly touched upon in the paragraphs above, have made the relationship between archaeologists and the objects they study increasingly ambiguous. Objects are central to archaeological research, but are at the same time associated with significant issues. Some of these issues are of a practical, others of a more fundamental nature. As soon as an object is excavated or otherwise retrieved, issues of ownership manifest themselves. Archaeologists usually no longer claim ownership of the objects that they unearth, but rights to keep or display them are often disputed between the owner of the land or the site, the local community, and the local, regional, and national authorities. Other parties to get involved may include descendant communities and international organizations considering selected objects world heritage. Such disputes can escalate when objects are inherently valuable, such as those made of precious metals; attractive to museums and private collectors; or appear historically and culturally significant, such as those bearing inscriptions.[22] Ownership also comes with responsibilities, including appropriate storage and timely conservation or restoration. The costs of these can far outweigh the monetary value of the object.

The possession of ancient objects can be demonstrably illegal or obviously unethical; however, in most cases issues of ownership are much less clear. For instance, many of the ancient objects excavated or on display in museums around the world were grave gifts, objects specifically meant for a deceased individual to use in the afterlife and thus never intended to change ownership ever again or return to the world of the living. If we acknowledge that the dead can still own objects, nobody can rightfully claim ownership of such objects. If we instead understand the dead to be bereaved of such rights, the ownership of their belongings can and often does become a matter of passionate debate.

One can of course argue that the finder of objects is their rightful owner—as applies to certain cases of the salvage of shipwrecks in international waters—or that they instead belong to the lawful owner of the land, as is usually the case for natural or mineral resources. For archaeological objects, however, these solutions are frequently not considered sufficient or acceptable. These are instead often claimed by regional or national governments or groups of individuals that experience a connection to the ancient owners, usually local stakeholders or descendant communities. Apart from the question whether ownership of objects should be considered a genetic property, it remains difficult to assess how deep into the past this extends. Were the images in the cave of Lascaux painted around fifteen thousand years ago by remote ancestors of the French, or did the genealogical lines fade enough over time to make these two groups as closely related as any other two groups of humans? The same question can be asked about the monument at Stonehenge, built around 4,500 years ago and thus in time much closer to us than to the paintings in Lascaux, which in turn are closer to us than to the paintings in the cave of Chauvet, also in southern France (Figure 31.2). This issue gets increasingly complicated as time spans decrease, and especially for more or less moveable objects, many of which have changed hands several times, often at great expense of money or human suffering. These transactions furthermore frequently lack accurate records of the chain of custody.

An illustrative example of this is the Nebra sky disk, an ancient bronze disk found by treasure hunters in 1999 in the Ziegelroda Forest near Leipzig, Germany. The disk had been decorated with pieces of gold, which appeared to have been attached at different times. Their shapes are generally interpreted to represent a full moon (or the sun), a crescent moon (or a solar eclipse), a cluster of stars, and three enigmatic objects. The disk is likely associated with the Bronze Age Unetice culture, dating to around 1600 BCE. After being unearthed the disk was sold several times, at vastly increasing prices, until it was appropriated by the authorities. The two men who unearthed it were apprehended and as part of a plea agreement revealed where they had found the disk, together with a number of other ancient objects. The disk is now kept in the Landesmuseum für Vorgeschichte, the archaeological museum of the German state of Saxony-Anhalt in Halle (Saale), and was included in the UNESCO Memory of the World Register in 2013 as one of the most important archaeological finds of the twentieth century.

The recent history of the Nebra sky disk above is rather typical for an ancient object of great value and significance, but what is less common is that the state of Saxony-Anhalt proceeded to claim the copyrights of the disk and won two court cases preventing others from using its imagery. After these rulings were overturned by higher courts, the state registered the disk imagery as a trademark with the Intellectual Property Office of the European Union. Even though the disk is around 3,500 years old and considered world heritage, the desire of the museum to claim ownership to this extent is illustrative of the human craving to possess splendid or meaningful objects. Many similar examples can be found, often further complicated by painful vestiges of colonial history.

In Egypt, the narrative from ancient times onward has always been one of continuity. Pharaohs and other rulers legitimized their position of power by claiming that it was handed down to them from the past. Among their main responsibilities when in power was to maintain order in the world, including the daily rising of the sun and the yearly flooding of the fields by the Nile. This ideology of continuity, or rather a fabricated continuity, convinced many early Egyptologists and still most visitors to the country today. That the ideology is still alive was evident in the large event in April 2021 surrounding the move of twenty-two royal mummies (eighteen kings and four queens who ruled Egypt between 1550 and 1100 BCE) from the Museum of Egyptian Antiquities on Tahrir Square to the newly built National Museum of Egyptian Civilization, near Fustat, which was the first capital of Egypt under Muslim rule between 641 and 750 CE, centered around the still active mosque of 'Amr Ibn al-'As, the first mosque in Egypt. After being paraded through Cairo, the mummies were welcomed into their new home by Abdel Fattah al-Sisi, the current president of Egypt, standing straight, all alone at the raised entrance of the museum. This clearly meant to demonstrate both the legitimacy of his position, as a direct descendant of the ancient rulers, and his physical and mental strength.

In contradiction to these narratives, the religion, language, culture, economy, genetic composition, geography, and climate of Egypt have changed continuously. This raises the question whether the people currently living in the region should indeed be considered the descendants and heirs of the Egyptians who lived during the Old Kingdom (2700–2200 BCE), and how either of these groups relate to those that lived in Egypt during the New Kingdom. It is difficult to comprehend the vast expanses of time involved (Figure 31.2). If we imagine going back from today to the day we were born, to 1000 CE, and then Year 0, and then the same amount of time back again, the Old Kingdom had already come to an end, and the pyramids in Giza were already almost five hundred years old. Directly related to this is the question of how long objects can be considered associated with the local population and at which point in time they should be considered the heritage of humanity as a whole. "Although this formulation [of ancient object being world heritage], which embodies many of the universalist ideas of the Enlightenment, will not please those relativists who would maintain that every group should be free to do what it wants with its own heritage, it reflects the reality of the modern world, in which the whole of humanity is becoming inextricably interrelated."[23]

Finally, ownership comes with responsibilities as well as privileges. Responsibilities include preservation, housing, conservation, and restoration; among the privileges are opportunities to amend their meaning, form, or function, as well as to decommission or even completely destroy them. Instances of iconoclasm and *damnatio memoriae,* both intended to alter history retroactively, are attested throughout human history and invariably involve modifying or destroying material objects. In 1951 the head and body of a more than life-size statue were found during the excavation of the foundation layers of the first–second century CE Temple of Baalshamin in Hatra (modern al-Hadr in Iraq). The statue could be identified by an Aramaic inscription on its pedestal reading: "The image of King Uthal, the merciful, noble-minded servant of God, blessed by God."[24] After extensive restoration the statue was put on display in the nearby Mosul Museum.

In February 2015 the statue was again destroyed, along with many other artifacts kept in the museum, this time not by disgruntled subjects of the king or invading armies, but by Islamic extremists who considered it a pagan idol and proudly posted video footage of their destructive activities online. These events caused outrage in Europe and the United States, fueled by concerns for the destruction of world heritage, but also by anti-Islamic sentiments and by the availability of modern media. The statue of King Uthal became a symbol of the destruction of the Mosul Museum, and using existing imagery artist Morehshin Allahyari created the digital files necessary to print a three-dimensional copy of the statue.[25] These were subsequently widely circulated, and printed versions were part of larger exhibitions in Toronto, Canada (Trinity Square Video, February–March 2016) and Turin, Italy (Museo Egizio, March–September 2018).

The statue of King Uthal was destroyed and restored twice by its *de facto* owners, albeit lastly the owners of just digital imagery of the statue. The footage of the final destruction, however, is eerily similar to the footage of civil rights activists toppling and destroying "The Boys Who Wore Gray" (Durham, NC) and "Silent Sam" (Chapel Hill, NC)—in August 2017 and 2018, respectively—because they were convinced that these statues represented an objectionable history or philosophy. Different than the fragments of the statue of King Uthul, however, the fragments of these statues were removed from their original location and placed in storage away from public access or view. Scientific and scholarly enterprises should obviously not be without reflection on humanistic values and ethical norms, and the differences and similarities between these two cases, serving as a paradigm for many more, warrant many more and more dispassionate discussions between all stakeholders.

If ultimately the choice is made to restore what has been destroyed, it remains to be decided which stage in the history of the objects is to be aimed for.[26] If this is the stage just before the final destruction, restoration will necessarily have to include replicating the damage done by time and previous generations. Alternatively, the decision can be made to restore objects as they appeared just after being completed. This would, however, deny them their history and raise the question why not to paint and dress most ancient statues.[27] This would go against all modern aesthetic sentiments and most certainly raise considerable resistance.

These issues were eloquently summarized by Willem-Alexander, King of the Netherlands, in a recorded speech explaining why the newly restored Golden Coach would remain retired for the foreseeable future. Between 1903 and 2015 this coach was used during the annual opening of the parliamentary year. Its side panels were painted by Nicolaas van der Waay (1855–1936), the one on the left showing tribute being brought from the Dutch colonies at the time.

Our history contains much to be proud of. At the same time, it also offers learning material for recognizing mistakes and avoiding them in the future. We cannot rewrite the past. We can try to come to terms with it together. This also applies to the colonial past. There is no point in condemning and disqualifying what has happened through the lens of our time. Simply banning historical objects and symbols is certainly not a solution either. Instead, it takes a concerted effort that goes deeper and lasts longer. An effort that unites us rather than divides us. . . . Listening to and understanding each other are essential conditions for achieving reconciliation and taking away pain in people's souls. I know that we can do it, even if it is a long and difficult road."[28]

One way to approach this quandary is to create digital, virtual-reality reconstructions of objects and sites,[29] allowing users to travel through space and time to appreciate various iterations. This at the same time renders the actual state of preservation and physical location of the objects less relevant.

Every decision to create, modify, decommission, restore, or destroy any object is necessarily consciously or subconsciously based upon more or less transient opinions, religious beliefs, or political convictions. The actual choices made and actions taken are what archaeologists ultimately study and reflect upon. We study these objects as they come down to us through time, with all the marks and scars that history bestowed upon them. Much relevant information is actually in such blemishes, rather than in surfaces that are unscathed and pristine. To conclude and circle back to the title above this section: "When we concentrate on a material object, whatever its situation, the very act of attention may lead to our involuntary sinking into the history of the object. . . . Transparent things, through which the past shines!" (Vladimir Nabokov, 1972, *Transparent Things,* Chapter 1).

In the above paragraphs I have provided a very brief overview of this volume and the history of archaeology, from well before this term was coined, and how the latter created the confines that the modern discipline all too often finds itself in. The issues afflicting past and present-day archaeology are now passionately debated and at times heavily criticized, to the extent that this threatens to create a new, confining box that may limit our interpretative framework, in a way not dissimilar to the intense discussions between processual and post-processual archaeologists at the end of the twentieth century. Many of these complex issues are touched upon in the chapters in this volume, as well as by the authors in some of their other publications, and by many of those that they make reference to.

In the remainder of this chapter I will go beyond a veritable introduction to this volume and aim to place two of the more pressing issues in a wider perspective. In the section "The Time Machine" I examine our efforts to come to terms with the colonial history of the discipline, and modern societies in general. In the section "Crime and Punishment" I discuss the ongoing and necessary evaluation and judgment of the opinions and behavior of practitioners of archaeology, both past and present. The sections below reflect my personal opinions, based on my individual experiences and observations, and necessarily suffer from an incomplete dataset and my particular biases. To create a framework, I will start with three parables, none of which I can claim as my own creation.

THE TIME MACHINE

Imagine making scrambled eggs for breakfast. You break two eggs in a pan with melting butter and when the eggs start coagulating you begin stirring. After a short while, you stop briefly to change hands or to adjust the heat (up or down, they are after all your eggs and your mental imagery). As you resume your stirring the eggs become liquid again and separate back into whites and yolks (Figure 31.5). Although there are no superficial reasons why this can only occur in your imagination, we all know intuitively that this will never actually happen in the world around us.

The thought-experiment above is widely used by physics and chemistry teachers to demonstrate entropy, the second law of thermodynamics, or the denaturation of proteins. Without going into the scientific or philosophical nuances, of which there are many, I use it here to illustrate the irreversibility of time, or rather of the events that take place over the course of history. It is obviously impossible to turn back time or to undiscover, uninvent, or even unthink things, at least on a human timescale.[30] What is, however, eminently possible is to alter a course of events, at the very least at a personal level. You can decide to add black pepper or parsley to your scrambled eggs (or both, or neither) and serve them on a slice of toasted sourdough bread or in a buttered bun, among a myriad other

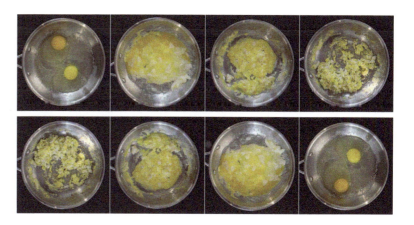

Figure 31.5. The scrambling (top) and un-scrambling (bottom) of two eggs. The sequence at the bottom never occurs in our daily experience.

options. You cannot, however, decide to unscramble and poach them instead.

In 1492, the year that both the Jews and the Arabs were ejected from the Iberian Peninsula, Cristoforo Colombo (now generally referred to as Columbus), a Genoan navigator working for the Spanish crown, led three small vessels from Spain to the islands of Cubao (Cuba) and Ayiti (Hispaniola), sailing across the Atlantic Ocean for the first time since the Vikings briefly settled in L'Anse aux Meadows in Newfoundland, Canada, about five hundred years earlier. Columbus would more or less safely repeat this crossing three times to explore the Caribbean region (Figure 31.6), until returning to Spain for the last time in 1504. These voyages had dramatic consequences.[31] From the newly established Spanish outposts in the Caribbean, the Aztec Empire in Mesoamerica was conquered by about five hundred men, led by Hernán Cortés, between 1519 and 1521. This was followed, between 1532 and 1572, by the conquest of the Inka Empire in South America by Francisco Pizarro heading about 150 men.

The subsequent exchange of goods, animals, and people—first with Europe and, after establishing the Manila–Acapulco galleon trade from 1565 onward, also with Asia—resulted in the mixing of the plant and animal species that evolved in isolation

Figure 31.6. On his fourth and last journey from the Old World to the Americas and back (1502–04) Columbus sailed along this stretch of the coast of Mesoamerica.

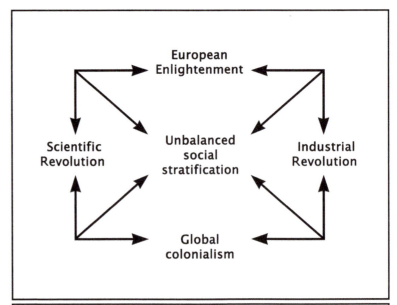

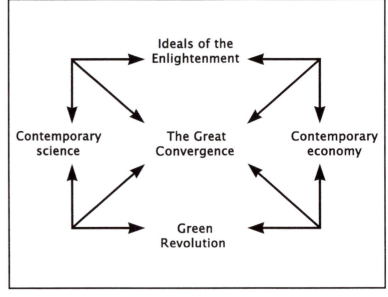

Figure 31.7. Very schematic overview of some of the entangled processes resulting in our modern world between around 1650 and 1950 (top), and since around 1950 (bottom). *Top: after Berlin 1979; Horkheimer and Adorno 1972; bottom: after Mahbubani 2013; Pinker 2018; Radelet 2015.*

since tectonic movement separated the continents around 150 million years earlier. Within two hundred years this so-called Columbian Exchange firmly established maize (corn), potatoes, tomatoes, and turkeys in the Old World, as well as cattle, horses, rice, wheat, and barley in the Americas, among many other plant and animal species. Next to such domesticated species, which were actively transplanted by humans, this exchange also included weeds, non-domesticated animals, traveling as stowaways, and pathogens affecting plants, animals, as well as humans. Immaterial but equally important changes include the spread across the globe of Christianity, in all its different varieties, as well as Indo-European languages, most notably English and Spanish, often completely replacing existing languages and religions. The most deplorable and disruptive aftermath was the trans-Atlantic slave trade, which between 1502 and 1859 disrupted societies on both sides of the Atlantic Ocean and gave rise to immeasurable human suffering the effects of which still very much reverberate today.

Irrespective of the many and complex moral and ethical aspects of these events, the question can be posed why the trip across the Atlantic Ocean was first made from east to west, and not in the opposite direction. In other words, why did Spanish vessels sail to Cuba and Hispaniola before Aztec vessels arrived in, for instance, Ireland or Portugal?[32] Furthermore, how could such small and unruly groups of adventurers subdue established powerful empires,[33] and why did the arrival, around the same time, of European vessels in China, India, Indonesia, and Japan lead to markedly different chains of events? Contact between what are now referred to as the Old World and the Americas, and the subsequent exchange of plant and animal species as well as cultures were likely inevitable, given the story of humanity, and would also have occurred without the voyages of Columbus. It is obviously impossible to envision when and how this would have happened, or what the world could have looked like, nor if the events as they actually happened represent the worst or the best possible outcome. It remains a valuable scholarly exercise, however, to investigate the structures and mechanisms responsible for the events as they did happen (Figure 31.7). At first the developing colonial enterprise was justified rather than explained by economic and geopolitical motives, although these concepts and terms did not exist at the time.

Early on, contact with leaders and thinkers in sub-Saharan Africa and the Americas had a profound influence on intellectual developments in Europe.[34] Combined with the dramatic increase in the institutionalization, globalization, and ruthlessness of the European colonial effort—progressively justified with racist arguments—world affairs were drawing more and more criticism from religious and ethical thinkers. Among the first and most often quoted is Jean-Jacques Rousseau (1712–78), one of the main actors within the European Enlightenment, who begins his comment on human society *Du contrat social; ou Principes du droit politique* (1762) by stating: "Man is born free, yet everywhere he is in chains." Two decades earlier, philosopher of politics Montesquieu (Charles-Louis de Secondat, 1689–1755) had written in *De l'esprit des loix* (1748) that "the state of slavery is in its own nature bad" (15.1), and later in the same volume expresses the hope that "there is not that climate upon earth where the most laborious services might not with proper encouragement be performed by freemen" (15.8). Many others were publicly critical of the human tragedies resulting from the international trade, capitalism, and colonialism of their days, including parliamentarian James E. Oglethorpe (1696–1785), philosopher Denis Diderot (1713–84), bishop Beilby Porteus (1731–1809), civil servant Granville Sharp (1735–1813) and deacon Thomas Clarkson (1760–1846). In 1839 Pope Gregory XVI issued papal bull *In supremo apostolatus* in which the Roman Catholic church resolutely denounces slavery and the slave trade. One of many visualizations of this point of view is the powerful and controversial painting *Slavers Throwing Overboard the Dead and Dying—Typhoon Coming On* (1840) by J.M. William Turner (1775–1851), now on display in the Museum of Fine Arts in Boston. After Charles Darwin published his theory of natural selection as the reason behind the origin of species in 1859, his insights were used as the foundation of a simplistic evolutionary rationalization of the *status quo.*

The third parable starts around 2010 when Joseph Henrich, Steven Heine, and Ara Norenzayan noted that many of the accepted paradigms of cognitive science, psychology, and economics varied considerably among different cultural and ethnic groups.[35] Their explanation is that much of the experimental research in these fields uses subjects recruited from students at universities in the United States and Europe. The large majority of these are from a single specific cultural background, whimsically identified as Western, educated, industrialized, rich, and democratic, or in short WEIRD (explicitly not intended to convey negative connotations or moral judgment). Repeating the same research outside the usual environment, for instance among native inhabitants of Oceania or parts of Africa (rather awkwardly referred to as "traditional societies"), revealed that human opinions and behavior depend much more on cultural backgrounds than previously acknowledged.

An example of two questions that reveal such fundamental differences is given in Table 31.1,[36] illustrated in Figure 31.8. Based on the information provided, most people with a WEIRD

Figure 31.8. How bad would it be if you took this bag (Table 31.1.)?

Scenario 1	Scenario 2
Two men, Bob and Andy, who did not know each other, were at a very busy outdoor market. There were lots of people. It was very crowded and there was not much room to walk through the crowd.	Two men, Rob and Andy, who did not know each other, were at a very busy outdoor market. There were lots of people. It was very crowded and there was not much room to walk through the crowd.
Andy was walking around and stopped to look at some items on display, placing the bag that he was carrying on the ground. Bob noticed Andy's bag on the ground.	Rob was walking around and stopped to look at some items on display, placing the bag that he was carrying on the ground. Another very similar bag was sitting right next to Rob's bag. This bag was owned by Andy, whom Rob did not know.
While Andy was distracted, Bob leaned down, picked up Andy's bag and walked away with it.	When Rob turned to pick up his bag, he accidentally picked up Andy's bag and walked away with it.
How good or bad was it what Bob did? - VERY BAD - BAD - NEITHER GOOD NOR BAD - GOOD - VERY GOOD	How good or bad was it what Rob did? - VERY BAD - BAD - NEITHER GOOD NOR BAD - GOOD - VERY GOOD

Table 31.1. Two scenarios that may reveal fundamental differences in the appreciation of events between individuals from Europe or the United States ("WEIRD" societies) and individuals from "traditional" societies. *Adapted from Henrich 2020, 49, Figure 31.8.*

background consider what Bob did in Scenario 1 as "very bad," and what Rob did in Scenario 2 as "neither good nor bad." Individuals with a different background, for instance those that grew up in Yasawa Island (Fiji), do not consider the scenarios too different, ranking both equally bad (or good). The explanation suggested is that those born and raised in Europe silently assume that they can somehow assess what made Bob and

Rob do what they did; that they can have knowledge about their thoughts or motives, which of course they ultimately cannot. Those born and raised in Oceania primarily consider the outcome, which represents a controllable fact (Andy lost his bag to either Bob or Rob). The mechanisms and reasons behind this simple fact are considered less relevant, also because they will necessarily remain hidden.

Two other notable differences are the readiness to donate blood for the benefit of anonymous strangers, which is significant in WEIRD societies and decreases with increasing

Figure 31.9. Left: how likely are you to donate blood for the benefit of anonymous strangers? Right: would you park here any time and not pay the fine?

WEIRD societies	"Traditional" societies
Bilateral descent	Patrilineal or matrilineal descent
No marriage with relatives	Intermarriage
Monogamous marriages	Polygamous marriages, often arranged
Neolocal	Patrilocal or matrilocal
Nuclear family societies	Kin-group societies
Mono- or atheistic	Ancestral rituals
Limited connection to place	Connection to place and history
Binary gender definitions	Gender fluidity
Emphasis on mental states	Emphasis on results of behaviors
Individual freedom	Strong social ties
Low conformity to traditions	Strong traditions
Guilt over shame	Shame over guilt
Cooperation with strangers	Distrust of strangers
Low in-group favoritism	High in-group favoritism
Analytical over holistic thinking	Holistic over analytical thinking

Table 31.2. General characteristics of Western-educated-industrialized-rich-democratic (WEIRD) versus "traditional" societies. After *Henrich 2020*.

proportions of cousin marriages used as an indicator for traditional societies,[37] illustrated in Figure 31.9, left. A second example is the relationship between behavior and cultural background when analyzing the inclination of diplomats from different countries to the United Nations in New York to pay their parking fines, which is voluntary as the city cannot enforce payment because of the protections provided by a diplomatic status,[38] illustrated in Figure 31.9, right. Diplomats with a WEIRD upbringing appear much more willing to do so voluntarily than those with another background.

Based on a plethora of similar research, Henrich inferred a number of properties associated with WEIRD and traditional societies (Table 31.2).[39] Whereas Jared Diamond (1997) explains the course of history mostly by differences in the natural environment—including the largest expanse of different climatic zones on different continents and the presence or absence of sizable, yet navigable bodies of water—Henrich identifies these difference in culture as the main reason. He surmises that the long-term focus of European Christianity on both monogamy between unrelated partners and written traditions resulted in a culture different from that in most other regions in the world. Over the centuries this made European society increasingly organize itself around neolocal nuclear families while becoming progressively literate. This resulted in a tendency toward independent thinking and cooperation with strangers, and ultimately the European Enlightenment, which was profoundly influenced by non-European thinkers,[40] the Scientific Revolution, the Industrial Revolution and the Green Revolution (Figure 31.7), but also in global colonialism, until about 1950, followed by the Great Convergence.[41]

Next to large-scale disruption and great suffering, the colonial enterprise also spread the "weird" ideals of the Enlightenment across large parts of the world, which ultimately resulted in a significant reduction of human sacrifice, child marriage, public torture executions, nepotism, lawlessness, and irrationality. In many places these were substituted, albeit often belated and incompletely, with water and food security, the rule of law, and evidence-based medicine. During the last century these developments were complimented by efforts to replace child labor with universal education, as well as the introduction and growing accessibility of a myriad previously unimaginable yet life-changing inventions, including cars, washing machines, oral contraceptives, televisions, airplanes, and cellphones.

The above three parables may serve to illustrate that the communal values related to parking tickets being paid, as a proxy for belief in the rule of law, blood being donated, as a proxy for indiscriminate altruism, and bags remaining with their owners, as a proxy for generalized empathy, were integral to the ideals of the European Enlightenment which resulted from and were disseminated across the world by the colonial enterprise. This happened because of an intricate array of complex reasons that remain difficult to impossible to untangle. Finally, time cannot be reversed, nor can historical events be undone, and even if this were somehow possible the question remains if we really want to.

The course of history as it happened resulted in the Columbian exchange, the trans-Atlantic slave trade, the Jewish Holocaust, and the atomic bombs that destroyed Hiroshima (6 August 1945) and Nagasaki (9 August 1945), among many other deplorable outcomes, including the irretrievable loss of many non-European languages, cultures, and knowledge. On the other hand, it gave rise to contemporary society, science, and technology, including sophisticated production techniques for food and increasingly complex devices, expedient transportation technology, as well as modern medicine, education and communication. Efforts for change should focus on global actions to mitigate the deteriorating environment and climate, conflicts, and social injustice—including poverty, inequality,

and racism—which require strengthening and implementation of the insights and ideals of the Enlightenment (Figure 31.7), rather than abandoning them. We have to accept and come to terms with the fact that they were part of global colonialism, similar to the way in which, for instance, the Spanish language established itself in large parts of the Americas, and Christianity took hold in sub-Saharan Africa. These new and constantly changing arrangements cannot be unscrambled (Figure 31.5).

Criticism of the Enlightenment goes back to its very origin in the mid-eighteenth century, partly because neither its start and end points nor its goals were ever clearly defined. The ideals of the Enlightenment, however, are unquestionably based on a faith in science, humanity, and progress. They are enshrined, for instance, in the national mottos of countries as diverse as France (Liberté, Égalité, Fraternité) and Brazil (Ordem e Progresso). One important expression of these ideals is the all-inclusive dissemination of knowledge and the power associated with it. From the Encyclopédie of Denis Diderot (1713–84) to Wikipedia (2001–present), these are taken out of the hands of religious and governmental elites and offered to the general public. Relatively quickly this contributed to the independence of the European settlers in North America from the British crown (1776) and the French Revolution (1789–99), which initially seemed to end with rise to power of Napoleon Bonaparte, but continued with the revolts throughout Europe in 1848 and the subsequent, more persistent changes.

During the twentieth century the complex array of historical events that resulted in our modern world were justifiably critically scrutinized by, among others, Max Horkheimer (1895–1973), Theodor Adorno (1903–69) and Isaiah Berlin (1909–97). They conflated the Enlightenment and the Scientific Revolution with the Industrial Revolution and European colonialism (Figure 31.7, top), and identified the evil that they saw in the world as the direct result of this interaction.[42] Around the same time, however, changing structures gave rise to scientific and economic globalization, while the work of Norman Borlaug (1914–2009) and his colleagues resulted in the Green Revolution, which provided food security for many millions across the globe

(Figure 31.7, bottom). Together these resulted in a significant increase in wealth, health, safety, and freedom worldwide,[43] a development identified as the Great Convergence.[44]

In the introduction to his comprehensive, evidence-based, quantitative, and at times maybe overly optimistic evaluation of the Enlightenment, Steven Pinker (2018, 6) states that "the Enlightenment has *worked* [but] because this triumph is so unsung, the underlying ideas of reason, science, and humanism are unappreciated as well [whereas] the ideals of the Enlightenment are in fact stirring, inspiring, noble—a reason to live." Among the reasons for this discrepancy he notes that, "it's in the nature of progress that it erases its tracks, and its champions fixate on the remaining injustices and forget how far we have come."[45] "As our moral standard rises over the years, we become alert to harms that have gone unnoticed in the past."[46] However, "the pathways are manifold and tortuous, the effects are slow and then sudden, but in the fullness of time an idea from the Enlightenment can transform the world."[47] Unfortunately, "the second decade of the 21st century has seen the rise of political movements that depict their countries as being pulled into a hellish dystopia by malign factions. . . . These movements have been abetted by a narrative shared by many . . . in which the institutions of modernity have failed and every aspect of life is in deepening crisis—the two sides in macabre agreement that wrecking those institutions will make the world a better place."[48]

Richie Robertson, a chronicler of the Enlightenment, concurs with Pinker's assessments: "in an age dominated by fake news, widespread credulity, xenophobia and unscrupulous demagogues, it matters more intensely than ever to hold on to reliable knowledge, to be aware of our common humanity, and to pursue the possibility of human happiness."[49] "Even the most treasured ideas of the present day are open to constructive criticism. In this sense, those critics who polemicize against the values ascribed to the Enlightenment perform a valuable function, occasionally identifying actual flaws, more often by stimulating others to defend the Enlightenment. The critiques made by sceptical philosophers assist the process of enlightenment."[50]

When the founding fathers of the United States wrote "We hold these truths to be self evident," they were of course correct that what they considered truths were self-evident to them (being products of the Enlightenment). However, that "all men are created equal, that they are endowed by their Creator with certain unalienable rights, that among these are life, liberty and the pursuit of happiness. That to secure these rights, governments are instituted among men, deriving their just powers from the consent of the governed," may be far from evident to those less affected by the ideas of the Enlightenment because of history, colonialism, or Christian proselytizing.[51] Even those composing the Declaration of Independence in 1776 might now be embarrassed to note that they did not make a single reference to women anywhere. They would likely be horrified to learn that among their direct descendants are groups that actively seek to deny the unalienable rights they enjoy themselves to those that arrived in the country either well before or shortly after them.

There seem to be too many elements in some of the passionate proposals for decolonialization and social justice that appear based on the same nativist and populist thinking—antithetical to the Enlightenment ideals of the *liberté, égalité, fraternité* of the French Revolution and the self-evident truths in the Declaration of Independence of the United States—that in 2016 resulted in the United Kingdom voting itself out of the European Union and the United States voting Donald J. Trump into the office of president. We should try not to throw the baby out with the bathwater, but instead act in the spirit of the words which Bishop Nathan Baxter included in his homily during the national prayer service on 14 September 2001, commemorating the horrific events that happened three days earlier: "As we act, let us not become the evil that we deplore." This sentence was later that day quoted by congresswoman Barbara Lee in her explanation for voting against the Authorization for Use of Military Force Against Terrorists Act, which ultimately turned out to be the only vote against the proposal in the entire congress. It is vital to amend what must be considered wrong, but not by simply turning it upside-down and do to others what they previously did to us. A related warning was laid down by Martin Luther King in his Letter from Birmingham Jail (1963): "Injustice anywhere is a threat to justice everywhere. We are caught in an inescapable network of mutuality, tied in a single garment of destiny. Whatever affects one directly affects all indirectly."

Violence and oppression have always been part of human history and may even be among the reasons behind our success as a species.[52] The European colonial enterprise thus represents the rule rather than the exception. It was certainly exceptional in its scope and impact, but also because it carried the seeds of its own demise. Over the last decades these seeds sprouted, raising the standard of living to unprecedented levels,[53] a development that has recently come under threat of seemingly unfettered nativism and populism. It may be an unexpected recommendation in a book about archaeology—albeit archaeology outside the box—but now more than ever should we try not to be mired by the past, but rather use our understanding of previous generations in our efforts to salvage the future of humanity.[54] For this it is vital not to retreat back behind national, cultural, or ethnic borders, but instead to facilitate a freer movement across the world of goods, ideas, and people.[55] Global cooperation and collaboration will prove indispensable to addressing an inevitable future pandemic—comparable to the Spanish Flu, HIV/AIDS, and Covid-19—and the ongoing climate crisis.[56] This will only be possible if we manage to remove ourselves from judging our fellow humans and instead aim to create an informed opinion based on their recent behavior and the current content of their character.

This is not to say that initiatives to make archaeology more inclusive and socially relevant suffer from this fallacy, as may be evident from the chapters in this volume, but it is important to remain vigilant. For instance, one issue that may need additional discussion and reflection is the language in which scholarly articles on archaeological research are published. Increasingly, suggestions are heard to do this primarily in the current language in the region, for instance Arabic for research into ancient Egyptian remains and Spanish for ancient Andean remains. This does of course makes perfect sense for bureaucratic reports and popular publications, but both Arabic and Spanish are languages that came into the region with foreign invaders, in the seventh and sixteenth centuries, respectively, and are not directly related to ancient Egyptian, Quechua, or Aymara as spoken by the peoples that are the subjects of the research. This issue becomes even more complex for cultures with a much larger time-depth, of which the linguistic background remains uncertain, and modern languages with a relatively small native community, for instance research on Paleolithic remains published in Catalan or Hebrew. It is obviously courteous toward local stake-holders to learn and use a local language, but ultimately publishing the research in that language will in many countries inevitably imply a political choice, for instance the choice between Amharic and Tigrinya in Ethiopia. Furthermore, it is likely to isolate research and researchers from the international scholarly community.[57] It may at times be a better choice to use a scholarly *lingua franca,* such as Latin in the past, English today, and possibly Chinese in the not too distant future.

Explaining all the ills in the modern world by European colonialism, or colonialism in general,[58] may be an oversimplification of reality and contributes little to ameliorating the many global problems that we are facing. Abandoning the ideals of the Enlightenment,[59] or the associated democratic systems is certainly not a viable solution,[60] as evident from recent developments in Brazil, Great Britain, Hungary, Turkey, the United States, and Venezuela. We cannot change history or its outcome today any more than we can unscramble an egg, but from tomorrow onward we can start to try to make the world a better place for all.

Attention should be on the effort to move away from the arbitrary differences between individuals, such as skin color or the language that one speaks at home, and instead focus on the contributions that each participant can bring to the table or, more importantly, to help make incremental improvements to our contemporary society. For this we need to be inclusive, also toward those that do not share our opinions and might even actively oppose them.[61] Change should truly aim to enlighten our discipline, its practitioners, and the world at large. To conclude and circle back to the title above this section: "There is no intelligence where there is no change and no need of change" (H.G. Wells, 1895, *The Time Machine,* Chapter 13).

CRIME AND PUNISHMENT

A second ongoing development in archaeology is the evaluation and judgment of the opinions and behavior of its practitioners, past and present. This is obviously necessary and appropriate, but it is at the same time important to keep in mind that the best is often the enemy of the good. All people are multifaceted and none are infallible; even the infallibility of the Pope is associated with his office, not his person. As humans we are moreover able to learn until the last day of our life and can therefore at any time modify our attitudes and change our ways when given sufficient reasons and incentives. Furthermore, the focus currently seems to be too much on individual victims and perpetrators, and insufficiently on ways in which issues of inappropriate behavior can be discussed and addressed, or the structures that maintain an undesirable status quo. I hope to illustrate the complexities of these issues with a few brief descriptions of well-known historical examples, after which I will discuss in some more detail one of the most debated cases, that of the life, political views, and operas of Richard Wagner.

In Rome, Italy, at the beginning of the seventeenth century, painter Michelangelo da Caravaggio (1571–1610) led a boisterous, belligerent life which in 1606 culminated in Caravaggio killing Ranuccio Tommasoni in a sword fight.[62] Caravaggio subsequently left Rome for Naples and Malta, where he painted *The Beheading of Saint John the Baptist* (1608) at the request of the Knights of the Hospital of Saint John to serve as an altarpiece for Saint John's Co-Cathedral in Valletta, where it still hangs today. The character of the artist and the subject matter of what is considered one of the most important works of Western art are obviously problematic, but the beauty, meaning and influence of the painting remain near impossible to ignore.

Some decades later, sculptor Gianlorenzo Bernini (1598–1680) had an affair with Costanza Bonarelli, who at the time was married to one of his assistants. When he discovered that she was also romantically involved with his brother Luigi, he nearly killed his brother in a fist fight and had a servant disFigure the face of their lover with a razor.[63] Bernini also created *The Rape of Proserpina* (1621–22)—more correctly translated as *The Abduction of Proserpina*—which is kept in the Galleria Borghese in Rome. As in the case of Caravaggio, the subject and creator of this marble sculpture are questionable, but the astonishing way in which it manages to make cold, hard marble appear like living human flesh renders it very difficult to disregard.

More recent examples of troubled artists creating broadly influential work include John Lennon (1940–80), one of the four Beatles and together with Paul McCartney the driving artistic force behind the band and its success. In his relationships with women Lennon was excessively jealous and often possessive, which at times escalated into verbal and physical abuse.[64] His songs *Give Peace a Chance* (1969) and *Imagine* (1971) remain nevertheless popular within the progressive counterculture and are often used as the informal anthems of the peace movement. Reversely, the troubled and troubling personal life of Michael Jackson (1958–2009) has severely tarnished his legacy.[65] This does not, however, eliminate the impact that his songs *Beat It, Billie Jean*, and *Thriller* (all three released in 1982) had on subsequent popular music and dance, as well as on racial relations in the United States and beyond.

Similar incongruous accounts can be reported in the sciences. In 1905 and 1916, respectively, Albert Einstein (1879–1955) published his special and general theories of relatively. The radical and at times counterintuitive statements in these have time and time again proven to be correct, each time increasing their fundamental influence on the natural sciences and our understanding of the physical world around us. Less well known is that Einstein developed his revolutionary insights together with his first wife Mileva Marić (1875–1948), who is rarely recognized within the scholarly community and remains largely unfamiliar to the general public.[66] Einstein also famously changed his mind as the world around him changed. In an interview he first stated that "there is not the slightest indication that [nuclear energy] will ever be obtainable. It would mean that the atom would have to be shattered at will" (*Pittsburgh Post-Gazette*, December 1934), while less than five years later he wrote, "This new phenomenon [of nuclear fission] would also lead to the construction of bombs, and it is conceivable—though much less certain—that extremely powerful bombs of a new type may thus be constructed" (*Letter to President Franklin D. Roosevelt*, August 1939). Changing one's mind should not be considered a character flaw, but rather as sign of mental flexibly and intellectual or personal development.

Even more controversial and debated are the life and work of philosopher Martin Heidegger (1889–1976). In 1927 Heidegger published *Sein und Zeit*, widely considered one of the milestones in Western philosophy. In 1929 he accepted a position as professor at the University of Freiburg, where he remained for the duration of his academic career. Heidegger was elected president of the university in April 1933, a few months after Adolf Hitler rose to power. In May 1933, Heidegger joined the Nationalsozialistische Deutsche Arbeiterpartei, (NSDAP, or Nazi Party), of which he remained a member until the party was dissolved in October 1945. Although he stopped attending party meetings after he stepped down as president of the university in April 1934, Heidegger appeared to have remained a supporter of Nazi ideology and politics. After the Second World War he never commented on the atrocities that took place, nor did he apologize for his at least passive participation in these.[67] His most influential students include philosopher Hannah Arendt (who was Jewish and briefly Heidegger's lover), historian Ernst Nolte (who later specialized in comparing Nazism and Stalinism), and Marxist philosopher Herbert Marcuse. Partly because of this and despite his personal views, Heidegger's *Sein und Zeit* remains highly influential in Western philosophy.

Most in this context, however, may have been written about composer Richard Wagner (1813–83), his life and opinions, his operas, his influence on modern art, and the real or perceived connections of these with Nazi ideology.[68] Wagner had a relatively long and certainly a turbulent life, a large part of which was spent in search of success as a conductor and composer, and at the same time evading both his many creditors and arrest because of his political ideas and activities, which ranged from socialist to anarchist and from revolutionary to German nationalist. As a consequence, he spent more than a dozen years in exile in Switzerland, Italy, and France. His luck changed only in 1864, when he was in his early fifties, and Ludwig II, who was Wagner's greatest devotee and likely sexually attracted to him, became king of Bavaria and committed himself and the treasury of his kingdom to fund Wagner's past and future projects.

Over the course of his life, Wagner became increasingly reactionary and developed rabid antisemitic views. These were partly inspired by the fact that his two principal artistic and financial competitors, Giacomo Meyerbeer (1791–1864) and Felix Mendelssohn (1809–47), were both Jewish. The case of Meyerbeer is particularly noteworthy, as he had actively supported Wagner at the beginning of his career and inspired him artistically. Another factor were the racist opinions of Wagner's second wife Cosima Liszt, the daughter of pianist and composer Franz Liszt and previously married to Wagner's friend, conductor Hans von Bülow. Wagner and Liszt became romantically involved around 1863 and married in 1870, after she had given birth to their first child. Wagner's antisemitism culminated in his publication *Das Judenthum in der Musik* (Judaism in Music), first published in 1850 as a shorter article in the *Neue Zeitschrift für Musik* under the pseudonym K. Freigedank, and in 1869 as a much larger volume under Wagner's own name.

Among Wagner's early admirers was philosopher and cultural critic Friedrich Nietzsche (1844–1900). He became very close with Wagner and Liszt, but ultimately broke with them because of their antisemitic stance. He wrote several essays about the composer and his work, which were published as *The Case of Wagner* (1888), *Nietzsche contra Wagner* (1888), and *Richard Wagner in Bayreuth* (published posthumously in 1909). In the first of these he famously states, "Wagner is modernity in concentrated form; there is no help for it, we must first be Wagnerites," words which turned out to be prophetic. Another influential author enamored of Wagner was playwright and cultural critic George Bernard Shaw (1856–1950), who in 1898 published *The Perfect Wagnerite*. In this he analyzed Wagner's magnum opus *Der Ring des Nibelungen* (first preformed as a complete cycle in 1876) as a parable for

Figure 31.10. Piano reduction of the first measures of Richard Wagner's opera *Tristan und Isolde* (1865), showing the so-called Tristan chord (1–2), which sounded the beginning of modern, or rather modernist times.

the problematic issues resulting from industrialization and capitalist colonialism, an interpretation that again gained popularity toward the end of the twentieth century.

Their contemporaries Theodor Herzl (1860–1904)—who convened the First Zionist Congress in Basel in 1897 and is named the spiritual father of the Jewish State in the *Declaration of Independence* of Israel—as well as William Du Bois (1868–1963)—one of the founders of the National Association for the Advancement of Colored People and present at the foundation of the United Nations in San Francisco in 1945—were likewise enchanted by Wagner's music,[69] despite being aware of the despicable opinions of the artist. Furthermore, until modern times the works of Wagner are appreciated by many within the homosexual community, continuing from King Ludwig II of Bavaria to actor Stephen Fry and music critic Alex Ross.[70]

The opera *Tristan und Isolde* (1865), by many considered Wagner's masterpiece, opens with a chord progression that may have changed the course of history and was at the very least indicative of the beginning of a new era (Figure 31.10). This co-called Tristan chord consists of a dissonant F–B–D#–G#

morphing into the equally dissonant E–G#–D–B, briefly passing through F–B–D#–A and E–G#–D–A#. With these notes Wagner decisively and irreversibly departs from traditional harmony and anticipates twentieth-century atonality. The tension that is created by the Tristan chord is resolved only at the end of the opera almost four hours later, with the death of Isolde, although it almost happens in the love duet of Tristan and Isolde, before this is rudely interrupted. In his score Wagner elevates the importance of the sound and perception of the chords over that of their theoretical structure and succeeds in making the suspense that is created at the very beginning last until the very end. Much has been written about this chord,[71] and its historic significance seems to have been experienced, more or less consciously, by many who heard it performed during the final quarter of the nineteenth century.

Between the death of Wagner in 1883 and the beginning of the First World War in 1914, his works had a profound influence on Western art,[72] validating the prophetic words of Nietzsche that Wagner is modernity in concentrated form. Prominent examples include painters Édouard Manet (1832–83), Paul Cézanne (1839–1906), John Singer Sargent (1856–1925), Hilma af Klint (1862–1944), and Wassily Kandinsky (1866–1944), as well as authors Marcel Proust (1871–1922), Willa Sibert Cather (1873–1947), Thomas Mann (1875–1955), James Joyce (1882–1941), and Virginia Woolf (1882–1941).

Perhaps most famously, J.R.R. Tolkien (1892–1973) combined his academic knowledge of Nordic myths and sagas, his Roman Catholic faith, and his aversion to both fascism and democracy to recreate the narrative at the basis of Wagner's *Der Ring des Nibelungen.* The result was the trilogy *The Lord of the Rings* (1954–55), which, with *The Hobbit, or There and Back Again* (1937) as its preface, also mirrors the form of Wagner's Ring cycle (three operas, with a fourth, *Das Rheingold,* labeled to be a *Vorabend,* a 'preliminary evening'). Tolkien, however, tells a sanitized version of the old stories and Wagner's interpretation of these, lacking the sexual tension, the deeply felt human emotions—including all-consuming love and greed—and the devastating ending, all of which are fundamental to the ancient as well as the nineteenth-century originals.[73]

In no discipline, however, is the influence of Wagner's work as obvious as in music and especially in the incidental music in motion pictures. In the *Festspielhaus,* the opera house that Wagner designed and had built in Bayreuth, Germany, the depth of the orchestra pit does not allow the public to see the musicians. With this he anticipates the music that accompanies most movie scenes without anybody questioning where it originates. At times, fragments of Wagner's music are used more or less unaltered, for instance in Alfred Hitchcock's *Murder!* (1930), Franklin Schaffner's *The Boys from Brazil* (1978), David Fincher's *The Curious Case of Benjamin Button* (2008), and most famously the music from the beginning of the third act of *Die Walküre* in Francis Ford Coppola's *Apocalypse Now* (1979). More in general, all film music from its inception onward is heavily indebted to Wagner's remarkable talent for connecting music and melodies with what is happening on stage in order to invoke and enforce emotions in the spectator.[74] Also outside the cinema, many wedding ceremonies worldwide include the music of the bridal chorus from the third act of Wagner's *Lohengrin* (1850), often combined with parts of the wedding march from Mendelssohn's *Ein Sommernachtstraum* (1842), which is remarkable given the discordance between the two composers and the unhappy ending of the brief marriage of Elsa and Lohengrin.

Wagner died a few months before the birth of Benito Mussolini, six years before the birth of Adolf Hitler, and more than thirty years before the introduction of fascism in Italy (with the formation of the Fascio d'Azione Rivoluzionaria in 1915 and the publication of the *Manifesto dei fasci italiani di combattimento* in 1919) and of national socialism in Germany (with the formation of the Deutsche Arbeiterpartei in 1919 and its change into the NSDAP and adaptation of the fascist 25-Punkte-Programm in 1920). The association of Wagner and his work with fascism is mostly the result of the rise to power of Adolf Hitler,[75] who admired both the man and his work, and the choices made by Wagner's heirs, including Houston Chamberlain (1855–1927), who was married to Eva von Bülow, one of Wagner's daughters.

Apart from the character of Sixtus Beckmesser and the infamous last lines of Hans Sachs, both in *Die Meistersinger von Nürnberg,* there is little in Wagner's operas that directly reflects his political opinions.[76] Instead, the general theme at the basis of his work is how the tremendous power of selfless love is able to triumph over greed, ambition, and fate, albeit often at the cost of its own demise. Although these themes are present in most operas, Wagner differs from other opera composers in that he was always committed to educate rather than entertain his audience. Together with the complexity of the music, these may be among the reasons why "Wagner's popularity actually declined on German stages during the Nazi era."[77] This was certainly true for Martin Heidegger, who embraced Nazi ideology but did not approve of the inclusion of Wagner's work, which he considered to represent weak, feminine aesthetics.

Ever since the end of the Second World War, Wagner's music has been controversial because of its perceived or real connections with antisemitism, on the one hand, and its fundamental influence on modern European art on the other.[78] Among the better and more accessible discussions of this controversy is the documentary *Wagner & Me* (2009), in which British actor and comedian Stephen Fry tries to reconcile his love for Wagner's music with his Jewish heritage and the loss of family members in the Holocaust. Fry documents a very personal search that includes a conversation with a Holocaust survivor and visits to the Nazi parade ground in Nuremberg as well as Wagner's house and grave in Bayreuth. In a more whimsical fashion a similar effort was made by American actor and comedian Larry David in "Trick or Treat" (2001), the third episode of the second season of television series *Curb Your Enthusiasm.* The conclusion of these interpreters of our times is shared by Alex Ross (2020, 432), when he laments "Hitler's success in convincing posterity that the composer belongs exclusively to the extreme right."

It may be all too easy to reject categorically all the art and science mentioned above, and much beyond, simply because of the faults and mistakes of their creators, as well as those inspired by them, or instead choose to ignore their faults completely and appreciate their creations in splendid isolation. However, it may instead be exactly in the tension and friction between the two that new insights can arise, allowing us to expand the understanding of our humanity. It would of course be a fallacy to think that there could be human beings without flaws and at the same time an indication of humility and civilization to leave decisions on crime and punishment to courts of law and not to public opinion.

The examples above purposefully do not include archaeologists and only discuss individuals long deceased, in which case accounts can be closed and the balance drawn up. In most other situations we do need to remain critical and vigilant and concentrate on the structures and institutions that enable and sustain undesirable opinions and behavior, rather than solely focus on individual victims and perpetrators. It may be more effective not to search relentlessly for retribution or revenge, but rather engage those with which we do not agree with an open-minded discussion and try to convince them to change their ways, while at the same time being prepared to amend our own opinions. There is no shame in changing one's mind, rather the contrary. It must instead be considered a show of strength and intelligence to internalize new insights. To conclude and circle back to the title above this section: "Pain and suffering are always inevitable for a large intelligence and a deep heart. The really great men must, I think, have great sadness on earth" (Fyodor Dostoevsky, 1866, *Crime and Punishment,* Part 3, Chapter 5).

In conclusion, when attempting to think or venture outside the box of archaeology we do of course need to explore what exactly constitutes that box, who created it, what is keeping us trapped inside, and what we expect to gain from our escape. The authors of the chapters in this volume each approach these questions in their own way, from their own unique perspective, and each with their own specific priorities and biases. No firm or overarching conclusion or position is reached, as this was never the aim of this project, and we would like to encourage our readers to make their own inferences. It may be clear, however, that archaeology as a discipline is relevant when we address certain pressing contemporary issues, and at the same time that simply abandoning the box in which it thrived, and out of which this volume sprouted, might prove counterproductive.

It will be more effective to make fundamental improvements, while getting rid of the rotten parts. This will require earnest soul-searching and thoughtful discussions, to which this volume hopes to add some arguments, albeit at times in lateral or whimsical ways. For a process of sustainable rejuvenation it will be vital to look beyond the increasingly short news cycle and instead into more time-depth, both into the past—which is our expertise—and into the future, for which we might be slightly better prepared than most. Our aspirations to approach social justice will be better served by the social sciences than by social media. Archaeology, and in its own limited way this volume, aspire to play their part in this endeavor. All those involved in this volume hope to provide a little guidance along the way out of the confines of the past toward a slightly better future. "In a world that, as a result of increasingly powerful technologies, has become too dangerous and is changing too quickly for humanity to rely to any considerable extent on trial and error, knowledge derived from archaeology may be important for human survival."[79]

ACKNOWLEDGMENTS

Sincere thanks are due to the peer-reviewers and Editorial Board of the Cotsen Institute of Archaeology Press for their expedient and insightful comments on earlier versions of this volume. I would furthermore like to express my gratitude to all the authors, as without all their hard work this book would never have seen the light of day. Special thanks are due to Peter Gould, who found the image on the cover.

NOTES

1   Acabado and Martin 2020, Agbe-Davies 2010, Atalay 2012, Barton 2020, Bousema et al. 2022, Burke et al. 2021, Chirikure 2020, Effros and Lai 2018, Fagan 2006, Flannery 2005, Hamilakis and Duke 2016, Jameson and Musteață 2019, Kelly 2015; Kintigh et al. 2014, Lane 2015, Lydon and Rizvi 2016, Ogundiran 2020, Raja et al. 2021, Scerri et al. 2020, Schmidt and Pikirayi 2016, Wendrich 2010a, 2010b, 2018.

2   The text and images in this volume should be considered a continuous narrative extracted from the minds or brains of the individual authors. Their archaeological character is reflected in the reversed numbering of the chapters and pages, meant to evoke the archaeological reality in which the highest numbers usually represent the oldest layers, structures, and finds, coming first in the narrative describing their relationships. As with almost all ideas, I cannot claim this one to be entirely my own. It first dawned on me while reading Matt Parker's (2020) book on the impact of errors made by relying too much on modern technology. In this volume the page numbers are reversed, for reasons that remain unexplained, something that I only noticed when using the index for the first time. This idiosyncrasy reminded me of Gary Zukav's (1979) book on modern physics in which each chapter is labeled Chapter 1, and of Mark Haddon's (2003) psychological novel *The Curious Incident of the Dog in the Night-Time,* in which the chapters are numbered with consecutive prime numbers referring to the Asperger syndrome affecting the protagonist. A little later I learned about Stephen King's (1982) thriller *The Running Man,* originally published under the pseudonym Richard Bachman, in which the chapters are numbered in reverse sequence (counting down from 100 to 000), and of Chuck Palahniuk's (1999) satirical novel *Survivor,* (his second after the more famous *Fight Club),* in which both chapter and page numbers appear reversed. Later it was pointed out to me that in both Alain Damasio's novel *La Horde du Contrevent* (2004) and *The Books of Jacob* (2014) by 2018 Nobel laureate Olga Tokarczuk the pages are numbered in reverse order (in the latter case as a subtle reference to Jewish literature published in Hebrew). Much of what we take for granted appears upon closer inspection based on conventions. For example, the currently almost universally used system to represent numbers was developed in Europe in late Medieval times by adapting the place-value system used in ancient India, which arrived in Europe through mutual contacts with the Arab world. Arabic numerals are combined into larger numbers by noting down the smallest units first, followed—according to the Arabic convention of reading and writing from right to left—by the numerals representing the tenths, the hundreds, the thousands, and so on. When this system was introduced in Europe to replace the awkward Roman and Cistercian systems, not only were the Indo-Arabic symbols used—albeit significantly amended—but also the Arabic order when combining these into larger numbers. Given that the direction of reading and writing European languages is from left to right, this means that in these the symbol representing the largest amount is written first and the units last.
A second example is that ancient Egyptians would be very upset by our modern maps of their homeland, as these show the Nile Delta and the Mediterranean Sea at the top and the First Cataract near Aswan (Syene) at the bottom, suggesting that the Nile flows up the contour of the landscape. The ancient map of Wadi Hammamat, in the Egyptian Eastern Desert between the Nile Valley and the Red Sea (drawn on a large sheet of papyrus around 1150 BCE by Amennakhte, son of Ipuy, for a quarrying expedition ordered by Pharaoh Ramesses IV and now kept in Museo Egizio, Turin), is indeed drawn with south at the top and north at the bottom, allowing the Nile to flow in the correct direction. This was especially relevant from an Egyptian perspective in which imagery is considered to be more than a representation of reality, but rather to be a mode of reality in its own right.
In Europe, the first numbered pages occurred only at the beginning of the fifteenth century, well after the first numbered chapters and even after the first index (Duncan 2021). With the increasing number of entirely digital publications page numbers as well as an index are again losing their importance. As the aim of this volume is to pull archaeology out of its box it seems justified to break with a few selected conventions to unsettle its readers without hampering their comprehension and enjoyment of the narrative.

3   Barnard forthcoming, Bennett 2010, De Muijnck 2013, Gosden and Marshall 1999, Hodder 2012, Ingold 2013, Malafouris 2013, Siefkes 2012.

4   d'Errico et al. 2003, Finlayson 2019, Hardy et al. 2020, Wragg Sykes 2020.

5   Trigger 2006, 40–48.

6   Tallis 2003, 234.

7   Peresani et al. 2013.

8   Karlshausen and De Putter 2017.

9   Kelly-Buccellati 2012.

10 Fowler 2003, 12, Gartner 2016, 15.

11 Trigger 2006, 40–48.

12 von Falkenhausen 2013, 2015.

13 Genoways and Andrei 2016, Impey and MacGregor 2018.

14 Carbonell 2012, Fowler 2003.

15 Trigger 2006, Schnapp 1996.

16 Nigra et al. 2015.

17 Trigger 2006, 540–48.

18 Buccellati 2017, Hodder 2012, Ingold 2013, Malafouris 2013, Schiffer 1987, Zubiaurre 2019.

19 Arnold et al. 2012, Farrier 2020, Ferrell 2006, Gonzalez-Ruibal 2019, Graves-Brown et al. 2013, Harrison and Schofield 2010, Rathje and Murphy 2001.

20 Atalay 2012, De León 2015, Effros and Lai 2018, Fowles 2016, Gould 2018, Hamilakis and Duke 2016, Jameson and Musteață 2019, Lydon and Rizvi 2016, Schmidt and Pikirayi 2016.

21 Ablitt and Smith 2019, Aycock 2016, Bailey 2017, Bowdler 1996, Bruner et al. 2016, Coolidge et al. 2015, Gant and Reilly 2018, Gere 2001, 2003, Griffiths and Wei 2018, March 2017, Miller 2021, Miller et al. 2019, Norris 2019, Paju 2018, Parry and Gere 2006, Pearson and Shanks 2001, Phillips 2019, Supernant et al. 2020.

22 Barnard forthcoming, Silverman 2011.

23 Trigger 2006, 545.

24 Fukai 1960.

25 Thompson 2018.

26 Scott 2016.

27 Brinkmann et al. 2010.

28 Text and translation from the original Dutch by the Royal House of Orange-Nassau, https://www.youtube.com/watch?v=W9vWfWS9RPc, January 13, 2022.

29 Denker 2017, Grün et al. 2004, Wendrich et al. 2014.

30 Page 1994.

31 Mann 2006, 2011.

32 Diamond 1997, Mann 2006.

33 Moseley 2001, Sharer and Traxler 2006.

34 Graeber and Wengrow 2021.

35 Henrich et al. 2010; Henrich 2020.

36 After Henrich 2020, 49.

37 Henrich 2020, 213.

38 Henrich 2020, 215.

39 After Henrich 2020.

40 Graeber and Wengrow 2021. It may well be that the collective human mind was ready for ideals like liberty, freedom, and rationality, as it was for Epipaleolithic and Mesolithic industries, agriculture, and writing, which seem to have occurred in several places at around the same time. Such ideals are unfortunately very fragile and leave few if any traces, while considerable efforts at their violent suppression and physical destruction have erased most of what remained.

41 Mahbubani 2013, Pinker 2018, Radelet 2015.

42 Berlin 1979, Horkheimer and Adorno 1972.

43 Pinker 2018.

44 Mahbubani 2013, Radelet 2015.

45 Pinker 2018, 215.

46 Pinker 2018, 207.

47 Pinker 2018, 213.

48 Pinker 2018, 5.

49 Robertson 2021, xxii.

50 Robertson 2021, 780.

51 Henrich 2020, 398–407.

52 Graeber and Wengrow 2021, Henrich 2015, Wragg Sykes 2020.

53 Mahbubani 2013, Pinker 2018, Radelet 2015.

54 Graeber and Wengrow 2021.

55 De León 2015, Goldin et al. 2011, Hamilakis 2018, Powell 2015.

56 Banerjee and Duflo 2019, Kahl and Wright 2021, Mações 2021.

57 Griffiths 2021, Salomone 2022.

58 The English word colony comes from the Latin *colonia,* which referred to a newly founded Roman settlement outside the Latin and Sabine regions in modern central Italy, beginning around 400 BCE. Similar settlements away from the heartland had already been founded around the Mediterranean Sea by the Phoenicians and the Greeks, from 850 BCE and 700 BCE onward, respectively. Starting in 632 CE (11 AH), the southern littoral of the Mediterranean Sea and the Levant were in turn conquered by Islamic tribes from the Arabian Peninsula. From 1299 onward the region became part of the Ottoman Empire, which was founded by Turkish people who had migrated from central

Asia centuries earlier. After 1798 they competed for control of the area with French and British governments.

The history of humanity is characterized by migration and displacement (Daniels 2022, Goldin et al. 2011, Graeber and Wengrow 2021). The successful colonization of the world beyond eastern Africa by anatomically modern humans *(Homo sapiens)* started around 200,000 years ago, ultimately reaching Iceland (c. 850 CE), Hawai'i (c. 1200 CE), and New Zealand (c. 1250 CE). On their way they adapted by rapid cultural changes, rather than by speciation (Henrich 2015), and replaced all other hominoids (Finlayson 2019, Wragg Sykes 2020), many other mammal species (including other primates), and at times also previously arrived groups of *H. sapiens.* The hunter-gatherers in Europe, for instance, were replaced by Neolithic groups between 6500 and 4000 BCE, which in turn were replaced by Indo-European peoples between 4000 and 2000 BCE. Ultimately these would colonize much of the world, spreading their languages and culture far beyond their traditional heartland.

Very similar developments took place on other continents. For instance in Africa, where from 1000 BCE onward Bantu-speaking peoples appear to have migrated east and south from northwestern sub-Saharan Africa, ultimately assimilating with or completely replacing previously present cultures. Between about 1300 and 1850 the Yoruba people controlled the Oyo Empire, in modern Benin and Nigeria, likely the largest and most powerful of the ancient states on the continent. The largest ancient empire in the New World was that of the Inka, which occupied most of the Pacific coast of South America from around 1435 until the arrival of Spanish conquistadors in 1526. The last major colonial enterprise was the expansion of Japan into much of eastern Asia between 1931 and 1945. Emphasis has since shifted toward the independence and self-determination of the nation states that resulted from the extended period of worldwide disruption between 1500 and 1945. Although physical confrontations between different groups are far from eradicated, competition for control now more often takes place in the cultural domain.

59 Mahbubani 2013, Pinker 2018, Radelet 2015, Robertson 2021.
60 Graeber and Wengrow 2021, Harari 2018, Pinker 2018.
61 Duarte et al. 2015.
62 Howard 1983.
63 Mormando 2011.
64 Lennon 2005.
65 Taraborrelli 2009.
66 Esterson et al. 2019.
67 Wolin 1991.
68 Carr 2007, Ross 2020.
69 Ross 2020, 230–76.
70 Ross 2020, 302–321.
71 Nattiez 1990.
72 Dabrowski 1995, Mahaffey 1988, Newark and Wassenaar 1997, Ross 2020, 322–99, Turner 1998.
73 Hiley 2004, McGregor 2001, Ross 2020, 641–49.
74 Ross 2020, 562–608.
75 Pinker 2018, 396–400.
76 Carr 2007, 172–91, Ross 2020, 230–65.
77 Ross 2020, 539.
78 Bruen 1993.
79 Trigger 2006, 548.

BIBLIOGRAPHY

Ablitt, Jonathan and Robin J. Smith (2019), Working out Douglas's Aphorism: Discarded Objects, Categorisation Practices, and Moral Inquiries, *The Sociological Review Monographs* 67(4), 866–85, DOI:10.1177/0038026119854271.

Acabado, Stephen B. and Marlon Martin (2020), Decolonizing the Past, Empowering the Future: Community-Led Heritage Conservation in Ifugao, Philippines, *Journal of Community Archaeology and Heritage* 7(3), 1–15, DOI:10.1080/20518196.2020.1767383.

Agbe-Davies, Anna S. (2010), Concepts of Community in the Pursuit of an Inclusive Archaeology, *International Journal of Heritage Studies* 16(6), 373–89, DOI:10.1080/13527258.2010.510923.

Arnold, Jeanne E., Anthony P. Graesch, Enzo Ragazzini, and Elinor Ochs (2012), *Life at Home in the Twenty-First Century: 32 Families Open Their Doors,* Los Angeles (Cotsen Institute of Archaeology Press).

Atalay, Sonya (2012), *Community-Based Archaeology: Research With, By, and For Indigenous and Local Communities,* Berkeley (University of California Press).

Aycock, John (2016), *Retrogame Archeology: Exploring Old Computer Games,* Cham (Springer).

Bailey, Douglas W. (2017), Art/Archaeology: What Value Artistic–Archaeological Collaboration? *Journal of Contemporary Archaeology* 4(2), 246–56, DOI:10.1558/jca.34116.

Banerjee, Abhijit V. and Esther Duflo (2019), *Good Economics for Hard Times,* New York (PublicAffairs).

Barnard, Hans (forthcoming), "What was the Nicest Thing You Ever Found? An Essay on the Meaning of Objects," in: Anke Hein, Rowan K. Flad, and Bryan Miller, eds., *The Art and Archaeology of Ritual and Economy in East Asia: Festschrift in Honor of Lothar von Falkenhausen's 60th Birthday,* Los Angeles (Cotsen Institute of Archaeology Press).

Barton, Daniel C. (2020), Impacts of the Covid-19 Pandemic on Field Instruction and Remote Teaching Alternatives: Results from a Survey of Instructors, *Ecology and Evolution,* DOI:10.1002/ece3.6628.

Bennett, Jane (2010), *Vibrant Matter: A Political Ecology of Things,* Durham and London (Duke University Press).

Berlant, Lauren and Kathleen Stewart (2019), *The Hundreds,* Durham and London (Duke University Press).

Berlin, Isaiah (1979), *Against the Current: Essays in the History of Ideas,* London (Pimlico, edited by Henry Hardy).

Bousema, Teun, Leonard Burtscher, Ronald P. van Rij, Didier Barret, and Kate Whitfield (2022), The Critical Role of Funders in Shrinking the Carbon Footprint of Research, *Lancet Planetary Health,* 6 (1), e4–e6, DOI:10.1016/S2542-5196(21)00276-X.

Bowdler, Sandra (1996), Freud and Archaeology, *Anthropological Forum* 7(3), 419–38, DOI:10.1080/00664677.1996.9967466.

Brinkmann,Vinzenz, Oliver Primavesi, and Max Hollein, eds. (2010), *Circumlitio: The Polychromy of Antique and Medieval Sculpture,* Munich (Hirmer Publishers).

Bruen, Hanan (1993), Wagner in Israel: A Conflict among Aesthetic, Historical, Psychological, and Social Considerations, *Journal of Aesthetic Education* 27(1), 99–103.

Bruner, Emiliano, Marina Lozano, and Carlos Lorenzo (2016), Visuospatial Integration and Human Evolution: The Fossil Evidence, *Journal of Anthropological Sciences* 94, 81–97, DOI:10.4436/JASS.94025.

Buccellati, Giorgio (2017), *A Critique of Archaeological Reason: Structural, Digital, and Philosophical Aspects of the Excavated Record,* Cambridge (Cambridge University Press).

Burke, Ariane, Matthew C. Peros, Colin D. Wren, Francesco S.R. Pausata, Julien Riel-Salvatore, Olivier Moine, Anne de Vernal, Masa Kageyama, and Solène Boisard (2021), The Archaeology of Climate Change: The Case for Cultural Diversity, *Proceedings of the National Academy of Sciences* 180 (30), e2108537118, DOI:10.1073/pnas.2108537118.

Carbonell, Bettina M., ed. (2012), *Museum Studies: An Anthology of Contexts,* Chichester (John Wiley and Sons, second edition).

Carr, Jonathan (2007), *The Wagner Clan: The Saga of Germany's Most Illustrious and Infamous Family,* New York (Grove Press).

Chirikure, Shadrek (2020), Issues Emerging: Thoughts on the Reflective Articles on Coronavirus (Covid-19) and African Archaeology, *African Archaeological Review* 37, 503–507, DOI:10.1007/s10437-020-09402-w.

Coolidge, Frederick L., Thomas Wynn, Karenleigh A. Overmann, and James M. Hicks (2015), "Cognitive Archaeology and the Cognitive Sciences," in: Emiliano Bruner, ed., *Human Paleoneurology,* Cham (Springer), pp. 177–206.

Dabrowski, Magdalena (1995), Kandinsky Compositions: The Music of the Spheres, *MoMa* 19 (Spring), 10–13.

Damasio, Alain (2004), *La Horde du Contrevent*, Clamart (La Volte).

Daniels, Megan J., ed. (2022), *Homo Migrans: Modeling Mobility and Migration in Human History,* Albany (State University of New York Press).

De León, Jason (2015), *The Land of Open Graves: Living and Dying on the Sonoran Desert Migrant Trail,* Oakland (University of California Press).

De Muijnck, Wim (2013), The Meaning of Lives and the Meaning of Things, *Journal of Happiness Studies: An Interdisciplinary Forum on Subjective Well-Being* 14, 1291–1307, DOI:10.1007/s10902-012-9382-y.

DeMarrais, Elizabeth, Christopher Gosden, and Colin Renfrew, eds. (2005), *Rethinking Materiality: The Engagement of Mind with the Material World,* Cambridge (McDonald Institute).

Denker, Ahmet (2017), Palmyra As It Once Was: 3D Virtual Reconstruction and Visualization of an Irreplaceable Lost Treasure, *The International Archives of the Photogrammetry, Remote Sensing and Spatial Information Sciences* XLII-5/W1, DOI:10.5194/isprs-archives-XLII-5-W1-565-2017.

d'Errico, Francesco, Christopher Henshilwood, Graeme Lawson, Marian Vanhaeren, Anne-Marie Tillier, Marie Soressi, Frédérique Bresson, Bruno Maureille, April Nowell, Joseba Lakarra, Lucinda Backwell, and Michèle Julien (2003), Archaeological Evidence for the Emergence of Language, Symbolism, and Music: An Alternative Multidisciplinary Perspective, *Journal of World Prehistory* 17(1), 1–70, DOI:10.1023/A:1023980201043.

Diamond, Jared (1997), *Guns, Germs, and Steel: The Fates of Human Societies,* New York (W.W. Norton and Company).

Duarte, José L., Jarret T. Crawford, Charlotta Stern, Jonathan Haidt, Lee Jussim, and Philip E. Tetlock (2015), Political Diversity will Improve Social Psychological Science [with Comments and Reply], *Behavioral and Brain Sciences* 38, E130, DOI:10.1017/S0140525X14000430.

Duncan, Dennis (2021), *Index, A History of the,* London (Allen Lane).

Effros, Bonnie and Guolong Lai, eds. (2018), *Unmasking Ideology in Imperial and Colonial Archaeology: Vocabulary, Symbols, and Legacy,* Los Angeles (Cotsen Institute of Archaeology Press).

Esterson, Allen, David C. Cassidy, and Ruth L. Sime (2019), *Einstein's Wife: The Real Story of Mileva Einstein-Marić,* Cambridge (Massachusetts Institute of Technology Press).

Fagan, Brian (2006), So You Want To Be An Archaeologist? *Archaeology* 59(3), 59–64.

Farrier, David (2020), *Footprints: In Search of Future Fossils,* New York (Farrar, Straus and Giroux).

Ferrell, Jeff (2006), *Empire of Scrounge: Inside the Urban Underground of Dumpster Diving, Trash Picking, and Street Scavenging,* New York and London (New York University Press).

Finlayson, Clive (2019), *The Smart Neanderthal: Bird Catching, Cave Art, and the Cognitive Revolution,* Oxford (Oxford University Press).

Flannery, Kent V. (2005), On the Resilience of Anthropological Archaeology, *Annual Review of Anthropology* 35, 1–13, DOI:10.1146/annurev.anthro.35.081705.123304.

Fowler, Don D. (2003), A Natural History of Man: Reflections on Anthrolopogy, Museums, and Science, *Fieldiania: Anthropology* 36 (New Series), 11–21.

Fowles, Severin (2016), The Perfect Subject (Postcolonial Object Studies), *Journal of Material Culture* 21(1), 9–27, DOI:10.1177/1359183515623818.

Fukai, Shinji (1960), The Artifacts of Hatra and Parthian Art, *East and West* 11, 135–81.

Gant, Stefan and Paul Reilly (2018), Different Expressions of the Same Mode: A Recent Dialogue Between Archaeological and Contemporary Drawing Practices, *Journal of Visual Art Practice* 17(1), 100–120, DOI:10.1080/14702029.2017.1384974.

Gartner, Richard (2016), *Metadata,* Cham (Springer).

Genoways, Hugh H. and Mary A. Andrei, eds. (2016), *Museum Origins: Readings in Early Museum History and Philosophy,* London and New York (Routledge, revised edition of the 2006 orginal).

Gere, Cathy (2001), William Harvey's Weak Experiment: The Archaeology of an Anecdote, *History Workshop Journal* 51, 19–36, DOI:10.1093/hwj/2001.51.19.

———— (2003), A Brief History of Brain Archiving, *Journal of the History of the Neurosciences* 12(4), 396–410.

Goldin, Ian, Geoffrey Cameron, and Meera Balarajan (2011), *Exceptional People: How Migration Shaped Our World and Will Define Our Future,* Princeton (Princeton University Press).

Gonzalez-Ruibal, Alfredo (2019), *An Archaeology of the Contemporary Era,* London and New York (Routledge).

Gosden, Christopher and Yvonne Marshall (1999), The Cultural Biography of Objects, *World Archaeology* 31(2), 169–78, DOI:10.1080/00438243.1999.9980439.

Gould, Peter G. (2018), *Empowering Communities through Archaeology and Heritage: The Role of Local Governance in Economic Development,* London (Bloomsbury Academic).

Graeber, David and David Wengrow (2021), *The Dawn of Everything: A New History of Humanity,* New York (Farrar, Straus and Giroux).

Graves-Brown, Paul, Rodney Harrison, and Angela Piccini, eds. (2013), *The Oxford Handbook of the Archaeology of the Contemporary World,* Oxford and New York (Oxford University Press).

Griffiths, James (2021), *Speak Not: Empire, Identity and the Politics of Language,* London (Zed Books).

Griffiths, Rupert and Lia Wei (2018), Reverse Archaeology: Experiments In Carving And Casting Space, *Journal of Contemporary Archaeology* 4, 195–213, DOI:10.1558/jca.32392.

Grün, Armin, Fabio Remondino, and Li Zhang (2004), Photogrammetric Reconstruction of the Great Buddha of Bamiyan, Afghanistan, *The Photogrammetric Record* 19(107), 177–99, DOI:10.1111/j.0031-868X.2004.00278.x.

Haddon, Mark (2003), *The Curious Incident of the Dog in the Night-Time,* London (Jonathan Cape) and New York (Doubleday).

Hamilakis, Yannis (2018), *The New Nomadic Age: Archaeologies of Forced and Undocumented Migration,* Sheffield and Bristol (Equinox).

Hamilakis, Yannis, Aris Anagnostopoulos, and Fotis Ifantidis (2009), Postcards from the Edge of Time: Archaeology, Photography, Archaeological Ethnography (A Photo-Essay), *Public Archaeology* 8(2–3): 283–309, DOI:10.1179/175355309X457295.

Hamilakis, Yannis and Philip Duke, eds. (2016), *Archaeology and Capitalism: From Ethics to Politics,* London and New York (Routledge, first published in 2007 by Left Coast Press, Inc.).

Harari, Yuval N. (2018), *21 Lessons for the 21st Century,* London (Jonathan Cape).

Hardy, Bruce L., Marie-Hélène Moncel, Celine Kerfant, Matthieu Lebon, Ludovic Bellot-Gurlet, and Nicolas Mélard (2020), Direct Evidence of Neanderthal Fibre Technology and its Cognitive and Behavioral Implications, *Scientific Reports* 10(1), 4889, DOI:10.1038/s41598-020-61839-w.

Harrison, Rodney and John Schofield, eds. (2010), *After Modernity: Archaeological Approaches to the Contemporary Past,* Oxford (Oxford University Press).

Henrich, Joseph (2015), *The Secret of Our Success: How Culture Is Driving Human Evolution, Domesticating Our Species, and Making Us Smarter,* Princeton (Princeton University Press).

——— (2020), *The WEIRDest People in the World: How the West Became Psychologically Peculiar and Particularly Prosperous,* New York (Farrar, Straus and Giroux).

Henrich, Joseph, Steven J. Heine, and Ara Norenzayan (2010), The Weirdest People in the World? *Behavioral and Brain Sciences* 33(2–3), 61–83, DOI:10.1017/S0140525X0999152X.

Hiley, Margaret (2004), Stolen Language, Cosmic Models: Myth and Mythology in Tolkien, *Modern Fiction Studies* 50(4), 838–60, DOI:10.1353/mfs.2005.0003.

Hodder, Ian (2012), *Entangled: An Archaeology of the Relationships between Humans and Things,* Chichester and Malden (John Wiley and Sons).

Horkheimer, Max and Theodor W. Adorno (1972), *Dialectic of Enlightenment,* New York (Herder and Herder, translation by John Cumming of the 1947 German original)

Howard, Hibbard (1983), *Caravaggio,* New York (Harper and Row).

Impey, Oliver and Arthur MacGregor, eds., 2018, *The Origins of Museums: The Cabinet of Curiosities in Sixteenth- and Seventeenth-Century Europe,* Oxford (Ashmolean Museum, revised edition of the 1985 original).

Ingold, Tim (2013), *Making: Anthropology, Archaeology, Art and Architecture,* London and New York (Routledge).

Jameson, John H. and Sergiu Musteață, eds. (2019), *Transforming Heritage Practice in the 21st Century: Contributions from Community Archaeology,* Cham (Springer).

Kahl, Colin and Thomas Wright (2021), *Aftershocks: Pandemic Politics and the End of the Old International Order,* New York (St. Martin's Press).

Karlshausen, Christina and Thierry De Putter (2017), Un oursin pour le dieu: L'oursin de Tjanefer (Turin Suppl. 2761), *Rivista del Museo Egizio,* DOI:10.29353/rime.2017.1068 (online document in French with an English abstract).

Kelly, Robert L. (2015), The Abyss: An Academic Archaeologist Looks at the Future, *Society for American Archaeology: Archaeological Records* 15(4), 12–17.

Kelly-Buccellati, Marilyn (2012), "Apprenticeship and Learning from the Ancestors: The Case of Ancient Urkesh," in: Willeke Z. Wendrich, ed., *Archaeology and Apprenticeship: Body*

Knowledge, Identity, and Communities of Practice, Tucson (University of Arizona Press), pp. 203–23.

King, Stephen (1982) , *The Running Man,* New York (Signet Books, originally published under the pseudonym Richard Bachman).

Kintigh, Keith W., Jeffrey H. Altschul, Mary C. Beaudry, Robert D. Drennan, Ann P. Kinzig, Timothy A. Kohler, W. Fredrick Limp, Herbert D.G. Maschner, William K. Michener, Timothy R. Pauketat, Peter Peregrine, Jeremy A. Sabloff, Tony J. Wilkinson, Henry T. Wright, and Melinda A. Zeder (2014), Grand Challenges for Archaeology, *American Antiquity* 79(1), 5–24, DOI:10.7183/0002-7316.79.1.5.

Lane, Paul J. (2015), Archaeology in the Age of the Anthropocene: A Critical Assessment of Its Scope and Societal Contributions, *Journal of Field Archaeology* 40(5), 485–98, DOI:101179/2042458215Y.0000000022.

Lennon, Cynthia (2005), *John: The Extraordinary Story of a Man, a Legend and a Marriage,* New York (Crown Publishers).

Lydon, Jane and Uzma Z. Rizvi, eds. (2016), *Handbook of Postcolonial Archaeology,* London and New York (Routledge, first published in 2010 by Left Coast Press, Inc.).

Maçães, Bruno (2021), *Geopolitics for the End Time: From the Pandemic to the Climate Crises,* London (Hurst).

Mahaffey, Vicki (1988), Wagner, Joyce and Revolution, *James Joyce Quarterly* 25(2), 237–47.

Mahbubani, Kishore (2013), *The Great Convergence: Asia, the West, and the Logic of One World,* New York (Public-Affairs).

Malafouris, Lambros (2013), *How Things Shape the Mind: A Theory of Material Engagement,* Cambridge (Massachusetts Institute of Technology Press).

Mann, Charles C. (2006), *1491: New Revelations of the Americas Before Columbus,* New York (Alfred A. Knopf).

—— (2011), *1493: Uncovering the New World Columbus Created,* New York (Alfred A. Knopf).

March, Paul (2017), Playing with Clay and the Uncertainty of Agency: A Material Engagement Theory Perspective, *Phenomenology and Cognitive Sciences* 18, 133-51, DOI:10.1007/s11097-017-9552-9

McGregor, Jamie (2001), Two Rings to Rule them All: A Comparative Study of Tolkien and Wagner, *Mythlore* 29(3/4, 113/114), 133–53.

Miller, Daniel (2021), A Theory of a Theory of the Smartphone, *International Journal of Cultural Studies* 24(5) 860–76, DOI:10.1177/1367877921994574.

Miller, Daniel, Elisabetta Costa, Laura Haapio-Kirk, Nell Haynes, Jolynna Sinanan, Tom McDonald, Razvan Nicolescu, Juliano Spyer, Shriram Venkatraman, and Xinyuan Wang (2019), Contemporary Comparative Anthropology: The Why We Post Project, *Ethnos* 84(2), 283–300, DOI:10.1080/00141844.2017.1397044.

Mormando, Franco (2011), *Bernini: His Life and His Rome,* Chicago (University of Chicago Press).

Moseley, Michael E. (2001), *The Incas and Their Ancestors: The Archaeology of Peru,* London (Thames and Hudson, second revised edition).

Nattiez, Jean-Jacques (1990), *Music and Discourse: Toward a Semiology of Music,* Princeton (Princeton University Press, translation by Carolyn Abbate of the 1987 French original).

Newark, Cormac and Ingrid Wassenaar (1997), Proust and Music: The Anxiety of Competence, *Cambridge Opera Journal* 9(2), 163–83, DOI:10.1017/S0954586700005243.

Nigra, Benjamin T., Kym F. Faull, and Hans Barnard (2015), Analytical Chemistry in Archaeological Research, *Analytical Chemistry* 87, 3–18, DOI:10.1021/ac5029616.

Norris, Lucy (2019), Waste, Dirt and Desire: Fashioning Narratives of Material Regeneration, *The Sociological Review Monographs* 67(4), 886–907, DOI:10.1177/0038026119854273.

Ogundiran, Akinwumi (2020), The Covid-19 Pandemic: Perspectives for Reimaging and Reimagining Archaeological Practice, *African Archaeological Review* 37, 471–73, DOI:10.1007/s10437-020-09408-4.

Page, Don N. (1994), *Information Loss in Black Holes and/or Conscious Beings?,* online document, https://arxiv.org/abs/hep-th/9411193.

Paju, Elina (2018), Plugging in Through Clothing: How Children's Clothes Influence Perception and Affective Practices in Day Care, *The Sociological Review* 66(3) 527–41, DOI:10.1177/0038026117703906.

Palahniuk, Chuck (1999), *Survivor,* New York (W. W. Norton).

Parker, Matthew T. (2020), *Humble Pi: A Comedy of Maths Errors,* London (Penguin).

Parry, Bronwyn and Cathy Gere (2006), Contested Bodies: Property Models and the Commodification of Human Biological Artefacts, *Science as Culture* 15(2), 139–58, DOI:10.1080/09505430600708036.

Peresani, Marco, Marian Vanhaeren, Ermanno Quaggiotto, Alain Queffelec, and Francesco d'Errico (2013), An Ochered Fossil Marine Shell From the Mousterian of Fumane Cave, Italy, *Public Library of Science ONE* 8(7), e68572, DOI:10.1371/journal.pone.0068572.

Pearson, Mike and Michael Shanks (2001), *Theatre/Archaeology,* London (Routledge).

Phillips, Susan A. (2019), *The City Beneath: A Century of Los Angeles Graffiti,* New Haven (Yale University Press).

Pinker, Steven (2018), *Enlightenment Now: The Case for Reason, Science, Humanism, and Progress,* New York (Penguin Random House).

Powell, Benjamin, ed. (2015), *The Economics of Immigration: Market-Based Approaches, Social Science, and Public Policy,* Oxford (Oxford University Press).

Radelet, Steven (2015), *The Great Surge: The Ascent of the Developing World,* New York (Simon and Schuster).

Raja, Nussaïbah B., Emma M. Dunne, Aviwe Matiwane, Tasnuva Ming Khan, Paulina S. Nätscher, Aline M. Ghilardi, and Devapriya Chattopadhyay (2021), Colonial History and Global Economics Distort Our Understanding of Deep-Time Biodiversity, *Nature Ecology and Evolution,* DOI:10.17605/OSF.IO/6WC7A.

Rathje, William L. and Cullen Murphy (2001), *Rubbish! The Archaeology of Garbage,* Tucson (The University of Arizona Press).

Renfrew, A. Colin, Christopher Gosden, and Elizabeth DeMarrais, eds. (2004), *Substance, Memory, Display: Archaeology and Art,* Cambridge (McDonald Institute).

Robertson, Ritchie (2021), *The Enlightenment: The Pursuit of Happiness, 1680–1790,* New York (Harper).

Ross, Alex (2020), *Wagnerism: Art and Politics in the Shadow of Music,* New York (Farrar, Straus and Giroux).

Salomone, Rosemary (2022), *The Rise of English: Global Politics and the Power of Language,* Oxford (Oxford University Press).

Scerri, Eleanor M.L., Denise Kühnert, James Blinkhorn, Huw S. Groucutt, Patrick Roberts, Kathleen Nicoll, Andrea Zerboni, Emuobosa Akpo Orijemie, Huw Barton, Ian Candy, Steven T. Goldstein, John Hawks, Khady Niang, Didier N'Dah, Michael D. Petraglia, and Nicholas C. Vella (2020), Field-Based Sciences Must Transform in Response to Covid-19, *Nature Ecology and Evolution,* DOI:10.1038/s41559-020-01317-8.

Schiffer, Michael B. (1987), *Formation Processes of the Archaeological Record,* Albuquerque (University of New Mexico Press)..

Schmidt, Peter R. and Innocent Pikirayi, eds. (2016), *Community Archaeology and Heritage in Africa: Decolonizing Practice,* London and New York (Routledge).

Schnapp, Alain (1996), *The Discovery of the Past: The Origins of Archaeology,* London (British Museum Press, English translation by Ian Kinnes and Gillian Varndell of the 1993 French original).

Scott, David A. (2016), *Art: Authenticity, Restoration, Forgery,* Los Angeles (Cotsen Institute of Archaeology Press).

Sharer, Robert J. and Loa P. Traxler (2006), *The Ancient Maya,* Stanford (Stanford University Press).

Siefkes, Martin (2012), The Semantics of Artefacts: How We give Meaning to the Things We Produce and Use, *Image: Zeitschrift für interdisziplinäre Bildwissenschaft* 16 (Themenheft Semiotik), 61–91.

Silverman, Helaine, ed. (2011), *Contested Cultural Heritage: Religion, Nationalism, Erasure, and Exclusion in a Global World,* New York (Springer).

Supernant, Kisha, Jane E. Baxter, Natasha Lyons, and Sonya Atalay, eds. (2020), *Archaeologies of the Heart,* Cham (Springer)

Tallis, Raymond (2003), *The Hand: A Philosophical Inquiry into Human Being,* Edinburgh (Edinburgh University Press).

Taraborrelli, J. Randy (2009), *Michael Jackson: The Magic, the Madness, the Whole Story, 1958–2009,* New York (Grand Central Publishing).

Thompson, Erin L. (2018), Recreating the Past in Our Own Image: Contemporary Artists' Reactions to the Digitization of Threatened Cultural Heritage Sites in the Middle East, *Future Anterior* 15(1), 44–56.

Tokarczuk, Olga (2021), *The Books of Jacob*, London (Fitzcarraldo Editions, English translation by Jennifer Croft of the 2018 Polish original).

Trigger, Bruce G. (2006), *A History of Archaeological Thought*, Cambridge (Cambridge University Press, second edition).

Turner, Norman (1998), Cézanne, Wagner, Modulation, *Journal of Aesthetics and Art Criticism* 56(4), 353–64, DOI:10.2307/432126.

von Falkenhausen, Lothar (2013), "Antiquarianism in East Asia: A Preliminary Overview," in: Alain Schnapp, Lothar von Falkenhausen, Peter N. Miller, and Tim Murray, eds., *World Antiquarianism: Comparative Perspectives,* Los Angeles (Getty Research Institute), pp. 35–66.

—— (2015), "Antiquarianism in China and Europe: Reflections on Momigliano", in: Suoqiao Qian, ed., *Cross-cultural Studies: China and the World: A Festschrift in Honor of Professor Zhang Longxi,* Leiden (Brill), pp. 127–51.

Wendrich, Willeke Z. (2010a), "From Practical Knowledge to Empowered Communication: Field Schools of the Supreme Council of Antiquities," in: Ran Boytner, Lynn Swartz Dodd, and Bradley J. Parker, eds., *Controlling the Past, Owning the Future: The Political Uses of Archaeology in the Middle East,* Tucson (University of Arizona Press), pp. 178–95.

—— (2010b), "Egyptian Archaeology: From Text to Context," in: Willeke Z. Wendrich, ed., *Egyptian Archaeology,* Chichester (Wiley-Blackwell), pp. 1–14.

—— (2018), Mutuality in Exploring the Past: Ethno-Experimental and Community Archaeology, *Journal of Ancient Egyptian Interconnections* 17, 188–201.

Wendrich, Willeke, Bethany Simpson, and Eiman Elgewely (2014), Karanis in 3D: Recording, Monitoring, Recontextualizing, and the Representation of Knowledge and Conjecture, *Near Eastern Archaeology* 77(3), 233–37, DOI:10.5615/neareastarch.77.3.0233.

Wolin, Richard, ed. (1991), *The Heidegger Controversy: A Critical Reader,* Cambridge (Massachusetts Institute of Technology Press).

Wragg Sykes, Rebecca (2020), *Kindred: Neanderthal, Life, Love, Death and Art,* London (Bloomsbury Sigma).

Zubiaurre, Maite (2019), *Talking Trash: Cultural Uses of Waste,* Nashville (Vanderbilt University Press).

Zukav, Gary (1979), *The Dancing Wu Li Masters: An Overview of the New Physics,* New York (William Morrow).

THE BOX PROJECT AND OUTSIDE-THE-BOX ARCHAEOLOGY

WILLEKE WENDRICH

Whereas previously, the entire emphasis was on the past social groups being studied, more and more archaeologists now practice with, in, and for, living 'communities.'. . . Our concepts of community must take into account ways in which communities are constituted, their non-homogeneity, and how we might become integrated into them. . . . It is when we enter into communion with individuals and groups outside the discipline that archaeology begins to become a truly inclusive practice. (Agbe-Davies 2010, pp. 373–74)

The Box Project was the last exhibition funded and published by businessman, archaeologist and philanthropist Lloyd Cotsen (1928–2017). In this project thirty-six artists were invited to create a work with fiber that would fit into a box measuring either 14×14×3 or 24×14×3 inches (36×36×8 or 61×36×8 centimeters). It was word play and an outside-the-box challenge to artists, provoking their inspiration by strictly limiting the size and scale in which they were invited to work. Restriction as stimulation for the expansion of works of textile art, as amply demonstrated by the highly original creations shown in the exhibit and preserved in the catalog (Figure 30.1).[1] In the volume in hand the opposite approach is taken by archaeologists and artists in order to investigate the boundaries of archaeology, not only by thinking outside the box, but by addressing an audience outside the box of archaeology, and academia. By showcasing unexpected objects and approaches, by including different ways of interacting with material remains of the past, this book provides a surprisingly accessible subject matter. What at face value can appear whimsical does in fact provide meaningful considerations of our material surroundings, while several of the more serious research approaches go hand in hand with unexpected insights that range from heartwarming to life-altering.

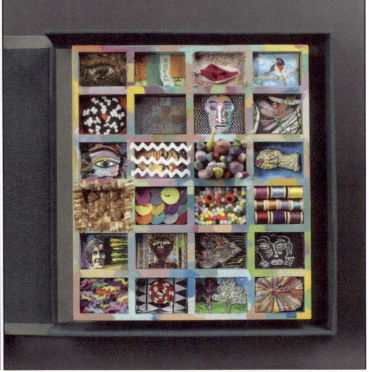

The advantage of an exhibit in small boxes is that it travels well: it packs up easily and can be unpacked in different venues for various audiences. Outside-the-box archaeology too travels well in the sense that it is eminently suitable for a range of readers beyond the archaeological profession. There are those who have been fascinated by treasure, discovery and the glimmer of gold, only to realize later that archaeologists are much more interested in cigarette butts. There are others who may have considered archaeology a useless pastime, but who may to their surprise discover that they have an interest in archaeology after all because it is dealing with deeply human questions and concerns. As reflected in the epigraph at the head of this chapter it is now becoming increasingly clear that archaeology as a discipline should come out of its box and spend more time and effort on public engagement. Unpacking archaeology will show that the field should not limit itself to the past, but expressly address the present and the future. Archaeology is not an endeavor for scholars only, but needs to be in constant conversation with the world.

This is achieved in the first place by involving local stakeholders and the interested general public in archaeological research,[2] as well as by demonstrating that archaeological methods and theories can be applied to address a variety of contemporary issues.[3] Given the nature of the discipline, local and indigenous communities should have a voice in the aims and approaches of archaeologists.[4] Known under various terms, community-based archaeology shares power and interacts explicitly with indigenous and local communities living near or in close relation with more or less ancient material remains. A mutual approach begins with speaking in a language that is free of jargon, addressing problems that speak to non-specialists, including descendant communities, and working with objects that might not intuitively appear archaeological.

Figure 30.2. An archaeology of life at home in the twenty-first century. *Adapted from Arnold et al. 2012: 102.*

Furthermore, archaeologists have much to contribute to the discussions concerning the Anthropocene, now mostly dominated by geologists,[5] as well as the political and humanitarian debates on migration streams across the Mediterranean Sea,[6] and the border between Mexico and the United States.[7]

A second, equally pressing issue is the need to recognize that archaeology developed within the framework of the European colonial enterprise and that the discipline has yet to break free from the reprehensible box of its own past.[8] The Cotsen Institute of Archaeology is actively contributing to this development, in its fieldwork and teaching, as well as by reaching out to colleagues,[9] scholars in general,[10] and the general public (Figures 30.2 and 30.3). A final, more pragmatic reason for such fundamental reflections is the need to make a case for public support for archaeological research and training.

Figure 30.1. Contributions to *The Box Project* by Gere Kavanaugh (top, *Untitled*, 2010, 24×14×3 in), Masae Bamba (bottom left, *Reborn*, 2009, 14×14×3 in), and Mary Bero (bottom right, *Compendium*, 2013, 14×14×3 in). *Adapted from Stapleton et al. 2016: 237,310, 157, respectively; photographs by Bruce M. White Photography, Copyright Lloyd Cotsen/Cotsen Foundation for Academic Research, 2016.*

Archaeology, which can be defined as the study of human behavior, development, interaction, and history as inferred from material remains, is fundamentally a multidisciplinary field of research. Archaeologists habitually combine archaeological, anthropological, and humanistic research methods with analytical techniques adapted from the natural sciences.[11]

Many archaeologists are aware of the need to move out of their scholarly ivory tower and break down the barriers between their scholarly enterprises and the rest of the world. Traveling across the globe to study the ancient history of other, often distant regions is no longer acceptable without meaningful interactions with local and regional stakeholders, as well as descendant communities elsewhere. Scholars and scientists are currently becoming aware of the issues associated with their privileged access to training, information, and resources. This brings a realization that multiple viewpoints have been silenced by a dominant paradigm. The correction of this situation is overdue, and requires a conscious self-reflexive attitude of the discipline. One element of the myopic stance of archaeology was the exclusive focus on elite society, both ancient and modern, as represented by a disproportional interest in temples, tombs, and treasure. A shift of attention to settlement and household archaeology, and the study of ancient landscapes and climate, has shown that understanding the issues that humanity faces today requires a study of the *longue durée*, of developments that last longer than human memory, history, or even archaeology can fathom.

Figure 30.3. An archaeology of life at home in the twenty-first century. *Adapted from Arnold et al. 2012: 11–12.*

OUTSIDE-THE-BOX ARCHAEOLOGY

This volume and its contributors aim to push this envelope by exploring the edges of archaeology—and beyond—in an effort to make archaeology relevant in non-traditional ways. Its goal is to showcase projects and ideas that broaden the applicability of archaeology by either using archaeological approaches to present-day subjects, or reflecting on present-day problems using lessons learned from the past. By illustrating the fascinating and pertinent nature of archaeological research, this book truly takes archaeology outside the box.

Context is central to archaeology and it is therefore relevant to mention that this introduction was written in the midst of the 2020 Covid-19 pandemic and the Black Lives Matter protests. Most chapters in this volume predate this unprecedented time. It seems fitting, therefore, to insert some words and images here on the effects that these worldwide phenomena are likely to have on the archaeological and geological records, as well as on archaeology as a discipline.

Obvious examples of what we might encounter as the material results of the worldwide pandemic include the large amounts of facemasks and disposable gloves ending up in landfills, which will eventually transform into geological layers,[12] as well as in the environment, where they at times are accidentally consumed by animals or used as nesting material. Locally—for instance in New York (United States), Manaus (Brazil), and Qom (Iran)—mass graves have been dug and filled with victims of the virus, reminiscent of the medieval 'plague pits' across Eurasia.[13] Subtler are the considerable changes in human mobility, ranging from the daily commute to intercontinental air travel (Figure 30.4), resulting in dramatically reduced pollution and seismic background noise.[14]

Other changes that have been noted, but not yet fully understood, include dramatically altered daily routines (ranging from having lunch at home to adopting a pet), a reduced crime rate but an increase in domestic violence, a drop in premature births, a shortage in coins, reports of wild animals entering urban environments, among many others. Such changes may well be reflected in the archaeological record, to be studied by future colleagues, especially if they result in lasting changes within contemporary human society and thus its material remains. It seems that some of the current events accelerate and engrain previously existing trends, such as flexibility in working place and hours, automation of industries and transport, and developments toward a more sustainable economy. All this may result in a subtle horizon in the archaeological and geological records, similar to the thin layer of iridium marking the transition between the Cretaceous and the Paleogene periods (the K–Pg or K–T transition, around 66 million years ago).

The dramatic changes in all aspects of our daily life will likely also result in unexpected yet important contributions to the arts and sciences. Examples from the past include *The Decameron: Prince Galehaut (The Human Comedy)*, compiled by Giovanni Boccaccio (1313–75) during the first wave of Black Death in Europe (1346–53), or the seminal work on the nature of light and gravity done by Sir Isaac Newton (1642–1727) during the Great Plague of 1665–66. These outbreaks were not caused by a virus, but by the bacterium *Yersinia pestis,* which

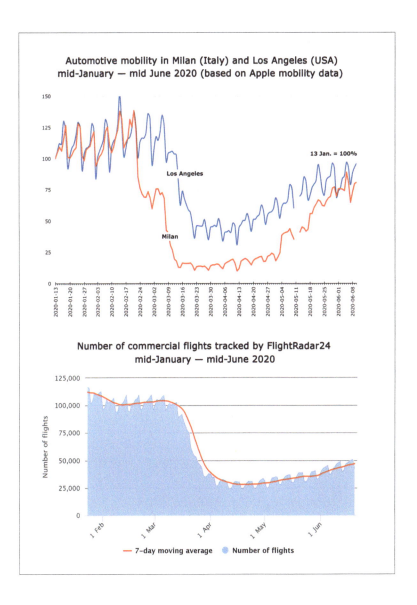

Figure 30.4. Changes in human mobility in the first half of 2020.

was spread across continents by infected fleas and rats, contrary to the more recent Great Influenza of 1918–1919 and the 2020 Covid-19 pandemic.

The more or less authoritative advice to stay at home and the widespread closing of restaurants, bars, schools, and public spaces have resulted in significant behavioral changes, but also

Figure 30.5. *The Black Experience* mural in the Ackerman Union building (UCLA), painted by Marian Brown, Neville Garrick, Andrea Hill, Jane Staulz, Joanne Stewart, Michael Taylor, and Helen Singleton in 1970, just after its restoration in 2013–14. *Photograph by Rebecca Kendall.*

Figure 30.6. Detail of Figure 30.5, showing how larger figures are filled in with images reflecting the history of Black people in the United States, including representations of, among others, Angela Davis, Frederick Douglass, Martin Luther King, Harriet Tubman, and Malcolm X. *Photograph by Rebecca Kendall.*

exposed existing gross racial and economic disparities to a much wider audience. In 2020, the Black Lives Matter movement had existed for more than seven years—following the killing of Trayvon Martin in 2013—well before the deaths of George Floyd, Breonna Taylor, and Ahmaud Arbery created a nationwide movement. Much of the material remains of the protests may prove to be ephemeral, such as the art that has been created on boarded up store fronts constructed to protect businesses from the violence in the wake of peaceful demonstrations, but changes in society may leave enduring marks.

Archaeology as the study and contextual analysis of material remains is relevant to understanding the present and recent past. At the University of California–Los Angeles (UCLA) the changing attitudes toward black lives is exemplified by the creation, hiding, and revealing of *The Black Experience,* a 3×8 meter (10×27 feet) mural depicting the struggles and achievements of African-Americans in the United States. This mural was painted in 1970 on the first floor of the Ackerman

Union building on the UCLA campus by students Marian Brown, Neville Garrick, Andrea Hill, Jane Staulz, Joanne Stewart, Michael Taylor, and Helen Singleton (Figures 30.5 and 30.6). With this work of art they aimed to add to the nationwide protests against the shooting at Kent State University of four students protesting the Vietnam War by the Ohio National Guard on 4 May 1970. After more than twenty years, in 1992, the remodeling of the area necessitated the building of a wall, hiding the mural from view for the next twenty years. Between December 2013 and February 2014 the area was renovated and the mural again exposed. Funded by the Associated Students UCLA and with assistance of students and faculty of the Cotsen Institute, the mural was subsequently carefully cleaned and restored.

At the time of writing it remains unclear how substantial the changes in society will prove to be and how long they will persist. Some of these changes are just beginning, such as a fundamental move to greater social equality and economic sustainability. All of us need to contribute to these efforts to ensure that they will go sufficiently far to become recognizable in the material record, which will hopefully show, for instance, architectural changes that reflect a more honest division of living space, and remains of sustenance and material belongings indicating a more just and equal society.

The volume in hand aims to make a small contribution to these necessary and inevitable developments. I do hope that you will read it with a smile, rather than a serious frown. And I expect that you will take it up time and again, because there are lessons to be learned and inspiration to be gained from changing your perspective.

NOTES

1   Stapleton et al. 2016.

2   Jameson and Musteață 2019, Schmidt and Pikirayi 2016.

3   Graves-Brown et al. 2013, Harrison and Schofield 2010.

4   Agbe-Davies 2010, Atalay 2012, Wendrich 2018.

5   Barnes et al. 2013, Erlandson and Braje 2013, Farrier 2020, Krauss 2015, Lane 2015, Palsson et al. 2013, Pétursdóttir 2017.

6   Fabre and Sant Cassia 2007, Hamilakis 2016.

7   De León 2015, Zubiaurre 2019.

8   Hamilakis and Duke 2016, Lydon and Rizvi 2010/2016.

9   Effross and Lai 2018.

10 Arnold et al. 2012.

11 Rainey and Ralph 1966, Seaborg 1964.

12 Farrier 2020.

13 Antoine 2008, Alfani and Murphy 2017.

14 Lecocq et al. 2020.

BIBLIOGRAPHY

Agbe-Davies, Anna S. (2010), Concepts of Community in the Pursuit of an Inclusive Archaeology, *International Journal of Heritage Studies* 16(6), 373–89, DOI:10.1080/13527258.2010.510923.

Alfani, Guido and Tommy E. Murphy (2017), Plague and Lethal Epidemics in the Pre-Industrial World, *Journal of Economic History* 77(1), 314–43, DOI:10.1017/S0022050717000092.

Antoine, Daniel (2008), The Archaeology of "Plague," *Medical History* 52(S27), 101–14, DOI:10.1017/S0025727300072112.

Arnold, Jeanne E., Anthony P. Graesch, Enzo Ragazzini, and Elinor Ochs (2012), *Life at Home in the Twenty-First Century: 32 Families Open Their Doors,* Los Angeles (Cotsen Institute of Archaeology Press).

Atalay, Sonya (2012), *Community-Based Archaeology: Research With, By, and For Indigenous and Local Communities,* Berkeley (University of California Press).

Barnes, Jessica, Michael R. Dove, Myanna Lahsen, Andrew S. Mathews, Pamale D. McElwee, Roderick McIntosh, Frances Moore, Jessica O'Reilly, Ben Orlove, Rajindra K. Puri, Harvey Weiss, and Karina Yager (2013), Contribution of Anthropology to the Study of Climate Change, *Nature Climate Change* 3(6), 541–44, DOI:10.1038/nclimate1775.

De León, Jason (2015), *The Land of Open Graves: Living and Dying on the Sonoran Desert Migrant Trail,* Oakland (University of California Press).

Effros, Bonnie and Guolong Lai, eds. (2018), *Unmasking Ideology in Imperial and Colonial Archaeology: Vocabulary, Symbols, and Legacy,* Los Angeles (Cotsen Institute of Archaeology Press).

Erlandson, Jon M., and Todd J. Braje (2013), Archeology and the Anthropocene, *Anthropocene* 4(1), 1–7, DOI:10.1016/j.ancene.2014.05.003.

Fabre, Thierry and Paul Sant Cassia, eds. (2007), *Between Europe and the Mediterranean: The Challenges and the Fears,* Basingstoke and New York (Palgrave MacMillan).

Farrier, David (2020), *Footprints: In Search of Future Fossils,* New York (Farrar, Straus and Giroux).

Graves-Brown, Paul, Rodney Harrison, and Angela Piccini, eds. (2013), *The Oxford Handbook of the Archaeology of the Contemporary World,* Oxford (Oxford University Press).

Hamilakis, Yannis, ed. (2016), Forum: Archaeologies of Forced and Undocumented Migration, *Journal of Contemporary Archaeology,* special thematic issue 3(2): 121–293, DOI:10.1558/jca.32409.

Hamilakis, Yannis and Philip Duke, eds. (2016), *Archaeology and Capitalism: From Ethics to Politics,* London and New York (Routledge, first published in 2007 by Left Coast Press, Inc.).

Harrison, Rodney and John Schofield, eds. (2010), *After Modernity: Archaeological Approaches to the Contemporary Past,* Oxford (Oxford University Press).

Hodder, Ian (2012), *Entangled: An Archaeology of the Relationships between Humans and Things,* Chichester (John Wiley and Sons).

Jameson, John H. and Sergiu Musteață, eds. (2019), *Transforming Heritage Practice in the 21st Century: Contributions from Community Archaeology,* Cham (Springer).

Krauss, Werner (2015), "Anthropology in the Anthropocene: Sustainable Development, Climate Change and Interdisciplinary Research," in: Heike M. Greschke and Julia Tischler, eds., *Grounding Global Climate Change: Contributions from the Social and Cultural Sciences,* pp. 59–76, Dordrecht (Springer Science and Business Media).

Lane, Paul J. (2015), Archaeology in the Age of the Anthropocene: A Critical Assessment of Its Scope and Societal Contributions, *Journal of Field Archaeology* 40(5), 485–98, DOI:101179/2042458215Y.0000000022.

Lecocq, Thomas, Stephen P. Hicks, Koen Van Noten, Kasper van Wijk, Paula Koelemeijer, Raphael S.M. De Plaen, Frédérick Massin, Gregor Hillers, Robert E. Anthony, Maria-Theresia Apoloner, Mario Arroyo-Solórzano, Jelle D. Assink, Pinar Büyükakpınar, Andrea Cannata, Flavio Cannavo, Sebastian Carrasco, Corentin Caudron, Esteban J. Chaves, David G. Cornwell, David Craig, Olivier F.C. den Ouden, Jordi Diaz, Stefanie Donner, Christos P. Evangelidis, Läslo Evers, Benoit Fauville, Gonzalo A. Fernandez, Dimitrios Giannopoulos, Steven J. Gibbons, Társilo Girona, Bogdan Grecu, Marc Grunberg, György Hetényi, Anna Horleston, Adolfo Inza, Jessica C.E. Irving, Mohammadreza Jamalreyhani, Alan Kafka, Mathijs R. Koymans, Celeste R. Labedz, Eric Larose, Nathaniel J. Lindsey, Mika McKinnon, Tobias Megies, Meghan S. Miller, William Minarik, Louis Moresi, Víctor H. Márquez-Ramírez, Martin Möllhoff, Ian M. Nesbitt, Shankho Niyogi, Javier Ojeda, Adrien Oth, Simon Proud, Jay Pulli, Lise Retailleau, Annukka E. Rintamäki, Claudio Satriano, Martha K. Savage, Shahar Shani-Kadmiel, Reinoud Sleeman, Efthimios Sokos, Klaus Stammler, Alexander E. Stott, Shiba Subedi, Mathilde B. Sørensen, Taka'aki Taira, Mar Tapia,

Fatih Turhan, Ben van der Pluijm, Mark Vanstone, Jerome Vergne, Tommi A.T. Vuorinen, Tristram Warren, Joachim Wassermann, and Han Xiao (2020), Global Quieting of High-Frequency Seismic Noise Due to Covid-19 Pandemic Lockdown Measures, *Science* 369, 1338–43, DOI:10.1126/science.abd2438.

Lydon, Jane and Uzma Z. Rizvi, eds. (2016), *Handbook of Postcolonial Archaeology,* London and New York (Routledge, first published in 2010 by Left Coast Press, Inc.).

Nigra, Benjamin T., Kym F. Faull, and Hans Barnard (2015), Analytical Chemistry in Archaeological Research, *Analytical Chemistry* 87, 3–18, DOI:10.1021/ac5029616.

Palsson, Gisli, Bronislaw Szerszynski, Sverker Sörlin, John Marks, Bernard Avril, Carole Crumley, Heide Hackmann, Poul Holm, John Ingram, Alan Kirman, Mercedes P. Buendíak, and Rifka Weehuizen (2013), Reconceptualizing the 'Anthropos' in the Anthropocene: Integrating the Social Sciences and Humanities in Global Environmental Change Research, *Environmental Science and Policy* 28(1), 3–13, DOI:101016/j.envsci.2012.11.004.

Pétursdóttir, Þóra (2017), Climate Change? Archaeology and Anthropocene, *Archaeological Dialogues* 24(2), 175–205, DOI:10.1017/S1380203817000216.

Rainey, Froelich and Elizabeth K. Ralph (1966), Archeology and Its New Technology, *Science* 153(3743), 1481–91, DOI:10.1126/science.153.3743.1481.

Schmidt, Peter R. and Innocent Pikirayi, eds. (2016), *Community Archaeology and Heritage in Africa: Decolonizing Practice,* London and New York (Routledge).

Seaborg, Glenn T. (1964), Science and the Humanities: A New Level of Symbiosis, *Science* 144(3623), 1199–1203, DOI:10.1126/science.144.3623.1199.

Stapleton, Lyssa C., Matilda McQuaid, Bruce W. Pepich, and Jenelle Porter (2016), *The Box Project: Works from the Lloyd Cotsen Collection,* Los Angeles (Cotsen Occasional Press).

Wendrich, Willeke (2018), Mutuality in Exploring the Past: Ethno-Experimental and Community Archaeology, *Journal of Ancient Egyptian Interconnections* 17, 188–201.

Zubiaurre, Maite (2019), *Talking Trash: Cultural Uses of Waste,* Nashville (Vanderbilt University Press).

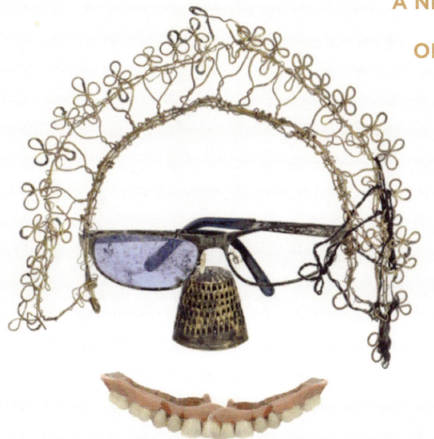

BUILDING AND BURNING EXPERIMENTAL STONE AGE HOUSES

ANNELOU VAN GIJN

RECONSTRUCTING HOUSES: WHAT'S THE USE?

Open-air museums are present all over Europe and beyond, attracting large crowds interested in what the past looked like.[1] Why should we build more of such houses and farms? Most of the structures built in the context of these (often commercial) centers were focused on getting the houses finished, with less attention to the actual building process leading to the final product. Instead, my research team wanted to document the entire *chaîne opératoire*, quantifying labor time, the amount of tool use and building materials, as well as studying the interconnectedness between these. We also wanted to give students and volunteers a chance to connect with the materials and tools used in the past, to give them a sensory experience away from computers and modern machines. And, last but not least, we wanted to push the limits of our restricted (academic) perspective of the past by exploring different technological solutions, drawing inspiration from the comments of the public, craftspeople, and, very importantly, from our dialogue with the materials we were working with.

The first house we built was located in the National Forest of Horsterwold, in the Flevopolder in the Netherlands. The forester here wanted a place to serve lemonade to the school children for whom he, together with Stone Age craftsman Diederik Pomstra, was organizing excursions in the forest, showing them how to live in and from nature. The latter suggested that such a tea house should be primal as well, and brought the Leiden Laboratory for Material Culture Studies and the forestry service together.

The house plan we chose for our experimental reconstruction was one from the site of Haamstede-Brabers, dating to around 2500 BCE by calibrated radiocarbon analysis and attributed to the late Neolithic Vlaardingen culture. This archaeological culture refers to sites that are for the most part located in the Rhine and Meuse deltas and which are characterized by a diversity in location, subsistence base, and choice of flint.[2] The house measured 9.1 × 3.8 meters (29.9 × 11.5 feet) and was not crosscut by earlier or later structures (Figure 29.1).[3] It was also relatively simple and straightforward, at least at first sight. However, already in the planning stage we encountered several problems; first of all, where was the entrance to the house? And where were the walls placed, along the outer posts or along the row of stake holes parallel to it?

THE FIRST HOUSE: WHAT DID WE LEARN?

Building the first house was really one gigantic learning experience (Figure 29.2), despite the presence of Hans de Haas and Leo Wolterbeek, both experienced in the reconstruction of prehistoric houses. We were using only replicas of Stone Age tools, banning short cuts with modern metal or mechanized tools, something that everyone, including our two experts, had to get used to. These Stone Age tools included ground stone and flint axes and adzes; bone axes, chisels, and adzes; antler wedges and adzes; and various wooden tools such as digging sticks. We collected building material from the nearby surroundings, selecting oak, elm, alder, and hazel trees as construction wood. Willow was used for the wattle-and-daub walls. As roofing material we used fresh summer reeds, harvested in late summer when they reach their maximum height. We folded bundles of reeds across the batten, a fast technique that does not require binding material.[4]

All the labor involved, as well as all the building materials, was to be quantified, a laudable intention, but one that quickly became an almost overwhelming task. Because all the tools that were used in the experiment were to be included in the reference collection for microwear analysis,[5] their complete biographies were documented. This required that each time a tool was chosen to be used, the task involved (including the contact material and the motions), time, gender, and right or left handedness of the user, as well as a subjective assessment

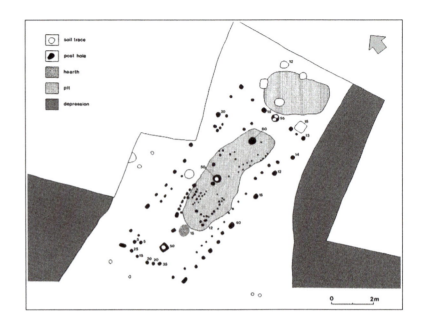

Figure 29.1. The archaeological house plan from the site of Haamstede-Brabers, the Netherlands, on which our two experimental reconstructions are based. *Adapted from Verhart 1992.*

of its effectiveness, were noted. In order to link tools with parts of the building process we also documented the number of the post, posthole, or other part of the construction that was involved. This made it possible to reconstruct a complete scheme of the *chaîne opératoire,* showing the network of labor input, tools used, and building material involved. Casts were taken after major tasks and whenever resharpening had to take place, documenting each stage of tool use for future microwear analysis. We are still facing the task of performing such an analysis on several hundreds of well-documented casts.

After four weeks the house was finished (Figure 29.3). It turned out to be an easier job than we envisaged. We think that a small family could actually build this type of house on their own, without really needing support from outsiders. So, what did the building process teach us? It taught us that Stone Age tools are far more efficient than many of us tend to think. You can cut down an oak with a diameter of 30 centimeters (12 inches) in twenty minutes using an axe made of

Figure 29.2. Some images of the building process: a) cutting down an oak tree with a quartzite axe; b) making the frame of the house; c) making the wattle and daub walls; and d) covering the roof with fresh summer reeds *All photographs by the Laboratory for Artefact Studies, Leiden University, the Netherlands.*

Figure 29.3. The house in Horsterwold, Flevopolder, the Netherlands: a) in 2012 after four weeks of labor input; and b) in 2015 when we had added several constructions, ovens, and craft zones and the site had developed into a small hamlet. *All photographs by the Laboratory for Artefact Studies, Leiden University, the Netherlands.*

quartzite or fine grained basalt. Of course this requires expertise in handling such a tool, something some students actually acquired surprisingly quickly. Using digging sticks to dig the postholes was also very illuminating in that it is possible to make a tightly fitting hole perfectly matching the post. This raises questions about the shape of postholes we find in our sites, which usually are far wider than the post inside it. We now think that these are actually the result of replacing the posts when they rotted, a process that already happened after four to five years with our house. Another surprising find was the observation that flint axes were far less effective and efficient than axes of ground stone. The latter did not need any resharpening during the course of the building process, did not break or even chip, all in contrast to the much less durable flint axes. Flint flakes, so ubiquitous in our excavations, turned out to be used very sparsely: they were briefly picked up to make a cut through bindings or other softer materials and were therefore frequently (briefly) reused and largely multifunctional. Most of these flakes rarely accumulated discernable wear traces over the course of the building project.

Another interesting insight was the importance of pain and discomfort. Despite the initial occurrence of blisters, none of the students complained about chopping down trees, trampling mud for plastering the walls, or any of the other tasks involved. With one exception: obtaining the enormous amount of reeds needed to cover the roof. We collected these in late August and we were pestered by heat, mosquitoes, humidity, and above all despair about this seemingly never-ending task. None of the different kinds of techniques or tools appeared comfortable and efficient enough to allow for some ease and optimism, and we were faced with our first (and only) student uprising. Collecting the 246 bundles of reed needed—actually an absolute minimum—was therefore the most painful aspect of the process and illustrates how work per se is not a problem, but pain, discomfort, and maybe even boredom can be. Using only Stone Age tools also taught us the importance of planning ahead. It was far more difficult to adjust a wooden post or a rafter with a bone or stone adze or axe than with a mechanical saw or even a metal axe. We therefore regularly used fire to burn away parts or sections of posts in order to adjust them to their position in the overall structure.

The Horsterwold house was used for various purposes (Figure 29.4). The Faculty of Archaeology of Leiden University used it for carrying out experimental fieldwork for masters students. Several graduate students used the location for long-term experiments. The forestry service organized school excursions, making use of the educational packages that we had developed. The house even occasionally functioned as a retreat for stressed captains of industry who could spend a weekend there in order to reconnect with nature. The Horsterwold building project also had a group of devoted groupies, who came back time and again, even staying over-night on cold winter nights. After all, it was a little paradise, located besides a beautiful little lake, very remote by Dutch standards, and without any modern comforts.

BURNING DOWN THE HORSTERWOLD HOUSE

After seven years the Horsterwold house needed some serious upkeep. It had gradually lost its social relevance, with fewer school classes coming in and local interest waning. We decided that we had to end the biography of the house and what bet-ter way to do so than to burn it down (the act of destruction is discussed in some detail by Doug Bailey, Chapter 1 in this volume). The house was furnished with a bedding of straw and hides and some wooden roughly hewn benches; ceramic ves-sels were filled with different contents like water, grains and hazelnuts; a roast and a large fish were hung above the fire-place; a quern with grain kernels was positioned close to the hearth; and some flint nodules were placed near the central posts (Figure 29.5a, b). The position of all of these objects was documented before setting the house on fire.

We wanted to simulate a normal accident, setting the house on fire from the inside. However, this took more effort than we had expected. We had to make a large fire in the hearth and only when the actual flames reached the reed roof did it catch fire

Figure 29.4. Some of the ways in which the house and its surrounding area were used: a) to show visitors and schoolchildren about Stone Age crafts and foodways; b) to carry out scientific experiments, here with the use of different kinds of fuel, with Leiden University archaeology students from the Department of Archaeological Sciences. *All photographs by the Laboratory for Artefact Studies, Leiden University, the Netherlands.*

(Figure 29.5c). But then it went fast: within a few seconds the fire rolled along the roof ridge and in less than four minutes the house was largely burned and the flames died down.[6] Only parts of the roof that had been covered in moss took a bit longer to catch fire and also continued to smolder (Figure 29.5d, e). Our thermocouples told us that the fire reached 987°C (1,809°F) at one point. Parts of the construction, especially the thick wall posts, continued to smolder for at least another twenty-four hours; the next day we could still see some flames. A visit three days later showed that the last of the center posts, which had still been standing before, had finally collapsed, evidently because they had been slowly burning from within. The fire had been an intense sensory experience, even for those of us who make fires frequently. The speed at which the entire house burned down was impressive. After the fire had taken its toll, the remnants of our house were a sad and almost spooky sight (Figure 29.5f). Certainly a fire like this, whether ignited intentionally or accidentally, must have formed an equally intense experience for onlookers and participants in the past.

Although we had hoped to leave the house for a few years before excavating it, the forestry service had other plans, so we had to excavate everything only three months later (Figure 29.6). Even after this short period nature had already taken over. Large parts of the ruins were overgrown with a variety of plants, mice had moved the last unburned hazelnuts around, and a fox had dug through one of the collapsed loam walls to remove the underlying roast. This had exposed one of the ceramic vessels in the house and a helpful visitor had saved it by placing it under a nearby tree. The excavation was basically a regular one, employing the normal procedures, but of course we knew what to expect. Obviously the bedding of reeds and skins was gone, as were the wooden digging sticks and the benches. However, most of the ceramics survived largely intact, even where the walls had collapsed

Figure 29.6. Excavation of the burned house. *Photograph by the Laboratory for Artefact Studies Leiden University, the Netherlands.*

on top of them. The bone tools could be retrieved, and even the burned remains of one of the baskets could be excavated. The flint nodules had fractured into hundreds of small fragments. One of the primary objectives was to see whether we could reconstruct the place of the burned wooden remains of the original structure.[7] This was possible in the majority of the cases.

THE SECOND HOUSE: WHY BUILD IT? NEW INSIGHTS

When the press came to the official opening of the Horsterwold house, we were asked by a reporter from the town of Vlaardingen why we were building a 'Vlaardingen house' in the Flevopolder. It should have been built in Vlaardingen. This shows that even an abstract construct like an archaeological culture, in our case the Vlaardingen culture, can evoke a sense of identity and ownership. And so it happened. In 2016

Figure 29.5. Burning down the Horsterwold house: a and b) the furnishings of the house prior to burning; c) a large fire had to be made in the hearth in order for the house to catch fire; d and e) the progress of the fire; and f) the sad remains just after the fire. *All photographs by the Laboratory for Artefact Studies, Leiden University, the Netherlands.*

Figure 29.7. The house reconstruction at Vlaardingen-Broekpolder in progress. *Photograph by the Laboratory for Artefact Studies, Leiden University, the Netherlands.*

we built a second reconstruction of the same house plan, this time in the Vlaardingen-Broekpolder (Figure 29.7). We worked closely together with the Federatie Broekpolder,[8] a group of volunteers who, along with our students, were instrumental in finishing the construction.[9] The house forms part of the new open-air center of Masamuda,[10] which is specifically aimed at showing how people lived in the deltas of the old Rhine and Meuse rivers through time.

Building the second Vlaardingen house, we made different choices with regards to the placing of the walls and various details of the building process, and we modified the documentation process, having learned from our previous experience (Figure 29.8). The stone axes and adzes, the wooden digging sticks, many of the bone and antler chisels, and some of the bone adzes were still usable and were used again for this house. Interestingly, the labor time and the time the tools were used in various activities was pretty similar to the first house. The Horsterwold house took around 325 working days and 327 hours of tool use, that at Vlaardingen-Broekpolder

Figure 29.8. Some details of the Vlaardingen-Broekpolder reconstruction: a) the east façade; b) the lock of the eastern entrance; and c) the doorframe covered with red deer skins stitched together and onto the frame with retted lime bark. *All photographs by the Laboratory for Artefact Studies, Leiden University, the Netherlands.*

352 days of labor and 376 hours of tool use. Although we were more knowledgeable and thus more effective, we also made the roof thicker and made some other improvements in comparison to the Horsterwold house, which took additional time to accomplish.

This house is used twice a week by volunteers, who use it as a base for their activities like laying out fields, carrying out various tasks within the area, and doing small repairs. The site is open to the public and visitors are shown around. It is also used by researchers of the Department of Archaeological Science of Leiden University for various scientific experiments.[11] The house will be the center for a new collaborative project between the Material Culture Studies group of Leiden University and Masamuda, with the title "Putting Life into Neolithic Houses: Investigating Domestic Craft and Subsistence Activities through Experiments and Material Analysis" (funded by Dutch Research Council grant NWO AIB.19.020).[12] Through workshops with knowledgeable craftspeople, experimentation, and microwear and residue analysis we hope to bring more detail and variation into the ways that Neolithic life is displayed in open-air centers. By having reconstruction drawings made by artists and disseminating these through Exarc.net,[13] we hope to get new inspiration that allows us to push the limits of our imagination. At the same time, public participation in archaeological projects is becoming ever more essential, and experimental archaeology is an excellent way of reaching out: doing things together and exploring the various technological choices of the past creates a scientific community in which both scientists and the general public can thrive.

ACKNOWLEDGMENTS

I would like to thank all involved in making these experiments possible: the National Forestry Service at Horsterwold, the city council of Zeewolde, the Federatie Broekpolder, Masamuda, and the Faculty of Archaeology, Leiden University. I especially want to mention Hans-Erik Kuipers and Andre Wels of the National Forestry Service and Jeroen ter Brugge and Sytse van der Hoek of the Federatie Broekpolder and Masamuda. At the Faculty of Archaeology I want to especially thank Eric Mulder, our laboratory assistant, as well as the student-assistants involved in these projects: Tobias Buitenhuis, Timothy Stikkelorum, and Jan Dekker. Of course, none of this would have been possible without my partners in crime Diederik Pomstra, Leo Wolterbeek, Annemieke Verbaas, and Hans de Haas. Students and volunteers, both in Zeewolde and in Vlaardingen, are thanked for their never-ending enthusiastic participation. The Prins Bernhard Cultuurfonds financed the experiment in the Horsterwold, the province of Zuid Holland and the Vlaardingen Council that of the reconstruction in the Vlaardingen-Broekpolder.

NOTES

1 https://exarc.net (accessed 28 February 2022).
2 Amkreutz et al. 2016, Van Gijn and Bakker 2005.
3 Verhart 1992.
4 Pomstra and Van Gijn 2013, Van Gijn and Pomstra 2016.
5 Van Gijn 2010.
6 Pomstra and Van Gijn 2020.
7 Full analysis of the excavated remains has not finished and will be reported in a forthcoming edited volume dedicated to experimental house building projects.
8 www.federatiebroekpolder.nl/archeologisch-erf (accessed 31 August 2020).
9 www.youtube.com/watch?v=kVkIeMAB6cU& (accessed 31 August 2020).
10 www.masamuda.nl (accessed 31 August 2020).
11 Kozowyk et al. 2017.
12 www.puttinglife.com (accessed 28 February 2022).
13 https://exarc.net/ (accessed 28 February 2022).

BIBLIOGRAPHY

Amkreutz, Luc, Leo B.M. Verhart, and Annelou van Gijn (2016), "Vlaardingen-Cultuur en Stein-Groep," in: Luc Amkreutz, Fred T.S. Brounen, Jos H.C. Deeben, Roy Machiels, Marie-France Van Oorsauw, and Bjørn Smit, eds., *Vuursteen Verzameld,* pp. 169–75, Amersfoort (Rijksdienst voor het Cultureel Erfgoed). [in Dutch]

Kozowyk, Paul R.B., Marie Soressi, Diederik Pomstra, and Geeske H.J. Langejans (2017), Experimental Methods for the Palaeolithic Dry Distillation of Birch Bark: Implications for the Origin and Development of Neandertal Adhesive Technology, *Scientific Reports* 7(8033), DOI:10.1038/s41598-017-08106-7.

Pomstra, Diederik and Annelou van Gijn (2013), The Reconstruction of a Late-Neolithic House Combining Primitive Technology and Science, *Bulletin of Primitive Technology* 45, 45–54.

Pomstra, Diederik and Annelou van Gijn (2020), De Dood van "Huize Horsterwold": De Experimentele Verbranding van een Huisreconstructie, *Archeologie in Nederland* 2020/3, 2–7. [in Dutch]

Van Gijn, Annelou. (2010), *Flint in Focus: Lithic Biographies in the Neolithic and Bronze Age,* Leiden (Sidestone Press).

Van Gijn, Annelou and Jan Albert Bakker (2005), "Megalith Builders and Sturgeon Fishers: Middle Neolithic B: Funnel Beaker Culture and Vlaardingen Group," in: Leendert P. Louwe Kooijmans, Harry Fokkens, Paul W. van den Broeke, and Annelou L. van Gijn, eds., *The Prehistory of the Netherlands*, pp. 281–306, Amsterdam (Amsterdam University Press).

Van Gijn, Annelou. and Diederik Pomstra (2016), "Huize Horsterwold: The Reconstruction of a Neolithic Houseplan Using Stone Age Equipment," in: Linda Hurcombe and Penny Cunningham, eds., *The Life Cycle of Structures in Experimental Archaeology; An Object Biography Approach*, pp. 177–86, Leiden (Sidestone Press).

Verhart, Leo B.M. (1992), Settling or Trekking: The Late Neolithic House Plans of Haamstede-Brabers and its Counterparts, *Oudheidkundige Mededelingen Rijksmuseum van Oudheden Leiden* 72, 73–99.

WHAT DID IT FEEL LIKE?

HOW SENSORY ARCHAEOLOGY IS CHANGING THE WAY WE UNDERSTAND THE PAST AND PRESENT

ROBIN SKEATES

When I was a student—initially captivated and subsequently bored by introductory lectures on archaeology, and later rubbing up against the boundaries of archaeological thought for my doctorate—I believed that all archaeologists should try to visualize, as vividly as possible, what it was like to live in past societies. We should aspire to be like photographers, and share our images widely, to bring the past alive for everyone. Now, some thirty years on, having traveled intellectually from material culture studies to visual culture, sensory studies, aesthetics, and beyond, I recognize the limitations of my original (visually-biased) way of seeing, yet still believe in an academic endeavor that, although not solely determined by present-day challenges, is obliged to inform our publics of our findings and feed their imaginations (see Chapters 30 and 31 in this volume). One way archaeologists can do this, I have come to think, is to ask the question, 'What did it *feel* like to live in past societies?'

This and related questions about past sensory perceptions and experiences, although growing in favor in contemporary archaeological theory, remain outside mainstream archaeological method and theory. Despite (or perhaps because of) this, they are worth considering, both on intellectual grounds and because—in my experience—people not trained in archaeology can readily relate to the bodily and emotional issues that they raise: personally (we all have bodies through which we make sense of the world around us), and in relation to their own and other cultures and societies (which impose diverse constraints on how we understand and what we actually do with our bodies). The questions are, in other words, relevant, and have the potential to highlight the relevance of archaeology to people today, both on individual and societal levels.

A eureka moment for me was when Michael Shanks (who has made a career out of outside-the-box archaeology)—in offering closing comments on a conference I had participated in on "Seeing the Past"—made the point that the meeting was in essence fundamentally flawed because of its visual focus at the expense of the other senses. I had recently written a book on *Visual Culture and Archaeology*, which sought to establish a new way of archaeological thinking about art and society, so I took Michael's comment very much to heart, and followed it up. I soon discovered the work of David Howes and Constance Classen on sensory studies, and spent a summer reading David's edited compendium (2005) *Empire of the Senses* cover to cover. This provided the conceptual starting point for my book on *An Archaeology of the Senses*,[1] and has led more recently to an edited volume with Jo Day on sensory archaeology.[2] Below, drawing on this latest book, I summarize some of the key tenets of sensory studies and sensory archaeology, before describing the ways in which I have begun to use these in my work on cave archaeology in Italy.

SENSORY STUDIES AND SENSORY ARCHAEOLOGY

The development of sensory archaeology has been influenced by the success of the sensory studies school, established by Howes and Classen in the early 1990s. This school of thought can be broadly characterized by a revelation that the senses are everywhere, yet generally taken for granted; a foregrounding of the senses as both object and means of study; as well as an emphasis on their sociocultural formation. The roots of the current archaeological interest in the senses lie in an array of archaeological studies published in the last twenty-five years. Only a few of these were dedicated to investigating ancient sensory regimes in a holistic manner. Instead, the majority touched on the senses, experience, and perception, often uncritically

accepting Aristotle's five senses model, and with arguments generally restricted to "the senses were there." Recent milestones in the growth of sensory studies in archaeology range from what might be characterized as archaeology *with* the senses, to archaeology *of* the senses. Instead of claiming a sensory turn for archaeology, or calling for the paradigmatic reconstitution of archaeological theory and practice as sensorial, I regard this continued proliferation of sensory studies in archaeology as helping to avoid their marginalization and facilitating their discussion and impact. With this background in place, I now want to outline some of the key concepts and debates of sensory archaeology.

SENSORIUM

The concept of sensorium has proved to be useful for thinking about the ways in which we make sense of the world around us and the ways in which different contexts shape our perceptions. It is similar to James Gibson's concept of affordances. The broad disciplinary span of archaeologists is leading us to acknowledge the sensorium also as a sociocultural construct.

SENSORY ORDERS

According to Constance Classen, each society espouses a particular sensory model—composed of sensory meanings, values, and hierarchies—according to which that society translates sensory perceptions and concepts into a worldview. This sensory model provides a basic perceptual paradigm to be followed by members of that society, but is also liable to be challenged by persons and groups who differ on certain sensory values. Archaeology can add to our knowledge of culturally diverse sensory orders.

SENSESCAPE

Sensescape is a term closely related to sensorium. It has been used by archaeologists in describing the sensory dimensions of culturally constructed landscapes.

WAYS OF SENSING

The term 'ways of sensing' likewise stems from a play on words and concepts; in this case John Berger's *Ways of Seeing*. In using this term, Howes and Classen have drawn attention to the practices of perception and the techniques of the senses used by members of particular cultures, especially for political ends.

THE SENSORIAL FIELD AND MULTI-SENSORIALITY

Central to the approach of Yannis Hamilakis (2013) to the senses is the idea of the sensorial field. This construct challenges the way in which sensory studies (and publishers) have often defined and analyzed the senses separately: one sense at a time. Instead, Hamilakis demands that we focus on the interrelationship of the senses, and on sensorial assemblages of experiences. A number of archaeologists have consequently placed an emphasis on multi-sensoriality. There are, however, arguments in favor of not entirely ruling out in practice the sense-divided perspective. David Howes argues that this divided approach helps us understand the origin and development of sensory studies, and that by studying the senses separately we can develop a deeper understanding of their differential elaboration and interplay in different cultural contexts.

AFFECT

'Affect' is a slippery term. Drawing on the affective sciences, Yannis Hamilakis and others use this term to refer to feeling, emotion, or specific emotional response. However, most archaeologists use the term more broadly, being concerned with the experiential and sensory properties and impacts of material things on people in the past and present. This ties in with Jane Bennett's concept of vibrancy.

SENSORY MUSEOLOGY AND HERITAGE

It is also worth reflecting on the institutionalized contexts of archaeological museums and heritage sites. Sensory and disability studies have criticized public museums as sight-centered institutions, where visitors are conditioned how to behave. In response, many museums have sought to democratize their spaces and exhibitions, in order to make their collections sensorially and conceptually more accessible and discursive to a wider range of stakeholders. This has included replacing "Do Not Touch!" with "Please Touch!" signage. Yet ethical and legal tensions remain, particularly when it comes to presenting and preserving archaeological heritage outdoors.

SENSUOUS SCHOLARSHIP

The idea of sensuous scholarship, first developed by the ethnographer Paul Stoller, questions how scholars undertake fieldwork and write about their experiences and calls for a sensory awakening.[3] This reflexive attitude has prompted some archaeologists to reconsider precisely how they undertake sensory studies. The difficulties of sensory studies in archaeology cannot be underestimated. However, hope is offered by an increasingly explicit range of research methods now being brought into the service of sensory archaeology.

RESEARCH METHODS IN SENSORY ARCHAEOLOGY

Critiques of previous academic traditions and studies that have denied the senses or failed to express them effectively are now well established. Archaeological sensory studies must then remain reflexive. A number of archaeologists have already attempted to remain sensorially self-aware throughout the workflows of archaeological practice, and they have subsequently sought to make sensorial details of the process of investigation a transparent part of published archaeological narratives. Incorporating thinking about sensoriality into existing archaeological research methods is of primary importance. Ethnographic insights and analogies can also add value, if used with caution. Direct bodily experience of the material remains of the past is also explicitly acknowledged as an important tool of sensorial archaeology. Experimentation and reconstruction can also help highlight, fill in gaps, and share our understandings of past sensorial experiences. A number of archaeologists also advocate the potential of digital visualization and virtual, augmented, and mixed reality, including acknowledging the decision-making processes involved in their creation, to help us think in new ways about the sensory dimensions of ancient sites and monuments. Using our imaginations to fill out and pull together our archaeological data on multiple scales is also something to be encouraged when seeking to understand the sensory dimensions of past people, places, and things.

Furthermore, given that we are all generally trained to think in constrained ways, creative input from contemporary artists can help to liberate us by providing food for thought and imagination. Related to this, a number of archaeologists now aim to evoke possible past sensory experiences, rather than to produce exact representations of them. In particular, the use of evocative writing, in contrast to conventional forms of scientific writing, can be effective in reanimating the past in multisensory ways. Empathizing with past people might be regarded by sceptics as a sensorial self-indulgence too far, particularly if it rests on an assumption that humans may feel and think in the same or very similar ways. However, as Liv Nilsson Stutz (2020) puts it, in relation to archaeologies of death and burial, by placing ourselves in this landscape we can at a deep level relate it to our own experiences of death and loss, and connect on a very human level to people in the past.

RISK-TAKING AND EXPERIMENTATION: THE BENEFITS OF SENSORY ARCHAEOLOGY

Ultimately, there is no single toolkit for sensory archaeology. Nor should there be—sensory archaeology is necessarily a work in progress. If we want to maintain a dynamic and innovative discipline of archaeology we have to take risks and experiment, by trying out some of these approaches in practice and then discussing whether or not they enhance our understandings of the past and of the present. Archaeologists who have tried clearly recognize the benefits of this shift in emphasis within sensory archaeology. Two good examples can be found in this volume, in the chapters immediately preceding and following this one: Annelou van Gijn (Chapter 29) underlines the sensory experience of experimentally building and burning down houses; while Christine Torill Lindstrøm (Chapter 27) codifies the arguably prescribed emotional experiences and personality traits represented by facial expressions on the Akrotiri wall paintings.

DOING SENSORIAL ARCHAEOLOGY

If my book on *An Archaeology of the Senses* was an exercise in armchair sensory scholarship, albeit enhanced by inspecting as many archaeological sites and museum collections as possible first hand (even though I was allowed to touch very little), my last two archaeological field projects—focused on later prehistoric burial caves and their associated landscapes in Italy—have been predominantly hands-on, and have provided exciting opportunities to experiment doing sensory archaeology away from the word processor. Essentially, we have adapted pre-existing archaeological methods to incorporate sensoriality into our work.

PERCEIVING AND EXPERIENCING SENSESCAPES

In the landscape, we have followed the lead of Sue Hamilton et al. (2006) in adapting phenomenological archaeology to undertake multi-sensory site catchment analyses around our excavated sites, at the same time as undertaking archaeological prospection work, and scientific studies of changes and continuities in the Mediterranean vegetation over time. This work has helped us characterize different sensescapes (ranging, in our study areas in Sardinia and Central Italy, from plateaus, to steep hillsides, to valley bottoms) and people's embodied and culturally variable perceptions and experiences of special places within them (Figure 28.1).

Figure 28.1. Our team excavates a mortuary deposit, placed below a former spring and covered by a stone cairn, in Su Cannisoni rockshelter, Sardinia (Italy). Out of all the caves we excavated in the Seulo landscape, this one felt the best to us, because of the panoramic view, shade from the summer sun, and fresh air. A few days after we took this photograph, the wind blew so hard along the rockshelter that our tripod fell and broke our surveying equipment, deepening our understanding of the distinct sensory personality of this place. *Photograph by the Seulo Caves Project.*

Figure 28.2. Archaeologist Agni Prijatelj crawls through Is Janus cave, Sardinia (Italy). We became somewhat habituated to negotiating this challenging cave system, but each of us developed a particular set of bodily techniques to do so, and I still remember the darkness and the ashes from prehistoric fires that covered us each time we went in and out of the cave. *Photograph by the Seulo Caves Project.*

EXPERIENCING RITUAL ARCHITECTURE, PLACES, AND PRACTICES

Within each of the caves that we excavated—all of which contained rich material evidence of mortuary and other ritual practices deposited in well-defined spaces—we have recorded and compared cave temperatures, relative humidity, and light levels throughout the year, in order to characterize their diverse sensorial affordances and personalities. While acknowledging changes in the morphology of these caves (due to major rockfalls, for example), we are fairly confident that—for the most part—their basic architectural forms have been relatively well preserved since prehistoric times. We have consequently interviewed our project members on their bodily and emotional experiences and memories of moving through and working in these caves, and then used this information to help imagine our way back into the multisensory experiences and perceptions of members of different prehistoric communities performing mortuary and other underground rituals within the distinctive sensoria of those caves.

In the case of Neolithic cult caves in Italy, Ruth Whitehouse (1992) has characterized these as relatively inaccessible, spatially zoned, cool, humid, dark, and resonant environments, elaborated with karst formations and symbolic installations that lent them an awe-inspiring sense of otherness and liminality—features that were exploited by ritual leaders, within particular sensory orders, for their physical and emotional

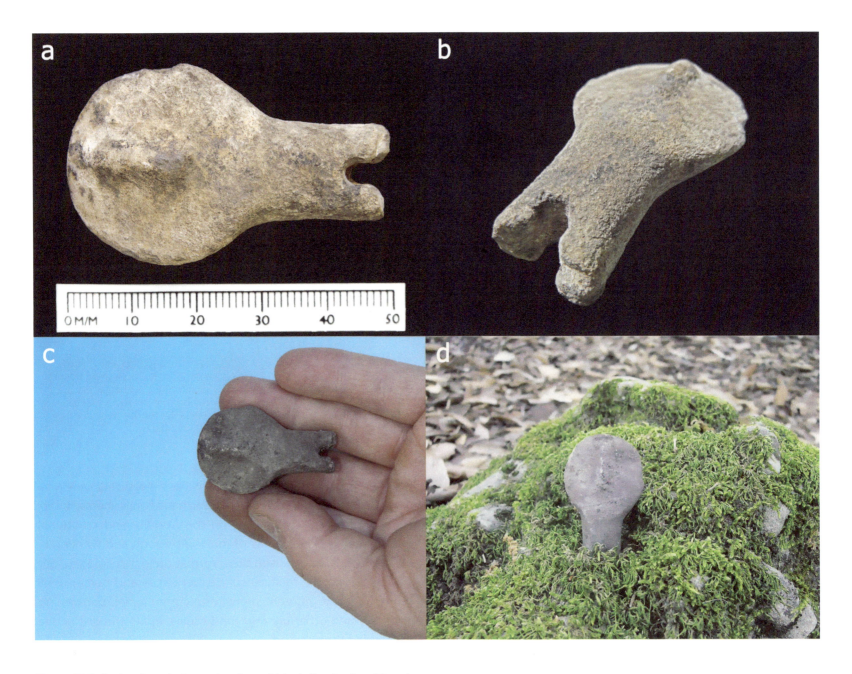

Figure 28.3. Contrasting photographs of a prehistoric figurine head from Is Janus cave: a) Jeff Veitch's professional archaeological photograph, taken for publication; b) another photograph by Jeff, which instead captures the texture of the stone and its working from an unusual angle; c) selfie showing how I preferred to handle the small artefact: resting gently between my fingers rather lying than in my palm; d) Agni Prijatelj's alternative photo of the anthropomorphic head, almost brought to life lying on a bed of moss in the magical woodland outside Grutta Is Janus ('Cave of the Fairies'). *All photographs by the Seulo Caves Project.*

impact on ritual participants. In our Seulo Caves Project in Sardinia,[4] we went on to present an even more nuanced view of how particular effects of light and darkness in ritual caves might have been actively used and experienced by later prehistoric people, and how these effects mediated between people's bodies, cave architecture, and cultural objects, including human remains (Figure 28.2).

PRODUCTION AND CONSUMPTION OF SENSUOUS CULTURAL MATERIALS

During the course of our post-excavation artifact studies and materials science analyses, we have also begun to think more about the multi-sensory properties of the artifacts and bones that we are recording, including how people might have manipulated and experienced these sensorially. A memorable example is the simple, symmetrical and detachable, stone figurine head that we found in a Neolithic deposit in Is Janus cave in central Sardinia. Informed by recent figurine studies, which acknowledge that the aesthetic properties of these special artifacts can appeal to the senses—particularly of sight and touch—and that they were subject to manipulation in performative contexts, we experimented photographing it in different ways (Figure 28.3).

THE CONTRIBUTION OF SENSORY ARCHAEOLOGY

Drawing together this combination of reflexive anecdote, academic literature review, and examples drawn from recent research projects, I would like to suggest that sensory archaeology can bring at least four significant benefits to the ways in which we understand the past and the present. First, it can highlight biases, limitations, and gaps in established scientific methods, interpretations, forms of writing, and illustration. Second, it can bring together and extend recent scholarly thought on the body, phenomenology, memory, emotion, and the senses. Third, it can encourage us to produce new,

full-bodied narratives of past people and their material remains. Fourth and finally, it can direct us to pay closer attention to the sensory properties, practices, experiences, and perceptions inherent in a range of archaeologically visible human behaviors, many of which remain with us today.

NOTES

1   Skeates 2010.
2   Skeates and Day 2020.
3   Stoller 1989, 1997.
4   Skeates 2016, Machause López and Skeates 2022.

BIBLIOGRAPHY

Berger, John (1972), *Ways of Seeing*, London (BBC and Penguin).

Hamilakis, Yannis (2013), *Archaeology and the Senses: Human Experience, Memory and Affect,* New York (Cambridge University Press).

Hamilton, Sue, Ruth Whitehouse, Keri Brown, Pamela Combes, Edward Herring, and Mike Seager Thomas (2006), Phenomenology in Practice: Towards a Methodology for a 'Subjective' Approach, *European Journal of Archaeology* 9(1), 31–71.

Howes, David, ed. (2005), *Empire of the Senses,* Oxford (Berg).

Machause López, Sonia, and Robin Skeates (2022), Caves, Senses, and Ritual Flows in the Iberian Iron Age: The Territory of Edeta, *Open Archaeology* 8, 1–29.

Nilsson Stutz, Liv (2020), "Sensing Death and Experiencing Mortuary Ritual," in: Robin Skeates and Jo Day, eds., *The Routledge Handbook of Sensory Archaeology*, pp. 149-163, London (Routledge).

Skeates, Robin (2005), *Visual Culture and Archaeology: Art and Social Life in Prehistoric South-East Italy*, London (Duckworth).

—— (2010), *An Archaeology of the Senses: Prehistoric Malta,* Oxford (Oxford University Press).

—— (2016), "Experiencing Darkness and Light in Caves: Later Prehistoric Examples from Seulo in Central Sardinia," in: Marion Dowd and Robert Hensey, eds., *The Archaeology of Darkness*, pp. 39–49, Oxford and Philadelphia (Oxbow Books).

Skeates, Robin and Jo Day (2020), *The Routledge Handbook of Sensory Archaeology*. London (Routledge).

Stoller, Paul (1989), *The Taste of Ethnographic Things: The Senses in Anthropology,* Philadelphia (University of Pennsylvania Press).

—— (1997), *Sensuous Scholarship,* Philadelphia (University of Pennsylvania Press).

Whitehouse, Ruth D. (1992), *Underground Religion: Cult and Culture in Prehistoric Italy,* London (Accordia Research Centre, University of London).

PSYCHOLOGY FROM THE BRONZE AGE

FACES, EMOTIONS, AND PERSONALITIES AT THERA

TORILL CHRISTINE LINDSTRØM

Art was a representation of the collective values of the society of which the viewer was a member.
(Nanno Marinatos 2014, p. 33)

Aber nicht allein in den momentanen Seelenzustand eines Menschen gewährt das Mienenspiel einen sichern Einblick, auch seine individuelle Eigenthümlichkeit lässt sich bis zu einem gewissen Grade daraus errathen. [The play of facial expressions not only affords a reliable insight into the momentary state of mind of a person, but to a certain degree his individual peculiarities can also be guessed from them.]
(Theodor Piderit 1886, p. 139)

FEELINGS ARE EPHEMERAL

Although archaeology is defined as the science of objects from the past, the lived lives of the individuals that produced and used these objects are what really intrigues us. Experimental archaeology provides numerous examples where prehistoric behaviors are reconstructed, re-enacted and experienced. The foci are mostly on the material processes, but also on the social and emotional experiences and feelings of the participants. But can we really grasp what prehistoric, or even historic, persons felt?

We could stop here and say that we are so embedded and imbued in our own bodies, feelings, and experiences, personal history, and cultural context, that we cannot transcend these contingencies. And indeed, historical films, made just a few decades back, now appear helplessly typical of the times in which they were made, not of the times that they are supposed to depict and describe. However, to the extent that humans are a species with species-specific, common characteristics,[1] it should be possible to start with common basic emotions and suggest some of the circumstances under which they may arise. In some instances, these might even be identifiable in archaeological materials, even though these may be difficult to interpret.

FACES FASCINATE, BUT DO THEY TELL US ANYTHING?

Depictions of human faces and bodies, produced in various materials—painting, sculpture, vase-paintings, textile, wood, stone, metal, among others—are probably what fascinate us most in archaeological findings. All of a sudden, we seem to look directly at people from ancient times. In the following, I will use the term 'picture' for all such representations of humans, regardless of the medium. Still, questions arise: how shall we perceive, understand, and interpret these representations? Were the depicted persons real or imagined? Can we use the images as sources of information about people from the period? Can ancient faces tell us anything about ancient people?

Psychological interpretations are the subject of a vast literature on portraiture and art-style within the history of art,[2] but one treatise stands out: the psychological description of the personalities of the Roman emperors based on their sculptured portraits written by the Norwegian classical archaeologist L'Orange (1967). He claimed that facial features can be used as data in their own right. However, no matter how fascinating L'Orange's study is, his interpretations were based solely on his own subjective impressions and intuition. The theoretical and methodological basis for analyzing facial expressions in reliable and valid ways was never developed within archaeology.

THE PICTURE AS DECEIVER AND REVEALER

Ancient pictures are often formal representations, executed in a stereotypical, traditional fashion: conventional ways in which a god, king, saint, worshiper, or any human being—real or imagined—should look and be presented. Actually, one can claim that most pictures, stereotypical or not, are constructions. Even our own private photos are seldom objective depictions of actual moments. We choose angle and background, we pose, we smile, we hide disturbing elements, and so on. Not to speak of pictures taken in the studio of a photographer. They show us at our best, our idealized selves: dressed up and made-up. Similarly, official pictures of royalty and political leaders are idealized constructions. Therefore, one may claim that all these pictures lie. Yet on the other hand, they tell another kind of truth: they show how these persons want to be seen and understood in their time and society. Portraits are at the same time normative representations and official icons. This opens up new ways of interpreting ancient pictures: they may tell us about the normative characters of rulers and other persons of high positions, as well as of other persons in the society. Pictures can show personality. The personality traits they were depicted to have had may tell us something about the normative personal qualities, personality traits, and ideals in the culture, and among the population in general. As Marinatos (2014) writes, "art was a representation of the collective values of the society of which the viewer was a member." But how can ancient faces be interpreted systematically?

CAN PSYCHOLOGY COME INTO THE PICTURE?

This is where psychology comes into the picture, quite literally. A test for registration and interpretation of facial expressions has been developed within psychology: the Facial Action Coding System,[3] which is used in research in numerous fields.[4] Archaeology is a discipline with multiple connections to other fields. Yet collaboration with psychologists has until now been sparse. This is, however, changing, particularly in cognitive archaeology and neuro-archaeology.[5] The turn toward exploring social behaviors and systems, beliefs, gender-roles, and attitudes has made psychology increasingly relevant within archaeology. Yet the combination of archaeology with psychology is often still regarded as being 'outside the box.'

The Facial Action Coding System is based on the human facial musculature (Table 27.1). Data recorded are degrees of contractions of these muscles, and their co-variation is clustered into recognizable emotional expressions. Particularly, the muscles around eyes and mouth have great relevance for emotional expressions. The application of this coding system across different cultures has been debated. Cultures have various reasons for expressing emotions and express them differently. Whether facial expressions show inner emotional states, or are determined by social conventions, has likewise been questioned.[6] Yet meta-analyses have shown that humans across cultures do indeed share some basic emotions and emotional expressions, and the proposed Facial Action Coding System has been shown to have reasonable good cross-cultural validity.[7] The basic emotions registered are: *anger, contempt, disgust, fear, happiness, sadness* and *surprise*. In addition, an intriguing finding is that emotional expressions appear related to personality.

Personality theories are numerous. Personality denotes the relatively stable characteristics of a person. Today, the Five-Factor Model Trait Theory of McCrae and Costa (1997) is one of the most widely accepted theories. It claims that personality can be described as a function of scores on five dimensions: *Agreeableness, Conscientiousness, Extroversion, Neuroticism*, and *Openness toward experience*. Each dimension refers to a set of related qualities. Like the Facial Action Coding System, the cross-cultural validity and relevance of the Five-Factor Model Trait Theory is debated. Yet the five dimensions are to a considerable extent registered and recognized as relevant personality traits across cultures.[8]

CONNECTIONS BETWEEN EMOTIONS AND PERSONALITY

As early as 1886 Theodor Piderit wrote that facial expressions provide not only insight into the momentary psychic state of a person, but that his or her individual peculiarity, up to a certain point, can be guessed from them.[9] In recent years, emotional expressions, as measured with the Facial Action Coding System, have been confirmed to connect to personality traits as defined by the Five-Factor Model Trait Theory. *Agreeableness* and *Extroversion* connect to expressions indicating a social approach: smiles and mirroring of expressions. *Conscientiousness* connects to smiles, but also to seriousness and embarrassment, conventionality, and adherence to social norms. *Neuroticism* connects to anger, hostility, aggression, fear, contempt, disgust, sadness, and generally to expressions of distress. *Openness toward experience* connects to positive emotions: smiles and laughter, alertness, concentration, curiosity, and also unconventionality and intelligence. This indicates that emotional expressions registered by the Facial Action Coding System can, to some extent, be related to the personality traits of the Five-Factor Model Trait Theory, and successfully be applied to art.[10]

WHAT DID I LOOK FOR, AND HOW?

Thera, also called Santorini, was a large volcanic island in the eastern Mediterranean Sea that suffered an enormous eruption around 1600 BCE. Large parts of the island were lost and the rest remained uninhabitable due to thick layers of tephra. Today, the Municipality of Thera consists of six islands of varying size, of which only two are inhabited. And indeed, except for a short-lived Phoenician settlement, the main island was uninhabited until the Dorian Greeks settled there in the ninth century BCE.

Yet hidden under the tephra, and well preserved by it, there were buildings with large-scale paintings. The excavation of the Bronze Age town, now called Akrotiri, started in 1870 by Ferdinand André Fouqué, was continued by Spyridon

Action unit	Descriptor	Muscular basis
1	Inner brow raiser	Frontalis, pars medialis
2	Outer brow raiser	Frontalis, pars lateralis
3	—	—
4	Brow lowerer	Depressor glabellae; Depressor supercilli; Corrugator
5	Upper lid raiser	Levator palpebrea superioris
6	Cheek raiser	Orbicularis oculi, pars orbitalis
7	Lid tightener	Orbicularis oculi, pars palebraris
8	—	—
9	Nose wrinkler	Levator labii superioris, alaeque nasi
10	Upper lid raiser	Levator labii superioris, caput infraorbitalis
11	Nasolabial fold deepener	Zygomatic minor
12	Lip corner puller	Zygomatic maior
13	Cheek puffer	Caninus
14	Dimpler	Buccinator
15	Lip corner depressor	Triangularis
16	Lower lip depressor	Depressor labii
17	Chin raiser	Mentalis
18	Lip puckerer	Incisivii labii superioris; Incisivii labii inferioris
19	—	—
20	Lip stretcher	Risorius
21	—	—
22	Lip funneler	Orbicularis oris
23	Lip tightener	Orbicularis oris
24	Lip pressor	Orbicularis oris
25	Lip part	Depressor labii; or relaxation of Mentalis or Orbicularis oris
26	Jaw drop	Massetter; Temporal and Internal pterygoid relaxed
27	Mouth stretch	Pterygoids; Digastric
28	Lip suck	Orbicularis oris

More grossly defined action units	
19	Tongue out
21	Neck tightener
29	Jaw thrust
30	Jaw sideways
32	Jaw clencher
32	Lip bite
33	Cheek blow
34	Cheek puff
35	Cheek suck
36	Tongue bulge
37	Lip wipe
38	Nostril dilator
39	Nostril compressor
41	Lip droop
42	Slit
43	Eyes closed
44	Squint
45	Blink
46	Wink

Table 27.1. Simplified Facial Action Coding System (action units). *After Ekman and Friesen 1978.*

Marinatos in 1967, and by Christos Doumas in 1974. Many of the paintings show persons involved in various activities and interactions (Figure 27.1). What can they tell us about themselves?

What I looked for was whether we can discern some of the collective ideals of the Thera Bronze Age society by analyzing these depictions of themselves, and in particular by analyzing their facial expressions (registered using the Facial Action Coding System), and relate this information to personality traits (defined by the Five-Factor Model Trait Theory). I used both quantitative and qualitative methods. The quantitative data collected by using the Facial Action Coding System were scored and registered by two independent researchers, with a high degree of agreement between them. The analysis was a qualitative dialectic process between the facial data and their connection with the behaviors and the body-postures of each person, interpreted as emotions and indicators of personality traits. Finally, this information was connected to the cultural context and what is known about Thera Bronze Age society from archaeological research.

The analyzed paintings come from four houses in Akrotiri, the Bronze Age town on Thera: the House of the Ladies, the West House, Xeste 3, and Building Beta. Reproductions of the paintings are on display in the Petros M. Nomikos Conference Center in Fira, the capital of the island. I visited the center in 2000 and took photographs of the paintings. These provided the data used here. Twelve female and nine male figures with visible and reasonably intact faces were analyzed. Some paintings from Akrotiri show naval scenes with boats, landscapes, cities, and people. These pictures are excluded from the analysis, partly because the people in them are small, sketchily painted, and without clear facial features; and partly because it is unclear whether these people were native to Thera and its culture. The paintings analyzed here show people and their faces in rather minute detail.

Figure 27.1. Painted persons in interaction in the Bronze Age town of Akrotiri on Thera (Santorini), Greece: figures F6 (saffron gatherers, top left); F7 (saffron gatherer) with F9 (mistress of animals, top right); M3 and M4 (boxing boys, bottom left); and M5 (naked boy) with M6 (naked boy with cloth, bottom right).

Their pictures come from rooms in houses where, according to Marinatos (2014), cultic activities took place, and may represent people from Thera involved in such activities. Exceptions are a figure interpreted as a goddess (F9, called "Mistress of Animals"),[11] and a black male (M9, called "The African"). The goddess, however, appears to be presented as an idealized

Theran young adult woman, and the black man could have been an inhabitant of Thera. The paintings are well preserved, and have undergone conscientious restoration. However, details may have disintegrated or been incorrectly restored. Therefore, any inferences about the validity of the registered facial expressions are drawn with great caution. The faces were literally analyzed at 'face value.'

WHAT DO THE PAINTINGS SHOW?

Of the twenty-one depicted figures, twelve (57 percent) were females and nine (43 percent) were males. All are in profile, a norm probably adopted at Thera from Egypt, or through influence from the Minoan culture on Crete. I established their genders from their body forms, particularly the presence or absence of breasts. Their approximate age I interpreted partly from their hairstyles—the hair of older women is made into a knot and covered—and partly from their body form.[12] The data are presented in Table 27.2 and the figures are shown in Figures 27.2–27.6).

There are no really old people in these paintings. F1 to F10 are young women, while F11 and F12 appear older and are probably married, as they are wearing headdresses. Among the nine men, only M7 can be considered older. No females appear to be pre-pubertal girls, whereas M3, M4, M5 and M8 are pre-pubertal boys. One woman (F11) and one older man (M7) appear a little plump; the image of body of the other older woman is too damaged to be evaluated. The rest, both females and males, have slim and athletic bodies.

All the males are naked, or wearing just a loincloth (M3, M4, and M7), while all the women, including the goddess F9, wear colorful clothes of high complexity, and some even transparent veils. Two males wear jewelry: M2 has a simple necklace, while M3 wears blue pearls around his neck and upper arm. In contrast, all the women are adorned with large and elaborate jewelry, in particular large earrings. They wear make-up, and some have red nail polish. All the males, except "the African" have hair that is completely or partially shaven; and two boys (M3 and M4)

have some long locks, but are otherwise shaved. Some women also have partially shaven heads, others have elaborate hairstyles, and two (F11 and F12) have their hair in buns.

Regarding the activities of the figures: many are hard to discern, as several paintings are partly destroyed (this pertains to F1, F11, F12, and M9). The others engage intensely in some activity: F2 carries an incense-burner, F3 walks or dances while holding a necklace in her hand, F4 sits with a hurt foot, F5 possibly dances with her head turned, F6–F8 gather saffron in buckets on steep hills, F9 (possibly a goddess) sits on a throne receiving saffron from a monkey provided by F8, F10 carries a bucket on her shoulder, and F11 and F12 are watching or overseeing some activity. Among the males, M1 and M2 carry fish, M3 and M4 are fighting (boxing?), M5 seems to attend M6, like a servant (or a slave?). M6 seems to have just snatched a cloth, possibly a towel, from the hands of M5, M7 is about to pour something out of a large heavy jar into a bowl that is held by M8, M8 holds a big bowl, possibly a washbasin, and finally M9 ("the African"), is outdoors under a palm-tree, but the image of his body is damaged so we cannot know what exactly he is doing.

The facial expressions are very vague and few. To modern eyes, the figures appear rather sketchily painted. Yet many of the lips, jaws, and brows indicate expressions. The positions of the heads differ, and when the activities of the persons, their gazes, and their body-postures are taken into consideration, several emotions can be discerned, some of which seem mixed. Most of the emotions are quite neutral (F2, F6, F8, F10–F12, M1, and M5–M9). These neutral emotions are on the faces of persons who are engaged in activities that require close attention and concentration. F3, F5, F7–F9, and M2 seem to show happiness or joy. Two (F9 and M9) seem somewhat surprised. Negative expressions are few. One person (F1) looks nervous or stressed, F4 looks a little sad or afraid (her foot is wounded), and two (M3 and M4) appear angry, or just act

Table 27.2. Facial expressions as facial action coding scores (action units), interpreted emotions, and possible personality traits expressed. *After Ekman and Friesen 1978.*

	Action units	Expression	Emotion	Personality
Females				
F1: Female figure 1	15, 25, 41	Mouth corner slightly down, lips slightly apart, eye looks up, neck bent slightly forward, red cheek	Fear? (worried? nervous?)	Neuroticism, Conscientiousness
F2: Woman with incense	1, 18	Inner eyebrow lifted, lips puckered	Neutral (concentrated)	Conscientiousness
F3: Woman with necklace	12, 25	Mouth corner slightly up, lips apart, looks a bit upward	Happiness (smiles? proud?)	Extroversion, Openness, Agreeableness
F4: Woman with injured foot	15, 25, 26	Mouth corner slightly down, lips apart, jaw dropped	Sadness (and fear?)	Neuroticism (in pain)
F5: Woman with veil	12, 17, 25	Mouth corner slightly up, chin thrust, lips slightly apart, head turned	Happiness (slight smile), (concentrated)	Conscientiousness, Openness
F6: Saffron gatherer 1	15, 16, 25	Lip corners slightly down, lower lip slightly down, lips apart	Neutral (talks?)	Conscientiousness, Extroversion
F7: Saffron gatherer 2	25	Lips slightly apart, smile-like curved upper lip, looks up	Happiness (slight smile? talks?)	Conscientiousness, Agreeableness
F8: Saffron gatherer 3	12?, 25	Mouth corners slightly up? Mouth closed, head bent backward, looks up at F9	Happiness? (smiles?) Neutral	Conscientiousness, Agreeableness?
F9: Goddess	6?, 25, 26	Cheek slightly raised?, lips apart, jaw slightly dropped	Happiness (smiles?) Surprise? Intense gaze	Conscientiousness, Agreeableness, Extroversion, Openness?
F10: Saffron gatherer 4	25	Lips slightly apart, head forward, carries bucket on shoulder	Neutral (concentrated)	Conscientiousness
F11: Female figure 2	23	Lips tightened	Neutral (concentrated)	Conscientiousness
F12: Female figure 3	23	Lips tightened	Neutral (concentrated)	Conscientiousness
Males				
M1: Fisherman 1	6? 25	Lips slightly apart? (mouth partly destroyed)	Neutral (smiles?)	Conscientiousness
M2: Fisherman 2	6, 12, 25	Raised cheek, mouth corner raised, lips apart	Happiness (smiles, proud)	Agreeableness, Conscientiousness, Openness?
M3: Boxing boy 1	4, 25?	Brow lowered, lips slightly apart, eye looks up, head low	Anger? (fights)	Neuroticism? (in aggressive act)
M4: Boxing boy 2	4, 23?	Brow lowered, lips tightened?, head slightly backward	Anger? (fights)	Neuroticism? (in aggressive act)
M5: Naked boy 1	25, 26	Lips apart, jaw slightly dropped, eye looks up	Neutral	Conscientiousness, Agreeableness
M6: Naked boy with cloth	25	Lips clearly apart, head turned, walks (eye destroyed)	Neutral (talks?)	Openness, Extroversion, Agreeableness?
M7: Adult male with jar	25	Lips clearly apart, head bent	Neutral	Conscientiousness
M8: Naked boy with bowl	25	Lips apart, looks up with head and eye	Neutral	Conscientiousness, Agreeableness
M9: The African	6?, 25	Cheek slightly raised, lips apart, looks up (only the head is preserved)	Neutral (Surprise?)	Conscientiousness?

Figure 27.2. Full figures and close-ups of the faces of painted figures F1 (female figure, top left), F2 (woman with incense, top right), F3 (woman with necklace, bottom left), and F4 (women with hurt foot, bottom right), from the Bronze Age town of Akrotiri on Thera (Santorini), Greece.

Figure 27.3. Full figures and close-ups of the faces of painted female figures F5 (women with veil, top left), F6 (saffron gatherer, top right), F7 (saffron gatherer, bottom left), and F8 (saffron gatherer, bottom right), from the Bronze Age town of Akrotiri on Thera (Santorini), Greece.

Figure 27.4. Full figures and close-ups of the faces of painted female figures F9 (goddess, top left), F10 (saffron gatherer, top right), F11 (female figure, bottom left), and F12 (female figure, bottom right), from the Bronze Age town of Akrotiri on Thera (Santorini), Greece.

Figure 27.5. Full figures and close-ups of the faces of painted male figures M1 (fisherman, top left), M2 (fisherman, top right), M3 and M4 (boxing boys, bottom), from the Bronze Age town of Akrotiri on Thera (Santorini), Greece.

Figure 27.6. Full figures and close-ups of the faces of painted male figures M5 (naked boy, top left), M6 (naked boy with cloth, top right), M7 (adult male with jar, bottom left), M8 (naked boy with bowl, bottom center), and M9 (the African, bottom right), from the Bronze Age town of Akrotiri on Thera (Santorini), Greece.

angry, as they are engaged in a fight, which might be ritual. Nobody displays disgust or contempt.

Regarding personality, as expressed by emotional display, this evaluation is clearly very tentative, perhaps even speculative. Yet, even if these depicted faces are not portraits, they still have expressions that give impressions of personal traits. Those showing rather neutral expressions, while involved in particular tasks, appear concentrated and conscientious. So, *Conscientiousness* is attributed to these. Those who seem to be smiling and perhaps talking, are attributed *Agreeableness.* Those who appear happy or engaged in a conversation, are seen as showing *Extroversion.* The very active individuals are attributed *Openness toward experience,* and finally, the possibly fearful and angry persons are attributed *Neuroticism.* In the Five-Factor Model Trait Theory neuroticism does not mean neurotic in the common sense, but encompasses negative emotionality in general.

CAN WE LEARN ANYTHING ABOUT BRONZE AGE THERA FROM THE PICTURES?

One can easily get the impression that the depicted individuals are somewhat void of expression, as they are shown according to the conventional style of the Bronze Age. Yet, the Theran artists showed more artistic independence and individuality in their paintings than artists in contemporary Minoan, Egyptian, and Mesopotamian cultures.[13] These faces from Thera are surprisingly different, vivacious, and show clear individual traits.

I must stress that I have evaluated and interpreted these pictures from Thera at face value. The painting style does not allow any deeper interpretation of the qualities and characteristics of the depicted persons. They were probably not meant to be portraits, but official icons possibly from, and within, a religious context. They probably do not express specific attributes of particular persons, but the more general attributes associated with the roles of such persons. During the execution of these roles, they express the preferred and prescribed emotions and personality traits: the way in which people should be and behave, and how they should present themselves to others. In short, they display their idealized selves according to the collective values of their culture. I believe that they were painted with this intention.

PICTURES OF PEOPLE ALWAYS HAVE AN EXPRESSION, AND ALWAYS LEAVE AN IMPRESSION

It is not possible to paint or draw a face without any expression. Just consider the simple line drawings by children of faces and stick-figures. The emotional expressions may be unintended, but in the eyes of the beholder expressions are seen and interpreted. They always have an expression and will always leave an impression. The Theran pictures are no exception. They seem simple at first glance, but on closer inspection they sparkle with vivacity and individuality. As these images were accepted by the Theran community, they must have shown expressions, and given impressions, that were in accordance with the values of the community. As such, they represent

intended self-representations of people from one of the most sophisticated Bronze Age societies in Europe. So what can they tell us about the ideas and ideals of Bronze Age Thera?

The main impression is that personality traits were quite equal among females and males, particularly among the young. The relative distribution of traits within the genders is also strikingly similar. *Conscientiousness* is particularly high (16 cases), followed by *Agreeableness* (8 cases) and *Extroversion* (7 cases). *Openness toward experience* ranks lower (5 cases) and at the bottom is *Neuroticism* (4 cases).

Conscientiousness refers to competence, orderliness, dutifulness, achievement motivation, self-discipline, deliberation, trustworthiness, and thoroughness. These are highly valued traits in our society today, and I think that it is uncontroversial to claim that these traits were also important on Bronze Age Thera. It seems hard to imagine a society having the latest technical achievements of its time and a flourishing trade, without this trait being present and cultivated among its members.

Agreeableness refers to friendliness, kindness, generosity, forgiving attitude, caring, empathy, sympathy, and altruism. *Agreeableness* is a trait that enhances social interaction and social abilities. It is a social glue in all societies.

Extroversion refers to consciousness directed toward the outer world more than to the inner world, feelings of being safe, interest for others, warmth, gregariousness, high activity, and enthusiasm. The presence of this trait on Thera is easy to explain: all happy and healthy young people tend to have these qualities. The introvert, shy, ruminating teenager is probably found also in all societies, but is hardly regarded as the ideal or preferred way of being, anywhere. These ancient paintings show young, extrovert Mediterranean persons full of life.

Openness toward experience refers to intellectual and behavioral fantasy and curiosity, to being adventurous, knowledge-seeking, in need of freedom, opportunistic, individualistic, courageous, unconventional, and creative. The traits *Agreeableness, Extroversion,* and *Openness toward experience* often coincide, as they do here. They seem to have been idealized traits in the young in this society. Again a reasonable finding, considering the Theran cultural situation: a flourishing, rich, and, for its times, modern society. Situated on a relatively small territory (an island) with trade as a major economic activity, Therans were dependent on both intense and peaceful relations with other peoples. No wonder that we find the triad of *Agreeableness, Conscientiousness*, and *Extroversion* expressed in their idealized icons. I had expected to find more *Openness toward experience*, because seafaring and trading over the long distances of the Mediterranean might require an adventurous willingness to take risks. However, considering the risks, and the skills needed to succeed, it seems equally reasonable that *Conscientiousness* was regarded as more important to cultivate.

Neuroticism refers to nervousness, carefulness, anxiety, compulsiveness, stubbornness, emotional inflexibility, need for conformity, little tolerance of ambiguity or change, need for orderliness, emotional instability, hostility, depression, self-consciousness, self-pitying, and vulnerability. In short, this trait encompasses all bad dispositions. It is associated with expressions of negative emotions (sadness, hostility, disgust, contempt, and fear). When a few figures here were found to express emotions related to this trait, these evaluations were based on expressions of very light fear, concern, and probably feigned aggression. I found no indication of strong and negative destructive emotions (reservation, restraint, disgust, contempt, hostility, and fear) that this trait encompasses. Actually, *Neuroticism* was found very little in both genders. On the contrary, social and positive emotions dominated.

To sum up, the personality traits, particularly among the young, as interpreted from their emotional expressions, give very positive impressions. They show responsibility through their expressions of *Conscientiousness*. They are very attractive with their expressions of the social traits of *Agreeableness* and *Extroversion*. They also show some explorative adventurous traits with initiative, curiosity, and activity through their *Openness toward experience,* and low aggressive, hostile, neurotic, and anxious qualities through their low expressions of *Neuroticism*. Older adults are few in this material. This means that proper across-age comparisons cannot be made. But the older adults also show *Conscientiousness.*

INFERRING CULTURAL CHARACTERISTICS THROUGH EXPRESSIONS IN THE THERAN PAINTINGS

Societies bring up their young not only according to the needs of the children, or the convenience of the parents, but also, perhaps primarily, in ways that fit the needs of the society. This means that if prominent characteristics are found in idealized representations of the young, these characteristics may represent values held by the society.

A prominent personality trait found in the paintings from Thera, regardless of the gender or age of the person depicted, was *Conscientiousness.* This may partly be because the persons were depicted in what is assumed to be a religious context. However, religiosity may have been an integrated part of their values and daily life.[14] A certain touch of unceremonious attitudes in the paintings supports this suggestion. People seem to be accustomed to interact with the divine sphere and were not notably terrified by divine presence and encounters with the divine: one young girl (F3) dances proudly toward an altar, another (F8) looks curiously up at the goddess (F9). Both a relaxed attitude and serious conscientiousness in relation to religion can coexist when religion is a natural part of everyday life. As Marinatos (2014) says, the divine and human spheres were often blended in the "Minoan mentality," and may also have been so in the Theran culture.

It is suggested that little importance was attached to warfare in Thera Bronze Age society.[15] As mentioned above, martial situations and equipment are totally absent in these analyzed paintings, and neither the men nor the women seem belligerent. As mentioned above, the painting of a fight between two boys was likely a ritual fight connected to fertility rites,[16] not a sign of *Neuroticism,* violence, or hostility. That the Bronze Age societies of Crete and Thera were pacifistic, feministic societies has been proposed,[17] but is unlikely. However, compared to other contemporary societies in the Middle East and later Greek societies, the lack of strong defenses on Thera and the few depictions of armies, battles, and armed men are striking. Yet it is clear that the painting called "The Naval Battle Scene" (if the scene is correctly interpreted by Marinatos 2014) shows that the Therans could fight back if attacked.

What is particularly striking in the all paintings though, are the beautiful, vivacious, partly naturalistic and partly ornamental, depictions of nature, including landscapes, animals, birds, plants, and flowers.

The person who is interpreted as a goddess (F9, "Mistress of Animals"),[18] and the offerings brought to her, add to this peaceful impression. The offerings presented in the paintings are not weapons or enemies (dead or alive), but rather fish, flowers (Crocus sativus), and jewelry. Fish was probably an important part of the diet on Thera. The crocuses were used to extract saffron, a highly valuable material for producing yellow dye as well as a pain-killing medicine, and was probably an important export article. The jewelry could be interpreted as a symbol of prosperity, but also as proper gifts to a lady. Marinatos (2014) suggests that this goddess was their prime deity and calls her the Mistress of Animals. Her picture is the only figure that has been interpreted as a deity in these excavated paintings. This female deity has some interesting features: she is not a typical fertility goddess displaying sexual attributes, pregnancy, or children. Instead, she is a woman displaying youth, beauty, and wealth; a goddess fitting a society where prosperity was not based on warfare or local agricultural fertility, but on trade, perhaps particularly of luxury articles and products.

I will claim that the paintings give an impression of a highly self-confident, economically expansive, and prospering society. If Theran society really was a leading seafaring and trading society, the cultivation of the personality traits of Conscientiousness, Agreeableness, and Openness toward experience certainly fit. To be able to communicate and trade with other peoples around the Mediterranean Sea and make new acquaintances certainly required extrovert and agreeable traits. To be able to navigate the Mediterranean Sea required conscientious cooperative skills and team-work among the crews, and it certainly required courage and adventurousness while encountering difficulties at sea: the Mediterranean Sea is not easily sailed. Finally, to be successfully involved in trade required, in addition to communicative skills, the trustworthiness and conscientiousness of good businessmen. In short, the traits expressed in the young men seem to fit the picture of

a successful, expanding, seafaring, trading society that was independent of warfare to secure and maintain its success.

What about the women? As mentioned above, different behaviors and qualities are often expected in females compared to men. This means that different characteristics are usually cultivated in the two genders, at least to some extent. It is therefore somewhat surprising to find approximately the same relative distribution of traits expressed in both genders. Conscientiousness and Extroversion are dominant, with Agreeableness next. These traits in the males are here proposed to be related to their seafaring expeditions. The women were hardly tradespeople, so these traits could have served other purposes in women. Apart from the characteristics inherent to Conscientiousness, which are probably highly treasured in both genders in all societies, the high incidence of Extroversion in women hints at a society in which women could be active and outspoken. In other societies where men spent a long time away from home—such as during the Viking period of Western Norway (790–1066 CE)—the women were in charge and exerted considerable power. The same could be the case on Bronze Age Thera. Young girls may have been brought up with the prospect of having to take on considerable responsibilities. Their images add to this impression. The young girls seem utterly self-confident. A particularly interesting feature of these young women is the way in which they approach and relate to the goddess. Their attitude when approaching the deity is certainly not one of fear and submission, but rather of pride and positive curious interest, perhaps even cooperation.

The adult women also show expressions of conscientious responsibility: their serious and stern expressions can be interpreted this way. If, as suggested above, women were in charge of the society during the periods in which many men were at sea, their expressions of concern and responsibility may simply indicate the serious role demands that adult women experienced on Bronze Age Thera.

Concerning the power, influence, and importance attributed to the two genders, the paintings indicate a considerable amount of equality between them, if not necessarily in the same activities, but in responsibilities and worth. Both genders worked: the men went fishing and the women gathered saffron. It is noteworthy that, apart from the goddess, there are no distinct indications of differences in status between the individuals, with exception of the young boy (M5) who might be a servant or a slave. If the prime deity on Thera was female, this could also be an indication of a high status for women. The females in these paintings are remarkably beautifully attired. Their exquisite clothing and jewelry give the impression that women were held in high esteem.

Another striking feature is the focus on bodily beauty and vivacity in both genders. The figures express responsibility and pride, assertiveness, but not aggressiveness, and they show respect for, not fear of, the divine world. To put it plainly, the Thera Bronze Age community, as presented in the paintings at Akrotiri, seems to have been a culture where personalities were allowed to develop in positive and healthy ways, where joy and aesthetic pleasures were treasured, and where both genders were held in high esteem. It should be noted that this conclusion may be an idealized one and that reality may have been different. However, it is based on these people's idealized self-presentations, showing, and showing off, how they wanted to be, their aspirations and ideals. If I have correctly analyzed and understood their self-representations, it is difficult to come up with a different conclusion.

Thera Bronze Age culture was remarkable in many ways. It was prosperous, technologically advanced, and a leading seafaring and trading society.[19] Yet, to my knowledge, no large central administrative centers, like the Cretan palaces, have been found in the excavations. It is therefore possible that the social organization at Thera may have been structured on a less hierarchical and more egalitarian basis. In fact, the art supports this notion. The individuality of the faces, the proud and confident bodily attitudes (even when approaching a divinity or an altar), the expressions of positive emotions, and the connections of these expressions to positive personality traits, all point in the direction of a society where each individual was valued as a person, and was not a member of a docile, suppressed population.

These psychological considerations, however vague, and possibly speculative, actually fit astonishingly well with what happened when the volcano of Thera erupted. In sharp contrast to the eruption of Vesuvius and the catastrophe of Pompeii in Roman Italy 1,700 years later—where most of the population died—the entire Theran population (with only a few exceptions) evacuated in good time. They reacted to the signs of minor earthquakes and ash-falls in adaptive coping ways. They even responded early enough to have time to put their larger belongings, such as big jars, in places where they might be safe (clearly hoping that they would return), and they had enough time to take their animals and portable valuables with them.

This kind of adaptive reaction to a volcanic threat is reported to be typical of societies with a flat organization. Societies where people are not subdued by strong leadership and prone to wait for orders will trust their own evaluations and take responsibility and initiate problem-solving cooperation.[20] As seafarers, the people of Thera were skilled in cooperation. In addition, one must not forget that they had one of the largest and best fleets of vessels of the time, with which they could escape the catastrophe. Moreover, because of their trading network, they probably had contacts and friends in many places around the Mediterranean Sea. In other words, they had places that they could escape and migrate to. This incredibly effective evacuation of Thera in the Bronze Age has long astonished archaeologists. Perhaps this outside-the-box analysis, using psychological theories and methodology, may shed new light on the extraordinary society of Bronze Age Thera.

NOTES

1   Buss 2001.

2   Brilliant 2013.

3   Ekman and Friesen 1978.

4   Ekman and Rosenberg 2005.

5   Overmann and Coolidge 2019.

6   Friedlund 1994.

7   (Berry et al. 2011).

8   Berry et al. 2011, Pervin 2003.

9   Piderit 1886, 139. See the epigraph at the head of this chapter for the
     exact quote.

10   Costa and Corazza 2006.

11   Marinatos 2014.

12   Marinatos 2014.

13   Doumas 1992, 1999; Marinatos 2014.

14   Marinatos 2014.

15   Doumas 1984, 1992; Gimbutas and Marler 1993.

16   Marinatos 2014.

17   Gimbutas and Marler 1991.

18   Marinatos 2014.

19   Doumas 1984, 1992.

20   Lindstrøm 2019.

BIBLIOGRAPHY

Berry, John W., Ype H. Poortinga, Seger M. Breugelmans, Athanasios
    Chasiotis, and David L. Sam (2011), *Cross Cultural Psychology:
    Research and Applications,* Cambridge (Cambridge University
    Press).

Brilliant, Richard (2013), *Portraiture: Essays in Art and Culture,*
    London (Reaction Books Ltd).

Buss, David M. (2001), Human Nature and Culture: An Evolutionary
    Psychological Perspective, *Journal of Personality* 69(6), 155–78.

Costa, Marco and Leonardo Corazza (2006), Aesthetic Phenomena
    as Supernormal Stimuli: The Case of Eye, Lip, and Lower-Face Size
    and Roundness in Artistic Portraits, *Perception* 35(2), 229–46.

Doumas, Christos G. (1984), *Thera: Pompeii of the Ancient Aegean:
    Excavations at Akrotiri 1967–79,* London (Thames and Hudson).

—— (1992), *The Wall-Paintings of Thera,* Athens (Kapon Editions:
    Thera Foundations).

Ekman, Paul and Wallace V. Friesen (1978). *The Facial Action Coding
    System (FACS): A Technique for the Measurement of Facial
    Action,* Palo Alto (Consulting Psychologists Press).

Ekman, Paul and Erika L. Rosenberg, eds. (2005), *What the Face
    Reveals: Basic and Applied Studies of Spontaneous Expression
    Using the Facial Action Coding System (FACS),* Oxford (Oxford
    University Press).

Friedlund, Alan J. (1994), *Human Facial Expression: An Evolutionary
    View,* San Diego (Academic Press, Inc.)

Gimbutas, Maria and Joan Marler (1993), *The Civilization of the
    Goddess: The World of Old Europe,* New York and San Francisco
    (HarperSanFrancisco).

Lindstrøm, Torill C. (2019), "Tephroarchaeology: Past, Present,
    and Future," in: Gina L. Barnes and Tsutomu Soda, eds.,
    TephroArchaeology in the North Pacific, pp. 161–274, Oxford
    (Archaeopress).

L'Orange, Hans Peter (1967), *Romerske keisere i marmor og bronse*
    [Roman Emperors in Marble and Bronze], Oslo (Dreyer Forlag).

Marinatos, Nanno (2014), *Art and Religion in Thera: Reconstructing a
    Bronze Age Society,* Firá (Editions Souanis Bros Co.).

McCrae, Robert R. and Paul T. Costa (1997), Personality Trait
    Structure as a Human Universal, *American Psychologist* 52(2),
    509–16.

Overmann, Karenleigh and Frederick L. Coolidge, eds. (2019),
    *Squeezing Minds from Stones: Cognitive Archaeology and the
    Evolution of the Human Mind,* Oxford (Oxford University Press).

Pervin, Lawrence A. (2003), *The Science of Personality,* New York
    (John Wiley and Sons).

Piderit, Theodor (1886), *Mimik und Physiognomik,* Detmold (Verlag
    der Meyer'schen Hofbuchhandlung).

RUMORS OF WAR AND WARRIOR REALITIES IN THE PERUVIAN ANDES

DANIELLE KURIN, VALDA BLACK, BEATRIZ LIZARRAGA, AND IVANNA ROBLEDO

What happens when archaeological discoveries contradict—or at least call into question—centuries of oral and written accounts from which an ethnic group derives their sense of place, history, and identity? How do archaeologists mediate between empirical evidence and the collective beliefs of living stakeholders? This chapter explores these contradictions through the lens of the Chanka, an indigenous ethnic group whose homeland is situated in the rural and rugged Andes of south-central Peru. We examine the historical trajectory of the Chanka people and reconstruct the history of the premier archaeological and tourist site in the region, a hillfort called Sondor.

THE MYTHIC HISTORY OF THE CHANKA PEOPLE

Our understanding of the Chanka people comes primarily from chronicles written soon after the Spanish conquest of Peru. These official histories were penned by soldiers, bureaucrats, nobles, and priests. These texts prioritize the history of the Inca, the most famous empire of South America. The informants for these texts were Inca-affiliated people, and the documents record perspectives that highlight Inca legitimacy and dominance. Common tropes deployed in these texts call into question the legitimacy of the Chanka homeland, reveal a violent and barbaric society led by warlords, and highlight the antagonistic relationship between the Chanka and the Inca. In the chronicling of the rise and fall of the Inca empire, the Chanka appear as literary foils and primordial rivals. The

Figure 26.1. Representations of the prototypical Chanka Warrior share common attributes. Warriors are tall, muscle-bound men in their prime, sling in hand, barefoot and nearly nude, save for a loincloth and puma-skin cape, and always posed in the act of active bludgeoning. The Warrior sculpture in the Plaza Mayor at San Jeronimo is typical (top). During local festivals, reenactments of Chanka myths feature actors who embrace and enhance the Warrior trope (bottom).

Chanka are depicted as bellicose warriors (Figure 26.1), whose thirst for lands, women, and lordship eventually brings them into direct opposition with the purportedly more savvy and civilized Inca elites.

According to the chronicles, the Chanka emerged during an era that Garcilaso de la Vega (1609–13/1968), an erudite mestizo historian, called the "Age of Warlike Men." This mythic dark age was marked by population expansion, military engagement, territorial conquest, and conflicts over natural resources. According to Pedro Cieza de Leon (1553/1996), a Spanish military captain, the Chanka lived in hilltop fortresses and raised their children in round, stone houses. They were governed by hereditary warlords and buried their dead in caves surrounded by treasure.

The names and deeds of Chanka leaders are still celebrated today. Descendants of the Chanka trace the origin to two founding brothers named Uscovilca and Ancovilca.[1] The founding Chanka brothers and their kinsmen migrated from distant lands and settled in a region called Anta Waylla, a Quechua name that means 'The Prairie of the Copper-Colored Clouds.' The invading Chanka exterminated the previously residing population.[2] Though settled in their new homeland, the Chanka soon yearned to conquer new lands. Jesuit priest Bernabé Cobó (1653/1964), relates that "a brave Indian named Ancohuallo," aided by six Chanka war captains named Mallma, Rapa, Yanavilca, Tecllovilca, Guamanguaraca, and Tomayguaraca,[3] subsequently conquered a huge swath of south-central Peru.

As decades marched on, the Chanka would make several attempts to subdue their arch rivals. Sometime after 1250 CE, Chanka war captain Tomayguaraca and his brothers-in-arms, Astoyguaraca and Huasco Tomayrimac, led thousands of warriors to rout the Inca,[4] pillaging villages and killing so many along the way that their spears were dyed red with blood. By the late fourteenth century CE, the Inca–Chanka War had reached its apogee, and the formidable Chanka once again turned their eyes east in what would become an apocryphal campaign to conquer Cuzco.

The imminent threat of an advancing Chanka battalion so flustered the old, doddering Inca Lord Viracocha that he fled Cuzco in fear, leaving his youngest son, named Yupanqui, and a couple of the boy's friends behind to defend the sacred city. Greatly outmatched, the young Yupanqui and his retinue nevertheless met the Chanka army on a plain outside the city walls, a place that would become known as Yawar Pampa, the 'Battlefield of Blood.' The fighting that took place there rivaled that of Thermopylae or Agincourt in both intensity and importance. The confrontation between Chanka and Inca was vicious and calamitous; hand-to-hand combat yielded casualties in the thousands.[5] Yet fortune would favor the Inca. After gaining the upper hand through supernatural intervention, Yupanqui finally killed the Chanka war captains and mounted their heads on tall spears. This act so dispirited the remaining Chanka warriors that they surrendered, rendering the Inca triumphant. Upon victory, the young Inca Yupanqui cemented his reputation as a singular, energetic leader and adopted a new regnal name: Pachacutic, meaning 'Reckoner and Transformer of the World.' With that act, the era of Inca imperial expansion began in earnest.

The battle of Yawar Pampa gave the Inca a decisive victory and became a seminal event in the conquest and consolidation of the nascent Inca empire. For the Inca, this was a nation-making movement. For the Chanka, the spectacular loss relegated them to a footnote in history, as but one more among the vanquished. Even in defeat, the ferocity and fate of the Chanka is forever fixed and deeply ingrained in descendant communities through acts of remembrance and reverence that persists to this day.

After the climactic Inca–Chanka War, historical accounts become murky. Some chroniclers report that all the Chanka were massacred. Others assert that the whole population fled down the Marañon River and into the Amazon jungle, never to be seen or heard from again. Somewhat less spectacular accounts suggest that the Chanka willingly accepted Inca colonization and oversight. Still other sources suggest the Chanka were intentionally displaced to distant corners of the Inca Empire, while foreign populations were forcibly resettled to local towns in Anta Waylla, with Sondor among the most important.

UNDERSTANDING THE CHANKA THROUGH BONE AND STONE

One way we can distinguish between popular myths and historical facts is through archaeological excavations in the Chanka heartland. Perhaps no other site in the region encapsulates the Chanka *Geist* like the ancient city of Sondor. Overlooking Laguna Pacucha, the largest freshwater lake in the south-central Andes, Sondor—situated at a breathless 3,300 meters (10,825 feet) above sea level—is the most famous, most visited, and most important archaeological site in the region (Figure 26.2). Doing field work at a site this well-known is sensitive work. Before breaking ground, archaeologists must ask permission to excavate and give offerings to the local ancestors in a ritual known as the *pagapu* (Figure 26.3). During the ceremony everyone follows the instruction of a local shaman, called a *yachaq,* who leads the chanting and libations. Offerings tend to be composed of sweets, liquor, and other treats. Participants chew coca leaves and pass around cupfuls of potent cane alcohol, flicking fingers full of fermented drops in the directions of the *apu*s—the mountain gods—that watch over Sondor and her supplicants. The communal participation in rites and an earnest belief in the ritual itself are key to a safe and successful field season (another example of this is discussed by Ruth Tringham and Annie Danis, Chapter 20 in this volume). Folks are always on the lookout for signs that the *pagapu* was well received. Or not. On several occasions, local coworkers were skeptical that the offerings had been accepted by the *apu*s. Foreman Don Feliciano marveled at how many foreign archaeologists were unsuccessful in navigating the challenging terrain. Slips and falls were seen as auspicious (and not the result of unskilled maneuvering along treacherous slopes carpeted by loose boulders amid a spiny sea of thorny plants). Fortunately, after a second offering of psalms, sweets, cigarettes, and alcohol, the gods were apparently satiated and our labors bore fruit.

Archaeological fieldwork at Sondor was aimed at illuminating the long history of the site, and reconstructing the lives of the people who lived there. Addressing those questions

Figure 26.3. Fieldwork is slow, meticulous, and deliberate, but ultimately intrusive (left). When excavating burials, knowledge of the human skeleton is crucial. So is a respect for ancestors. Offerings are placed at tomb openings to appease the dead and alleviate the spiritual offense of the excavation (right).

Figure 26.2. The archaeological site of Sondor (Peru). The Inca architecture—a plaza and niched walls—is in the foreground. In the background is a conical hill with ringed walls; at its summit is a shrine worshiped by inhabitants centuries prior to Inca arrival.

required us to exhume skeletons from their places of rest. Consequently, excavations centered on areas where the dead were likely buried, in this case house floors and small mortuary caves. This so-called bioarchaeological approach considers skeletons to be the primary unit of analysis. Our plan was to disinter, screen, and record all human remains and material culture. It was slow, meticulous work. After several unforgiving months in the dirt, we were able to recover the skeletons of a few dozen people as well as thousands of associated grave goods, including pottery, stone tools, metal jewelry, animal bones, and pieces of textile and braided sawgrass ropes that once formed the outer layers of ancient mummy bundles.

Back in the laboratory, we cleaned, stabilized and catalogued everything that came out of the ground, but our top priority were the precious human remains. This is because bones and teeth directly represent the life history of a person, recording both the mundane and extraordinary activities of both quotidian and sacrosanct life—from the food that people ate and the places that they migrated from, to the diseases that they endured and the violence that they suffered. These behaviors and occurrences all leave unique, indelible marks on bone amenable to analysis by specialists trained in human osteology, anatomy, paleopathology, and taphonomy.

One major task was to figure out exactly how many individuals were represented by the thousands of bones, and fragments of bone, that we recovered during excavations. That was easier said than done. A human skeleton has around 206 bones and 32 teeth. Graves that have a single, articulated skeleton are fairly easy to excavate and analyze. The puzzle quickly becomes challenging when a tomb contains more than one skeleton; more challenging still when skeletons are buried collectively and are also disarticulated, broken into small pieces, and all jumbled up like a macabre game of pick-up sticks. We assessed the skeletons and recorded data on biological sex, age-at-death, bony lesions indicative of disease, and any signs of trauma such as broken bones. We also documented conspicuous body modification traditions like artificial cranial deformation. Taken together, these classes of

DANIELLE KURIN, VALDA BLACK, BEATRIZ LIZARRAGA, AND IVANNA ROBLEDO demographic, physiological, and cultural data help us better understand how individual life histories articulate with the historical sequence of Sondor.

A VIOLENT REPUTATION WELL DESERVED

Our excavations at Sondor tested the veracity of characterizations of the Chanka drawn from the old colonial chronicles, which almost exclusively emphasize violent encounters between young male combatants. Our investigations showed that some of the skeletal data was consistent with the folklore. For instance, about half of all Chanka people excavated experienced violence in the form of head wounds, and nearly a third were cut down due to deadly skull fractures. But our analysis also showed that the Chanka were *not* a monolithic group. While violence certainly existed in Chanka society, our data show that not everyone suffered equally. In fact, Chanka skeletons from Sondor and other contemporaneous sites—representing around three hundred people—suggest that Chanka society maintained internal caste-like divisions between groups of people.

One of the most notable distinctions was the schism between the *rumpu uma*—people with natural, round heads—and the *çaytu uma*, those with long, artificially deformed heads. Both groups worked side by side during life and were buried together after death. Yet, for reasons not yet entirely clear, Chanka people with round heads led relatively peaceful lives, while their long-headed counterparts were singled out for violent attack. Their head wounds were more numerous and more deadly, and one out of every six was the victim of multiple attacks. More than any other factor, homicidal blows were the cause of excess mortality among otherwise healthy young men and women, and also among vulnerable noncombatants like children, the elderly, and the infirm. The high ratio of fatal to survivable wounds suggest lethal intent: assailants focused on kills rather than casualties. Another unique feature among this group were the gaping wounds on the base of scores of skulls—telltale execution blows. Dozens also had

their faces physically obliterated by repeated, bone-crushing, overkill trauma. Collectively, these corresponding lines of evidence confirm that prior to Inca conquest, Chanka people sought to intentionally hurt and kill one another. So, while the archaeological data largely support Chanka trauma tropes, the skeletons themselves revealed greater nuance than provided by lore alone.

UNCOVERING THE HISTORY OF SONDOR

The story of Sondor begins some thirteen centuries ago, well before the Inca held sway over much of western South America. In those days, another great empire, known as the Wari, governed the territory that became the cradle of the Chanka people. At Sondor, villagers lived under the auspices of the Wari empire, imitating and importing artifacts that reflected imperial taste and styles. People were healthy and life was peaceful. However, when the Wari empire mysteriously collapsed between 1000 and 1100 CE, all traces of its influence at Sondor also disappeared. Sacred mummies were sacked from ancestral altars, Wari-era skeletons that had been buried under house floors were exhumed, and the remodeling of Sondor into a defensible hilltop fortress began in haste.

Right around the time that the Battle of Hastings was raging a world away (1066 CE, on the southeastern coast of Great Britain), the people that came to be known as the Chanka initially established a village on the eastern ridge of Sondor. The village was a dense complex of agglutinated patio groups and circular houses hewn of stone haphazardly quarried from the local bedrock. It was home to hundreds of families and several thousand people. Just west of the village is the Muyumuyu, an exquisitely-terraced conical hill. The summit is crowned with a majestic rock outcropping. In the pre-Hispanic era, this outcrop was considered a *huaca*, a natural shrine that could be reaching by ascending an elaborate 260-step staircase, with a double-jamb entryway signaling consecrated space. Nevertheless, life at Sondor was far from idyllic. The Chanka lived along the contours of a cold mountain ridge out of necessity, and not by choice. Sondor lacks nearby water sources, and there is scant evidence of Chanka investment in infrastructure or public works projects or urban planning. Rather, like other nearby settlements, Sondor evinces defensive features, including ramparts, baffled entries, imposing walls, ditches, limited access points, lookouts, and weapon caches.

Life for people at Sondor changed dramatically in the early fifteenth century CE when Inca expeditionary forces and imperial diplomats arrived. The motive for the conquest was clear. As a principal settlement on the Royal Inca Highway, Sondor would have been a crucial stop for bureaucrats, trade caravans, and conscripts. To cement their status, the Inca constructed a number of intrusive buildings on the western ridge. Characteristic Inca architecture includes enclosed patios called *kancha*s, ritual–administrative complexes known as *kallanka*s, and mummy niches fashioned in finely pillowed masonry. Excavations within the Inca buildings at Sondor yielded the skeletons of possible *capacocha*s: children selected for sacrifice. Further evidence of Inca incursion still lies plainly on the surface of the site. The ground is scattered with fragments of Inca pottery, including distinctive *aryballo*s used to store maize. The artifacts looted from Sondor that now populate private collections throughout the region are overwhelmingly and undoubtedly Inca in origin. The village on the east side of Sondor is replete with Inca, Chanka, and hybrid ceramics, but also pottery from faraway territories. All told, the archaeological data suggest the Chanka and the Inca coexisted at Sondor for around 150 years. So, unlike the stories reported in colonial chronicles, the decline of Sondor was probably not characterized by ethnic cleansing and repopulation. Rather, it appears that the site served as an integrative nexus typified by Inca and Chanka cohabitation, as well as the possible immigration of people from more distant lands.

Intriguingly, dry and dense legal documents written soon after the Spanish invasion of Peru suggest Sondor was not just populated by the Chanka and Inca, but by other groups of people who hailed from the distant fringes of the now-fragile empire. An *encomienda* land grant ceded to conquistador Diego Maldonado by Francisco Pizarro reveals that as late as 1539 CE the Chanka heartland hosted a plurality of ethnic groupings and social classes. The *encomienda* notes that Sondor, in particular, was populated by Inca *orejone*s (nobles) and *tukuyriku*s (officiating administrators), as well as *yunga*s (lowland cloud forest people), *mamacona*s (single women who served the state), and other tribes from the Andean hinterlands. There were even conscripts from the faraway Chachapoya jungles of northeastern Peru. This is not surprising. The proto-historic cultural diversity at Sondor that the Spanish observed was the result of a well-documented Inca economic and political strategy of both forced resettlement and corvée labor.[6]

The *encomienda* illuminates a multicultural dimension to Sondor that shimmered in the century of Inca conquest and consolidation. Yet soon after, the Spanish resettled the population of Sondor into Spanish-style towns, and the site became part of the property of Emilio Montez, a wealthy landowner. Montez's once elegant lake-front hacienda was home to a private museum featuring an exquisite collection of artifacts from Sondor.[7] Sadly, the stately mansion had been mostly destroyed by 2010 and its graceful colonial architecture was replaced by a grotesquely designed police barracks painted a cartoonish lime-green. And like the now-occulted hacienda, the Inca riches of Sondor found a similar fate: Montez sent the bounty of Sondor to Chicago, for the 1893 World's Fair and Columbian Exposition, and he later sold the collection to the Field Museum, where it remains to this day.

THE CURIOUS CASE
OF THE CHANKA LOVERS

Archaeologists need to be ever-mindful of how their discoveries are interpreted by stakeholders and descendants (Figure 26.4). Such was the case with a particular pair of spectacular skeletons excavated at Sondor. For weeks, Peruvian bioarchaeologist Beatriz Lizarraga and her team had been meticulously excavating a rock-shelter grave. Moving earth one spoonful at the time, the crypt gradually yielded its secrets. Slowly but surely the dust gave way, revealing the

DANIELLE KURIN, VALDA BLACK, BEATRIZ LIZARRAGA, AND IVANNA ROBLEDO

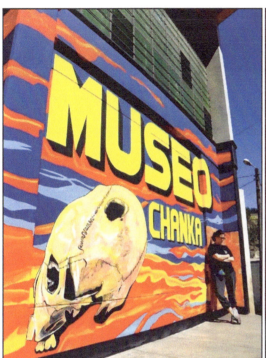  

Figure 26.4. Portrayals of Sondor and the Chanka people at the local museum. The mural on the façade of the museum faithfully depicts an actual cranium from the collection (left). Despite the awkward pose, a Chanka Warrior mannequin is dressed and equipped in reproductions of actual finds (center). In an inventive maquette of Sondor, the 'stones' that form the ringed walls in the model are actually tiny amaranth seeds (right).

smooth, compact surfaces of human bones. Unlike most burials at Sondor, which consisted of chaotic and commingled beds of bone, Beatriz noted that these elements were articulated. The skeletons had not been disturbed since the time their once-fleshy bodies were entombed side by side during a single event centuries earlier. As a fuller picture emerged, Beatriz found herself staring at two complete skeletons. They had been placed on their backs in a fetal position, their knees drawn up under the ribs, a clear sign of a distinctive embalming technique whereby the viscera are removed, and the legs are bent and inserted into the chest cavity. Simple offerings had

been placed in the grave, including ceramic vessels that were found to contain remnants of food and drink for the afterlife. The bodies had been covered in earth, protected by boulders, and forgotten for five hundred years.

"The Last Stand of the Chanka Lovers!" newspaper headlines proclaimed the next morning. Within days, television, radio, and print media throughout Peru began broadcasting news of a fabulous new find at Sondor that would engender a new narrative about the Chanka people. Why? Because when the public gazed upon the grave, they saw two skeletons, arms seemingly clasped around one another in wistful embrace (Figure 26.5). Or maybe it was a death grip. Either way, the skeletal pair were assumed to represent a moment of poignant death crystalized in time, a Peruvian Pompeii of sorts. Consequently, a romantic tale emerged that emphasized enduring love in a time of conflict. Indeed, the Chanka had defied the Inca, and these ancient individuals were surely the personification of that resistance, representing a last stand at Sondor, akin to the biblical Siege of

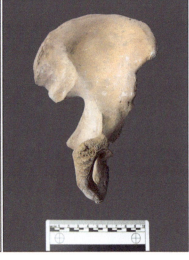

Figure 26.5. A natural tension exists between archaeological findings and popular narratives. Expertly excavated burials drew sensationalized and speculative media attention (top). Reports averred a pair of skeletons were embracing paramours (bottom left). In actuality, based on features of the pelvis (bottom right), both skeletons were male, and before entombment, each was posed in a fetal position, held in place by mummy-like wrappings, which decayed long ago.

Megiddo. Perhaps, folks speculated, this noble pair had ended their lives willingly, a Cleopatra and Mark Antony of the Andes, who were so committed to one another that they chose death rather than suffer the violent fate that awaited any and all who opposed Inca might. The instantly famous Chanka Lovers were quickly and widely acknowledged as conclusive proof that Chanka men and women loved ferociously and lived fiercely, and would rather die free than live in subservience.

Or not. For the apparent paramours still had one more secret to reveal, and it was an intriguing surprise. Back in the laboratory, Beatriz furrowed her brow. She had laid out the two skeletons on long dissection tables, reassembling them bone by bone. She started with the cranium and mandible. She could immediately tell by the wear and tear in the bones and teeth that both individuals were adults, and that one was older than the other. Both skeletons displayed broken bones consistent with intentional assault, but the older one exhibited more injuries than the younger one. This pattern is to be expected in a sanguinary society where wounds tend to accumulate over time: the longer someone is alive, the longer they are exposed to conflict. That both skeletons died of blunt force trauma to the head indicated their demise was indeed violent, but given the locations of the lethal blows, the manner of death was not suicide, but rather homicide.

For each skeleton, Beatriz next laid out the seven cervical (neck) vertebrae, twelve thoracic vertebrae, and five lumbar vertebrae, which snaked down the table. On either side, she placed the twelve gracefully bowed rib bones. Next came the sternum, scapulae (shoulder blades) and clavicles (collar bones), followed by the sacrum and pelvis. With the axial skeleton complete, Beatriz then arranged the extremities. The long, tubular arm bones (humerus, ulna, and radius), and lanky leg bones (femur, patella, tibia, and fibula) were capped by the itty-bitty bones of the hands and feet.

Stepping back, Beatriz could now appreciate each fully extended skeleton. It was then that something struck her. Something that had not been visible when the hyper-flexed finds were still covered by centuries of soil. First, she investigated the skulls. Beatriz traced her fingers over the robust brow ridges.

She thumbed the rounded half-moons that form the upper eye orbits and tapped the blocky mastoid processes, the bony nodules located just behind the ears. She swept her palm over the rugose ridges of bone on the back of the skulls that served to anchor the muscles of the neck. Turning to the mandibles (lower jaw bone), she noted their bulkiness, and she felt the eminent chins. Her hands were telling her something was askew with these so-called Chanka Lovers. Beatriz then moved down to inspect the bones of the hip. For both individuals, the shape of the pelvic bones were shallow and high; the angle of the greater sciatic notch (a U-shaped area of bone located behind the ball-and-socket joint on the hip) was acutely narrow, and the tail of the sacrum jutted forward. Neither skeleton exhibited the soft and delicate features of a Chanka woman. Rather the skulls were big and blocky and bulky, and the hips were shaped in such a way that would have made bearing children a physical impossibility. Ivanna Robledo, a skilled osteologist, and Valda Black, an expert in skeletal biology, noticed these bony patterns as well. The three came to a potentially contentious consensus: both of the skeletons were males.

Now what? Fuss had been broadcast and ink had been spilled in a viral—yet inaccurate—story about an Andean Cleopatra and her Antony, who perished for love when threatened by war. The challenge at hand was to tactfully and respectfully reconcile conflicting narratives without sacrificing scientific facts. Acts of violence were intimately associated with being Chanka, but sentimental relationships (especially those between partners of the same sex) and tender displays of affection were not. At its core, Chanka popular identity is largely predicated on hyper-masculinity, strict gender roles, and reverence for brave and bellicose Spartan strongmen. A new—more accurate—interpretation was needed to explain the enigmatic pair.

In the end, the bones never changed, but the narrative about them did. Now, the pair are appropriately heralded as the Chanka Brothers, instead of the Star-Crossed Lovers. For descendant communities, the manifestation of a fraternal bond formed a better fit with their understanding of Chanka origins, expansion, and leadership, and better conforms to the archaeological and historical data that has been recovered to date. Ambiguities and romanticism aside, the find contributed a new voice to the chorus of Chanka history, one that revealed the basic humanity of people long hailed as singularly belligerent and brutal.

AN EPILOGUE OF LOVE AND WAR

Far from being exterminated or banished at the end of the Inca–Chanka War or perishing under the weighty yoke of colonial (and later republican) rule, Chanka people maintained a continual presence at Sondor. Today, the ancient terraces of the site still serve as agricultural plots and the gentle slopes of Sondor provide pasture where lazy llamas graze. In the abutting villages of Cotahuacho and Pacucha, descendants of the prehistoric inhabitants of Sondor continue to live off the land like their Chanka ancestors, eking out a mostly peaceful existence as subsistence farmers. And to this day, the people of the south-central Peruvian highlands proudly claim descent from the Chanka.

Nowhere is this connection more conspicuous than in Anta Waylla, the place long considered the cradle of Chanka culture. In the towns and cities of this region, reminders of Chanka prowess remain. In every central plaza, colonial fountains have been replaced by garish fiberglass installations of Chanka warriors in attack mode, surrounded by vicious felines. The local television station, Chanka-Vision, occasionally broadcasts *The Last Chanka Warrior*, a popular locally-produced action film, or reruns of *Survivor: Sondor*, a nationally televised reality show. On Soccer Sundays, folks disembark at the Chankas Express bus station, walk down Avenida Chanka to get to the Los Chankas stadium to watch a match. The off-season brings the Chanka Rally, where off-road stock cars whiplash around hairpin turns as engines growl and squealing tires spit up clouds of dust. During holidays, schoolchildren don hyper-stylized iterations of Chanka battle dress and parade proudly. They are followed by a float with the reigning Miss Chanka, selected as much for her poise as her potato-peeling prowess. Arguably the most breathtaking events are the yearly reenactments of Chanka battles. With Sondor serving as stage, hundreds of locals take part in this choreographed event; thousands of spectators attend. The tale of the warriors is still repeated with gusto, but now there is more nuance and a greater recognition of the brilliant spectrum of culture-history that vividly colors Chanka identity.

ACKNOWLEDGMENTS

This chapter is dedicated to our friends and collaborators, Sarah Jolly and Ricky Nelson. We graciously thank the individuals—especially Yuval Bar-Zemer, Hans Barnard, Ran Boytner, Nene Lozada, and Willeke Wendrich—and institutions that supported various stages of this research including the Institute for Field Research, Washington State University, National Geographic, and the National Science Foundation.

NOTES

1   Sarmiento de Gamboa 1572/2007.
2   de Murúa, 1613/2008.
3   de Betanzos 1557/2004.
4   Pachacuti Yamqui Salcamaygua 1613/1993.
5   Betanzos 1557/2004.
6   Rowe 1945.
7   Bauer et al. 2010.

BIBLIOGRAPHY

Bauer, Brian S., Lucas C. Kellett, and Miriam A. Silva (2010), *The Chanka: Archaeological Research in Andahuaylas (Apurimac), Peru,* Los Angeles (Cotsen Institute of Archaeology Press).

Cieza de León, Pedro (1996), *La crónica del Peru,* Madrid (Historia 16, new edition of the 1553 original).

Cobó, Bernabé (1964), *Historia del nuevo mundo,* Madrid (Ediciones Atlas, new edition of the 1653 original).

de Betanzos, Juan (1996), *Narrative of the Incas,* (University of Texas Press, translation of the 1557 Spanish manuscript by Roland Hamilton, edited by Dana Buchanan).

de la Vega, Garcilaso (1968), *Comentarios reales: El origen de los Incas,* Madrid (Bruguera, new edition of the 1609–13 original).

de Murúa, Martín (2008), *Historia general del Piru: Facsimile of J. Paul Getty Museum Ms. Ludwig XIII 16,* Los Angeles (Getty Research Institute Publication Program Publications, facsimile of the 1613 original).

Markham, Clements E. (1871), On the Geographical Positions of the Tribes Which Formed the Empire of the Yncas, with an Appendix on the name "Aymara," *Journal of the Royal Geographical Society of London* 41, 281–338.

Pachacuti Yamqui Salcamaygua, Joan d.S.C. (1993), *Relacion de las antiguedades deste reyno del Piru,* Lima (L'Institut français d'études andines, new edition of the 1613 original by Pierre Duviols and César Itier).

Rowe, John H. (1945), Absolute Chronology in the Andean Area, *American Antiquity* 10(3), 265–84.

Sarmiento de Gamboa, Pedro (2007), *The History of the Incas,* Austin (University of Texas Press, new edition of the 1572 original by Brian S. Bauer, Vania Smith, and Jean-Jacques Decoster).

ARCHAEOLOGY AND CONTEMPORARY CAPITALISM

PETER G. GOULD

When I was approached to produce a chapter on the subject of archaeology and contemporary capitalism for a volume on outside-the-box archaeology, the prospect so intrigued me that I accepted readily. After all, while I have been a PhD-carrying archaeologist for several years now, I spent the prior thirty years as an economist and, most of that time, as a corporate chief executive officer: a capitalist. While such credentials either immediately qualify or terminally taint me to pursue this subject, I have straddled these two worlds for much of my life and the prospect of engaging with both was compelling.

Only later did the question dawn on me: what is the box that archaeology and capitalism are supposed to be out of? The chapters in this volume address innovative archaeological practice or conventional archaeological practice in novel settings. How does capitalism fit in? Moreover, not many years ago Yannis Hamilakis and Philip Duke's (2007) *Archaeology and Capitalism* comprehensively criticized the ethics of the embrace of capitalist forces by archaeology. Is there something new to say?

On reflection, I conclude that there is, in fact, a box archaeology needs to escape. *Archaeology and Capitalism* was born in the first decade of the 2000s and was focused on the ethical conflict between the obligations of archaeology to living people and scholarly truth, on one hand, and the practices and mores of twentieth-century capitalism on the other. But the world has changed. In this third decade of the twenty-first century, technology has simultaneously shrunk, interlaced, and fragmented the world in unanticipated ways. For better or worse, capitalism is changing in the new century and archaeology is not immune to the effects of those changes. Twentieth-century ideas are fast being overtaken by twenty-first–century realities. It is time to inquire anew whether we have boxed ourselves into obsolescent perspectives on the ethics, politics, and practice of archaeology in a capitalist world.

THE TWENTIETH-CENTURY CAPITALIST BOX

What are the contours of what we might call the twentieth-century capitalist box (Figure 25.1)? Let us first stipulate that, without question, archaeology is irredeemably embedded in the capitalist system. Excavation and employment depend heavily on construction projects. Government support for heritage preservation and management is driven largely by the lure of the tourism industry. The universities that train us all and employ some of us, the museums we work in, the research projects we wish to pursue; all increasingly depend on the philanthropic priorities of wealthy capitalists. In other words, every facet of the discipline, in every place in the world, is indebted to, dependent upon, or under threat from the dynamics of global capitalism.

The relationship of archaeology with capitalism has always been checkered. Its roots are in antiquarian curiosity, which carried off the patrimony of unwitting colonies to fill the 'universal museums' in the Western world. Archaeologists were complicit in helping justify the great colonial project of the nineteenth century that exploited the global south for the benefit of a few in Europe and the United States. Archaeologists have become deeply embedded in the global tourism market, both underpinning and benefiting from the exploitation of heritage for fun and profit. It is true that archaeologists and heritage experts have succeeded at making the preservation of ancient ruins, heritage structures, and cultural practices essential elements of global, national, and local government policy. In the process, we have erected an industry of excavators, international consultants, academics, museum specialists, conservators, and bureaucrats, creating employment for tens of thousands of archaeologists around the world. Yet, despite being embedded in capitalism at every stage, in every era, and in every part of the world, the embrace by archaeology of the world of business is at best ambivalent and often hostile in the extreme. Indeed, the collaboration of archaeology with capitalism has tainted the field in its own eyes.

Figure 25.1. Is the capitalist box a prison? *Photograph by Scott Webb, Pexels.*

Hamilakis and Duke's *Archaeology and Capitalism* was an expression of that ambivalence and hostility, of the self-consciousness of archaeologists who must reckon simultaneously with their dependence on capitalism and their disdain for its consequences. Their book was a comprehensive appeal for the discipline to step away from casual acceptance either of the often disgraceful link of archaeology to historic nationalism and imperialism, or of its present-day engagement with globalized neoliberal capitalism. For a discipline looking back at the end of the twentieth century, Hamilakis and Duke's book helped to set out the ethical boundaries at the time for the interaction of archaeologists with capitalism. Those boundaries—in principles and in practice—define the dimensions of the capitalist box in which archaeology finds itself today.

THE PRINCIPLES DIMENSION

The nationalist, even racist, past of archaeology has given way to a combination of shame and anger, translated into an expanding critique of past practice and current attitudes, and to the emergence of ethical rights and wrongs that lean decidedly toward the interests of subaltern populations whether they be the poor, indigenous groups, minorities, or the politically oppressed. Particularly among anthropologists, and especially in the western hemisphere and the antipodes, ethical archaeology works with the disenfranchised against state and capitalist interests.

Chapters in Hamilakis and Duke constitute a catalog of the failings of the discipline to which this set of values is a response. Hamilakis, in his chapter, objected to the concept of stewardship of the archaeological record, whether already exposed or still-to-be-excavated archaeological sites, the protection of which has been a basic ethical precept of twentieth-century archaeology. Hamilakis argued that stewardship inappropriately entrenches private property within the public resource that is archaeology, and elevates the interests of archaeologists, who arrogate the mantle of expert or steward, above the needs of living people. In a brief introduction to the chapters on capitalist practices within archaeology, Duke argued for the need to make archaeology a truly ethical and emancipatory practice, and objected to the promulgation of Western ideas, such as tribal museums, that are alien to indigenous peoples. A chapter by Alice Kehoe critiqued the deep association of archaeology with global capitalist expansion and complained that commercialization has led the discipline "to pander to lurid vulgar taste . . . when as anthropological archaeologists we think the public should learn more about everyday life and commoners' lots, to compare and contrast with their own lives".[1]

This critique is echoed throughout the literature, both from archaeologists with Marxist leanings,[2] and from those with less pronounced views.[3] If the practice of archaeology has been coopted and contorted by the demands of nationalist politics, commercial marketing and finance, and global tourism, the prescribed antidote is an ethical praxis that redirects the focus of archaeology away from the rich, ruling classes of the world and toward the needs, desires, and priorities of the subaltern. This has led to an insistence that archaeologists must do archaeology in a different way, which takes us to the practical dimension of the capitalist box.

THE PRACTICE DIMENSION

Like others in the field,[4] the authors in *Archaeology and Capitalism* attempted to trace the outlines of an ethical practice in archaeology. Given the profound imbrication of the field with capitalism, this is no trivial challenge. The vast proportion of archaeologists in the United States, Europe, and to varying degrees elsewhere, are employed by commercial businesses specializing in rescue excavations, regulatory compliance work, and remediation in advance of commercial construction. They are, in a very real sense, part of the capitalist machinery of economic development. Archaeologists have lost the independence enjoyed by wealthy eighteenth-century antiquarians. Paul Everill complained in his chapter in Hamilakis and Duke that compensation and working conditions in commercial archaeology have reduced highly educated and skilled archaeologists to near-proletarian economic status. In field research, Dean Saitta argued for an emancipatory archaeology that redirects practice toward the interests, needs, and perspectives of indigenous peoples, the working poor, and others "who historically have had little use for archaeology as traditionally practiced."[5] Such an approach implies redirecting the focus of research to matters of concern to groups such as those union members whose history Saitta's chapter addresses. In other contexts, this concern has led to calls for multivocal research, and often to sharing research design and excavation work with indigenous people or others who are disenfranchised in the capitalist economy.[6]

The dependence of archaeology on tourism for funding and public interest led Alice Kehoe to decry marketing capitalism and the drive for tourism that replaced multi-layered historical and cultural complexities with sanitized presentations curated for a self-indulgent public. In his chapter. Neil Silberman lamented the emergence of "McArchaeology," of heritage sites (Figure 25.2) transformed from a legacy with cultural and social meaning to a consumable service on a par with movies and theme parks, often distorted for political ends. To Silberman and many others, this process both devalues the heritage and undermines its ultimate sustainability. The most egregious transformation of archaeology and heritage into a consumable is the conversion of artifacts themselves—vital sources of data to the archaeologist—into chattel traded in the great auction houses and procured by looters whose vandalism renders valueless sites once ripe for scientific study. Whether due to the loss of knowledge or the loss of innocence, ethical practice keeps many archaeologists a good distance from anything smacking of corporate support, adaptation to the consumer market, or simplified interpretation.

TWENTY-FIRST CENTURY CAPITALISM

The unease within archaeology about its entanglement with capitalism is partly ideological, but it also reflects a discipline that operates within models that evolved in the last century. Particularly in the era following the Second World War, governments accepted that archaeology and heritage were public goods and assumed the roles of regulator, controller, employer, and funder of archaeology, while philanthropists provided support motivated by personal enthusiasms that recall the

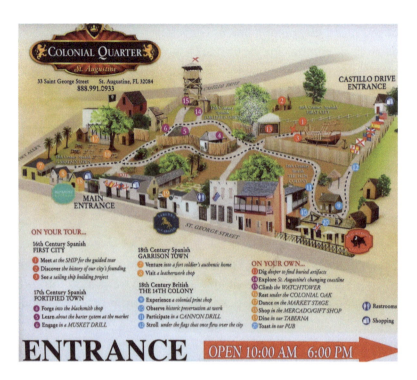

Figure 25.2. McArchaeology? The Colonial Quarter attraction, St. Augustine, Florida. *Photograph by the author.*

antiquarian era. The success of archaeologists at encouraging governments to become regulators of preservation meant that corporations were compelled to hire archaeologists to satisfy government mandates. In the last quarter of the century, though, this government-managed public-good model has collided with neoliberal ideology that idealized markets and was skeptical of the capacity of governments to perform. Private market-rooted solutions became the preferred approach to social challenges. However, the consequences of privatization were often disappointing, unleashing the critical perspectives embodied in the capitalist box that Hamilakis and Duke framed for the end of the twentieth century.[7]

Now we stand partway into the twenty-first century, and capitalism is in a peculiar moment. Neoliberal catechisms are being shredded by their own failure and by changes in technology, the economy, and politics. Political upheaval confronts

Figure 25.3. The odor of chaos is in the wind. *Photograph by Markus Spiske, Unsplash.*

every government everywhere, and no industry is immune from the tumult of market disruptions. The maldistribution of income, laden with the prospect of social division and economic malaise, has become a focal point for activists, as have the problems of systemic racism and imminent environmental crisis (Figure 25.3). A global pandemic confronts the globe with a catastrophe of unique dimensions. There is a noticeable odor of chaos in the wind. These are circumstances that archaeology can choose to exploit or risk being overwhelmed by.

Consider the following five examples (Figure 25.4):

1) The concentration of corporate and individual financial wealth has accelerated astonishingly since 2000, with social and economic implications that frighten even economists.[8] Nonetheless, with the growth of entrepreneurial crowd-funding platforms, we increasingly see the capacity to aggregate small contributions of time or money from masses of people to disrupt those who dominate the economy. How can archaeologists exploit this?

2) Likewise, political power increasingly seems concentrated among a wealthy and connected elite. The persistence of Brexit, Donald Trump, Russian oligarchs, and impudent technology billionaires are markers of the degree to which neoliberal economic policies and their beneficiaries manage to remain empowered even though widely disparaged and discredited by events. Nonetheless, we have experienced the extraordinary capacity of ill-financed popular movements riding on new technologies to undermine the political elite. Look no further than the Color Revolutions in Eastern Europe, the Republican Tea Party, or the success of Democrat Alexandria Ocasio-Cortez in the United States. How can archaeologists exploit this?

3) Cultural vehicles, such as publishing, performing arts, movies, and television, are increasingly concentrated in the hands of a few dominant commercial or nonprofit entities, while scholars find paywalls and high prices constrain the promulgation of their research. Nonetheless, technology-enabled individuals, able to generate and disseminate content, are real competitors to the titans of corporate communications. YouTube, with its free content, is among the most-watched media outlets. Free access to digitized collections has undermined museums as hegemons of knowledge or curation. Bootleg academic books are widely distributed on websites of dubious provenance, while academic websites circumvent journal paywalls. Defending monopolies is getting harder and harder. How can archaeologists exploit this?

4) Riding on economies of network scale and scope, corporations like Google or Amazon are swallowing competitors to create near monopolistic enterprises. Nonetheless, their own technologies have fragmented work, freeing the skilled to freelance and to start small businesses, or to work from home, share jobs, or otherwise build lives outside of conventional corporate structures. The Covid-19 pandemic has amped-up these trends irreversibly. Large-scale technology is undermining large-scale enterprise. How can archaeologists exploit this?

5) The consolidation of wealth in the top 1 percent has skewed philanthropy toward the values and methods of the ultra-rich. Culture is losing philanthropic ground to grand

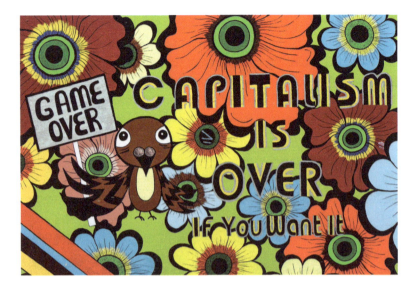

Figure 25.4. How do archaeologists respond to the crisis facing capitalism? *Photograph by Koushik Chowdavarapu, Unsplash.*

OUTSIDE THE BOX: ARCHAEOLOGY AND CONTEMPORARY CAPITALISM

The shortcomings of capitalism are well documented: its tendency toward monopoly, dishonesty, exploitation, resource destruction, persistent poverty in the face of great wealth, and the corruption of the polity. Critiques at the end of the last century like Hamilakis and Duke's identified real and troubling issues. And yet, the disruptive innovations described in the prior paragraphs are also the fruits of capitalist businesses. There is another side to capitalism. At its best, capitalism is a process of competitive interaction that harnesses a fundamental human desire to advance one's lot in life. Capitalism is constantly adapting in order to meet people's needs with the least possible wastage of scarce resources. Capitalism thrives on upheaval that liberates creativity, catalyzes innovation, and restructures human relations in an unending drive to improve lives while making a profit. Although imperfect and often late, capitalism can and does respond to the changing needs of the world. In the present moment of crisis and change, archaeology has an opportunity to define a better future by harnessing to its own ends the creatively destructive tendencies of twenty-first–century capitalism.

I offer six suggestions:

1) We need to embrace what markets tell us (Figure 25.5). Markets are signaling devices conveying information about what society values and what it does not. Markets are short-term oriented and far from perfect, especially when valuing intangibles such as cultural heritage. But markets dominate every economy globally and will for any conceivable future. We need to learn to interpret the signals and respond. Archaeologists should not plead for special treatment. We should not presume that the value of what we do is obvious. Today, scarce financial resources are being allocated away from archaeology. This is the signal that what we do is not valued as much as other demands on human and financial resources. We need to listen to the market, and to respond with innovations in practice that demonstrate the value of archaeology and heritage. This can come through commitment to aggressively engaging the public with our work; through radical transparency about what we

projects to eradicate diseases or solve other great social problems. Cultural organizations increasingly face demands that they measure the value of social benefits heretofore regarded as inherently unmeasurable. Nonetheless, that sort of philanthropy must contend with the internet-enabled capacity of Kickstarter, Go-Fund-Me, or DigVentures in archaeology to secure financing for novel, even odd ideas outside of conventional philanthropic channels. I ask once again, how can archaeologists exploit this?

Turmoil and fragmentation—in technology, economics, and politics—characterize twenty-first–century capitalism. Recall that the Chinese character for 'crisis' contains one character meaning 'dangerous' and another meaning 'a changing point.' Creative thinking about how to avoid the danger and exploit the potential change flowing from the emerging capitalist crisis can open new vistas for archaeology. That is where the journey outside the box begins.

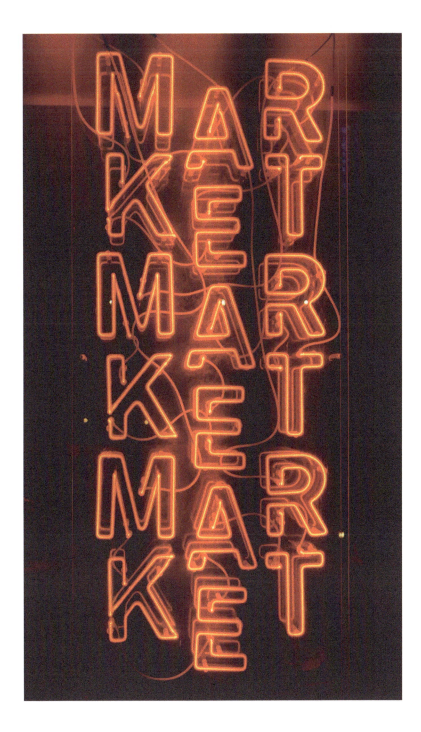

Figure 25.5. Markets still drive the world; use them for good. *Photograph by Karine Germaine, Unsplash.*

do, why, and how; and through recognition that activism—with individuals, communities, and governments—is at the core of changing perceptions of the value of archaeology.

2) To do this, we need to embrace the public. Only living people can benefit from what archaeologists do. We need to recognize that people who do not share our passions are not the great, unethical unwashed. They simply have other priorities, other interests, other pressures on their lives. We should seek to meet them where they live with humility. Objections to market capitalism are at best obsolete and at worst arrogant. Marketing is about tuning the offer to satisfy human desires. We need to understand what the public needs from archaeology and heritage—not what we think they should want—and innovate to provide it creatively. Museum buildings are not the only, or even the best, way to tell stories that resonate with people. Public archaeology, practiced as a one-way lecture by the expert to the ignorant, is passé. Listening to the public, responding to people's real needs from archaeology, and delivering museums, sites, programs, and literature that meet those needs is the only way to make archaeology relevant in the twenty-first century. This may well mean focusing on very local activities—"community-based" archaeology—at the expense of mega-projects that bring attention to proponents but mean little to the populace. Archaeologists who understand and effectively meet the needs of ordinary people—in capitalist jargon our customers—are engaged in smart marketing, not ethical capitulation.

3) Archaeologists need to embrace entrepreneurship, risk-taking, change and, yes, failure. Archaeologists in general are more comfortable in a trench than in a boardroom, but exceptions are arising beyond commercial cultural resource management companies. The Sustainable Preservation Initiative, where I have been a board member, is a non-governmental organization that funded community groups in emerging countries to build businesses in order to generate support for local heritage. That process proved hard to scale but we learned how to train bottom-of-the-pyramid entrepreneurs, so the Sustainable Preservation Initiative has rebranded itself as Escala Initiative and opened its online business skills training

Figure 25.6. Crowd-power: regular people doing real archaeology for a social enterprise. *Photograph: DigVentures, Ltd.*

platform to serve all poor entrepreneurs, not just those adjacent to archaeological sites. CoDiFi Inc. commercialized new technology for recording archaeological field data through a B (for Social Benefit) private corporation that is now expanding outside the archaeological niche to any fieldwork industry. The Institute for Field Research is a nonprofit organization building an economically viable platform to expand opportunities for field schools to find students and for students to experience archaeology. DigVentures, of which I am a part owner, is a Social Enterprise in the United Kingdom pursuing public archaeology with measurable social impact through the power of internet-enabled crowd sourcing and crowd funding.

Archaeology needs many more entrepreneurial experiments, some of which are going to fail, because experimentation and innovation are the only way twenty-first–century structures can emerge in archaeology (Figure 25.6).

4) We need to embrace collaborating with corporations—on constructive terms. The uproar was deafening over the ill-conceived initiative of the World Archaeological Congress to collaborate with Rio Tinto.[9] But let us not throw out all collaborations because of one misjudgment. Corporate leaders increasingly recognize that they must satisfy a broader public, not just their shareholders, if they are to survive in the future. The capitalist crisis is their crisis. Corporations will work with us and even change their behavior if collaboration enhances or protects their brands in the eyes of their increasingly diverse and demanding customers and stakeholders. To be sure, constructing positive collaborations with profit-motivated businesses requires a steely, critical ethical eye. But to abandon partnerships entirely is to walk away from resources and positive impacts available at large scale from no other source.

5) Archaeologists need to validate their own impact. New, hyper-wealthy philanthropists are biased toward demonstrated social impact based on entrepreneurial solutions. Like the signals from the market, this so-called impact philanthropy asks us to demonstrate our value to society. Archaeologists have been conspicuously inept at this. Public archaeology has resisted serious, methodical research. Museums act as if counting the people who visit conventional galleries or participate in school projects are effective contributions to communities. Archaeologists instinctively want to give priority to researching and preserving sites and artifacts, but when money is scarce choices must be made and we must make choices that demonstrate our impact. After all, wealthy philanthropists generally are both capitalists and skeptics. They want to maximize the good they can do with their money. More crucially, traditional foundations and government agencies, especially in Europe, are coming to share this view and demand impact assessments in their grants. There is no practical alternative today to responding to the demand for meaningful measures of positive social change arising from the work of archaeologists.

If archaeologists can define and demonstrate their value,[10] access to impact-driven resources will make a huge difference to our practice. In the process, we will make archaeology and heritage management better disciplines.

6) Finally, we need to embrace nontraditional scholarship in archaeology. This means adding courses that help future practitioners understand how economic value, impact philanthropy, entrepreneurial organization, and other twenty-first–century capitalist ideas can be applied in archaeology. Students want jobs, and archaeology jobs in the future will be deeply impacted by the trends outlined here. We need to adjust curricula in order to equip them for those jobs and train them to lead the changes that contemporary capitalism will demand of our field. In hiring and tenure decisions, universities should assign value to community-focused projects, to entrepreneurial experimentation, and to open-source publications that people actually read. At the Sustainable Preservation Initiative, we learned the hard way how current standards of success in academia constrain the enthusiasm and capacity of archaeologists to lead community-development initiatives. There needs to be a tenure-track premium, not a penalty, for pursuing projects that help living people, that impact public policy, or that bring the wisdom of other social science disciplines into archaeology classrooms.

Ten years into my career as an archaeologist and heritage economist, I have come to recognize a split personality in the field. There is growing acceptance of our ethical obligations—to communities, to indigenous people, to humans in general—that can supersede allegiance to the archaeological record or scholarly convention. But there also is resistance to changing the paradigm in which we operate as scholars and practitioners so that we may truly benefit people. Technology is driving wrenching changes in the capitalist system. We should neither avert our eyes nor criticize from a distance. Rather, we should engage vigorously. The current turmoil in the world around us presents a unique opportunity to bring ethics and practice together in new ways, stripped of ideological baggage and focused on the liberating potential for archaeology to really make a difference in the world.

NOTES

1   Hamilakis and Duke 2007, 173.
2   McGuire 2008.
3   Graham et al. 2000.
4   Gnecco and Lippert 2015, Scarre and Scarre 2006.
5   Hamilakis and Duke 2007, 267.
6   Colwell-Chanthaphon and Ferguson 2008.
7   Harvey 2005.
8   Picketty 2020.
9   Shepherd and Haber 2011.
10 Wilkins 2019.

BIBLIOGRAPHY

Colwell-Chanthaphonh, Chip and Thomas J. Ferguson, eds. (2008), *Collaboration in Archaeological Practice,* Lanham, New York, Toronto and Plymouth (AltaMira Press).

Gnecco, Cristóbal and Dorothy Lippert, eds. (2015), *Ethics and Archaeological Praxis,* New York, Heidelberg, Dordrecht and London (Springer).

Graham, Brian, Greg J. Ashworth, and John E. Tunbridge (2000), *A Geography of Heritage,* London and New York (Arnold Publishers and Oxford University Press).

Hamilakis, Yannis and Philip Duke, eds. (2007), *Archaeology and Capitalism,* Walnut Creek (Left Coast Press).

Harvey, David (2005), *A Brief History of Neoliberalism,* Oxford and New York (Oxford University Press).

McGuire, Randall H. (2008), *Archaeology as Political Action,* Berkeley, Los Angeles and London (University of California Press).

Picketty, Thomas (2020), *Capital and Ideology*, Cambridge and London (The Belknap Press of Harvard University Press).

Scarre, Chris and Geoffrey Scarre (2006), *The Ethics of Archaeology,* Cambridge (Cambridge University Press).

Shepherd, Nick and Alejandro Haber (2011), What's up with WAC? Archaeology and "Engagement" in a Globalized World, *Public Archaeology* 10(2), 96–115.

Wilkins, Brendon (2019), A Theory of Change and Evaluative Framework for Measuring the Social Impact of Public Participation in Archaeology, *European Journal of Postclassical Archaeologies* 9, 77–100.

STUFF AND HTTPS://BELOWTHESURFACE.AMSTERDAM

URBAN WASTE FROM THE RIVER AMSTEL, MIRROR OF THE CITY OF AMSTERDAM

JERZY GAWRONSKI

Archaeologists work with material debris to reconstruct the past. Their finds consist of broken items, either discarded as waste or lost unintentionally, and closely connected with the daily routines of people. Despite the manifold ways that lead to the formation of archaeological sites and finds, the material deposits share one common feature: they are mute—sherds do not communicate in words like the letters of an ancient historical text. Therefore, archaeologists classify the material remains into ordered data to give meaning to their finds and consequently to the site or location from which they originate. This chapter deals with the classification of finds from the River Amstel that were retrieved during the construction between 2003 and 2018 of a new metro line—the North/South Line—in Amsterdam, the Netherlands. The River Amstel runs through the historical (medieval and early modern) center of Amsterdam. The excavation of the riverbed by the archaeological department of Monuments and Archaeology of the City of Amsterdam resulted in approximately 700,000 identified finds.

As a municipal project, the archaeological research had a strong public scope, to reach not only fellow science colleagues, but also the citizens of Amsterdam and the users of the metro, including commuters, tourists, and visitors. For the public and scientific valorization of the finds, a number of unconventional analog and digital products were created. This chapter discusses the photographic catalog *Stuff,*[1] which displays 13,000 finds, the public display of ten thousand finds in two showcases in one of the metro stations, and the website https://belowthesurface.amsterdam, which presents twenty thousand finds.

For each product, a specific design format was developed to create a new language to tell archaeological stories. Because in the end, archaeology is all about storytelling. More than written historical sources, archaeological objects have a strong visual impact. New and exciting design options were explored beyond the classical archaeological classification systems to render meaning to material culture and to visualize the River Amstel as a new source of archaeological narratives on urban life.

THE METRO

The North/South Line is a 9.7 kilometer (6 mile) metro connection between the north and the south of Amsterdam, which are separated by the IJ, the ancient harbor in front of the historical town. Where possible, the 7.1 kilometer (4 mile) long underground route in the historic city center followed the existing open infrastructure to avoid damaging buildings. The open spaces in the center consist of streets, but also of partly open and partly filled in waterways, including Stationsplein—part of the IJ—Damrak and Rokin—part of the riverbed of the Amstel— Vijzelgracht, and a seventeenth-century canal (Figure 24.1). The tunnels were drilled at a depth of 20 to 30 meters (66 to 99 feet) below the Amsterdam Ordnance Datum (defining the normal water level in the city), deep below the wooden foundation piles of the buildings next to the metro route, which reach an average of 12 meters (39 feet) below the ordnance datum. From a civil engineering point of view, the building project was highly innovative and even experimental, as at the time there was no experience of boring tunnels through a soft subsoil of sand and clay under a historic city center such as that of Amsterdam.

The challenges of the North/South Line were not confined to civil engineering, but applied equally to the archaeological research, which was organized by the office of Monuments and

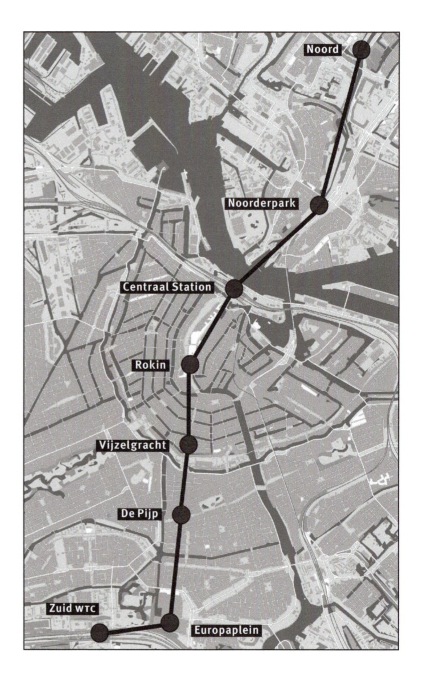

Figure 24.1. Route of the North/South Line; the Damrak building site is part of Central Station, together with Rokin and Vijzelgracht, situated in the historical center of Amsterdam. *Adapted from Gawronski and Kranendonk 2018: 12; design: Willem van Zoetendaal.*

Archaeology of the city of Amsterdam and formed an integral part of the construction program. The archaeological implications for the construction sites in the city center were assessed in the early stages of planning. The tunnel itself was not the primary archaeological site, as is it was technically near impossible for archaeologists to work ahead of the tunnel-boring machine. The tunnel cuts through different levels from several landscape periods dating from 124,000 to 10,000 BCE (the geological epoch of the late Pleistocene). Between roughly 12 and 25 meters (39 and 82 feet) below the ordnance datum the soil layers belong to a steppe landscape (the Weichselian or last Ice Age period, around 114,000–10,000 BCE) and from approximately 25 meters (82 feet) below the ordnance datum are the shores of a warm sea, the Eemian Sea (around 124,000–114,000 BCE). The archaeological research focused on the soil layers in the upper 12 meters (39 feet), belonging to the Holocene epoch (10,000 BCE until present), of the six vertical excavation pits for the stations along the route.

RIVER ARCHAEOLOGY

Four of the six construction sites—Stationsplein, Damrak, Rokin, and Vijzelgracht—that were selected for archaeology were situated in former or existing streambeds. The two main sites were Damrak and Rokin, which yielded 99 percent of all finds (Figures 24.2 and 24.3). These sites make the archaeological project of the North/South Line essentially a river archaeology project, involving a systematic examination of the bed of the River Amstel.[2] Streambeds in general comprise large archaeological potential because of the simple fact that material remains can sink to the bottom of rivers, canals, or open water, where they can pile up in large quantities over time, depending on the dynamics of the water environment.

Archaeologists were first alerted to the research potential of streambeds by the nascent discipline of underwater archaeology in the 1960s. The upsurge of finds and discoveries from lakes, rivers, canals, and their banks raised general awareness of the scientific value of streambeds as repositories of

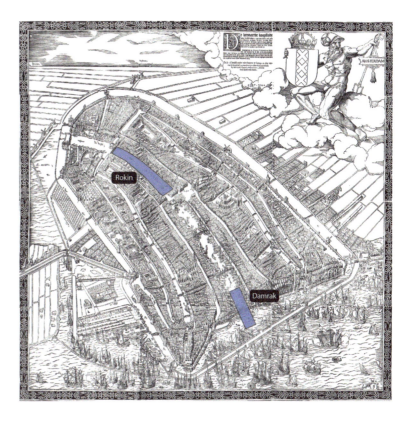

Figure 24.2. Historical map of Amsterdam from 1544 by Cornelis Anthonisz, with the River Amstel as the vital artery of the city (Amsterdam City Archives, 010001001032). The tunnel of the North/South Line follows the open waterway of the River Amstel in the historical city center and the construction sites of Damrak and Rokin are situated in the riverbed. *Adapted from Gawronski and Kranendonk 2018: 14; design: Willem van Zoetendaal.*

archaeological finds, while excavations of reclaimed waterways and harbors served to strengthen this idea. In recent years, several other metro construction projects that transect water zones also yielded rich archaeological sites, such as the excavations of the Roman harbor in the Rhine near Cologne while building the Nord–Süd Bahn between 2003 and 2012, and those of the Byzantine Harbor of Theodosius in Istanbul during the construction of Yenikapi metro station between 2004 and 2013.[3] The special archaeological nature of banks and underwater sites has been recognized not only by science but even

Figure 24.3. The richest deposits of finds in the river were uncovered above approximately 6.5 meters (21 feet) below the ordnance datum. Cross-section of the upper part of the Amstel riverbed at Rokin, consisting of modern sand of the infill—R6: ground level to 3 meters (10 feet) below the ordnance datum—and organic layers with seventeenth-, eighteenth-, and nineteenth-century urban waste—R5: 3 to 6.5 meters (10–21 feet) below the ordnance datum. *Photograph: City of Amsterdam, Monuments and Archaeology; source: https://belowthesurface.amsterdam, accessed February 29, 2020.*

in art, such as Mark Dion's *Tate Thames Dig* in 1999. Dion used the banks of the River Thames in London as a backdrop for an installation by collecting finds there at low tide, thus representing the river as a source for archaeological materials.[4]

By far the largest group of archaeological finds from these riverbed sites is linked to a universal aspect of human behavior, namely, the habit of dumping refuse in water. It is an easy way of getting rid of waste, as it immediately disappears out of sight or is carried away by the current. The debris, specifically in an urban setting, can be extremely varied, of both domestic and industrial origin. As such, it can be spatially related to activities that are associated with a building or structure, a workshop or an installation along the shore. Apart from archaeological remains, which are connected with activities on land, there is also a category of finds that are primarily associated with shipping activities and vary from items that have fallen overboard to parts of ships or complete shipwrecks. Yet another group consists of items, mostly personal belongings, that were not dumped intentionally but somehow lost accidentally in the water.

Apart from the physical aspect of archaeological material sinking into the water, underwater deposits differ from those on land in the diverse origin and generally mixed nature of the finds. The chance of finding concentrations of material remains is highest in the beds of urban canals, due to high habitation density and the frequency with which inhabitants and workshops discarded their unwanted stuff in water. In a water-rich city such as Amsterdam, this was certainly the case. The many historical rulings in the city on the disposal of refuse in waterways go back as far as the fifteenth century and clearly attest to the widespread practice of this illegal form of waste disposal and the difficulties in curbing it.

PROCESSING FINDS INTO DATA

Altogether 697,235 archaeological finds were retrieved from the metro excavations, mainly from the Damrak and Rokin sites, including complete objects and many fragments (Table 24.1, Figure 24.4). These are documented in 134,282 individual records in a digital relational database that is compiled from multiple separate data tables. Each record consists of a number of fields in which the separate attributes of a find are recorded, based on specific data tables. In principle, one record contains two categories of information: fieldwork data and object data. Fieldwork data is practical and comprises, for instance, the date on which the find was recovered and its location within the excavation.

Object data are more varied and relate in the first place to the perceived attributes of a find, such as its dimensions, material, production method, type of decoration (important, for instance, for differentiating pottery), the number of fragments or parts within a record (for instance, the sherds of a single pot), or the extent to which an object is complete.

Site	Number of finds	%	Number of records	Total weight (gr)
Damrak NZD1	465,536	66.7	43,045	8,010,552
Rokin NZR1 and NZR2	229,943	33	90,258	13,347,833
Other sites	1,756	0.3	979	344,719
Total	697,235	100	134,282	21,703,104

Table 24.1. The total number of archaeological finds from Damrak, Rokin, and other sites of the North/South Line project, including the number of records in the database and the total weight of the finds. *Adapted from Gawronski and Kranendonk 2018: 20; design: Willem van Zoetendaal.*

A second group of object data is derived from interpretations. These extrinsic data concern functional, chronological, and spatial attributes of the find.[5] Functional data record what an object was used for. A functional reconstruction of the find is one of the primary goals of artifact studies. These functional interpretations may vary in complexity. The most basic functional meaning is to define the purpose of the complete original object, as archaeological finds in general are broken and consist of fragments. So when a find consists of the foot of a vase, the function of the object is given as "vase" and not "foot." A second functional meaning is linked to the broader context in which the artifact was used, for instance a household item or a tool. These functional features serve to create larger categories of finds. To the functional feature the chronology of the find can be added. The chronological attribute is determined by the year or time period when it was made or used. A dating can be deduced from the object itself if it is representative of a certain type from a certain period, or else from its relation with other finds of known date, which thus provide a relational chronology. The spatial non-fieldwork features relate to the location where the object was made or in case of import, its place of origin, which in turn can be linked with the type of material and the production technique. This applies in particular to pottery; for example, if the material is porcelain the place of origin could be China.

Figure 24.4. Processing the finds from the Amstel in the archaeology workshop. *Photograph by Wim Ruigrok.*

DAMRAK AND ROKIN DATA

The two main archaeological sites of Damrak and Rokin show some striking patterns regarding the quantity and dating of the finds. An initial distinction can be made on numerical grounds: the yield of 465,536 finds from the riverbed at Damrak is double that of the 229,943 finds from the entire excavation at Rokin, constituting respectively 66.7% and 33.3% of the total yield. Comparison of the types of material reveals a similarity in the type of objects that were discarded in the river at both locations (Table 24.2). The bulk of the finds consists in both cases of pottery (350,491), followed by bone (126,367), metal (91,849), leather (58,597), clay pipes (26,225), glass (21,218), and building ceramics (10,405). There were very few finds in any of the other categories. However, there were also differences between the two sites. Although there were half as many finds at Rokin, the average weight per find at Rokin was 3.5 times greater than that of the Damrak finds. The difference in weight indicates that the finds at Damrak were

Category	Damrak number of finds	Damrak number of records	Damrak weight (gr)	Rokin number of finds	Rokin number of records	Rokin weight (gr)
CER (ceramics)	201,823	16,947	3,326,919	148,668	50,334	8,581,922
FAU (fauna)	111,198	4,538	2,889,223	15,169	3,948	947,878
MTL (metal)	74,867	10,308	1,221,127	16,982	14,556	834,118
LEE (leather)	45,775	2,278	2,939	12,822	5,255	6,451
CPY (pipe clay)	15,088	3,239	898	11,137	6,382	3,195
GLS (glass)	7,586	1,674	88,389	13,632	4,971	784,453
BWM (building ceramics)	2,494	880	133,788	7,911	2,949	971,760
HT (wood)	1,175	985	167,714	810	627	25,925
KSC (clay sculpture)	120	120	2,196	7	6	383
KST (synthetics)	641	369	7,697	51	42	2,320
PLT (botanical)	1,790	270	5,064	536	166	4,483
STN (stone)	1,032	514	110,317	1,468	437	1,133,720
TW (rope)	73	51	326	133	101	2,791
TXT (textile)	753	585	10,895	389	289	2,162
VST (flint)	549	137	27,702	1	1	11
Other	572	150	15,358	227	194	46,261
Total	465,536	43,045	8,010,552	229,943	90,258	13,347,833

Table 24.2. Distribution of the finds from Damrak and Rokin per material category. *Adapted from Gawronski and Kranendonk 2018: 22; design: Willem van Zoetendaal.*

Figure 24.5. Finds from Damrak, dating from the fourteenth to the twentieth century. *Photograph: City of Amsterdam, Monuments and Archaeology, Wiard Krook; source: https://belowthesurface.amsterdam, accessed February 29, 2020.*

more fragmented. These simple comparisons of quantity and weight offer an initial indication of different waste disposal practices due to the specific topographical context of each site. Damrak, at the mouth of the River Amstel, reflects the disposal of bulk waste, and Rokin, situated in the urban heart of the city, shows the disposal of complete household items. Another factor determining the statistical outcome is the collection method. At Damrak the excavated soil was disposed through a sieve, which yielded a comparatively large number of small finds, including a relatively large number of virtually indestructible metal objects, compared with Rokin where the finds were collected by hand and traced by metal detectors.

Regarding the dating of the finds, both sites share the common feature of a long-term and almost continuous chronology. As Rokin was only filled in 1937 and Damrak was still open water during the excavation in 2005, the finds date not only from the medieval and early modern period, but are also related to the modern era, linking urban material culture from a historic context to the present day (Figure 24.5). Nevertheless, there were also some striking differences in find dating between the two sites. The chronological data shows that the bulk of the Damrak material dates from 1450 to 1600 (Figure 24.6). The peak in the first half of the sixteenth century can be put down to the construction in the first quarter of that century of a land abutment to a bridge in the river mouth, which was filled with urban waste. This bridge, called the New Bridge, was first mentioned in 1365 but was built at an earlier date and is

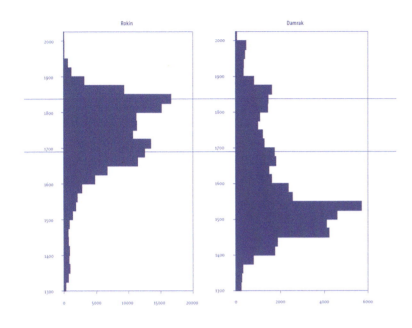

Figure 24.6. Distribution in blocks of twenty-five years of the dated finds from Damrak and Rokin. *Adapted from Gawronski and Kranendonk 2018: 22; design: Willem van Zoetendaal.*

still in use.[6] Another factor that affected the chronology of the finds is the construction of the massive wooden floor of a lock in the New Bridge in 1681, sealing the streambed beneath the bridge. The Rokin finds, on the other hand, mainly date from the period 1650–1850. The more recent dating can be attributed largely to the dredging operations carried out from 1600 onward to maintain navigable water levels, which cleared the waterways of material remains from earlier periods. Thus the two sites give a further insight into the material culture in the city during these eras. Despite their different dating, the two locations show the same pattern between 1600 and 1900, with a similar (slight) peak around 1650–1725 and 1800–1875. This dating pattern may well mirror major economic cycles, such as the blossoming of trade and the city in the seventeenth century, stagnation and decline in the eighteenth century, and the renewed opportunity and growth brought by the Industrial Revolution in the nineteenth century.

URBAN CLASSIFICATION

In view of the great potential of the Damrak and Rokin finds for urban storytelling a classification scheme was developed through which the varied finds from the riverbed would reflect the city as an entity. As discussed, cataloging archaeological remains is based on the selection of one specific feature of a find from the database. Which criterion is selected and what meaning is given is for the archaeologist to decide. Ultimately, archaeological meaning is a subjective perception even though it is based on calculated and objective information. This applies even more to an archaeological catalog, because this entails by definition a selective arrangement of the finds. The central structure of a catalog can only be based on one criterion or attribute at a time. Various catalog systems exist. For instance, to convey an era, the objects can be presented chronologically, or, for a spatial presentation, arranged according to where they were produced or how they were distributed at the site. Archaeological catalogs tend to be functional overviews in which objects are grouped according to their function or purpose, very often in conjunction with the material that they were made of.

The ambition of the classification of the Damrak and Rokin finds was to turn the riverbed of the Amstel into a material mirror of the city, analogous to the water surface that reflects the city along its bank on calm windless days. Therefore, a classification of material remains was developed around the functional, spatial, logistical, economic, and cultural characteristics that typify an urban center. A city sets itself apart from non-urban communities in its scale and in the diversity with which these characteristics are given expression. A city such as Amsterdam can be broken down into ten main functional features, which were added to the finds database for an urban ordering of the archaeological remains. This ordering structure is based on classifications used for large museum collections, and these in turn are based on the assumption that every artifact originally assumed a specific role and place in the interaction between people and their surroundings.[7]

From their individual functional properties the objects can be allocated to one of ten main urban categories of the overall classification system. The ten urban categories are:[8]

1. Buildings and structures: the city is a spatial phenomenon with a built environment that is shaped by the constructed amenities of urban life, such as city walls, churches, hospitals, and theaters.

2. Interiors and accessories: the city provides a living environment that is reflected in the furnishings of interiors, including furniture and permanent fixtures.

3. Distribution and transport: the city functions as an infrastructural junction for the transportation of goods and people by water, land, and air.

4. Craft and industry: the city is a center of multifarious production with the capacity to upscale from an artisanal to an industrial level.

5. Food processing and consumption: the city is a subsistence environment where people provide for their daily needs themselves.

6. Science and technology: the city is a center of knowledge serving the advancement of science and technology.

7. Arms and armor: the city provides citizens with a safe environment, generally in tandem with law enforcement and the use of arms.

8. Communication and exchange: the city is an environment conducive to the exchange of ideas, goods, and news. This is what sets urban culture apart. Social and cultural processes in such diverse areas as information transfer, religion, art, monetary transactions, and (product) quality guarantee fall into this category.

9. Games and recreation: the city is an environment where people relax and enjoy free time.

10. Personal artifacts and clothing: the city is a place made up of individuals with both a private life and a life as a member of the urban community. Anything that distinguishes a person as an individual, from prostheses to jewelry, falls into this category.

THE PHOTOGRAPHIC CATALOG STUFF

The urban classification system was used as the basis for different products to present archaeological finds in varying settings and contexts. The first was a classic archaeological product—a printed find catalog—but unconventional because of its systematics and layout, which were developed in view of the sheer quantity of finds.[9] The published collection comprised a total of 665,412 objects. In approximately 73 percent of the finds (482,502 objects), the significance could be traced to a (pre-)urban context. Each prototype or each series of similar but individual objects among these finds is reproduced in the 11,279 photographs in this catalog, which was given the title *Stuff*. The challenge was to make the results of the archaeological excavations visually accessible. While the scientific ordering system supplied by the archaeologists was the starting point of the catalog, the visual experience was realized by the designer and the photographer. *Stuff* distinguishes itself from mainstream archaeological catalogs because of the close cooperation between archaeologist, photographer, designer, and printer—a trustful cooperation in which each discipline had its own and equal say resulting in a visual strong experience, telling a story of material sequences of urban life by serial images of finds.

At first glance, *Stuff* is a never-ending stream of different, more or less recognizable objects that invites us to browse and explore our own associations and reconstructions. However, behind the cascading images lies an archaeological story that gradually emerges out of the visual structure of the catalog, thanks to Willem van Zoetendaal's lucid and seductive design. The photographs tell their own story, prompted not by text but by their arrangement in chapters and sections according to the different functions that a city fulfils as a living organism. The material remains are primarily organized according to the role the object once assumed within these different urban functions. The finds derive their significance from the functional and chronological relation with the city assigned to them in the catalog. Basic catalog information, like find number, size, and dating, was allocated to each find in a vertical bar left of the object photograph, contributing to a cascade-like design grid that made this large quantity of visual information accessible (Figure 24.7). Each singular image had a powerful visual effect because of the unmatched eye for detail, color, and texture of photographer Harold Strak, who documented more than 20,000 finds during the project. To underline the basic practice of archaeologists who by excavating do nothing less than read the book of the earth, the printer (Rob Stolk, Amsterdam) used custom-made paper with a semi transparent effect, showing the contours of the finds on the next pages, simulating find layers in the soil.

TWO SHOWCASES AT ROKIN STATION

Archaeology was part of the art program of the North/South Line project. Each station features artwork with a specific theme by different artists. The theme of Rokin Station in the heart of the historic city was history and archaeology. The commission for the platform walls of this station was awarded to the British–French partnership Daniel Dewar and Grégory Gicquel. They constructed a monumental mosaic in different kinds of stone in two 110 meter-long (360 foot) strips with thirty-three enlarged images of everyday modern objects inspired by archaeological finds, together representing a sentence telling a layered story:

The crocodile, the melodica, the pike fish, the high heel pump, the sportswear shoe, the rear derailleur, the tie, the sandal, the ballpoint pen, the pipe, the shrimp, the garden tiger moth, the pair of dice, the leopard frog, the sewing machine, the Welsh Corgi Pembroke dog, the calico cat, the flat-twin car engine, the rattlesnake, the French horn, the teapot, the wetsuit, the handheld fan, the mallard, the diving flipper, the paintbrush, the nutcracker, the whelk shell, the fishing lure, the foxglove, the umbrella, the dragonfly, and the badminton racket.

In addition to the artwork on the platform, two permanent displays of real-life archaeological finds were incorporated in the architectural design of the metro station by Benthem Crouwel Architects. The archaeological team in cooperation with the artists was responsible for the content and production of these showcases, which were situated between the escalators at the south and north entrances to the platforms. The basic principle of the public display was to show as many archaeological finds as possible to reflect the abundance of the material deposits in the River Amstel, while treating each object autonomously with its own unique meaning, ordered in the non-hierarchical urban functional classification scheme. The two massive glass display cases—12 meters long and 3.34 meters wide (39 by 11 feet) at the north entrance and 14 meters long and 3.59 meters wide (46 by 12 feet) at the south entrance, both tapering down to a width of 2.06 meters (6.75 feet)—contain a total of 9,500 archaeological finds selected from durable, mainly inorganic, materials such as ceramics, glass, and metal (Figures 24.8 and 24.9). The objects are attached with thin brass pins to the sloping bottom of the showcases, which follow the incline of the escalator (a gradient of 30 degrees), inducing the impression of a free fall of material remains. As each display is categorized, a hidden visual order is created in the apparent chaos of objects, which lack any written explanation. The north display shows the categories (from top to bottom):

Food processing and consumption, Science and technology, Arms and armor, Communication and exchange, Games and recreation, Personal artifacts and clothing;

and the south display the themes:

Building and structures, Interiors and accessories, Distribution and transport, Craft and Industry.

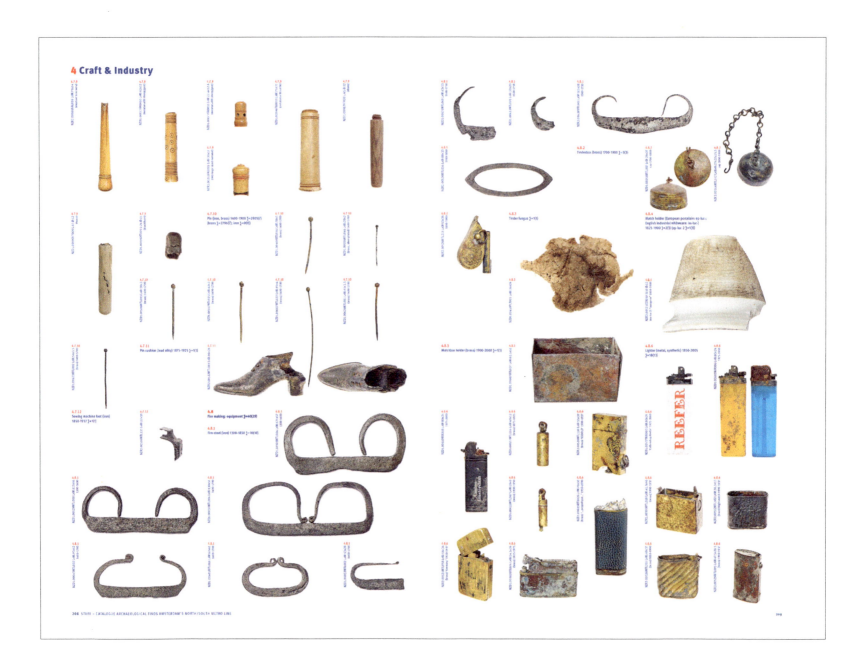

Figure 24.7. Spread of two pages from the chapter "Craft and Industry" in *Stuff*, with finds related to fire-making between 1300 and 2005. *Adapted from Gawronski and Kranendonk 2018: 208–209; photographs by Harold Strak.*

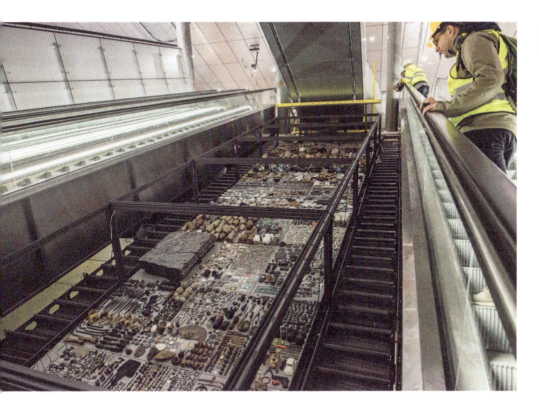

Northern showcase **Southern showcase**

Figure 24.8. The showcase between the escalators at the north entrance of Rokin Station. *Photograph: City of Amsterdam, Monuments and Archaeology, Ranjith Jayasena; source: https://belowthesurface.amsterdam, accessed February 29, 2020.*

Figure 24.9. The layout of the two showcases at Rokin Station, with 9,500 finds. *Photograph by Harold Strak; geographical information system: City of Amsterdam, Monuments and Archaeology, Jort Maas, Bart Vissers; source: https://belowthesurface.amsterdam, accessed February 29, 2020.*

WEB PORTAL HTTPS://
BELOWTHESURFACE.AMSTERDAM

To accompany the two displays a multipurpose archaeological website https://belowthesurface.amsterdam was developed by the Department of Archaeology and the Chief Technology Office of the city of Amsterdam. Although the station constitutes an accessible public museum, which can be visited for the price of a metro ticket, the displays lack background information on the finds. Visitors and travelers are, unlike in most regular museums, unprepared for the archaeological experience and the objects flash past, as the escalators do not stop. Belowthesurface.amsterdam provides digital access to both displays, which are rendered in the website as a geographical information model linked to the database. In this way details of each of the 9,500 finds on display can be accessed, either in the station itself by smart phone, or at home using a computer (Figure 24.10). The core of the website is a timeline database, invented and designed by Fabrique and programmed by Q42, which enables the visitor to scroll through the finds from 2005 to more than 100,000 years ago. Alongside the timeline finds can be searched by material, function, or location. The website contains more than 27,000 photographs of 19,000 finds. To zoom in on the different finds, Q42 applied Micrio, an international image interoperability framework compatible platform (image viewer and image server) for telling visual, interactive narratives with high-resolution images. The site can be used for fun or to do archaeological research, as the complete dataset (135,000 records) of all finds of the archaeological project is incorporated in belowthesurface.amsterdam. Not only are the finds accessible in a passive way, but one can create a digital showcase of favorite finds. Each find in the timeline database can be selected and added to a personal showcase that can be published online. In belowthesurface. amsterdam, archaeological finds can be used both as scientific datasets on our past and as visual elements in creative display adventures. Different people from all over the world have created their own showcases (3,223 by February 2020),

BELOW THE SURFACE

THE ARCHAEOLOGICAL FINDS OF THE NORTH / SOUTHLINE

CREATE YOUR OWN DISPLAY WITH THE FINDS

EXPLORE THE DISPLAYS INSIDE THE ROKIN METRO STATION

Figure 24.10. Homepage of the website belowthesurface.amsterdam, containing three different functions: timeline database of 19,000 finds, the two showcases at Rokin Station, and creating your own showcase. *Source: https://belowthesurface.amsterdam, accessed February 29, 2020.*

discovering a creative entry to science. As each element of the visual showcase composition stays linked to the archaeological database, belowthesurface.amsterdam combines scientific curiosity with creative self-motivation, thus creating new ways to experience archaeology and the material past.

CODA

In their endeavor to explore new and unconventional ways to present their finds and data, the archaeologists had to work together with partners like artists, photographers, and designers. Trust proved to be the most vital and basic prerequisite for this outside-the-box archaeological endeavor. By trusting the creative input of non-archaeological partners, the straitjacket of traditional archaeological cataloging can be avoided and new visual ordering paradigms for archaeological finds can be looked for without nullifying or neglecting current scientific standards.

NOTES

1. Designed and published by Willem van Zoetendaal with photographs by Harold Strak (Amsterdam 2018), this book was awarded the Golden Letter at the Best Book Design From All Over The World Festival (Leipzig 2019) and the Cornish Family Prize for Art and Design Publishing (Melbourne 2019).
2. Gawronski and Kranendonk 2010, 2018.
3. Kocabaş 2015.
4. Coles and Dion 1999.
5. Gawronski 2012, 8–13.
6. Gawronski 2012, 30.
7. Blackaby et al. 1988.
8. Gawronski and Kranendonk 2018, 27–28.
9. Gawronski and Kranendonk 2018.

BIBLIOGRAPHY

Blackaby, James R., Patricia Greeno, and The Nomenclature Committee (1988), *The Revised Nomenclature for Museum Cataloging: A Revised and Expanded Version of Robert G. Chenhall's System for Classifying Man-Made Objects,* Nashville (American Association for State and Local History Press).

Coles, Alex and Mark Dion, eds. (1999), *Archaeology*, London (Black Dog Publishing).

Gawronski, Jerzy, ed. (2012), *Amsterdam Ceramics: A City's History and an Archaeological Ceramics Catalogue 1175–2011*, Amsterdam (Bas Lubberhuizen).

Gawronski, Jerzy H.G. and Peter Kranendonk (2010), Der Fluss als Spiegel der Stadt: Archäologie und Amsterdams Nord-Süd-Bahn, *Skyllis* 10(2), 169–78.

——— (2018), *Stuff: Catalogue Archaeological Finds Amsterdam's North/South Metro Line*, Amsterdam (Van Zoetendaal Publishers; design: Willem van Zoetendaal; photography: Harold Strak).

Kocabaş, Ufuk (2015), The Yenikapi Byzantine-Era Shipwrecks, Istanbul, Turkey: A Preliminary Report and Inventory of the 27 Wrecks Studied by Istanbul University, *International Journal of Nautical Archaeology* 44(1), 5–38.

WHAT REMAINS OF PAQUIUS PROCULUS

VIDEO GAME BODIES IN VIRTUAL POMPEII

DAVID FREDRICK, RHODORA G. VENNARUCCI, AND WILLIAM LODER

GIVING BODY TO DATA

In July 2020, the Virtual Pompeii Project at the University of Arkansas administered a way-finding experiment in virtual space to thirty-one subjects. The subjects were directed to find their way through digital reconstructions of four houses in Pompeii, following one of four scenarios: free exploration–decoration off, free exploration–decoration on, object discovery–decoration off, or object discovery–decoration on. The subjects completed a survey about the experience upon conclusion of the experiment. As part of this survey the subjects in the fourth scenario (object discovery–decoration on) were presented with four screenshots from each house, and asked the following question: "In which location did you discover the vase?" An example of this question is presented in Figure 23.1, as posed for the House of Paquius Proculus.

This question seems simple. It was designed to test the ability of the subjects to remember where in each house they discovered the vase, as the houses in the series grew bigger and more complex. The houses ran in order: House of the Large Altar (VI 16 15-17), House of the Prince of Naples (VI 15 7-8), House of Paquius Proculus (II 7 1), House of the Small Fountain (VI 8 23-24). But we would like to call attention to the assumptions and relationships built into this question, as they bear directly on the use of video game technology to construct experiences of past environments, and the emergence of a new kind of phenomenology based not on the physical body of the archaeologist in a landscape, but a hybrid body of the video game player in a virtual environment.

First there is the pronoun 'you.' This 'you' is apparently in two places at once: sitting at a laptop or desktop playing through the Virtual Pompeii application, and also embodied within that application, with a 'head' upon which a camera is

Figure 23.1. Question 12, "In which location did you discover the vase?" from the post-navigation response form for the third house in the series, the House of Paquius Proculus (II 7 1).

mounted (like eyes), that turns in response to mouse or touch-pad movements, and 'feet' that evidently carry 'you' through the environment in response to input to the W-A-S-D or arrow keys. These digital feet touch the floor, and your digital 'shoulders' will bump the walls, with colliders establishing a physical limit around your digital body. As first-person game play has become a common media experience, most game players do not reflect on their identification with the player character, and the relationship this creates between their physical body and the digital body not just on the screen, but seemingly in it. Hence our question was not confusing to our subjects, who were able to ask themselves, "where did *I* discover the vase?" and answer the question without pausing to consider the ontology of this *I* that is made up of the intertwined physical and digital video game body.

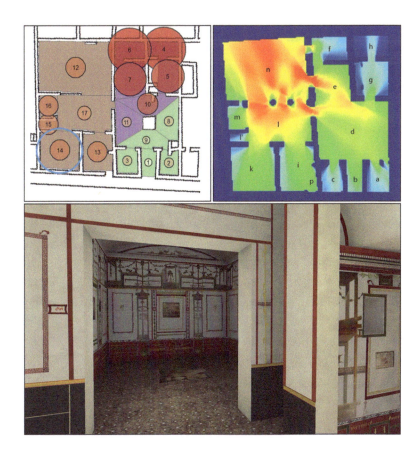

Figure 23.2. House of the Prince of Naples (VI 15 7-8), room k: eigenvector centrality (top left), visual integration (top right), and decoration (bottom).

The nature of the relationship between the gamer's physical and digital bodies is nevertheless complex, and increasingly relevant as archaeologists begin to use real-time game engine environments, explored by human subjects, to test theories about behaviors and experiences in past cultures (the archaeology of gaming software is briefly discussed by John Aycock and Katie Biittner, Chapter 8 in this volume). For Virtual Pompeii and its parallel project, Virtual Roman Retail, player exploration of the digital environments offers a way to test movement patterns predicted through the analysis of the spatial plans and visual characteristics of the streets, shops, and houses. It is a

way of *embodying spatio-visual data*, which would otherwise be difficult or impossible. Developing these data is one thing that enables us to form hypotheses about patterns of movement and interaction, but putting these hypotheses to the test is another thing. Tests that would use real human subjects, in the physical houses or streets of Pompeii, are neither practical nor repeatable. Further, in the digital environments we can control many variables (light and time of day, presence or absence of decoration, vegetation and water features, different soundscapes) and measure how they impact the movement choices of our subjects. The use of post-exploration surveys allows us to capture and compare a range of qualitative responses to the experience of these digital environments, with which we can develop profiles for what the spaces inside these houses 'feel' like.

This methodology immediately raises objections: our subjects are not really 'Roman,' and they were not really 'there' with their physical bodies. These objections are valid. The digital houses and shops are proxies for the real houses and shops, our human subjects are proxies for the Roman subjects, and the video game bodies of these subjects are proxies for the living bodies of humans in these spaces. We are guilty as charged, and we would only say in our defense that proxy phenomenology is all we have. For instance, we could say that room k in the House of the Prince of Naples has modest eigenvector value within the network, and modest visual integration, while its decoration has high visual complexity and interest (Figure 23.2). Therefore, we might predict that the house owner and their higher-status guests often used this room. But no matter how objective and scientific that might sound, we would need these data to *become embodied* to see if what they suggest about movement in the environment compares to the navigation patterns of x number of living humans, if not the technofantasy of Romans brought back to life. To dig deeper into the embodiment of environmental data through player testing, we will ground our discussion in Material Engagement Theory and sensory archaeology, and present an overview of results from the first experiment pass by the Virtual Pompeii Project in 2018.[1] While this experiment was conducted through a desktop app, we are looking forward to global crowd-sourced testing using a web-based app in fall 2021. We will then explore the potential of more specifically game-like approaches as pioneered through the Virtual Roman Retail project for virtual reality (VR), leading to a discussion of game-play narrative design for archaeology that ties these two projects together.

SENSES AND THINGS

Recent work on the phenomenology of video games has emphasized that the game body is hybrid, constructed through the flow back and forth between the gamer's physical body and their in-game body. No matter how deep the immersion or sense of presence created by the game, the physical body does not go away.[2] In fact, game designers and artists lean on the sensory history of the players' bodies to *evoke*, rather than literally recreate, a fuller sensory immersion in the game. Visual hyper-realism is not necessary for this evocation. In fact, less here can be more, and some of the most sensorily effective games combine meaningful object interaction with a more abstracted art style to engage players with their worlds across the senses. The 'walking simulator' *Gone Home* (Fullbright 2013), for instance, invites the player to interact with cassette tapes of 1990s riot grrrl bands as part of reconstructing the history of the player character's (Katie) missing younger sister, Sam. Even though you do not see your own hands, you can 'pick up' the tapes, rotate them, insert them into a tape machine, and press 'play' to listen. The pace of these actions, and the tactile pops, squeaks, and clicks of the machine, induce you to feel these actions in your fingers and hands, which are of course actually engaged with a keyboard and mouse or console controller. While controlled through these small-scale interfaces, the things of games very frequently evoke the touch, sound, smell and taste of the things of the world through the mechanics of their interactions, drawing on the sensory and sensuous history of the player's physical body to do so.

The gamer's body is thus fundamentally synesthetic, as the digital body and consciousness are distributed across the range of things with which that digital body can interact. This hybridity reproduces in a simulated, abstracted form the model of cognition as extended among and between things proposed by Lambros Malafouris and Colin Renfrew (2010), for both archaeologists and the cultures they study. It is also consonant with Yannis Hamilakis's theory (2014) of the senses as a mobile and dynamic field, with flow back and forth between the body-mind and the world. Central to both Malafouris and Renfrew's Material Engagement Theory and Hamilakis's approach to sensory archaeology is a rejection of the Cartesian dichotomy between mind and body that has dominated the history of Western thought. Both approaches also reject a firm division between self and world, and, in Hamilakis's case, firm divisions between one sense and another. In this regard, both clearly look back to the emphasis in phenomenology on embodiment and locatedness: the archaeologist cannot finally occupy a disembodied and completely objective view on the evidence. At the same time, video games cannot be reduced to the celebratory performance of a violent, colonializing, phallocentric, hyper-visual Western sensorium. When archaeologists pick up a game engine, that baggage is there, but the diversity of video games, particularly those produced by smaller, independent studios, in themes, audiences, and development teams, opens avenues for challenging the dominant culture that previously defined the medium.

WAYFINDING SURPRISES IN THE ROMAN HOUSE

Turning back to the Virtual Pompeii Project, we realized we needed a way of modeling the environment of Pompeii holistically and comprehensively in order to predict movement and behavior within these environments. This is not a question of further physical excavation, but rather excavation of the data contained in the plan of the city and the extensive documentation of its artwork, in particular the eleven-volume publication *Pompei: pitture e mosaici*,[3] which is the single most important source for decoration in Pompeii. This project asks of this data: what kind of artwork is found in what kind of space in Pompeii?

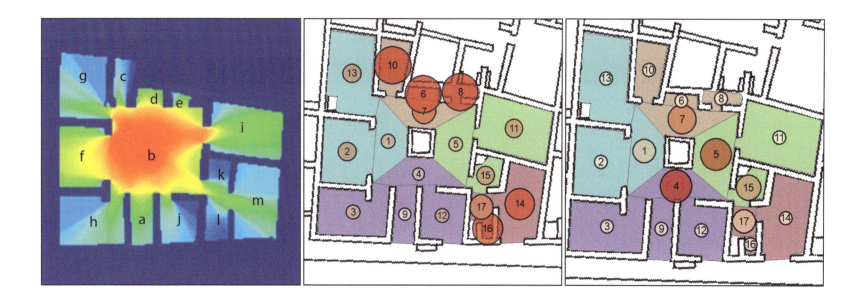

Figure 23.3. House of the Large Altar (VI 16 15-17): visibility graph (left), network topology eigenvector scores (center), betweenness scores (right).

How do the spaces and decoration work together to shape patterns of movement and behavior? What did this feel like?

As a way into these questions, we first put together a methodology and testing procedure in spring 2018. On the predictive side, we viewed the houses as spatial networks, with each room as a node and each door as an edge. This allowed us to calculate values for each room using metrics familiar from social network analysis, primarily betweenness, closeness, eigenvector, hub, and authority. A room with high betweenness or hub scores is likely to receive a lot of pass-through traffic, while a room with high eigenvector or authority scores is more likely a high-value destination. Recognizing that central features like *impluvia* (water catchment basins in the atrium) or gardens in the peristyle deflect movement around them, we assigned multiple nodes to these spaces. We combined the network topologies with visual integration graphs, which take the form of a heat map that shows the comparative visibility of spaces within a structure, as shaped by the structure's own architecture. An example of this approach for the House of the Large Altar is produced in Figure 23.3.

The combination of the network topology scores with the visibility graph would suggest higher pass-through traffic on the left side of the atrium, while 'room f,' on the left side of the atrium with high visual integration, would receive the highest traffic of the peripheral rooms. 'Room g,' in the top left corner of the plan, being relatively isolated visually, would receive comparatively low traffic. As shown in Figure 23.4, when the virtual houses were navigated by human subjects, these predictions turned out to be partly true, but also wrong in some significant ways.

In the experiment, users performed the navigation test on a desktop computer, playing through a build published by the Unity3d game engine. The build included code that tracked player location and rotation each frame (roughly 40–60 times per second), allowing the generation of the heatmaps and the ability to replay each player's journey from their first-person point of view. Whether the subjects were assigned the free exploration or object discovery scenario, they did not visit room f very often, with decoration off or on, but room g, in the upper left, was the most visited room. This is, in fact, where the vase was located in the object discovery scenario, but even in the free exploration scenario room g received a high amount of

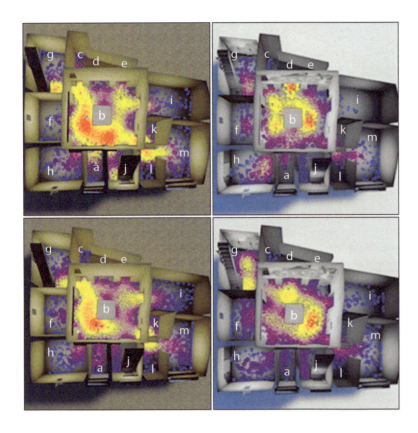

Figure 23.4. House of the Large Altar (VI 16 15-17): heat maps of player movement in each of the four experiment scenarios: free exploration–decoration off (top left), free exploration–decoration on (top right), object discovery–decoration off (bottom left), and object discovery–decoration on (bottom right).

Figure 23.5. Which way do I turn around the *impluvium*?

traffic. In addition to this surprising outcome, it is evident that decoration plays an enormous role in shaping player navigation, as it shifts movement patterns dramatically from the left side of the atrium (where they were predicted) to the right side, with an additional hot area on the far side. Despite the claims made by space syntax, space alone is not the machine that drives human movement in structures, and neither are viewsheds.

This points to the fact that players were presented with conflicting cues for navigation: decoration off they went one way, decoration on they went another, as the network topology and visibility characteristics pulled them in one direction

and decoration pulled them in another. This conflict is not just in the digital model, it is in the physical house. As basic as this seems, it points to the importance of phenomenology—the qualitative response forms—as a part of the experiment, to try to get a sense of what this conflict feels like (Figure 23.5).

Another very surprising outcome from our first experiment iteration is demonstrated most clearly in the results from the House of Paquius Proculus (Figure 23.6). Whether the scenario is free exploration or object discovery, the presence of decoration clearly and significantly impacts movement, in a way we did not and could not have predicted with network topology, viewsheds, or visibility graphs. With decoration off, there is significant traffic across and within the garden space, including a hotspot at its center. This matches what is predicted through the network topology and visibility graph. However, with the decoration on, this traffic largely evaporates. In part, this could be explained through the function of the decoration as an attractor or landmark, but it also seems to reflect a more basic effect: the presence of decoration acts as a check on exploration, and seems to message to the players that they should stay on the beaten path around the peristyle. Which is to say, even in these digital recreations of Roman houses, players seem to have a sense of rules and transgression. If decoration encourages them to stick to 'expected' lines of movement (paths), they must have a sense of what those expectations are.

This brief review of experiment outcomes thus far concludes with another surprise, this time from the qualitative data of the post-navigation response forms. With the decoration off, players were able to pick out the correct house plan from a set of four possible plans with a high degree of accuracy (69.6 percent for free exploration, 66.6 percent for object discovery; Table 23.1). With decoration on, their accuracy declined significantly (28.6 percent for free exploration, 55.6 percent for object discovery, declines of 41 percent and 11 percent respectively). Nonetheless, players in the decoration-on scenarios reported that the decoration helped them understand where they were and improved their confidence in navigation. This conflict between cognitive understanding of the plan, which declined with the presence of decoration, and spatial confidence (the feeling that the decoration positively

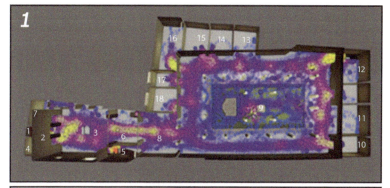

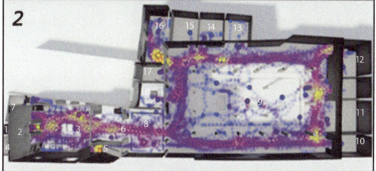

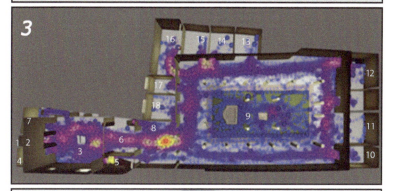

Figure 23.6. House of Paquius Proculus (I 7 1): heat maps of player movement in each of the four experiment scenarios: free exploration–decoration off (1), free exploration–decoration on (2), object discovery–decoration off (3), and object discovery–decoration on (4).

	Free exploration			Object discovery		
	Decoration off (11 subjects)		Decoration on (7 subjects)	Decoration off (11 subjects)		Decoration on (9 subjects)
House of the Large Altar	73%*	29%	**−44%**	55%	67%	**+12%**
House of the Prince of Naples	82%	43%	**−39%**	73%	44%	**−28%**
House of Paquius Proculus	54%	14%	**−40%**	73%	56%	**−17%**
Average	70%	29%	**−41%**	67%	56%	**−11%**
*Percentage of subjects who correctly identified the house plan in the post-navigation survey.						

Table 23.1. Selection of the correct plan of the house out of a set of four house plans.

improved their ability to navigate) definitely deserves further investigation. However, it already hints at the ability of contemporary emotions, assessed through a phenomenology of 'playing' three-dimensional (3D) digital environments, to point to Roman emotions in the navigation of the physical structures, even if indirectly and imperfectly. Which way do I turn? What are the 'rules' of this space, and how freely can I explore? How do I know where to go?

FROM WAYFINDING EXPERIMENTS TO EMERGENT PLAY

Looking ahead, the Virtual Pompeii Project has added a WebGL application to the desktop application that was used in the 2018 experiment. This is significant because the WebGL application is playable natively through the major browsers, with the same ability to collect player movement and rotation data, thus allowing remote testing of hundreds or thousands of subjects. Through WebGL, contemporary player exploration of virtual sites from the past can be crowd-sourced, and this has very large implications for phenomenological approaches in archaeology. As noted above, it is true that no one of the

potentially thousands of subjects testing the application will be an ancient Roman. It is equally true that no one archaeologist is an ancient Roman, and this latter group remains a very narrow demographic slice, overwhelmingly white, of European, North American, or Australian origin, and until recent decades largely male. 'Romans' themselves were of course not so, but rather highly diverse in ethnicity, cultural identification, religion, sexual experience, and gender construction. By crowd-sourcing the testing of archaeological sites through virtual space—video game space—diverse proxy phenomenology offers a way to approach the diversity of ancient Rome through the responses of a diverse global subject group, whose combined quantitative and qualitative data offer a manifold perspective on the site that is not possible for a lone archaeologist in a landscape, or even archaeologists collectively (see Peter Gould's call for archaeologists to embrace the public in Chapter 25 of this volume). Beyond this, because of the many variables that can be controlled through a game engine, in repeatable, shareable ways, there are methods for constructing hypotheses about movement and behavior that can be tested. Emergent game play is a well-known concept in game design, as players will discover means of playing around and against the rulesets as designed. Designers will even intentionally craft their play spaces and rules to foster this possibility, affording their players agency and creative scope to produce game play outcomes that were not formally determined. We might think of the current moment of game engine use within archaeology as one of emergent play, as the rulesets for developing testable scenarios are unclear and elastic, and video game bodies are hybrid, synesthetic, and in evolution along with the video games themselves. One direction of that evolution involves the use of VR by the Virtual Roman Retail project, and the development of connections between sensory archaeology and the investment of contemporary retail in sensory experiences and virtual technologies.

A SENSORY APPROACH TO THE ROMAN SHOP

The late twentieth century witnessed the emergence of experiential retailing, a type of commerce in which shops market immersive and memorable consumer experiences to add value to their products.[4] Stimulating the senses through the design of the shop is a key component of this commodification of retail experience today, but asking how ancient shops engaged consumers through their senses in the past is still novel because shopping behavior has historically been considered the hallmark of modern retailing. Virtual Roman Retail argues, however, that the process of consumption in ancient Rome was multisensory, complex, and imbued with social and cultural signifiers. In fact, before the Industrial Revolution and the advent of mass marketing, a consumer's sensorial appraisal of the environment of the shop, and its products was a (the?) critical factor in shaping consumer behavior.[5] The primary interest of Virtual Roman Retail, therefore, is to understand how consumer experience was enacted through the design of a Roman shop.

While the physical remains of the Felt Shop of Verecundus (IX 7 7)—the focus of this experiment—reflect how the design of an ancient shop may have engaged the consumer's different senses, as with the houses in Virtual Pompeii, on-site exploration of the shop is hindered due to restricted access and poor preservation. Digital technologies offer innovative, if indirect, avenues for experiencing this shop environment that are simply impossible with an in-person visit today. Based on

Figure 23.7. The Felt Shop of Verecundus (IX 7 7), showing the façade of the shop and the hypothetical design of its interior as they appear to the player when looking across from the south side of the via dell'Abbondanza.

the model of Virtual Pompeii, Virtual Roman Retail integrates object interaction with a faithful but abstracted 3D visualization of a Roman shop that activates the sensory memories of a player to evoke immersion in a past sensescape within a digital environment. In 2019 the project developed an application in the Unity3d game engine that reconstructed the shop using photogrammetry models captured on site, excavation records, plans, and photographs, as well as comparative evidence from other excavated shops on the same street (Figure 23.7).

By exploring what it felt like to shop in Pompeii, this project aims to put sensory archaeology into practice (see also Robin Skeates's Chapter 28 in this volume).[6] A sensory approach to Verecundus's shop, however, necessitates a platform that allows for a greater range of experiential flow,[7] and specifically better haptic feedback, than the desktop application currently used for the houses in Virtual Pompeii. For this reason, we designed our application for use on the Oculus Quest. The Quest consists of a lightweight untethered VR headset with built-in speakers and two hand-held controllers, which together track the player's body movements, including—important to note—hand gestures, in real-time (Figure 23.8). This heightens the sense of hybrid embodiment already found in video games played through keyboard and mouse or console controller interfaces.[8] In its current stage, our VR application leverages the augmented mimetic movement capabilities and haptic perception of the Quest to provide the player with the experience of walking down a street in Pompeii and browsing objects in a shop.

EMERGENT PLAY IN THE ROMAN SHOP

When our application starts, you find yourself surrounded by 3D architectural façades, standing on the northern sidewalk of the via dell'Abbondanza and facing west toward the Forum, a few meters down from the Felt Shop of Verecundus. The wide field of vision of the Quest and perspectival first-person view augment the perception of 'being there,' and for the project directors who have often traipsed this stretch of Pompeii in the summer, the brightly lit virtual street evokes memories of heat, sweat, and crowds. At present, however, you have the street to yourself, and you may notice that it is oddly quiet here. The project is working on designing an active soundscape to suggest the rich acoustic environment of the via dell'Abbondanza, the most heavily trafficked thoroughfare in Pompeii.

Due to the untethered nature and immediate kinesthetic feedback of the Quest, when you start walking in the physical world, your digital body moves in the same direction and at the same pace in the virtual world; when you turn your head or your body in the physical world, your digital body mimics these movements. This mode of movement helps to overcome the disorientation and motion sickness sometimes associated with using a VR application. Shifting the input interface from fingers on a keyboard or controller to the whole body, without the encumbrance of a cable connected to a computer, deepens the sense of hybrid embodiment and allows you to experience how the shop may have appeared, in time and space relative to your own moving physical/digital body, to a Roman pedestrian passing along the street. As you move toward the shop, you

Figure 23.8. Students explore virtual worlds with the Oculus Quest in the Tesseract Center for Immersive Environments and Game Design at the University of Arkansas.

may notice a sudden change in light caused by the awning that shades the entrance of the shop.

Leaning on synesthesia, the project is in the process of designing historically informed lighting scenarios for the street to explore how bright sunlight, with additional visual cues evoking the heat of a summer afternoon in Pompeii, may lead players to escape this digital glare (and implied heat) by seeking the 'cool shade' of the interior of the shop. We can also test the impact of the awning (which can be toggled off and on) on this behavior. Within a meter or so of the shop entrance, you catch an oblique view to your right of the brightly colored frescoes adorning the façade (Figure 23.9). If you choose to stop and inspect the frescoes in more detail, you will see that they advertise the felt production process and textile products of Verecundus, the shop owner, who is proudly depicted on his shop front.

Moving forward to stand in front of the wide-open entrance of the shop you see tables set up at the threshold—typical of Roman shops—on which the shopkeeper has displayed a selection of merchandise in the hopes of enticing you to stop and

Figure 23.9. The Felt Shop of Verecundus (IX 7 7), showing the façade of the shop and the entrance as they appear to the player when passing by the shop from west to east on the via dell'Abbondanza. Note the shop scene fresco depicting a commercial exchange in the lower register left of the entrance.

browse. Haptic perception would have been an important part of shopping in ancient Rome: by browsing and repeatedly handling a variety of objects in the shops, consumers developed an embodied, sensory skillset useful for discerning qualities of design and workmanship in non-standardized goods.[9] Put another way, the skilled Roman consumer would not value an item by sight alone; instead, consumer cognition was shaped by feeling, smelling, and even tasting (especially perishables) the product with their bodies. Verecundus sold fancy felted dining slippers along with other high-end textiles in his shop. Because shoe-sizes were not standardized in ancient Rome, trying on the slipper would have been extremely important before buying it. While handling the shoe to judge the feel and density of the felt, the consumer may have noticed the smell of ammonia from the urine or other mordants used in the dyeing process. This mind-body-sense-thing feedback loop that shaped consumer behavior in the shop speaks directly to the concept of extended cognition in Malfouris and Renfrew's

Material Engagement Theory (2010) and Halimakis's emphasis on sensorial flows (2014) discussed above.

To simulate this browsing behavior, you can interact with objects in the shop. The Quest controllers not only track hand gestures but provide haptic feedback that compensates for lost sensations in the virtual environment like physical touch, and act as a bridge between your hybrid physical/digital bodies and worlds. You can reach out your arm to pick up one of the slippers on the table by pressing the buttons on the handgrip with your index and middle fingers once your digital hand 'touches' the shoe (Figure 23.10). While keeping the buttons on the controller pressed down, you can lift the slipper off the table for closer inspection. Although your physical hand is gripping a hard plastic controller, not a soft felt slipper, the visuo-tactile correlation of the gestures between physical/digital arm and hands, as well as the act of grasping something physical in your hand, make the digital object feel material. This effect can be enhanced by coding objects differentially to exhibit more or less attraction to the controller during the pick-up action, making the slipper "feel" lighter in contrast to heavier objects. Digital objects can also be coded with visual and even auditory cues to evoke differences in their qualities. As discussed above in the example of cassette tapes from *Gone Home* spatialized audio works closely with input interfaces in video games to increase the perceived materiality of digital objects. Just as browsing taught the Roman consumer necessary tactile skills for navigating commercial exchanges, repeated interaction with a diversity of digital objects helps you, the player, embody a new haptic skill set useful for assessing digital materials in the digital environment.

Back in the application, when you look up from the merchandise, you see a female shopkeeper watching you browse from behind the shop tables. Roman shopkeepers often occupied this position so that they could watch over the items on display and be at the ready to engage with a potential buyer, answering questions and negotiating a price. Now that you are peering deeper into the shop, you also notice a wooden bench set against the wall in the shadowy interior, an invitation for you to enter the shop and stay for a while. The positioning

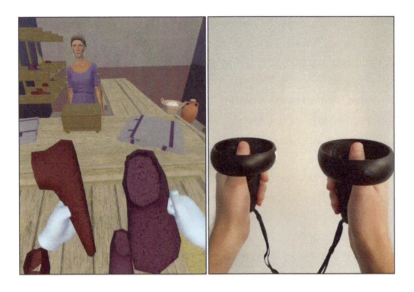

Figure 23.10. Virtual hands browse items on the shop counter in the Felt Shop of Verecundus (IX 7 7) (left) and physical hands holding the Oculus Quest controllers that track hand movement in real time (right).

WHAT REMAINS OF PAQUIUS PROCULUS AND VERECUNDUS

While we acknowledge that Roman sensescapes were socially and culturally constructed, and their experience by Romans is something we cannot directly recreate, these projects study the embodied experiences of humans alive today to encourage new ways of thinking about how the spatiality and decoration of Roman streets, shops, and houses shaped cognition and behavior in the past. Edward González-Tennant (2016) noted the importance of the "walking simulator" genre of video games as a potential model for archaeologists as a way of presenting real-time 3D visualizations of sites to the public, as the genre is driven by player discovery of information through exploring the game environment at 'normal' walking speed, rather than the hyper-accelerated action and exaggerated super-bodies of the first-person shooter. We would push this a step or two further by noting first that the pace of the walking simulator constructs the hybrid relationship between physical body and digital body differently than the shooter, as this game body moves at the walking speed of 'my' body, and does not have an exaggerated capacity for running, jumping, flying, sensing. This pushes the player toward a more limited, embodied position in the environment, rather than a mastery that would stand apart from it. Second, while the narrative of the walking simulator does advance through information discovery, via environment exploration and object interaction, its interest is driven by the archaeology of emotion, especially those wrapped up in trauma, loss, and survivance in the family. For instance, in *What Remains of Edith Finch* (Giant Sparrow 2017), the death or disappearance of each member of the Finch family, is accessed through exploration of the memorial shrine of their bedroom. By playing through each of these narratives, the player fills in the strange genealogy of this family, culminating in the birth of Edith's son, Christopher. While Edith dies in childbirth, Christopher turns out to be the player character, and, together with the notebook genealogy, all that remains of Edith Finch.

of the tables, shopkeeper, and bench in our digital shop is modeled after the shop scene fresco from the façade that depicts a commercial exchange between the female shopkeeper and a male customer. This scene and the interactive scenario of our application underscore how Roman shopkeepers designed their shops to encourage browsing behavior and social interaction.

Although Virtual Roman Retail plans to use subject testing like Virtual Pompeii, safety during the Covid-19 pandemic is currently a significant concern. Once we can safely start VR testing in our laboratory, the player data collected will help us address a series of questions about consumer experience: what, if anything, about the visual messaging of the shop engages the player and for how long? Are they first attracted by the façade décor or the objects on the tables? Do they approach and linger at the tables in the entrance, or do they try first to enter the shop? Which objects do they interact with and for how long? What were their affective responses and perceptions of the shop and its goods, and how did sensory stimuli impact those responses and perceptions?

On the one hand, then, we are exploring the ability of 3D models published through a game engine to test and iterate statistically derived predictions of movement in Roman houses, streets, and shops. On the other hand, all that remains of the house owner Paquius Proculus and the shop owner Verecundus is more than indirect traces of how they, or their customers, or their *familia*, might have moved through these spaces. Beyond this lie the emotional worlds of everyday Romans seemingly beyond our recovery, which of course they are, in any direct sense. Taking a cue from walking simulators, however, we might imagine game scenarios that begin to lead players at least a little way into those worlds, scenarios whose game play data and qualitative response forms, gathered from a diverse, global audience, can shed indirect insight on the emotional colors of that world.

It is the morning of the Nones of April, 825 years after the founding of Rome (roughly 5 April 72 CE). You are the wife of a formerly enslaved freedman of the emperor Vespasian, and you yourself were once also enslaved. Your husband has been dispatched to the Bay of Naples to check on the progress of reconstruction in Pompeii a decade after the powerful earthquake in 62 CE, and to check on local politics and loyalties. You are staying at the house of Caius Cuspius Pansa, a young politician running for the office of aedile, north of the Forum of Pompeii, but this evening you have been invited to dinner at the house of Publius Paquius Proculus, a friend and close supporter. While your husband's position in the imperial household is significant, you both prefer to travel humbly. You yourself are a woman *sui iuris*, under your own legal control, and you have significant wealth, independent of your husband—a fact of which you must occasionally remind him. Today you and your husband are making your way on foot down the via dell'Abbondanza with your enslaved attendant Leander, a tall man in his mid-twenties from central Asia Minor, fluent in Latin, Greek, and several dialects of Aramaic, as are you. As you near the house of Proculus, your husband realizes two things: first, he would like to visit the *fullonica* (laundry shop) of Stephanus, as the gossip of this business, and the taverns nearby, can offer surprising political insight; second, he has forgotten his dining slippers. As a laundry and taverns

are not appropriate terrain for you (at least, not anymore), he peels off to make these stops, while you and Leander proceed east down the street, searching for a felt shop...

Player Choice/Behavior: do you approach or avoid the fountain on the street corner? Potential source of useful neighborhood gossip and information, but also pestering words and even physical contact, though Leander is of sufficient size . . . .

Player Choice/Behavior: do you notice the electoral graffiti (*CIL* IV 7201) by the door of Proculus's house? It names your host (Pansa), and you note that phrase, "if there is any glory for one living a modest (Latin: *verecunde*) life . . . ." Maybe Leander is more observant here than you.

Player Choice/Behavior: how do you pick out the Felt Shop of Verecundus, across the street from the house of Proculus? Which environmental cues lead you there? Once you realize the owner's name, as announced in his shop decoration, means 'Mr. Modesty,' does this ring a bell?

Player Choice/Behavior: Once near the entrance of the shop, do you choose to stay on the sidewalk, before the table, or do you choose to enter the shop? Or do you leave Leander in front of the table outside near the door, and move inside yourself? While handling the felt slippers and assessing their quality, how do you direct the conversation with the shop attendant? Toward the issue of 'modesty' and the relationship Verecundus might have with Proculus?[10] If you sense friction there between the freedman shop owner and the higher-class house owner, how deeply do you pursue? As the shop front faces out to the front door of Proculus's house, there may be useful information here . . . .

This scenario unfolds as an experiential trajectory shaped by player choice, some choices spatial, some choices social, some speaking to the player's sense of vulnerability and trust with respect to Leander. Presented in the more embodying and haptic platform of VR (limited in terms of number and diversity of test subjects), or crowd-sourced to a diverse global audience through WebGL, this experiment begins to color in, however indirectly, the emotional range of plausible street experiences in ancient Pompeii. Were the experiment extended to the dinner party in the house of Proculus, it could be similarly charted through a set of interactive moments involving decoration, objects, and conversation trees. Developed through emergent play between games, game engines, and archaeology, scenarios like these indeed offer a different kind of phenomenology. The strength of the experiment lies in its diversity, in its ability to at least begin to sketch out, through game play data and qualitative response forms, what a Roman street, or house, or social encounter might feel like outside the box of traditional academic research—through the bodies, personal histories, and cultural contexts of the many human ones who are *not* white classical archaeologists of European or North American origin.

NOTES

1   Fredrick and Vennarucci 2021.

2   Keogh 2018.

3   Pugliese Carratelli and Baldassarre 1990–99.

4   Pine and Gilmore 1999.

5   Dyer 2014.

6   Tringham and Danis 2019, 55.

7   Shinkle 2008, 908.

8   Shinkle 2008.

9   Smith 2012.

10 Hartnett 2017, 293–94.

BIBLIOGRAPHY

Dyer, Serena (2014), Shopping and the Senses: Retail, Browsing and Consumption in 18th-Century England, *History Compass* 12(9), 694–703.

Fredrick, David and Rhodora G. Vennarucci (2021), Putting Space Syntax to the Test: Digital Embodiment and Phenomenology in the Roman House, *Studies in Digital Heritage* 4(2), 185–229.

González-Tennant, Edwin (2016), Archaeological Walking Simulators, *The Society for American Archaeology Archaeological Record* 16(5), 23–28.

Hamilakis, Yannis (2014), *Archaeology and the Senses: Human Experience, Memory, and Affect,* Cambridge (Cambridge University Press).

Hartnett, Jeremy (2017), *The Roman Street: Urban Life and Society in Pompeii, Herculaneum, and Rome*, Cambridge (Cambridge University Press).

Keogh, Brendan (2018), *A Play of Bodies: How We Perceive Videogames*, Cambridge (Massachusetts Institute of Technology Press).

Malafouris, Lambros and Colin Renfrew (2010), *The Cognitive Life of Things: Recasting the Boundaries of the Mind*, Cambridge (McDonald Institute for Archaeological Research).

Pine, B. Joseph and James Gilmore (1999), *The Experience Economy*, Boston (Harvard Business School Press).

Pugliese Carratelli, Giovanni and Ida Baldassarre (1990–99), *Pompeii Pompei: Pitture e mosaici* (11 volumes), Rome (Istituto della enciclopedia italiana).

Smith, Kate (2012), Sensing Design and Workmanship: The Haptic Skills of the Shopper in Eighteenth-Century London, *Journal of Design History* 25(1), 1–10.

Shinkle, Eugenie (2008), Video Games, Emotion and the Six Senses, *Media, Culture and Society* 30, 907–15.

Tringham, Ruth and Annie Danis (2019), "Doing Sensory Archaeology: The Challenges," in: Robin Skeates and Jo Day, eds., *The Routledge Handbook of Sensory Archaeology*, London (Routledge), pp. 48–75.

THE MUSEUM HOTEL ANTAKYA

AGAINST THE COLLAR FOR TEN TOUGH YEARS

EMRE AROLAT

FIRST TOUCH

I did not know whether to laugh or cry. As far as I could understand, she had given up on becoming a veterinarian, which she had been talking about for a while. Now she wanted to be an architect. I suggested she come with us on the weekend. She had never seen Antakya. "I am sure you will find it interesting," I said, "It's a special place, with layers and layers of history and religions. Mosques, churches, and synagogues, all side by side.[1] Four thousand years old, they say it was one of the three largest cities in the ancient world. Of course, it's not easy to see that looking at it today. But it doesn't matter, maybe we'll have the opportunity to cross the border and go to Aleppo as well.[2] It takes less than two hours. I've never been there either. They call it 'The Queen of the East.' A friend of mine praised it to the skies the other day. He could not say enough, he went on and on about how its grand bazaar was so well preserved and how

the meal he ate of hummus, baba ghanoush, and tabouli was so delicious.[3] And of course, there is the Umayyad Mosque.[4] Remember I showed you pictures yesterday of a courtyard surrounded by colonnades? A magnificent space. We'll see that too while we're there."

I wake up to the sound of the wheels of the plane sharply hitting the tarmac. I had been working on the new housing project that we designed in Lisbon. I only finished at midnight. I am very excited about this project. It is always this excitement that brings out the energy in me. However tired I am, the new sun rising each day brings my body alive again. I fell in love with the inimitable spirit of Alcântara the minute I saw it anyway.[5] I guess that is the best thing about doing projects in different places. The in-depth research about new countries, new cities, and regions. These are rare opportunities. Even if you feel hopeless because you see how little you know, and the more you learn the more anxious you feel, in the end you arrive somewhere. If you work hard enough, never give up, give it the sensitivity that it deserves, and in the end you say, "Okay. I think I begin to understand."

The process is painful every time, but pleasurable too. Whether everyone suffers this much, I do not know. Maybe they feel as much self-doubt. Each and every time I drown in the same ignorance, the same feeling of poverty in knowledge. Then little by little my surroundings begin to light up. The vast area called context. Layer upon layer, and so very complex. It is not an easy thing to comprehend the whole all at once. If you concern yourself only with what you see at first and do not look into the background, you get into serious trouble. Why? Who? When? Who with? From where? You have to ask a flock of questions and examine every nook and cranny of the problem from all angles. And painstakingly sort through the thousands of sources that you have collected to research the thing. Yes, it is incredible how the digital world has made it so much easier to access information. But this heap of information you get in a flash has to be approached with caution. You cannot believe everything you see; you pick through it and realize that most of it is garbage. But that is okay. I am only too glad to have it. Younger generations do not know how we used to spend weeks hunting down just one book. Such-and-such library, such-and-such institute, asking this friend and that friend for favors. Breathlessly. And then all you found were a few paragraphs that you could use. And now? Crazy speed. Two strokes on the keyboard and the world is at your feet.

There was a time when this district was considered far outside Lisbon. Nowadays, although it is swiftly on the way to becoming a new sub-center, its nineteenth century industrial sprit is still quite legible. "Swiftly" by Portuguese standards, of course. Lisbon is not Istanbul, New York, or London. First, we did a few months' worth of strict analytical research. Then we worked day and night. For weeks. On the one hand, investors expect us to create an attractive choice answering demands current to the new world, and on the other, there is our desire to somehow preserve the spirit special to the atmosphere where the project will be built. And we did it, I think. Now I

feel better. Friends at the Istanbul office are putting the last touches and the project will be sent to Lisbon today.

I am having trouble getting myself to wake up. The sun hits the plane exactly at the point where we are seated. I can see she has just woken up too. She is finding it hard to open her eyes too. "You see what I mean," I say. "The profession has these silly aspects to it as well. But I think it depends on how you look at the work as a whole. I haven't slept in days, but I'm happy. We did the best we could, and I believe that in the end we produced a project firmly knit into its context. And I think it can answer the current tendencies of the local market nicely. I hope it will be built; it would be our first project in that region. In any case, let's forget that for now. I am beginning to get excited about what we will see shortly." She looks at me blankly as if it is of no interest to her. She obviously thinks that I am talking nonsense. I tell myself the day will come when she will understand these things too.

It has been ten years. Easy to say. Yes, Zeynep studied architecture as she thought she would then. Now she stays up all night from time to time. All she thinks about is making the work she does as perfect as possible. I know the feeling well. Anxiety takes over as the first light of day turns the sky a pale blue. You have not even stirred from your seat all night long, seeking a better solution to some tiny detail no one else would notice. Sometimes I worry she is wearing herself out. A father cannot bear to see his daughter hurt. But I confess that I am at the same time happy for her. There is no greater privilege in life than being able to do the work that you love.

We settle into the upholstery of the black Mercedes that meets us at the airport. "You won't believe it, but this used to be a lake, stretching far as the eye can see. Lake Amik. It was partially drained and this area reclaimed. Amik Lake is now Amik Valley." She laughs. She looks at me as if I am kidding her. "No, it's really true. Later they built an airport. But the water table still rises sometimes. There are major overflows too. It even became a lake again a few weeks ago. The runways and so on were submerged in water, flights were canceled." Now she looks really perplexed. "Why? Is there nowhere else for them to go?" A good question. Nature always takes its revenge. But let's not get into that now. I do not want that pristine world of hers, that sense of justice she guards with her life, to be stained by things she hears from me. Although I know this is only putting it off, and to no avail. In a few years her fantasies, too, will be smashed. She will rebel against what is happening around her, as we all do. The terrible news she hears every day will terrify her. Let's leave it there for today.

Makeshift structures begin to appear on either side of us as we get onto the main road. Lately we are confronted by these structures in almost every city we visit. Knocked together without plan, without care. This was not what modern Turkey dreamed of. But the speed of urbanization that gradually increased from the 1950s onward ruined every city. And unfortunately, that became the vision for development of the state from then on. Short-sighted, even scrambling, shallow populist politics increased the pace of migration from country to city day by day. Just thirty years ago the rural population of Turkey was greater than its urban population. As a result of this extraordinary transition, today at least eight out of ten citizens live in a city.[6] Nothing can stand up to the demand this creates. The cities developed at this mad pace in a weird sort of spontaneity. Like a series of towns accidently attached side by side or end to end, following no plan, conforming to no perceivable rule. Unwholesome organisms, almost always ugly. "Don't look," I say. "It's always like this outside the center. The same landscape wherever we go."

We stop in front of a big iron gate. An area cordoned off by high panels on four sides. One cannot see inside. On the phone they said it was almost 20,000 square meters (215,000 square feet). It must be a small industrial area in the process of transformation. The pattern of building around it suffers from neglect. Most of the structures are obviously abandoned. On the other side of the road a group of people sit in the sun, sipping their tea and playing backgammon. It seems that they do not care about the dust and dirt lifted by the wind. The sputtering sound of a transistor radio perched crookedly on a stool beside them spreads over the street. "I dried the roses, I dried the roses, I rocked my love to sleep on my breast."[7]

Figure 22.1. The author visits the archaeological site on which The Museum Hotel Antakya was to be built for the first time in 2009. His daughter Zeynep, together with Necmi and Sabiha Asfuroğlu walk along the old riverbed.

The gate is opened noisily. A small part of the lot has not yet been dug up. The rest of the space is like a beehive (Figure 22.1). Hundreds of people in clothes of all colors are at work, but there is not one single machine in the entire area.[8] Everyone is working with their hands. A little further we stop in front of a construction site container. The man greets us with a warm smile in his eyes. "Welcome, welcome, you bring us joy," he says, extending his hand. He introduces those standing next to him one by one. "Mrs. Hatice,[9] our valued archaeology professor; Mrs. Demet,[10] from the Hatay Archaeological Museum team,[11] is also an archaeologist; and this is our young lady Sabiha,[12] my daughter. I swear we keep her working day and night here."

Well-steeped tea arrives as soon as we sit down at the table. I have always admired those who bring dozens of glasses of tea on a huge tray swinging from a chain without spilling any. Necmi Bey is so courteous.[13] He takes the trouble to ask each of us how we are one by one. "You have come a long way and you must be hungry." We say we ate on the plane and thank him. In fact, we were so fast asleep that we did not even notice breakfast being served. "Bring some of those pastries, my boy," he calls out to someone inside. It is as if he did not hear us. And maybe he knows we are lying.

Necmi Asfuroğlu is a well-known and respected business-man who is proud to have been born in Antakya and is in love with the place where he lives. We weathered many a crisis together. And we argued often these past ten years. To be frank, I confess that there were many times I wanted to part ways with him and because of that, with the project as well. But I always held back. The attraction of the place and the design won out every time, and now I am glad that it did.

After we have caught our breath and drunk tea we go out into the site. The area is 200 meters (650 feet) long. The breadth must be around 100 meters (325 feet). We walk as a group along a line between the ruins, curving slightly here and there, lengthwise from one end to the other. It is like a pedestrian path. It looks weird. The whole place is full of ruins, while this one meter (3 feet) wide line is empty (Figure 22.2). Platform pieces sheathed in marble catch the eye at the south-ern end. "This area was likely a place of public assembly in front of a large temple or official structure; it was encircled by columns. This is clearly legible from the traces of fire on the ground," Uğur Tanyeli said.[14] In fact, it was he who got me involved in this.

Figure 22.2. Composite aerial photograph of the archaeological site along Kurtuluş Boulevard, near the ancient Grotto of Saint Peter in Antakya, Turkey. Note the former river, used as an access way, dividing the area in half.

The field of archaeology has interested me ever since I was a child, but I somehow have never been able to internalize it. Is it only me? I doubt it. For some it is a sacrosanct, mysterious discipline, for others just old pieces of pottery. A person cannot really love a thing that they do not know well. Like it or not, you view it from a distance. And this is such a distance that most of the time what is said about archaeological finds seems to be made up, rumors, or even fairy tales difficult to believe.

But this place is something else. After just a few steps it catches a person and pulls them inside. It must be a kind of sense of discovery that I have never felt before that is making me so excited. Discoveries about the past, thousands of years old. Distant voices play in my ears, as if women are washing clothes in the lake. They laugh and joke with one another in a language I cannot quite understand. I seem to hear horses neighing beyond them. It gives me goose bumps.

"The line we are walking on is actually the bed of the Parmenius River, which flowed approximately northwest to southeast. That is why there are no archaeological remains here. The walls visible here are from the Hellenistic era, around the third century BCE. They probably functioned as dykes to hold back seasonal flooding of the river. If you look carefully, you can easily discern later additions to the old walls. They show that this area was used similarly in later periods."

As she talks excitedly, dozens of people are continuing the work of excavation with the greatest of care. And they are remarkably silent. Each of them carries a small instrument, some a fine brush, others only pen and paper. "As you can easily see, this here is a Roman-era bath," Hatice Hoca is saying (Figure 22.3). The truth is I cannot really see it that easily. I cannot be considered experienced in such things. And the supports of the furnace flooring were not as clearly visible then as when you look at it today. It is not an easy thing to bring pieces from different sections together, to see the whole picture, and give it meaning. She confuses me a bit more by saying, "We can date this bath to the mid-fifth century CE. It is a small-scale row type bath with channels for emptying water into the riverbed, a defending wall, units for hot and cold bathing, and

a hypocaust system." We talk among ourselves about how surprising it is that the wastewater infrastructure of the ancient city was so advanced.

Dozens of separate periods, variety upon variety of archaeological finds. And the mosaics dividing the lot in two from northeast to southwest would make you lose your mind. They are not yet fully uncovered, but they say it is the largest mosaic floor ever found in the region (Figure 22.4). Nine connected panels, each with a different geometrical motif, cover an area larger than 1000 square meters (10,750 square feet). The surface has been significantly warped by the earthquakes it has endured (Figure 22.5). In fact, the undulation is quite beautiful. It is as if a gigantic carpet is waiting to be uncovered.

She stops us again as we walk toward the northwestern edge and continues talking without taking a breath. "In this section there is a residential structure dated to the fifth century CE. Here, too, mosaic floors with figures and motifs have been discovered. You cannot see them all now because we have covered a large section to preserve them, but still you can read the overall plan. The floor of the main hall here is covered with mosaics. You can see the smaller rooms on either side, and the corridor cutting through the central hall." She moves the pen in her hand as if drawing what she is describing on the air. "Unfortunately, the mosaics in the central hall are not in good condition. Within the frame of the medallion right at the center of the floor there is female figure and a personification of Magnanimity. The male and female birds surrounding it are freely placed. The female figure holding a kind of baton in the center of the medallion is the personification of the Creative Spirit, the second of its kind in the Antakya mosaics. The other is in the Yakto Mosaic exhibited in the Hatay Archaeological Museum. In this corridor bordering the central hall there is a mosaic depicting wild animals. They are so beautiful, so delicately and masterfully done that you will not believe your eyes when they are uncovered."

We are told that many new objects large and small are found every day of the excavation. Coins from the Abbasid period, figurines from the Roman, Byzantine, Crusader, or Islamic periods, column capitals, vessels, oil lamps, jugs, and semiprecious

Figure 22.3. The remains of a mid-fifth century CE Roman bath in Antakya, Turkey. Note the foundations of the hypocaust floor and the residential stuctures in the backgound.

Figure 22.4. Parts of a large ancient mosaic floor in Antakya, Turkey.

Figure 22.5. Part of a two-thousand-year-old mosaic floor in Antakya, Turkey. The floor, warped by earthquakes, measures around 1000 square meters.

stones. The seals made of diorite with tiny designs are very interesting. A statue of an amazon from the second century is mentioned, and there is the legendary Eros of white marble.

Our walk lasts almost three hours. In the end we head toward one of the construction site containers. Necmi Bey is waiting for us in the shade of a tree by the door. With that ever-present smile of his he invites us all into the partition that has been transformed into a meeting room. Haluk Hoca has also arrived now.[15] They had said he was in Ankara. He finished his work early. "I came as fast as I could as soon as I heard you were coming. Just between us, the meeting was very dull," he says, smiling at me archly. May he rest in peace, he was one of the most gentlemanly human beings I have known in this world. It is such a pity that he was not able to see the project finished. Tea is served again. A young man with glasses and curly hair left to grow long comes in. Later I learn that he too is one of the archaeologists. He puts the box he is carrying down carefully at the center of the table. Suddenly everyone stands up all together. When I see how excited they are, I stand up as well. Inside the box there is a long, thin, scrappy piece of what must be baked clay. "Although some among us insist it must be early Roman, it is highly likely that this *unguentarium* is from the Hellenistic period," Hoca Abbasoğlu says in his velvety voice. He looks into my eyes. Clearly this object has an important story. I purse my lips and slowly nod my head, pretending I understand. An *unguentarium*, what might that be? Why does everyone find this tiny flask so important? I am bursting with curiosity but say nothing. I do not want to look like some stupid architect, especially not with Zeynep by my side.

Afterward there is a long silence in the room. Necmi Bey turns toward me, looking at me without speaking. Clearly, I am supposed to say something. But at that moment one of the archaeologists is swinging his leg under the table and my mind is fixed on the rustling sound it is making. And I am trying to think how to postpone the tedious speech I must give in a moment. Now what can I do to throw the ball out of bounds without offending anyone? Thousands of years of civilization have come and gone, apparently choosing this lot for a home. One on top of another. Layer upon layer. Is there supposed to be room left here for a hotel? What should one say now to this man? What can be said to make him give up on the idea?

I begin: "Necmi Bey, are you really sure that you want to build a hotel here?"

DONE AND DUSTED

Her gaze seems to be nailed to the spot. She stands motionless at the end of the bridge taking in the entire view of the area. Though I try not to show it, inwardly I am worried what she will say. In fact, this is the first time I am having such a moment with her. For years I wondered anxiously how my mother would react the first time she saw a work I designed. Now, with a similar feeling, I look into her eyes. "I can't believe it, Dad," she whispers. "Here it is, finished at last!" Yes, she was a high-school student when she came with me to Antakya ten years ago. This is the first time she has returned since then. "It is one of the best projects that you have done," she says, smiling.[16]

Necmi Bey did not give up. He not only threw himself into the fire, he pushed me into this weird adventure as well. Oh, Uğur Tanyeli! Did I not say that it all came out of his head, and this thing that for me lasted years began with one telephone call from him. "If only you would come and see this place. I am sure you will find it interesting," he said. I could not hurt his feelings; I had no way to say no. The great Tanyeli. I went, and I saw. That was it.

"Emre Bey, this has become something much more than an investment for me. It is a matter of honor. I was born here, I grew up here, and now I want to pay the debt I owe to this land. You see the great care we have taken, struggling here for months, and with such a quality team. Either I will do this or I will do this. I cannot even conceive of an alternative." It was hard not to be influenced by Necmi Bey's stubbornness and faith. I tried to emphasize how exhausting the task before us might be, the bureaucratic tedium we would probably have to face, and how it would be financially impossible to see a way back from the investment he would make. But my efforts were all in vain.

Figure 22.6. Architectural concept sketch of The Museum Hotel Antakya by the author.

Figure 22.7. Room units manufactured outside the construction site are put in place by cranes during the construction of The Museum Hotel Antakya.

It took more than three months to heat the concept project to the temper I wanted. I was happy with the intellectual framework of the design and the physical entity that emerged (Figure 22.6). But it was all but impossible for an average contractor to take charge of this project. The governing idea was based on the principle of generating a structure that would preserve the archaeological ruins without touching them at all. Try now to bring this before your eyes. On the riverbed that runs along the lot from end to end, and on the two lengthwise sides of the lot, points were to be found where there were no archaeological ruins. Wells two meters (6 feet) in diameter would be dug at these points in order to reach the firm ground nearly 25 meters (80 feet) below. And no construction machinery would be used to do this work. More than sixty wells with walls secured by a reinforced concrete sheath would be dug by hand under the supervision of an archaeologist; then, steel supports 1.2 meters (47 inches) in diameter and approximately 45 meters (148 feet) high, including the portion to remain underground, would be erected in these wells. Because

the ruins were scattered, these supports, each of them sitting on a different geometrical axis and approximately 40 meters (130 feet) apart, would be roofed by a gigantic steel platform 20 meters (66 feet) above the ground.

On the one hand, the platform would serve as a covering to protect the ruins from external influences, and on the other it would be a basis for indoor shared-use areas to be located on top of it. In this way all the shared functions we are accustomed to seeing on the ground floor of a conventional hotel—such as a restaurant, bar, night club, spa, gymnasium, and even a swimming pool—would be arranged on this platform at the top of the structure. Underneath it, a three-bedroom floor 10 meters (33 feet) above the ruins would be joisted to the steel structure.

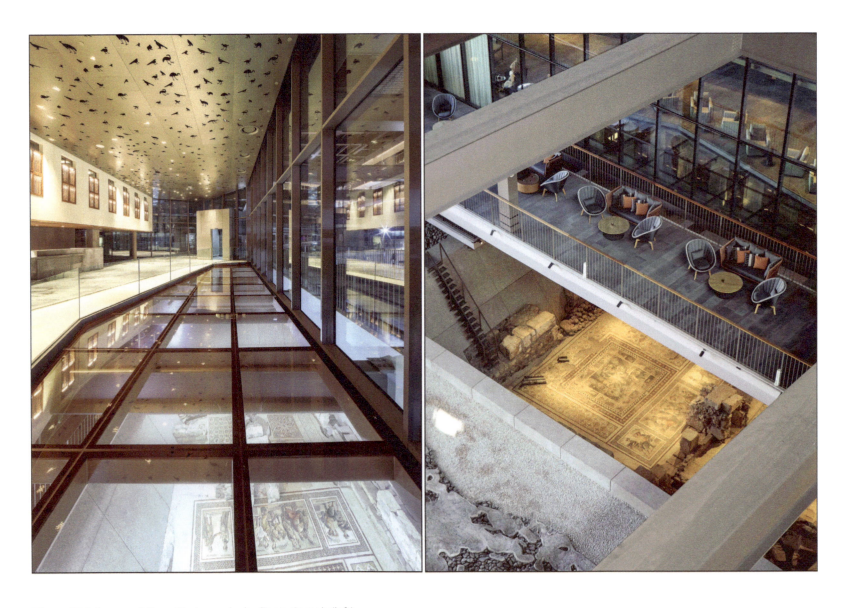

Figure 22.8. Layers of time. *Photographs by Engin Gerçek (left) and Emre Dörter (right).*

Figure 22.9. The Museum Hotel Antakya. *Photograph by Engin Gerçek.*

Room units to be manufactured outside the construction site using a prefabricated method would be transported to the lot one by one by large lorries and set down by cranes upon the joists as internally complete modules (Figure 22.7). These units would be detached one from the other and placed in such a way that guests could have visual contact with the archaeological area below (Figure 22.8).[17] A direct link would be constructed between the elevation of the external road, approximately 4 meters (13 feet) above the ruins, and the reception unit. The public museum, accessed from a lower level by taking advantage of the slope of the external road, would be formed by a kind of hanging concourse providing continuous experience of both the indoor exhibition unit and the entire area.

In such situations here we use the phrase, "Don't die, my donkey, don't die." This saying is used when one knows that something is very unlikely to succeed. That is how long the roads to be traveled and how steep the peaks to be scaled were. Only by some miracle can the donkey survive. What the phrase really expresses is a lack of faith. I must confess that when the concept project was laid out, that was the mood in the office. One usually sees such freak projects only in architecture school, where they are called experimental projects and done as homework assignments. Real life is something else. Whatever has a long reach—the powers-that-be, or what we call the system, some enemy, some kind of ogre—suddenly appears out of thin air to destroy the project or at least put it at risk, softening its corners, grinding down its jagged peaks and punishing its excesses. Such apparently irrational projects are rarely encountered on the mediocre, conformist paths of real life, where guarantees are demanded.

I glance into his eyes as I give my presentation. His glasses glint more brightly in the light of the projector. I have never seen his face so expressionless. I am thinking that as soon as I finish, he will get up and run away, never to be seen again. Now and then he steals a look at Uğur Tanyeli as if seeking salvation. Or so it seems to me. It is probably a tendency of mine to think that way. But Tanyeli's eyes are on the screen, watching the presentation attentively. He only raises his eyebrows once in a while. I finish the presentation by saying, "I know it's not going to be easy. Maybe you will even regret many times that you embarked on the project. But if it happens that we can complete it, if we can reach the end, you will have put your signature to a work that is at once radical and as sensitive as it is possible to be. This project has the potential to provide an original example of the relationship between the fields of archaeology and contemporary architecture, preservation, restoration, and urban archaeology on the one hand, and on the other, a new appreciation of the potential for private and public space use. As I said a moment ago, if we can see the day when the functions of hotel and museum are conducted simultaneously, even private land, with the help of the three-dimensional solution we have set forth, may attain the potential for public use, at least with regard to the whole of its ground plane. And we will have shown how socioeconomic classes that under normal conditions have no contact can mingle within one structure. When that day comes, I will believe I have done a good thing."

The Museum Hotel Antakya opened at the end of 2019 after ten years of feverish work (Figure 22.9).[18]

NOTES

1   Antakya is a county of Hatay province located in the east of Turkey's Mediterranean region. The Habibi Neccar Mosque, the Antakya Catholic Church, and the Antakya Jewish Temple are located on Kurtuluş Boulevard, the oldest street in this city founded as Antioch around 300 BCE according to ancient sources.

2   Aleppo is located 100 kilometers east of Antakya in Syria, which shares a border with Turkey.

3   Special to the Eastern Mediterranean region, tabouli, hummus, and baba ghanoush are traditional starters (mezes) of Levantine cuisine.

4   Aleppo Ulu Mosque, or as it is popularly known, Aleppo Umayyad Mosque, was built in 715 CE by the Umayyad Caliph al-Walid ibn Abd al-Malik. The architect was Hasan ibn Mufarraj al-Sarmini. The area where the mosque was built was once the Hellenistic Agora, and in the Byzantine era, the garden of Saint Helena Cathedral.

5   Alcântara is a civil parish of Lisbon, the capital of Portugal.

6   There has been massive internal migration in Turkey from rural areas to the cities since the 1950s, due to such factors as unemployment, unequal distribution of wealth, and the politics of agriculture and animal husbandry. This migration contributed additional momentum to urbanization.

7   "I dried rose petals" is a traditional folksong from the Hatay region.

8   No construction equipment was used because the area was being excavated according to archaeological standards. The enormous lot was excavated with thousands of brushes and dental tools.

9   Professor Hatice Pamir is the director of the scientific excavation, she is presently the chair of the Department of Archaeology at Hatay Mustafa Atatürk University.

10 Archaeologist Demet Kara, assistant director of the Hatay Museum, was a member of the excavation team throughout the process and made important contributions to the project.

11 The Hatay Archaeology Museum is the largest museum of mosaics in Turkey. The museum includes works from the Paleolithic, Neolithic, Chalcolithic, Bronze Age, Hittite, Hellenistic, Roman, Eastern Roman, Seljuk, and Ottoman periods.

12 Sabiha Asfuroğlu is founder of The Museum Hotel Antakya brand and the director of the Museum Hotel.

13 Necmi Asfuroğlu is an Antakya businessman and the investor of The Museum Hotel Antakya.

14 Professor Uğur Tanyeli, an academic architectural historian for more than forty years, was on the Scientific Committee during the first phase of the excavation for the Museum Hotel Antakya. He continues his work at various universities.

15 Professor Haluk Abbasoğlu, director of the recently defunct Istanbul University Faculty of Letters Department of Archaeology and of the Classical archaeology branch, made important contributions to the project as a member of its scientific committee.

16 https://emrearolat.com/project/the-museum-hotel-antakya/ (accessed 31 August 2020).

17 See also *The Economist,* November 16, 2019, pp. 75–76.

18 In 2009 the Antakya businessman Necmi Asfuroğlu decided to build a five-star hotel on the land he owns on Kurtuluş Boulevard, one of the main arteries of the city. The land is located within a Class Three Protected Archaeological Site. Within this framework the Hatay Archaeology Museum, by order of the Adana Cultural and Natural Properties Preservation Committee, had twenty-nine wells drilled to examine the archaeology of the area. In the light of data collected from the wells the decision was made to conduct archaeological excavations over the entire 17,132 square meters (184,407 square feet). The excavations were completed in 2010–11, employing nearly 120 workers, thirty-five archaeologists, and five restoration architects. In the process, it was decided that the project previously prepared by an architectural firm should be replaced with a new project that should not damage the unearthed archaeological remains. As a result of negotiations, an agreement was reached with EAA–Emre Arolat Architecture and, at the suggestion of that firm, the idea was adopted to build a Museum Hotel that would allow the public to view the archaeological finds, rather than build a conventional hotel. The Concept Project presented by EAA at the end of 2010 was based on the principle of determining points in the lot where no archaeological remains exist and having the upper structure supported by steel columns placed within wells to be dug at these points. With this aim thirty-six wells of 22–28 meters (72–92 feet) in depth were dug on the site, each one entirely by hand under supervision of an archaeologist. The work of installing the steel supports and other structural elements started in 2012 and continued into 2015. In the process, guest rooms manufactured outside the site were transported to the site and mounted in place using special cranes. An important characteristic of the project is the location of all social spaces on the platform that rests on the supports. Hotel and museum entrances and concourse routes are constructed so as to be independent of one another. Many surprises and difficulties emerged during the construction. The project was revised time and again during the placement of elevation joists and related work due to the discovery of archaeological finds in close coordination between archaeologists, art historians, and architects. Within this framework not only the architectural design but the joist system, the mechanical and electrical projects, and related technical calculations were revised dozens of times.

In 2011 a mosaic was discovered during the digging of column wells on points along the axis defined as G-2. As a result of this find, which amazed the archaeologists as well, the excavation area of this section was broadened under the supervision of the Cultural and Natural Properties Preservation Committee. During the excavation the 12×15 meter (39×49 foot) triclinium of a house, dated to the second century CE, was discovered at an average depth of three meters below ground. In the mosaic floor a central panel and the three small panels framing it depict mythological themes and creatures. A *nymphaion* emerged in another section of the space. The central panel is occupied by a winged Pegasus figure and three nymphs, and framed by panels containing animal figures. Three panels were discovered at the south end of the central panel. The eighth of the nine Muses (Ourania) is depicted in the large panel at the center, and the ninth (Calliope) in the side panel at the right, facing the ancient writer Hesiod. In the left panel there is a personification of the region of Boeotia and Mount Helikon, where all of the mythological figures on the mosaic reside. On the south side of the triclinium there is a *nymphaion* against a mosaic background, with panels depicting Eros figures fishing, an ocean scene, and adjacent geometric designs. A sleeping Eros relief and a freestanding Eros statue were also found during further work here. One of the most fascinating finds discovered in the lot thus became the cause of a very important change in the project, and the circulation strategy of the ground floor was revised accordingly.

Five consecutive cultural layers, from the Hellenistic to the Islamic period, along with many artifacts surviving to the present day from thirteen distinct civilizations, are on display as a kind of archaeopark within the scope of the Museum Hotel Antakya completed and opened in 2019. The expenses of all archaeological excavations, documentation, conservation, and restoration work, construction of all indoor and outdoor spaces of the museum, and implementation of its exhibitions were paid for by the investor, the Asfuroğlu Group, and upon completion of the construction the Museum was donated to the Ministry of Culture for public use.

PART II

THE ARCHAEOLOGY OF

LIVING MEMORY

21

USING ARCHAEOLOGY
TO UNDERSTAND HOMELESSNESS

LARRY J. ZIMMERMAN

Since 2003, I have been using archaeological field methods to study homelessness, looking especially at the material culture—the stuff—acquired, used, and discarded by people living rough in St. Paul, Minnesota, and in Indianapolis, Indiana. This may seem odd, because archaeologists usually study much older stuff. To most people the archaeo part in archaeology means ancient or prehistoric, and something doing an 'archaeology of five minutes ago' is not it. With rare exceptions, I have spent about thirty-five years of my career on the old stuff, studying the development of Pre-Contact Native American village life along the Missouri, Mississippi, and Ohio River basins in the Great Plains and Midwest regions of the United States. One exception, excavating in the abandoned gardens of a late nineteenth-century mansion in St. Paul, Minnesota, pushed my thinking and fieldwork away from standard archaeology into the archaeology of the contemporary. In making this transition, I have

learned six important points about archaeology that I hope will become apparent:

1. Many standard archaeological field methods work reasonably well for contemporary sites, but need minor modifications;

2. We do not always need excavation or complex theories to interpret what we see in homeless sites;

3. What we observe can be useful in support of people who live roofless if we can communicate it well to non-archaeologists;

4. Archaeology can challenge common misunderstandings and negative narratives about homelessness;

5. The general public seems to be interested in learning that archaeology can be useful for understanding the very recent past; and

6. An archaeology of the contemporary can earn its keep.

I have discovered that thinking of 'live' in the past tense—lived—distracted and limited me by pushing me toward social theories that have little that is immediately and specifically useful to ease the difficulties homeless people face. To make it worse, the many missing pieces in the study of the distant past emphasize what non-archaeologists tend to see as the weaknesses of archaeology, which leaves the stories archaeologists produce wide open to speculation or a claim that archaeology is just academic and not the real world. What this work has taught me is that using archaeology to study homelessness is absolutely real world.

"D'OH!": PROJECT ORIGINS AND MY HOMER SIMPSON MOMENT

How I almost stumbled into studying homelessness is all about how material culture is the real archaeology and not so much about time or the past. From 2002 to 2004, I was head of the Archaeology Department for the Minnesota Historical Society and monitored any ground disturbance at the more than 30 sites and museums operated by that society. Included was the James J. Hill House, a National Historic Landmark just a few blocks from the Minnesota History Center and downtown St. Paul, directly across the street from the massive Basilica of Saint Mary. Railroad magnate James J. Hill, the 'Empire Builder' who built and controlled the Great Northern Railway, completed the 3350-square-meter (36,000-square-foot) house in 1891. Built to impress potential clients, the three-acre estate included gardens, greenhouses, and other structures sloping down to the Mississippi River.[1] Two massive stone-faced walls broke the slope. Five years after Hill died in 1916, his family donated the property to the Archdiocese of St. Paul, which turned the house into a seminary, but neglected the gardens. The Minnesota Historical Society acquired the house and grounds in 1978. They restored the house but not the gardens, which became overgrown with brush and trees. The walls had deteriorated badly by the mid-1980s, and the construction of Interstate Highway 35E at the base of the slope required removal of garden buildings. In 2002, the Minnesota Historical Society decided to restore the gardens, but needed architectural details on the walls, especially for a mushroom-growing cave built into one wall. Getting that kind of information was standard archaeology and frankly, was not particularly thrilling, but that soon changed.

The University of Minnesota and the Minnesota Historical Society organized an archaeological field methods class around the project. A common first experience for students is to learn how to do a systematic surface survey and to collect any cultural materials visible on the surface of mapped collection units. The students immediately started asking if I wanted them to pick up all the junk, which I assumed was just accumulated litter from two decades along a major urban highway. As we studied the junk, my litter hypothesis evaporated. Lots of old clothing, rotten sleeping bags, broken alcohol bottles and cans, and even drug paraphernalia, showed a pattern of distribution that went too far upslope from the highway to be litter. The materials were concentrated in brushy areas and near the walls, where someone occasionally had pulled the stones out to make fire rings. Where this stuff came from soon started to make sense as we began excavations around the walls and in the mushroom cave. For decades, homeless people had been and still were using the abandoned gardens as camp sites (Figure 21.1). Most mornings we found a homeless man sleeping in the partly collapsed mushroom cave. He always ran away before we could talk with him. He usually left behind blankets and a large duffel bag. As we excavated the first meter (3 feet) of a test unit in the collapsed cave entrance, we found used cooking utensils, broken bottles, and other debris used by homeless people nearly all the way to the cave floor, where we found a late 1800s shovel blade, perhaps left by Hill estate gardeners. A few of us explored other parts of the gardens and found several places that appeared to be regular homeless camping areas.

As my crew was closing our excavations, we happened to hear a radio interview with a homeless woman and her daughter in San Francisco who had just found room in a shelter. When the interviewer asked the daughter how she liked it, she said something like, "It's okay, but I miss all my stuff." That was an

Figure 21.1. Left: the partly collapsed roof of the mushroom cave built into a garden wall of the Hill estate gardens in St. Paul became a convenient shelter for homeless people to sleep; almost every morning there would be blankets, food and drink remnants, and a duffle or garbage bag in which a homeless person kept personal items. Right: there were makeshift shelters in many brush or tree clusters on the Hill estate gardens such as this one in a depression where a tree had been uprooted; the two smaller poles would be covered with a large plastic tarp to create a shelter; the box contained food and cooking supplies; clothing was scattered in many places in and around the shelter.

epiphany for me, like a face-slapping Homer Simpson "D'oh!" moment that made me realize how stupid I had been: *Homeless people have stuff!* From that moment, what had seemed like junk took on much sharper patterning. I made a few notes and took a few photographs of the homeless materials and camping areas, but the garden wall project had priority. I remember thinking about the ironies of capitalism that homeless people had found places to live on the property of the Empire Builder, given over to a Catholic Archdiocese, and finally, a state historical society, something I discussed in the final paragraphs of the project report.[2]

Two months later I gave a talk about the Hill House garden project to board members of the Minnesota Historical Society. I dutifully went through my PowerPoint slides on the historical archaeology but had only a slightly interested audience. At the end I threw in photographs and observations about the current use of the gardens as a different kind of home and raised the possible use of archaeological methods to study homeless campsites. I included a bit of follow-up research on the homeless materials, especially where all the discarded clothing in the gardens came from. As it turned out, the Dorothy Day Center, a church-supported homeless day shelter was only a few blocks away. Homeless people could get clothing and supplies without having to put up with many of the residential homeless shelter rules that many homeless people do not like. A short walk would take them to secluded areas in the Hill House gardens. My audience seemed to perk up, and when I asked for questions, they went on for half an hour. Every question was about the homeless research, none about the Hill gardens, and several people felt compelled to tell me about nearby homeless campsites that they had encountered. Their interest was not lost on me: they had never thought of archaeology being used this way and were intrigued, a pattern that still goes on whenever I give a public talk about homelessness.

AN 'ARCHAEOLOGY OF FIVE MINUTES AGO' IN INDY

In 2004, I returned to academia at the Indiana University–Purdue University Indianapolis, on the western edge of city center. The Anthropology Department of that institution is oriented toward applied urban anthropology and expressed interest in a starting a homelessness research program. The St. Paul project had been entirely exploratory, so beginning formal fieldwork in Indy (a nickname for Indianapolis) took about two years. I discussed my research in classes, and with a few interested students, sought scholarly descriptions of homeless life in camps, which we quickly discovered were rare. Most fieldwork has been done in homeless shelters, with limited anecdotal descriptions of people living rough, which made a degree of sense because many scholars are associated with and funded by the homelessness 'industry,' the government, social welfare, and non-profit agencies interested in causes of homelessness, social institutions related to it, and plans to end or reduce the number of homeless people. Much of the information they use is survey and interview data acquired by talking with homeless shelter occupants and managers. Homeless shelters are mostly safe, easily accessible data collection points. My search for any detail about the stuff homeless people used in campsites came up nearly empty, with only photographs and sidebar descriptions in a few ethnographies or journalistic feature stories. However, a few videos—such as *Dark Days*, Marc Singer's classic documentary on homeless people living in unused tunnels in New York City—showed a rich material culture of cleverly repurposed, scavenged items. Made in 2000, just before the St. Paul project, *Dark Days* inspired a search for other images and videos. Since YouTube went live in 2005 more than 100,000 videos of homeless camps have appeared, eventually becoming an important source of material culture information.

Jessica Welch, a student who lived homeless in California for a time, asked about doing fieldwork in Indy. She made several insightful observations about California camps and knew of several camps just east of downtown Indy, about a mile from the Indiana University–Purdue University Indianapolis.

For her senior project, we developed a research design to survey within a ten-by-ten city block area. This cultural landscape of mixed small businesses, inner-city homes, and mostly neglected industrial sites is bisected by the north–south conjoined sections of Interstate Highways 65 and 70, as well as east–west railroad lines passing just south of downtown. Rail and city street over- and underpasses allow easy crossing of Interstate 65/70 to the city center and the shelters. The survey area was home to Wheeler Mission, a full-facility homeless shelter for men; Horizon House, a day-shelter for homeless people; a fast-food restaurant (Hardee's); and a 24-hour convenience store for highway travelers and locals. This proved to be an ideal landscape for living rough, with ready pedestrian access to downtown resources for food and panhandling, but also to a few welfare services and the large city and university libraries. The shelters provided showers and other hygiene facilities as well as food, mailboxes, and some clothing. Hardee's allowed some use of their restrooms and were a source of cheap food, but especially coffee accessible from early morning into the late evening from their service counter and drive-through window, with discarded Hardee's branded Styrofoam cups found almost everywhere we surveyed. The convenience store provided twenty-four-hour access to some foods, but especially inexpensive shorts: single cans of beer and small wine bottles. Most important were the many relatively private and secure places to sleep roofless or to create somewhat longer-term shelters. This is a vastly complex cultural landscape, which most homed people see as desolate and dreary, but with richness we barely realized until a student mapped access from one of the main campsites to key resources by following worn pathways and interviewing and accompanying occupants.

Over a two-year period, we categorized sixty-one sites within this landscape into three types.[3] Five were route sites, places where people had stopped for short periods of time, with no evidence of sleeping or camping, but with graffiti, remnants of fast or snack food, a few pieces of outerwear clothing, and human waste, often with an intense smell of urine. These were out-of-sight locations in alleys or near dumpsters and

We also located sixteen campsites, which showed intensive, longer-term use (Figure 21.2). Some had distinct areas for shelter and sleeping, with separate areas for food preparation and consumption. Prepared areas for cooking fires and for warmth were common. Five-gallon plastic buckets with bag liners and lids sometimes served as toilets, whereas another camp had a poop wall, a remnant concrete foundation that provided privacy. Durable shelters, such as tents or makeshift buildings, cardboard for sleeping on or under, and mattresses, pillows and blankets were visible.

Caches—suitcases, plastic garbage bags, shopping carts, and even coolers providing temporary storage for food, sleeping and camping gear, and personal items—were often hidden from view. Stuff was abundant and occasionally appeared reasonably well-organized.

STUFF WE FOUND, STUFF WE DID NOT FIND, AND WHAT THAT SHOWED US

The Indy sites led to simple notions of how archaeology might be useful. The abundant smaller trash that we found mirrored contemporary American life: remnants and packaging of fast and junk food, cooking and eating utensils, reading materials, pornography, clothing, and personal hygiene products from tampons to toothpaste. You name it, and it was there. At the same time, some small things did not readily make sense. For example, we found used toothbrushes, empty sample toothpaste tubes, single-use mouthwash bottles, and used personal deodorant containers in or near most short-term sites and campsites, but we also found many full, hotel-sized and branded shampoo and conditioner bottles, just thrown away. People choose to stay clean when they can, but why throw away shampoo, and where did the bottles come from? The explanation about why they were not used was simple, but not how they got there. Brushing teeth requires only small amounts of water, but hair washing takes much more. Water carried into camps weighs about 1 kg (2 pounds) per liter (2 pints), so carrying much to a camp can be burdensome.

Figure 21.2. This camp under the Davidson Street bridge in Indianapolis was a primary study location. The camp looks comfortable, with several tents for some occupants, while others slept in the open as with the person sleeping under the blanket on the mattress on the right by the bridge beams. A blanket over the beam could be pulled down for privacy. Bridge beams were used for storage. Cooking could be done on fires in the bright, open area at the left. The most recent camp here was home to seventy people, but the city evicted residents for the third time in 2015.

close to unoccupied buildings, but always near streets or along railroads. There was usually a continuous spread of litter, which made route sites difficult to delineate.

We located forty short-term sites only used for a night or two, with evidence of sleeping and food usage, but not cooking. Any shelters were simple but provided some weather protection or privacy. Most were made of plastic sheeting or cardboard, sometimes even clusters of tall weeds tied into tent-like structures at the top and cleared out underneath. One was under three side-by-side, permanently parked, rusting semi-trailers.

You can sign up for a weekly shower in one of the shelters, where ample shampoo is provided, rendering shampoo and conditioner useless in the camps. So where did the bottles come from? We asked people in the camps, who told us that people from the churches brought them. The church people that we talked with told us that they collected hotel bathroom personal care amenities from places where they stayed, then brought them to church so that outreach teams could distribute them in homeless camps.

Caring, churchgoing and homed people worry about homelessness, but first think about what they would need if they were homeless and rarely about the limitations of living in an actual homeless cultural landscape. Similarly, we found food cans that, if opened at all, had been bashed open with rocks, pried open with knives, or exploded in fires. Homed people are generous and provide tinned food, but what do they not bring? Can-openers. Including a P-38 can opener—a few cents each from military surplus stores—with a batch of cans could solve this problem. Better still, provide pull-tab food cans, which we found occasionally. People also donate prepared food, which is very generous, but when a woman brought a large, disposable pan of lasagna to a camp where our team was mapping, she did not realize that residents had no plates nor serving and eating utensils. Thankfully, a team member had camping gear in her car, so everyone ate. During the gardening season, people bring their excess raw vegetables. Tomatoes and carrots can be eaten with little preparation, but not large zucchini or turnips, which must be cooked. Such offerings are gratefully accepted, but the unusable produce goes into a trash heap on the edge of camp, attracting mice, rats, and insects.

WHAT STUFF DO HOMELESS PEOPLE NEED? JUST ASK THEM!

The simplest lesson that we learned was not to make assumptions about what people need. Once people got comfortable with having us around, we just asked what they needed or wanted. As the trash heaps grew in one camp, the most requested item was rat poison, but some less-common items surprised us. At the Davidson Street bridge camp, Chris asked for some AA batteries to operate his police radio scanner to see if cops were in the area. Women wanted tampons, so a student provided a large box of them. Patrick told me he wanted a baseball cap. He liked a cheap one in the nearby Salvation Army Center, so I gave him $10; he came back wearing the cap, gave me the change, and thanked me. We were curious, though, about what items consistently appeared in camps, so a student on our team who lived in his van for a year watched more than a hundred videos of homeless camps and carefully tagged and counted the items he saw. He then used a word cloud to visually represent the intensity of use of each item that he had observed. The variety of items was surprising, but as expected, essential shelter, sleep, food, and safety dominated. Another student looked at blogs written by homeless people. That homeless people write blogs seems surprising, but some have laptops while others use computers in public libraries—in Indy, some even use them for homeless activism.[4] One blog—with the title "The Survival Guide to Homelessness: The Interactive List of the Best"—was especially instructive as it listed top, brand-quality items to outfit your camp. The list is not what we expected but it explained some things. Comments by other homeless people about the list are endlessly fascinating. One explained why we found numerous pairs of shoes without laces. Shoelaces are commonly needed, as the blogger explains, but people do not provide shoes with laces because they think that the recipients will hang themselves or strangle someone else with the laces. He advised providing two pairs with each pair of shoes because they break easily, but also are useful for lots of other applications.

ANECDOTAL NEGATIVE NARRATIVES CAN BE OVERCOME WITH DATA

Shoelaces are one example of hundreds related to the powerful negative narratives—anecdotally developed stories, really—that Americans believe about homeless people. Such narratives can be easily challenged by our work.[5] The Institutional Research Board of the Indiana University–Purdue University Indianapolis—a federally mandated body to oversee research proposals to protect human subjects from harm, in our case homeless people—had its own negative narrative issues. For example, we wanted to provide cheap (<$10) disposable cameras for people to take pictures of where they went in a day. The board told us that giving a few individuals cameras "would make them targets for theft." I responded that most people in the Davidson Street bridge camp had better smartphones with cameras than I did. I wanted to offer $5 and $10 gift cards for Hardee's to homeless folks who were especially helpful. The board demanded a detailed plan of how much time spent with us would be required to earn each card, and then decided it was a bad idea altogether because "it would cause fights in the camp." Such narratives were actually linked stereotypes: that homeless people never have much of value and that they would steal or fight over anything, even low-value stuff. A few homeless people have money from regular jobs, but most usually at least have some, although not a lot and not very regularly. So many stereotypes are related to material culture, but many more judge personal qualities: being responsible for their own situations; being uneducated or stupid; being addicted or mentally ill; being unpleasant to be around; nobody likes being homelessness; the list goes on. As with most stereotypes, there is everything from a grain of truth to a truckload, but none are universal.

My favorite is that no one likes to be homeless. When I gave a lecture to more than eighty homeless people at the Carnegie Day Centre, a day shelter in Vancouver, one man challenged me immediately, telling me to stop using the word 'homeless.' "I am home-free," he said, contending that while I probably had a mortgage to pay or a lawn to mow, all he needed was food and a safe place to sleep. I admitted there was some wisdom in that. About 18 percent of roofless people are chronically home-free by choice.

IS THIS REALLY ARCHAEOLOGY OR SOMETHING ELSE?

Briefs snippets about homeless camp life provide only a glimpse of what goes into an archaeological study of homelessness.[6] Archaeology demands systematic rather than anecdotal approaches, like journalistic features that appeal to emotion more than objectivity. Archaeologists usually collect and classify material culture, but in contemporary campsites we chose not to disturb anything, not knowing what was still in use or whether an item might be reused or adapted by someone. The huge number of campsite objects defy reasonable collection and curation. From the surface survey in St. Paul and within our Indy survey area, we could have collected several thousand items of discarded clothing and bedding with conditions ranging from rotten and filthy to barely used (Figure 21.3).

Curation of artifacts for future study depends on available space, difficulty of caring for materials for extended periods, and funding to pay for it. Archaeologists often struggle with such problems, guessing what materials and what quantity might answer eventual questions, such as how many empty shampoo bottles or food cans you might need? In St. Paul, we retained only the excavated materials, but in Indy, we collected nothing because we had only a tiny laboratory and no curatorial space. Because we did not excavate, documentation of stuff had to be entirely photographic. Typical analyses of many contemporary materials offer other challenges.

The first mass-produced plastics appeared in the early 1900s and now seem ubiquitous, used for nearly everything. Quantities are enormous; decomposition over time is minimal. Courtney Singleton, an undergraduate student at the Indiana University–Purdue University Indianapolis and integrally involved in the Indy project, excavated a homeless campsite in Pelham Bay Park in the northeast corner of New York City for her PhD

Figure 21.3. This short-term site in Indianapolis has been used many times, with enough room for only one person. There is so much stuff that collection and even full documentation would be difficult without several photographs. Notice cigarette packages, a book, gloves, a newspaper, a sealed plastic bowl with food and a spoon, a single shoe with laces tied, a plastic tarp for sleeping on or under, and much more. Concrete wall remnants on two sides provide some privacy.

research at Columbia University.[7] Her struggles to collect and analyze plastics have been instructive due to both quantities and identifying types of plastic and functions. One of her questions to me says it all: "How do I deal with 100,000 fragments of Styrofoam?" My answer was not to. Just say there were lots of fragments of Styrofoam and speculate why. Trying to analyze types of plastic from broken fragments, Courtney determined that there were no good tools short of expensive chemical analysis. Determining function, especially from small parts, was equally difficult, but she crowd-sourced images on social media and got many useful responses. For archaeologists, how we analyze and keep artifacts is determined by our research questions, facilities, available techniques, funding, and in many instances, ingenuity, and in a few, a dumpster outside our laboratories.

Our St. Paul and Indy photographic documentation was substantial. Digital cameras make taking multiple exposures easy, quality image manipulation tools are abundant, and mass data storage is mostly safe and cheap. Capturing many photographs demands quality metadata, which takes time, careful tagging of images, and a willingness to dispose of unneeded exposures. The same applies to all the videos and blog entries that my team downloaded from the internet. As with artifacts, archaeologists must consider what information is in the medium and why we need it. Making maps also depends heavily on project research questions. We mapped sites in many ways, from formal total station maps for some piece-plotting—mapping locations of individual items—in the Davidson Street bridge camps to simple sketch maps. Google Earth and aerial photos provided good bases for plotting camp locations and routes from camps to resources or to other camps.

A huge problem for studying contemporary homeless camps is that the cultural landscape can change in a matter of days and in occupied campsites, in moments. One camp hidden in a brushy area along a railroad was a rich source of information. Pathways between it and several short-term camps were even visible on aerial photos. A week after a visit, all the brush and camps were entirely gone, removed by the railroad company. Still, new sites popped up regularly and were recorded. Historical records indicate homeless use of the Davidson Street bridge area for decades. During the five years of our study, precise camp locations within the area varied as did the number of occupants, with a maximum of seventy. During that time, the residents were evicted three times. Every day, a few occupants arrived and departed or changed their location within the camps. Activity areas for specific tasks like communal cooking changed place and size. Stuff people brought into camp varied; even the ways and places they disposed of garbage could change but were more stable than other activity locations. We even experimented with documenting microchanges in camp. Occupants who smoked cigarettes in bed usually flipped the butts away from sleeping areas. Knowing preferred brands, in the morning we mapped the butts into 10-centimeter (4 inch) units on a meter-square (3-foot-square) grid, which entertained the residents mightily. We frequently captured panoramic photographs and videos to log changes. In hindsight, I wish we had taken audio soundscapes over one or more twenty-four-hour periods for even more sensory data. Everything described above is done with normal archaeological methods, except the soundscapes.

Some might think that watching the lives of people and talking with them is unusual, but it is a standard contemporary archaeology method called ethnoarchaeology. Being members of the culture that produced people in the camps, we were familiar with most things people used, but what they meant to them might be completely different. We found a man's discarded Father's Day card with a poignant note from his children near one camp. Can we begin to understand its emotional content or why he threw it away? In another place we found a mattress with sheets, a bedspread, pillows, a small rug, and cached items (Figure 21.4). We understand the need for a place to sleep, but this was impractical except for wanting someplace at least temporarily resembling a remembered home. Because we are members of the same culture, we do not need complex social theories to understand most of what is going on, even many of the meanings. Mostly what we understand comes from our deep, shared recognition of the patterns we observe from the material culture and places we share with homeless people, something I call 'gut theory,' which is still theory, but in its simplest form. Interpretations are immediate and easy to translate. There are dangers to this approach, of course, such as the 'fallacy of the familiar.' Just because something seems familiar does not mean it is always

the same—especially in meaning—as what we know from our own experiences. We have learned to be cautious because we have observed substantial ethnic variation in homeless sites and have found seemingly familiar items combined to make tools we do not understand.

BIG DEAL! WHAT DO WE DO WITH THIS INFORMATION?

Why the public seemed so interested in our research puzzled me for a while. I have decided it is because many of us have commonly shared understandings of what 'home' means and we all can imagine ourselves being homeless. The Newsroom of the Indiana University–Purdue University Indianapolis issued a press release on our project, which brought a flurry of reprints in media as distant as Chile and Nigeria. *Archaeology* magazine eventually published a story on the project,[8] which brought even more attention and several interviews. Using homelessness as its core, Elizabeth Kryder-Reid (2019) and I taught a seminar in 2011 with the title "Issues in Cultural Heritage," for students from several disciplines. Emphasizing heritage activism, the class had several projects, including an on-campus exhibition of a few materials like those found in Indy homeless campsites. A photographic exhibition, *What Does Homelessness Look Like?,* in the Indianapolis Central Public Library, opened ahead of a forum that drew about two hundred people to talks by Jessica Welch and Courtney Singleton on the Indy project, and British archaeologist Rachael Kiddey (2017), who described her intriguing research on homelessness in York and Bristol. We booked several taxis to take a dozen occupants of the Davidson Street bridge camp to the exhibit and forum, followed by dinner with our students and speakers. That dinner was delightful and went a long way with our students and restaurant staff toward challenging the narrative that homeless people are unpleasant to be around. Later, students produced a small print-on-demand book, *Urban Heritage? Archaeology and Homelessness in Indianapolis*, to document our activities.[9] A few weeks after that, several students helped arrange

Figure 21.4. This campsite in the Davidson Street bridge area, entirely in the open, had a mattress, sheets, bedspread, and pillows, with a rug at its foot. Behind are cardboard pieces to reduce the lights from the traffic on Interstate 65/70. Small personal items and food line the fence. Under the sheet and plastic tarp around the tree is a cache of personal items protected from both weather and sight. Not visible, but in a bush near where the picture was taken was a stuffed toy cat with multiple colors, which could be easily seen by someone on the bed. Such efforts to make places seem 'homey' were not uncommon in our survey areas.

for homeless people to participate in a forum organized by Indiana Public Radio and the American Civil Liberties Union about plans to keep homeless people away from Lucas Oil Stadium and fans during the 2012 Super Bowl XLVI week. The purpose of the class was to translate homelessness archaeology research for the public in ways that challenged negative narratives and to advocate usable recommendations that might help marginalized people living rough.[10]

Archaeologists have been advocating greater public engagement and application of our discipline to understand contemporary social issues for at least seventy years.[11] The focus of the discipline, however, has been on protecting and interpreting heritage sites. While important, doing so has helped create a heritage industry. Only within the past few decades have archaeologists recognized a darker heritage, in which people who have been marginalized or have suffered have been ignored or selectively edited out of narratives to make nations or communities seem more palatable, as Indy and other communities keep trying to do with homelessness. Archaeology can help define a homelessness heritage by challenging negative narratives, can make useful recommendations to assist homeless people living rough, and can do more to 'earn its keep!'

NOTES

1   http://www.mnhs.org/hillhouse/learn (accessed 29 February 2020).

2   Zimmerman 2004.

3   Zimmerman and Welch 2011.

4   Karim 2014.

5   Zimmerman 2013.

6   Zimmerman 2015, 2016, Kiddey 2017.

7   Singleton 2021.

8   Albertson 2009.

9   Zimmerman and Kryder-Reid 2011.

10   Zimmerman et al. 2010.

11   Little and Zimmerman 2010.

BIBLIOGRAPHY

Albertson, Nicole (2009), Archaeology of the Homeless, *Archaeology* 62(6), 42–43.

Karim (2014), "Leaving the Bridge, Passing the Shelters: Understanding Homeless Activism through the Utilization of Spaces within the Central Public Library and the IUPUI Library in Indianapolis," Masters thesis in Anthropology, Indiana University, https://scholarworks.iupui.edu/handle/1805/5928.

Kiddey, Rachael (2017), *Homeless Heritage: Collaborative Social Archaeology as Therapeutic Practice*, Oxford (Oxford University Press).

Kryder-Reid, Elizabeth (2019), "Do the Homeless Have Heritage? Archaeology and the Pedagogy of Discomfort," in: Susan J. Bender and Phyllis Mauch Messenger, eds., *Pedagogy and Practice in Heritage Studies*, pp. 129–47, Gainesville (University Press of Florida).

Little, Barbara and Larry J. Zimmerman (2010), "In the Public Interest: Creating a More Activist, Civically-Engaged Archaeology," in: Wendy Ashmore, Dorothy Lippert, and Barbara Mills, eds., *Voices in American Archaeology*, pp. 131–59, Washington, DC (Society for American Archaeology Press).

Singleton, Courtney (2021), "Vague Dwelling: An Archaeology of The Pelham Bay Park Homeless Encampment," dissertation in Anthropology, Columbia University, https://academiccommons.columbia.edu/doi/10.7916/d8-x97c-6d63/download.

Zimmerman, Larry J. (2004), Archaeological Evaluation of the Hillside Gardens Areas at the James J. Hill House (21RA21), St. Paul, Minnesota, *Minnesota Archaeologist* 63, 118–36.

—— (2013), "Homelessness," in: Paul Graves-Brown, Rodney Harrison, and Angela Piccini, eds., *The Oxford Handbook of the Archaeology of the Contemporary World*. pp. 336–50, Oxford (Oxford University Press).

—— (2015), *Displaced and Barely Visible: Using Archaeology to Understand Homelessness,* https://www.academia.edu/41967923/Power_Point_Homelessness_and_archaeology (accessed February 29, 2020).

—— (2016), "Homeless, Home-Making, and Archaeology: 'To Be at Home Wherever I Find Myself,'" in Mikkel Bille and Tim Flor Sørensen, eds., *Assembling Architecture: Archaeology, Affect and the Performance of Building Spaces,* pp. 256–72, London (Routledge).

Zimmerman, Larry J. and Elizabeth Kryder-Reid, eds. (2011), *Urban Heritage? Archaeology and Homelessness in Indianapolis*, Cupertino (Bookemon), https://www.academia.edu/4145697/Urban_Heritage_Archaeology_and_Homelessness_in_Indianapolis

Zimmerman, Larry J., Courtney Singleton, and Jessica Welch (2010), Activism and creating a Translational Archaeology of Homelessness, *World Archaeology* 42(3), 443–54.

Zimmerman, Larry J. and Jessica Welch (2011), Displaced and Barely Visible: Archaeology and the Material Culture of Homelessness, *Historical Archaeology* 45(1), 67–85.

20

FORGOTTEN PRODUCTS OF LABOR

A RITUAL OF MANY LIVES

RUTH TRINGHAM AND ANNIE DANIS

This story starts with evictions. The first is the eviction of archaeological materials, once honored as valuable informants of the past, from the Archaeological Research Facility of the University of California, Berkeley. The second is the eviction of people living on a former landfill known as the Albany Bulb, just a few miles to the north.

In 1987 Ruth Tringham and a team of archaeologists transported Neolithic house rubble from Serbia to the University of California, Berkeley campus for analysis and storage. By 2018 the Archaeological Research Facility no longer wanted the rubble, which took up space in its extremely small storage area. The Albany Bulb is the resting place of similarly unwanted materials, discarded construction debris from its surrounding neighborhoods. This debris sheltered many Bay Area residents who, while experiencing what is commonly called homelessness, built homes out of it, until they were evicted in 2014. The Neolithic house rubble ultimately came to

rest on this strange peninsula jutting into the eastern edge of the San Francisco Bay through our recognition of meaningful parallels. None of these events overlapped in time, but their traces are now marvelously intertwined. This chapter outlines how that archaeological construction material came to end its life in the Albany Bulb and how we attempted to extend its value through connection with the history of homes there.

RUBBLE: OPOVO (RUTH)

The Neolithic house rubble (in Serbian *kućni lep*) that we used for this performance had gone through many transformations. It began life as the unfired clay skin of a house six to seven thousand years ago (4500–5000 BCE, Figure 20.1). The house was built in the wattle-and-daub construction technique in what is now called Opovo in modern Serbia. This is the

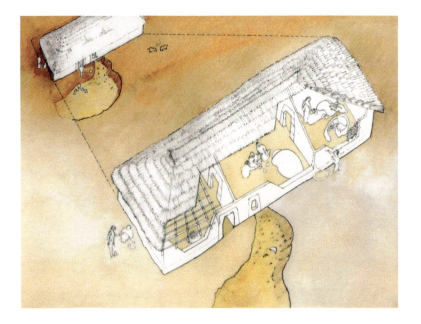

Figure 20.1. Cutaway architectural reconstruction of a late Neolithic house in southeastern Europe (based on the Vinca culture house excavated at Divostin, Serbia). *Tinted drawing by Catherine Chang.*

Figure 20.2. Close-up of burned clay rubble mass from House 2 at Opovo, Serbia, 1984.

technique described for some of the houses in Annelou van Gijn's Chapter 29 in this volume. Sometime later, the house was then burned by its Neolithic residents. This was not an unusual event; on the contrary, this was the norm for a thousand years or more in that period in the area of southeastern Europe.[1] The houses were burned deliberately and as single events, maybe as a ritual fiery end to the house, marking the ritual closure and protection for its former residents. The house walls and roof collapsed inward and fell on its contents; its wooden structure burned away but remained visible, ghost-like, as impressions in the clay. All that survived was the clay daub transformed into a red-orange ceramic-like mass (Figure 20.2), indestructible, forever visible, through which the house could be remembered.[2]

As the millennia passed, the value of the burned rubble as a memorial faded; modern farmers came to hate it, because it prevented their plants from growing properly. They dug it up and used it for filling potholes and ruts in the country roads. Archaeologists traditionally found the burned rubble useful as

marking the location of a Neolithic house. But they did not value it as a source of information on the house itself; they excavated it quickly and carelessly to get to the artifact-laden floors below. They did not keep the rubble, but dumped it back into the holes they had made.

Between 1983 and 1989, however, Ruth Tringham's team of archaeologists at Opovo valued the rubble very highly as a source of information on how and why the Neolithic residents burned their houses (Figure 20.3). They excavated, labeled, mapped, and analyzed every piece to be able to construct a fire map similar to an arson investigation (Figure 20.4).[3] To complete this research, Ruth brought back samples to the Archaeological Research Facility at the University of California, Berkeley (Figure 20.5).

The Serbian archaeologists were happy for her to do this, as for them the rubble had no value. But Ruth and her team treasured it, and further analyzed these pieces. Our research showed for the first time that the temperatures at which

Figure 20.3. Earlier life of the burned clay rubble. Excavation of the burned clay remains of House 1 in Opovo-UgarBajbuk, Serbia, 1984.

Figure 20.5. Ruth Tringham (on the right) and Annie Danis examine the rubble samples stored at the Archaeological Research Facility, University of California, Berkeley. *Photograph by Susan Moffat, 2019.*

Figure 20.4. Mirjana Stevanovic examining rubble fragments at Opovo for her PhD dissertation research, 1987.

clay-daubed houses at Opovo burned were so high (in many cases up to 1000ºC [1800°F], enough to vitrify the clay) that the house-fires must have been started, fueled, and maintained intentionally. This was confirmed by the fire-maps that Mirjana Stevanovic was able to produce from the analyzed samples.[4] The Opovo house fires were set in order to end the life of the houses, but in doing so they created a permanent memorial of the houses and their location on the landscape (usually just below the modern surface). The house fires did not produce garbage in the eyes of the residents, but objects of great value and meaning. The pile of rubble created by a funeral pyre for the house became as permanent a marker of ancestry and continuity as any grave marker.

PROVOCATION: EVICTION

Thirty years after their arrival in the United States, the rubble samples were evicted from their home in the Archaeological Research Facility, as part of the remodeling of the room where they had been stored (Figure 20.5). Those who had loved them had retired or gone back to Serbia. They were once again devalued as garbage and without a home. But building material is resilient and refuses to be forgotten.

Ruth was whining to Annie over coffee about what to do with the evicted rubble, now exclusively her responsibility. She had thought maybe to use it in her garden, or (as they do in Serbia) use it to fill in potholes in San Francisco. But Annie made an interesting connection: bricks at the Albany Bulb shared a use-history with the Opovo rubble, and art-making common at the Albany Bulb could inspire a more creative solution: a ritual performance to create an art work. There were many ways the Opovo rubble resonated with the Albany Bulb, including the dumping of unwanted materials, the creative afterlives of garbage, and the idea of home.

Figure 20.6. Boxer Bob shows off his "mansion" with million-dollar views of the Golden Gate Bridge (top). Amber poses inside her bedroom (bottom). *Photographs by Robin Lasser.*

RUBBLE: ALBANY BULB (ANNIE)

The Albany Bulb was formed by approximately 1.5 million cubic meters (2 million cubic yards) of construction debris dumped into the San Francisco Bay between 1963 and 1983 and is so called because of the dramatic neck and bulb layout. When the dump was decommissioned, it became a site of creative resistance to growing forces of displacement in California. People quickly discovered the joy of the views and the richness of the bedrock of the Albany Bulb, a diverse substrate of past homes and buildings: rebar, brick, concrete and stone. Dog-walkers,

Figure 20.7. Stockton and Richmond bricks identified by the Archaeology of the Albany Bulb project directed by Annie Danis. *Photograph by Annie Danis.*

lovers, artists, ravers, and trippers found themselves amid a landscape of familiar materials out of place.

Eventually some of these people built homes and public spaces, alongside a constantly evolving artistic landscape of painting, graffiti, found object sculpture, humor, politics, and mysticism. Over nearly thirty years of occupation hundreds of people camped and lived for days, weeks, months, and years at a time (Figure 20.6). But in 2014, the City of Albany evicted these residents to make way for park improvements that would minimize the visible traces of the landfill and erase the history of its long-term residents.[5]

Many of the bricks that are part of the landscape of the Albany Bulb were made by the Stockton and Richmond brick companies in the early twentieth century, as evidenced by their makers' marks. These bricks and their marks link the Albany Bulb of today to the industrializing landscape of the San Francisco Bay shoreline over the last hundred years (Figure 20.7).[6]

The bricks got a second life in the hands of Pat, who lived with his partner Carrie on the Albany Bulb until his death

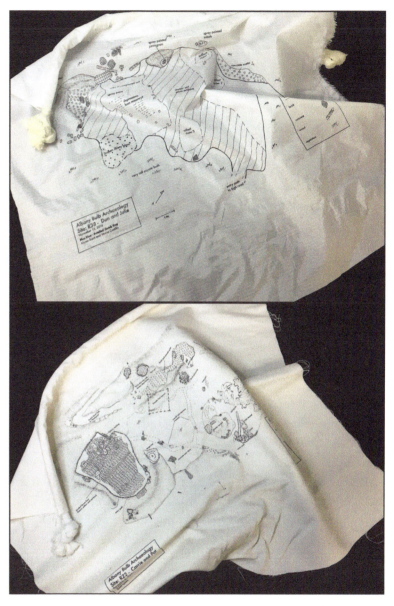

Figure 20.8. Site map of Pat and Carrie's place, screen printed on canvas by Annie Danis and collaborators for the Refuge in Refuse exhibition at the SOMArts Gallery in San Francisco, 2015.

(Figure 20.8), just before the evictions in 2014. Pat built a twenty-first-century floor out of the ubiquitous yellow and red twentieth-century bricks in the dump (Figure 20.9). According

Figure 20.9. Pat's brick floor (2013), photograph taken in 2019. *Photograph by Annie Danis.*

Figure 20.10. Mapping the route of the Forgotten Products of Labor ritual of redeposition at the Albany Bulb, California. *Satellite image by Open Street Maps, markup by the authors.*

to Amber Whitson, another former resident, the floor was one of Pat's last projects, and you can feel the labor of love just by looking at how each brick was perfectly aligned head to foot, resulting in a masterfully level platform that has by now weathered after being exposed for more than six years. Across from the brick floor an open space protected by the canopy of a large coniferous tree extended Pat and Carrie's home and was surrounded by brick-lined beds of decorative plants and trinkets. After he passed away in October 2013, a group of friends constructed a memorial message, fittingly out of bricks, in an area known as the "brick yard" just above Pat and Carrie's place, that reads, "We ♥ you Pat."

CONCEPT

From the parallel stories of the rubble from Opovo and the bricks at the Albany Bulb, we developed a performance that would join the two timelines and the two cultures (Figure 20.10). In so doing

we wanted to explore the issue of value: the value invested in the Opovo rubble by its makers and the archaeologists, which was taken away by time and limited space; the value invested in bricks by their original producers and by Pat's loving reuse, which was taken away by the acts of dumping and eviction.

Art-making at the Albany Bulb has been an informal but vibrant practice since it became a public place in the 1980s. In response to its present-day development as a groomed city park, community members have formed an organization to structure and encourage art and stewardship called Love the Bulb.[7] We developed a performance that would produce a reflection on the life histories of the Opovo rubble and Albany Bulb bricks through a series of site visits to the Archaeological Research Facility and the Albany Bulb in collaboration with Susan Moffit of Love the Bulb. The performance developed as a direct response to the materials themselves, to the home sites at the Albany Bulb, and to a dialogic process between Annie and Ruth as archaeologists and Susan as an invested steward of the Albany Bulb. We proposed the following performance

Figure 20.11. At the beginning of the Forgotten Products of Labor ritual on 2 September 2019, the group gathers at the the Cove, a tiny hidden amphitheatre-like space at the entrance to the neck of the Albany Bulb. *Photograph by Ward Long.*

Figure 20.12. Annie Danis and Ruth Tringham leading the Forgotten Products of Labor procession on 2 September 2019. *Photograph by Ward Long.*

as part of their annual BulbFest program, but ultimately presented it as a standalone event with an audience of former residents, Albany community members, artists, and archaeologists in September 2019.

THE PERFORMANCE

On a bright, windy day our audience assembles at "the Cove," a tiny hidden amphitheatric space at the beginning of the neck of the Albany Bulb (Figure 20.11). Ruth and Annie greet them with an introduction to the Opovo rubble and the ritual performance of depositing it at the Albany Bulb. The audience thus become participants (another example of this is discussed by Danielle Kurin et al. in Chapter 26 in this volume).[8] They are seated around a 90-kilogram (200-pound) pile of burned daub fragments and are invited to pick up several pieces from the pile and place them in two wheelbarrows outside the narrow

entrance to the amphitheater. Meanwhile, the first two people to emerge from the Cove are given jars and led by Annie to the beach to fill them with water; they must carry them for the duration of the procession. Ruth and Annie each take up the handles of a wheelbarrow and invite everyone to join in the procession that starts along the "upper road" of the causeway to the Bulb (Figure 20.12). Annie and Ruth push the wheelbarrows, leading the way, with the audience massed behind them and eventually around them. As they walk, Ruth and Annie chant questions in heterophony, encouraging the participants to join in the responses (although most are too shy to do so).

Why did we bring this to this place?
This place is full of industrial leftover
Nobody loves this place
This place is a dump
This place is home
This place is Ohlone land

Is this garbage, is this rubbish?
This is something valuable
This has a long history
This burned in a very hot fire
This is not rubble
This will last for years and years and years
This will grind down into dust
This sounds like a ringing
Walking on this is like walking on rubble
There are so many colors in my wheelbarrow
This smells like...
This is...

Do we despise this, do we value this?
We think...
We think this has no place in a museum
We think this place is perfect for this rubble
We think people should live here
We think this rubble should have a place to live
We think this might be the spot
We think this is the best
We think this is data

Who are we that bring this here?
We are archaeologists
We are dancers
We are residents of the Bulb
We are the women who burned the house
We are . . . .

Reaching our destination at the site of Pat and Carrie's former house, we rest in the shelter of its large tree (Figure 20.13). Annie points out the early twentieth-century brick that Pat used to create his beautiful house floor, and she traces it backward in time to follow the story of the brick from discard to its use in Albany homes, to its manufacturer in early 1900s factories, to its source in local clay.

The procession moves on to the hill behind Pat and Carrie's former home, "the Brickyard," where the memorial message

Figure 20.13. At the end of the Forgotten Products of Labor event, everyone gathers around Pat and Carrie's tree to watch the sunset and have a conversation. *Photograph by Ward Long.*

to Pat once stood. Annie and Ruth instruct the participants to take a piece of clay daub out of the wheelbarrows and ritually deposit the rubble, intermingling it amongst the modern bricks (Figure 20.14). As they lay them down, each participant dedicates the piece of rubble, naming a person, a thing, or a place to be memorialized. They repeat the process until all the rubble has been deposited. Then Annie and Ruth mix a mortar of Bay water and rubble dust from the bottom of the wheelbarrows. They smear it by hand onto the deposited rubble. Finally, Ruth closes the ritual performance with the words: "And now we have brought some closure to these bricks. Two different cultures have been brought together today through the prehistoric rubble and the historic bricks, and through the names that we have linked to them. Through this ritual we have created a little community and made this a very special place. These materials can never be transformed into any other form or substance. Here they have found a home. They will last for a very long time and with them, our memories."

Figure 20.14. The final Forgotten Products of Labor ritual of redepositing the Neolithic daub rubble among the debris of early-twentieth-century bricks of the Albany Bulb. *Photographs by Ward Long.*

REFLECTION: VALUE, FORGETTING, AND THE CONCEPT OF GARBAGE

History shows that what could be thought of as garbage at one time could, at another time, be revered as a source of wonder and memory. So it is with this place, the Albany Bulb. So it is, too, with the rubble from Opovo.

This performance is fundamentally about the resilience of materials to transform their value and their ability to hold memories. It illuminates an easily overlooked material at the Albany Bulb—bricks—and calls into question their value by contrasting them with the archaeological rubble from Serbia. The performance mobilizes the echoes of human residence of the Albany Bulb to show parallel histories of home and building across time and space that now are part of uniquely contemporary struggles about the category of material called garbage or rubbish (see also Chapter 14 by Anthony Graesch and Timothy Hartshorn in this volume). It shows the transformations that any material—whether prehistoric or quite recent—can go through in its life and afterlives as the context of attitudes toward it and values of it change through time.

While this was a solution to the problem of what to do with Ruth's rubble, it is also an ongoing provocation. Did our deposition of the rubble revalue it, as a material worthy of remembering? Did it devalue it, by associating it with a landfill? Did our connection of the rubble to brick highlight or erase the meaningful difference of value afforded to even the most mundane of archaeological materials versus the materials people used to build homes at the Albany Bulb?

The ritual itself is a kind of archaeological practice in reverse. A practice of deposition rather than extraction, an imbuing of personal meaning rather than the deduction of one. This was a way to embody the issue of the storage crisis in museum and archaeological collections, and a way to draw it into urgent debates about the housing crisis in our own community. The two evictions, of the rubble from its academic home, and of residents like Pat and Amber from the Albany Bulb, are of course extremely different. But they were able to speak to each other through performance.

After the final piece of rubble had been deposited Susan led a conversation under Pat and Carrie's tree (Figure 20.13). With the audience of artists, archaeologists, former residents, lovers of the Albany Bulb, and newcomers, we discussed the meaning of the performance: the value of materials and narratives of home. This, perhaps, is the best outcome of the work: a sustained, personal, and embodied reflection on what it means to throw things, histories, memories, or people away.

ACKNOWLEDGMENTS

Foremost among our acknowledgment of a debt of gratitude is to the former residents of the Albany Bulb, especially Amber Whitson, Pat and Carrie, and Susan Moffat of Love the Bulb. In addition we would like to acknowledge the role that Mirjana Stevanovic played in bringing these pieces of burned rubble back to Berkeley. Mirjana wrote her PhD dissertation on the burned houses of Opovo; she is now back in Serbia, her original homeland. Our thanks are also due to Professor Christine Hastorf, the director of the UC Berkeley Archaeological Research Facility; without her request to us to remove the samples from their storage space, we would not have had this event. Thanks also go to professors Laurie Wilkie and Rosemary Joyce who supported Annie Danis's initial research at the Bulb and to the team of graduate and undergraduate students from UC Berkeley and San Jose State University who participated in mapping homesites there after eviction (a full list is available at anniedanis.com/albanybulb). Finally to Erika Chong Shuch and Ghigo DiTommaso who, with Susan Moffat, explored the Bulb through performance as instructors of "SiteWorks: Exploring Place Through Design and Performance" at UC Berkeley.

NOTES

1 Stevanovic 1997, Tringham 2005, 2019.
2 See the three *Opovo Fire Story* movies in which the rubble is very much center stage: https://vimeo.com/showcase/8283473 (accessed 23 March, 2021).
3 Stevanovic 1997, Tringham et al. 1992, Tringham 2019.
4 Stevanovic 1997, Tringham 2005, 2019.
5 Danis 2022.
6 Danis 2020.
7 https://www.bulbfest.org/ and https://www.facebook.com/LovetheBulb/ (both accessed 29 February 2020).
8 *Forgotten Products of Labor: The Movie:* https://vimeo.com/533379764 (accessed 15 April, 2021).

BIBLIOGRAPHY

Danis, Annie (2020), *Landscapes of Inequality: Creative Approaches to Engaged Research in Archaeology,* PhD Dissertation, University of California, Berkeley.

—— (2022), "Home(less) Place and Home-making and at the Albany Bulb," in: Elena Sesma and Evan Taylor, eds., *Archaeology of the Contemporary in Old Places*, Arlington (Archaeological Papers of the American Association of Anthropology).

Stevanovic, Mirjana (1997), The Age of Clay: The Social Dynamics of House Destruction. *Journal of Anthropological Archaeology* 16, 334–95, DOI:10.1006/jaar.1997.0310.

Tringham, Ruth, Bogdan Brukner, Timothy Kaiser, Ksenija Borojević, Ljubomir Bukvić, Petar Šteli, Nerissa Russell, Mirjana Stevanović, and Barbara Voytek (1992), Excavations at Opovo, 1985–1987: Socioeconomic Change in the Balkan Neolithic, *Journal of Field Archaeology,* 19(3), 351–86, https://doi.org/10.1179/009346992791548860.

Tringham, Ruth (2005), "Weaving House Life and Death into Places: A Blueprint for a Hypermedia Narrative," in: Douglass Bailey, Alasdair Whittle, and Vicki Cummings, eds., *(un)settling the Neolithic*, pp. 98–111, Oxford (Oxbow Books).

—— (2019), *Fire: Friend or Fiend in Human History,* Third Annual Pitt-Rivers Lecture, Bournemouth University, https://www.academia.edu/42113549/Fire_Friend_or_Fiend_in_Human_History.

HOSTILE TERRAIN 94

USING AN ARCHAEOLOGICAL SENSIBILITY TO RAISE AWARENESS ABOUT MIGRANT DEATH ALONG THE US–MEXICO BORDER

NICOLE SMITH, GABRIEL CANTER, AUSTIN E. SHIPMAN,
CAMERON GOKEE, HAEDEN STEWART, AND JASON DE LEÓN

Those who understand the physical realities of the southern geopolitical boundary of the United States and the complexity of the global political economy recognize that building a wall along the US–Mexico border is not a rational idea. The imagined wall that some politicians have recently argued for would be prohibitively costly, an engineering impossibility, and unlikely to stop the flow of people. Currently, only around 18 percent of the 3145 kilometers (1954 miles) that make up this border has something that resembles a wall. Most of the terrain where these two countries meet is remote, depopulated, rugged, and unsupervised. Instead, vast portions of the border are demarcated by three-strand barbed wire fences, Normandy-style barricades, or nothing at all. The areas that do have significant fencing and other security measures are in and around urban ports-of-entry such as San Diego and El Paso. Walls and high-tech surveillance cameras abruptly stop on the outskirts of these urban zones. This discrepancy in security infrastructure between populated areas and uninhabited expanses of wilderness is not just a matter of cost. Leaving large portions of the border relatively open to undocumented migration is part of a Border Patrol strategy called Prevention Through Deterrence (PTD).

Officially launched in 1994, PTD is a policy that emphasizes hyper-security measures—such as high fencing, motion sensor cameras, and field agents—in unauthorized crossing areas around urban ports-of-entry with the goal that "illegal traffic will be deterred, or forced over more hostile terrain, less suited for crossing and more suited for enforcement."[1] For almost three decades this strategy has intentionally funneled millions of migrants toward the Sonoran Desert of Arizona, where people seeking illegal entry will walk for long distances, upward of 160 kilometers (100 miles), while negotiating a barren landscape characterized by extreme weather, dangerous animals, and other hazards. Mountains, rattlesnakes and dehydration have been conscripted by federal policy makers to deter migrants. The Sonoran Desert is America's border wall.

Much to the chagrin of the federal government, however, more than twenty years of research has shown that PTD has failed to stop migration while turning border crossing into a well-organized, dangerous and violent social process. Since 2000, over six million people have traversed the Arizona desert and as of February 2023, at least 3,977 people have lost their lives while en route.[2] Forensic work conducted in the Arizona desert indicates that the harsh environmental conditions can quickly destroy bodies before they can be recovered,[3] suggesting that the current death tally likely undercounts the actual number of people who have died while crossing.[4]

In 2019, the Undocumented Migration Project (UMP) began developing a global exhibition about migrant death called "Hostile Terrain 94" (HT94).[5] This participatory exhibition involves coordinating thousands of volunteers across six continents to write out the names and forensic information onto toe tags of the thousands of people who have died while crossing the border. These tags are then mounted onto a large map of the border between Mexico and Arizona in the exact location where remains were recovered. The goal of this project is to connect viewers to this distant and often difficult to comprehend phenomenon via a translation of archaeological and forensic data into a visual and spatial encounter that at its core is a tactile experiment in empathy. In this chapter we outline the structure and logic of HT94 and describe how an attention to materiality, artifacts, memory, time and space, what we deem an *archaeological sensibility*, is the foundation of this project.

BACKGROUND

Starting in 2009, the UMP has utilized a mix of ethnography, archaeology, visual anthropology and forensic science to document and understand various aspects of clandestine migration between Latin America and the United States.[6] Much of the archaeological research focused on collecting data from remote border regions such as the Sonoran Desert of Arizona where hundreds of migrant sites have been documented and more than thirty thousand artifacts used and discarded during the migration process have been analyzed.[7] One of the long-term goals of the UMP is to understand the connection between material culture and the embodied experiences of border crossers. In this context, an archaeological approach allows for the collection of new types of data on unauthorized migration (such as use-wear patterns on artifacts) that can be integrated into an overarching ethnographic narrative.[8]

The archaeological, ethnographic, and forensic data that the UMP has collected over the past ten years has raised awareness about PTD and its brutal impacts on the bodies of migrants, both living and dead. Our research has been published in numerous peer-reviewed articles and a book-length monograph. However, since 2013, we have increasingly sought to engage more directly with the general public through a variety of projects including a 2019 documentary film *(Border South)* and an exhibition called "State of Exception/Estado de Excepción," which ran from 2013 to 2017.[9] The centerpiece of the State of Exception exhibit was a wall of backpacks that included embedded speakers playing audio of border crossing stories, intended to humanize the numbers of people suffering in the desert. In 2018, the UMP developed a multi-media exhibition called "Hostile Terrain," which debuted at the Institute for Contemporary Art in Portland, Maine, followed by a show at the Phillips Art Museum in Lancaster, Pennsylvania. One element of this exhibition included a large map of migrant deaths in Arizona between the mid-1990s and 2018. This graphic is based on data from the Pima County Office of the Medical Examiner that has been made available online by the humanitarian group, Humane Borders.[10]

During the course of exhibition development, we struggled with how to translate this migrant death data (Table 19.1) into something that could better illustrate the full scale of this human tragedy. In our first attempt, migrant deaths were represented by red dots on a map of the US–Mexico border (Figure 19.1). After the installation of this piece, we found that the red dots on a wall were viewed by many museum attendees as anonymous data points that seemingly had the opposite effect of trying to humanize these deaths. In preparation for the opening of Hostile Terrain at the Phillips Museum in early 2019, we decided to replace the red dots on a map with custom toe tags for each recovered body. These tags contained data fields for name, age, reporting date, sex, surface management (whose land the bodies were found on), cause of death, body condition, county, and the latitude and longitude where remains were found. The tags were color coded, with manila representing bodies that have names associated with them and orange for unidentified human remains. This information was handwritten onto each tag by members of the UMP. It took nearly three months for the five members of our team to fill out all 2,999 tags.[11]

From the beginning of this process, conversations among our working group revolved around the emotional difficulty

Number	Name	Sex	Age	Date	Surface management
01-00082	unidentified	Male	unknown	15 Jan. 2001	Ironwood Forest National Monument
01-00266	unidentified	Female	unknown	13 Feb. 2001	Tohono Oodham Nation
01-00338	unidentified	Male	unknown	26 Feb. 2001	Tohono Oodham Nation
01-00548	unidentified	Male	unknown	2 Apr. 2001	Private
01-00591	unidentified	Male	unknown	10 Apr. 2001	Bureau of Land Management
01-00697	unidentified	Male	unknown	1 May 2001	Pima County Office of the Medical Examiner
01-00748	Cruz-Mendoza-Cruz, Fernando	Female	31	9 May 2001	Tohono Oodham Nation
01-00791	Sotelo-Mendoza, Alicia Adela	Female	46	17 May 2001	Tohono Oodham Nation
01-00823	Sanchez-Najera, Felipe	Male	53	May 23, 2001	Private
01-00861	unidentified	Female	unknown	May 29, 2001	Tohono Oodham Nation
01-00876	Beltran-Rojas, Daniel	Male	24	1 Jun. 2001	Tohono Oodham Nation
01-00878	Rosales-Pacheco, Armando	Male	25	31 May 2001	Bureau of Land Management
01-00888	Ayala-Zamora, Buenaventura	Male	45	2 Jun. 2001	Organ Pipe Cactus National Monument
01-00920	Bautista-Lopez, Roberto	Male	19	8 Jun. 2001	Tohono Oodham Nation
01-00931	Lopez-Guerrero, Anastacio	Male	38	10 Jun. 2001	Bureau of Land Management
01-00934	unidentified	Male	unknown	11 Jun. 2001	Sonoran Desert National Management
01-00946	unidentified	Male	unknown	13 Jun. 2001	Tohono Oodham Nation
01-00957	Espinosa-Cruz, Martin	Male	40	16 Jun. 2001	Tohono Oodham Nation
01-00971	Sala-Perez, Adela	Female	30	17 Jun. 2001	Tohono Oodham Nation
01-00979	Octaviano-Nieto, Guadalupe	Female	21	19 Jun. 2001	Ironwood Forest National Monument

Table 19.1. Sample of migrant death data for individuals recovered from the Sonoran Desert in 2001. Humane Borders 2020.

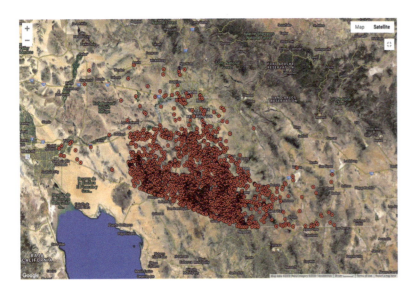

Figure 19.1. Migrant death map. *Humane Borders 2020.*

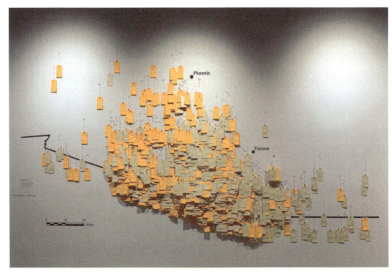

Figure 19.2. Hostile Terrain 94 at the Phillips Museum of Art at Franklin and Marshall College.

and intensity of writing the name of each individual, their cause of death, and the condition in which their bodies were found. Words and phrases such as "exposure," "hyperthermia," "fully fleshed," "skeletonization with disarticulation," and "mummification" were difficult to write even after five hundred times. Upon completion of the initial version of the wall map in Lancaster (Figure 19.2), our team was overwhelmed by the density of toe tags pinned on to the wall (Figure 19.3), and the violence and grief that those tags represented. The many personal reactions that our team had while making this tactile exhibition became the inspiration for the development of HT94 as a way to connect audiences around the globe emotionally and physically to the issue of migrant deaths.

The original intention of HT94 was to display the exhibition in ninety-four locations as a nod to the year that both PTD started and when the North American Free Trade Agreement was initiated, the latter resulting in an out-migration of millions of disenfranchised Mexican farmers. In January 2019 we made our first call for participating hosts via Facebook and Twitter. Within a couple of months, we received an outpouring of interest and it became clear that we would easily surpass our goal

Figure 19.3. Many tags overlap due to their close proximity on the map, creating a dense, three-dimensional effect.

NICOLE SMITH, GABRIEL CANTER, AUSTIN E. SHIPMAN, CAMERON GOKEE, HAEDEN STEWART, AND JASON DE LEÓN

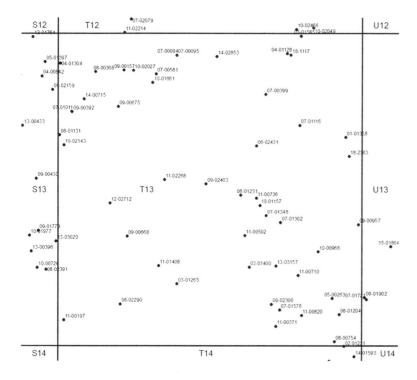

Figure 19.4. Sample grid square used to locate the precise location of each toe tag.

of ninety-four installations. In order to make HT94 accessible to as wide an audience as possible, we increased the number of available hosting sites to a maximum of 150 locations.

HT94 was originally designed to be installed over the course of six months (May through November 2020) leading up to the American presidential election, in more than 130 locations around the world, including Los Angeles, New York, Philadelphia, Seattle, Miami, Mexico City, San Pedro Sula (Honduras), San Salvador (El Salvador), and Lampedusa (Italy). With the onset of the Covid-19 pandemic, the timeline has been adjusted. While a few hosting partners continued with HT94 in the Fall of 2020, others have postponed until they feel comfortable participating in-person, which may shift events well into 2024.

The installation comprises a 4.5–6 meter-long (15–20 foot-long) map of the border between Mexico and Arizona with more than 3,800 handwritten toe tags; the maps may vary in

size depending on the availability of space at a given location. Tags correspond to a specific place on a large grid to ensure accurate placement of individual remains (Figure 19.4). Each map comes with an introductory wall text explaining the project and also features an augmented reality experience to accompany the map that can be accessed for free using a cellphone app. This allows the viewer to hear stories of people who have crossed the desert or lost loved ones to the process, visit locations where people have died, and receive a close-up look at artifacts that migrants have left behind.

ARCHAEOLOGICAL SENSIBILITY

Touching and seeing the world in relation to ourselves and the people, places, and things around us is crucial to the human experience. The former, touching, is likely fundamental to early childhood development.[12] In many ways, our natural inclination toward tactile and visual connections may inspire a human desire to use informal archaeological methodologies and practices in areas that are not inherently archaeological. Michael Shanks (2012, 25) describes this inclination as "a pervasive set of attitudes towards traces and remains, towards memory, time and temporality, the fabric of history." He also notes that archaeology is concerned with site, representation, and arrangement, and emphasizes that the way things are documented and engaged with is important to understand the past and how it relates to the present.[13] We argue that an archaeological sensibility—or a special attention to materiality, artifacts, memory, time, and space—can be used in a range of contexts and as a framework to understand contemporary human engagements with material culture. In some instances, this sensibility is subtle and does not necessarily involve excavating or collecting objects off the ground,[14] but instead a general attunement to an archaeological perspective. For example, Susan Phillips (2019, 5) remarks in her study of graffiti in Los Angeles that "words on a wall remain stagnant until people's stories begin to inform their interpretation. Uncovering fuses ethnography and archaeology and embraces a sometimes-chaotic stratigraphy where names and keywords are invitations to engage in multiple fields across time." In other instances, an explicit archaeological approach may be used to understand human relationships with objects as they happen in real time.[15] An archaeological sensibility is deeply rooted in HT94 through the application of three interrelated themes: counter-mapping, multi-sensory approaches, and memorialization.

COUNTER-MAPPING

Since the beginning of PTD, the United States Border Patrol has relied on maps and spatial data to weaponize the Sonoran Desert against migrants. Geographic Information Systems software assists Border Patrol agents in mapping rough terrain and determining the most optimal routes a person on foot might take.[16] Paired with other forms of surveillance such as remote sensors, lookout towers, and GPS devices, this generates a comprehensive body of spatial information that can be utilized to "provide immediate real-time information of suspected migrant activity."[17] Although vast areas of the US–Mexico border, like the Sonoran Desert, are without security infrastructure and seemingly open, these mapping and spatial technologies are employed as a means of remote surveillance crucial to policing these regions.[18]

While the Border Patrol uses mapping techniques as a form of oppressive power, geographers are increasingly reappropriating these traditional surveillance technologies in new and alternative ways.[19] Termed 'counter-mapping,' these strategies undermine dominant power structures enforced by institutional maps and bring otherwise erased narratives to the forefront.[20] The humanitarian organization Humane Borders embodies this spirit of counter-mapping. Mapping sites of migrant death and humanitarian water stations, Humane Borders designs and distributes posters warning potential undocumented migrants about the risks of crossing the desert.[21] In order to keep track of the human cost of border policies of the United States they also maintain a searchable map interface, the Arizona OpenGIS Initiative for Deceased Migrants, which provides spatial data regarding where deceased migrants are discovered and personal data about those individuals.

Mapping the myriad sites of recovered migrant bodies in order to emphasize the brutality of the desert and the border policy of the United States, this cartographic practice demonstrates an archaeological sensibility. HT94 has drawn on these data to construct the three-dimensional maps of the Arizona border where handwritten toe-tags are geolocated in the locations where remains were found. HT94 reinterprets spatial data provided by Humane Borders, not only by enlarging the map of migrant deaths into a 4.5–6 meter (15–20 foot) display, but by also (re)documenting the data collected for each death by copying these by hand onto individual toe tags. In each of our hosting locations, volunteers fill out the information and contribute to this (re)documentation, thus creating numerous unique handwritten versions of the same data set.

Once filled out, tags are geolocated on a map of the border region and hung from a red pin in the location where each person was found. The representation of migrant deaths on these tags functions as a physical connection point between the participants writing them and those who they are writing about. Many may come across individuals who share the same first or last name, age, or some other characteristic, such as when the body was found on the birthday of the writer of the tag. These shared details coupled with placing them onto the map may create a personal connection between the participant and a moment of the story of this deceased individual.

Prior to launching in July 2020, we organized eight prototypes in a range of locations including New York, Michigan, Ireland, and California. Many participants commented that migrant death in Arizona initially seemed distant and unfathomable, but by writing out information for the dead and potentially having some commonality with that person—such as the same name or age—connected them to the issue in an unexpected way. Moreover, participants of HT94 are offered a glimpse into the enormity of the humanitarian crisis occurring at the southern border of the United States by witnessing up close the number of lives that have been lost because of border policies. The accessibility of HT94 publicly highlights the scales of suffering between individual deaths and the larger issue unfolding along the US–Mexico border.[22]

NICOLE SMITH, GABRIEL CANTER, AUSTIN E. SHIPMAN, CAMERON GOKEE, HAEDEN STEWART, AND JASON DE LEÓN

MULTISENSORY APPROACHES

Cara Krmpotich (2019, 97) has recently noted the many ways that museums have shifted toward multisensory engagements in exhibitions, apart from prioritizing the visual. New art initiatives have sought to focus on tactility and empathy; emphasizing the embodied experience and the interactions between objects and humans.[23] The ability to touch, move, and analyze materials are all part of the archaeological process and the multisensory turn has been progressively utilized by archaeologists searching for new methods of interpretation (also discussed by Robin Skeates in Chapter 28 of this volume).[24] HT94 is similarly built upon sensory engagements and an attempt to connect participants to migrant death through the physical processes of writing and mounting toe tags. The construction and outcomes of the exhibition are wholly dependent on the participation of our hosting partners and their community members. Participants are able to physically handle these tags, transforming the digital data into something tangible. Through this act, toe tags transform into artifacts; they become something that holds a deep, complex history, representing a past that lingers in the present and implores a responsibility for the future.[25]

This tactile, participatory practice is comparable to sensory experiences in archaeology, but in some ways also mirrors the laborious nature of archaeological laboratory work. Participants are tasked with meticulously writing out the tags and are required to start again if they make a mistake. Many attendees at our prototypes sat for hours copying the information of the deceased, recognizing that however tedious, they felt it necessary and meaningful to continue writing. Additionally, it is important to note that HT94 exhibitions do not all occur within museum spaces. While many will, the majority of our shows take place in common, public spaces such as building lobbies or outdoor plazas. The public nature of the exhibition allows for a wide audience to engage with the materials in familiar spaces. The ability to touch and physically transform these tags paired with the overall location of the display establishes connections that would not otherwise be established behind the dull homogeneity of glass vitrines.[26]

Apart from touch and vision, HT94 also draws on sound. Embedded within the completed toe tag display are several QR codes (Figure 19.5) that can be scanned using the camera feature on any smartphone and will direct the user to various online content. This includes testimonials from family members who have lost loved ones after they attempted to cross the desert. We have also included QR codes with testimonials from participants of HT94 recorded through story-telling workshops that occur either before or during the installation of the exhibition. In these workshops people are given a platform to share their own stories of migration or their reaction to the exhibition. By including these stories, we emphasize that this is not a distant issue, and is deeply connected to and impacts communities across the globe.

The final version of HT94 includes an augmented reality component created by UMP collaborators Alex Suber and Alvaro Morales. While visiting the exhibition, viewers can point their cellphones at the toe tag wall and enter virtual portals that offer a glimpse into the stories of those who have crossed the Sonoran Desert via interviews, the unforgiving environment in 360° photographs, and the human cost of the journey evident from shrines and memorials for the deceased. The stories recorded include first-hand testimonies of undocumented migrants and their perspectives on crossing the border, interviews with humanitarian workers who have discovered human remains in the desert, and researchers who document the impacts of border policies.

NEGATIVE HERITAGE AND MEMORIALIZATION

While part of HT94 aims to educate those in the United States and around the world about America's border humanitarian crisis, much of this project is also about memorializing those who have died and standing in solidarity with migrants around the world. Families and communities affected by PTD are all too familiar with its consequences, and for many, the Arizona desert has become a site of what Lynn Meskell (2002, 558) calls negative heritage, "a conflictual site that becomes a repository of negative memory in the collective imaginary." However,

Figure 19.5. The QR code on the top left of this toe tag can be scanned with a cellphone camera and directs the participant to a RadioLab (WNYC) series discussing this individual.

NICOLE SMITH, GABRIEL CANTER, AUSTIN E. SHIPMAN, CAMERON GOKEE, HAEDEN STEWART, AND JASON DE LEÓN

Meskell also notes that as a site of memory, negative heritage can be mobilized didactically or alternatively be erased.

Over the course of several field seasons, the UMP conducted experimental forensic work using pig carcasses as proxies for human remains to study corpse decomposition and desert taphonomy.[27] These studies demonstrate that bodies decompose rapidly in the hot desert environment, and personal effects and skeletal remains are often scattered long distances or completely disappear due to animal scavenging activities. There are likely many bodies that are completely destroyed by environmental conditions before they can be recovered,[28] rendering this landscape a place where death is an everyday occurrence that often remains hidden or is erased by the natural environment.

Since 2009, the UMP has also employed an archaeological gaze to consider the objects left along the migrant trail—such as water bottles, distressed shoes and clothing, backpacks—as a tangible heritage-in-the-making.[29] This approach has been partly inspired by the fact that the remnants of undocumented migration are disappearing fast as the extreme desert environment quickly degrades this contemporary archaeological record. Moreover, in an attempt to clean up the desert, federal agencies and local citizens have been systematically collecting and disposing of all evidence of migration, speeding up the process of erasure.[30] At times, the UMP has acted as an archaeological salvage operation, recovering as much material culture as possible so as not to allow these significant narratives to be erased from history.

Modeled after these same salvage practices, HT94 is a platform to memorialize publicly and pay homage to migrants who have died in the desert. Many of the institutions collaborating with the project are hosting workshops where their local communities will come together to fill out the toe tags and spend time reflecting on these issues. We have named these workshops "Days of Witnessing and Remembering," emphasizing that this practice of writing the intimate details of how one died onto a tag is a process of memorialization. We also encourage participants of the installations to write notes on the backside of the tags. In our prototypes, people have

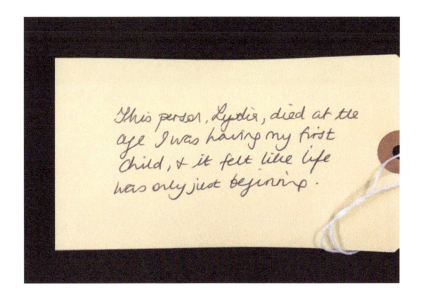

Figure 19.6. Note written on the back of a toe tag by a volunteer at the University of Pennsylvania.

inscribed personal letters to the individual on the tag offering their condolences, others have written poems, or talked about their own particular connections to death, dying, and grief (Figure 19.6). While the opportunity to write these notes can be perceived as cathartic, we hope this is also a way for people to draw connections between their realities and those of lost migrants while creating artifacts representing these moments of interaction.

Audiences are brought even closer to sites of migrant death through the augmented reality and the video footage associated with the exhibition. These digital features include photographs of shrines created by researchers and humanitarian workers in the desert where deceased migrants have been found (Figure 19.7). Without these memorials, there is often no in situ evidence that something tragic has occurred in these locations. Furthermore, many of the tags will be collected and archived by the hosts, while others will become part of a permanent traveling version of HT94, essentially a new archaeological collection of toe tags with representation from each hosting location.

Figure 19.7. A shrine created in the Sonoran Desert for a deceased migrant.

CONCLUSION

Translating archaeological data into an insightful narrative about the behavior of people from the past is no small feat. Archaeological inference requires an attunement to spatial relationships, chronology, and material culture in order to breathe life into pot sherds, lithics, and other physical remnants of human activity. This connects people to distant worlds populated by those who are no longer present. In many ways, this is what HT94 has attempted to do: translate forensic data into a tactile experience that for a brief moment connects an exhibition attendee with the lives of those who have died while migrating. Our initial goal was to facilitate a meaningful experience for exhibition participants that would simultaneously memorialize the dead while educating the public. It was only upon reflection that we came to see this endeavor as partly an archaeological one: a mediated experience that relies on notions of geolocation, time, depth, and touch to create a narrative about the tragic loss of life that has been occurring at the US–Mexico border since the 1990s. In recent years, archaeologists have made a strong case for the relevance of traditional archaeological methods and theories to excavate and understand the remains of modern cultural phenomena. In this chapter we have argued that an archaeological approach does not have to involve shovels or screens to make a serious contribution to understanding and connecting with the past. Embracing and explicating an archaeological sensibility in unexpected locations has the potential to introduce new audiences to the power of understanding ourselves and our shared human history through deep considerations of time, space, and materiality.

NOTES

1   United States Border Patrol, *Border Patrol Strategic Plan 1994 and Beyond,* https://www.hsdl.org/?view&did=721845, accessed 29 February 2020.

2   Humane Borders, *Migrant Death Mapping,* https://humaneborders.org/migrant-death-mapping/, accessed 13 February 2023.

3   Beck et al. 2014.

4   Martínez et al. 2014.

5   The figure 94 refers to both the year that Prevention Through Deterrence started and the year the North American Free Trade Agreement was initiated. The latter resulted in the migration of millions of disenfranchised farmers out of Mexico.

6   De León 2015, De León and Gokee 2018.

7   De León 2013, De León et al. 2015, Gokee and De León 2014.

8   De León 2013, 327.

9   De León and Gokee 2018.

10 https://humaneborders.org/migrant-death-mapping/, accessed 29 February 2020.

11 In January 2019, the number of migrant deaths was tallied at 2,999. Tragically, that number continues to increase and, as of February 2023, 3,977 bodies have been recovered and recorded in the Sonoran Desert of Arizona.

12 Winnicott 1953. We recognize that the visually impaired may be excluded from part of this experience while the importance of the sense of touch is often heightened.

13 Shanks 2012, 146–48.

14 Phillips 2019, Stallybrass 1993.

15 De León 2013.

16 Wayne Sweeney (2001), *US Border Patrol Maximizes Enforcement with GIS: ArcNews Online, Fall 2001,* https://www.esri.com/news/arcnews/fall01articles/usborderpatrol.html, accessed 29 February 2020.

17 Stewart et al. 2016, 164.

18 Stewart et al. 2016, 164.

19 Gokee et al. 2020, González-Ruibal 2008.

20 Stewart et al. 2016, Gokee et al. 2020.

21 https://humaneborders.org/migrant-death-mapping/, accessed February 29, 2020.

22 Gokee et al. 2020.

23 Gadoua 2014, Peers and Brown 2015.

24 Hamilakis 2014, Skeates and Day 2019.

25 Shanks 2012, 149.

26 Hamilakis 2014, 48.

27 Beck et al. 2014.

28 Beck et al. 2014, 9.

29 De León and Gokee 2018.

30 De León and Gokee 2018, 74.

BIBLIOGRAPHY

Beck, Jess, Ian Ostericher, Gregory Sollish, and Jason De León (2014), Animal Scavenging and Scattering and the Implications for Documenting the Deaths of Undocumented Border Crossers in the Sonoran Desert, *Journal of Forensic Sciences* 60(S1): S11–S20.

De León, Jason (2013), Undocumented Use-Wear and the Materiality of Habitual Suffering in the Sonoran Desert, *Journal of Material Culture* 18(4): 321–45.

——— (2015), *Land of Open Graves: Living and Dying on the Migrant Trail,* Oakland (University of California Press).

De León, Jason and Cameron Gokee (2018), Lasting Value? Engaging with the Material Traces of America's Undocumented Migration "Problem," in: Cornelius Holtorf, Andreas Pantazatos, and Geoffrey Scarre, eds., *Cultural Heritage, Ethics and Contemporary Migrations*, pp. 70–86, London and New York (Routledge).

De León, Jason, Cameron Gokee, and Ashley Schubert (2015), "By the Time I Get to Arizona": Citizenship, Materiality, and Contested Identities along the US–Mexico Border, *Anthropological Quarterly* 88(2): 445–79.

Gadoua, Marie-Pierre (2014), Making Sense through Touch, *The Senses and Society* 9(3): 323–41.

Gokee, Cameron and Jason De León (2014), Sites of Contention: Archaeology and Political Discourse in the US–Mexico Borderlands, *Journal of Contemporary Archaeology* 1(1): 133–63.

Gokee, Cameron, Haeden Stewart, and Jason De León (2020), Scales of Suffering in the US–Mexico Borderlands, *International Journal of Historical Archaeology* 24(4): 823–51, DOI: 10.1007/s10761-019-00535-6.

González-Ruibal, Alfredo (2008), Time to Destroy: An Archaeology of Supermodernity, *Current Anthropology* 49(2): 247–79.

Hamilakis, Yannis (2014), *Archaeology and the Senses: Human Experience, Memory, and Affect*, Cambridge (Cambridge University Press).

Krmpotich, Cara (2019), "The Senses in Museums: Knowledge Production, Democratization, and Indigenization," in: Robin Skeates and Jo Day, eds., *The Routledge Handbook of Sensory Archaeology,* pp. 94–106, London and New York (Routledge).

Martínez, Daniel E., Robin C. Rienecke, Raquel Rubio-Goldsmith, and Bruce O. Parks (2014), Structural Violence and Migrant Deaths in Southern Arizona: Data from the Pima County Office of the Medical Examiner, 1990–2013, *Journal on Migration and Human Security* 2(4): 257–86.

Meskell, Lynn (2002), Negative Heritage and Past Mastering in Archaeology, *Anthropological Quarterly* 75(3): 557–74.

Peers, Laura and Alison K. Brown (2015), *Visiting with the Ancestors: Blackfoot Shirts in Museum Spaces,* Edmonton (Athabasca University Press).

Phillips, Susan A. (2019), *The City Beneath: A Century of Los Angeles Graffiti,* New Haven (Yale University Press).

Shanks, Michael (2012), *The Archaeological Imagination,* London and New York (Routledge).

Skeates, Robin and Jo Day (2019), "Sensory Archaeology: Key Concepts and Debates," in: Robin Skeates and Jo Day, eds., *The Routledge Handbook of Sensory Archaeology,* pp. 1–17, London and New York (Routledge).

Stallybrass, Peter (1993), Worn Worlds: Clothes, Mourning, and the Life of Things, *The Yale Review* 81(2): 35–35.

Stewart, Haeden, Ian Ostericher, Cameron Gokee, and Jason De León (2016), Surveilling Surveillance: Counter-mapping Undocumented Migration in the USA–Mexico Borderlands, *Journal of Contemporary Archaeology* 3(2): 159–74.

Winnicott, D.W. (1953), Transitional Objects and Transitional Phenomena; A Study of the First Not-Me Possession, *The International Journal of Psychoanalysis* 34: 89–97.

ON AIR

AN ARCHAEOLOGICAL RIFF ON MONTSERRAT'S WORLD-FAMOUS 1980S RECORDING STUDIO

KRYSTA RYZEWSKI AND JOHN F. CHERRY

I don't know where I'm a-gonna go
When the volcano blow
(Jimmy Buffet, "Volcano," recorded at AIR Studios in 1979)

In the context of the tiny British Caribbean island of Montserrat, Jimmy Buffet is more prophet than pop star. Shortly after Sir George Martin, the 'fifth Beatle,' opened Associated Independent Recording (AIR) Studios in May 1979 as a luxurious workplace for A-list musicians, Buffett and members of his Coral Reefer Band traveled to Montserrat to record their upbeat, Caribbean-infused song "Volcano." The skyline behind AIR Studios was dominated by the peaceful green slopes of the long-dormant Soufrière Hills volcano, serving as picturesque inspiration for the ninth album of the band; a catastrophic eruption seemed just a figment of their imagination.

The tranquility that musicians enjoyed at AIR Studios was disrupted by a series of devastating eruptions beginning in 1995. These destroyed Plymouth, the capital city of Montserrat, killed nineteen people, and rendered more than half the island an uninhabitable off-limits exclusion zone until today. The hypothetical anxiety over displacement that Buffett sang about in "Volcano" became a reality for the Montserratian population. Caught by surprise, local residents worried about where they could go to escape the deadly pyroclastic flows and ash-falls; eventually, two-thirds of them left the island permanently.

When the volcano awoke, the fate of AIR Studios was already sealed. Six years earlier, in September 1989, category-4 hurricane Hugo swept across the island and destroyed more than 90 percent of the buildings on Montserrat. Although AIR Studios fared better than most, gaping holes and loose

shingles on its roof invited rain, tropical vegetation, and animals into the buildings and their wooden floors soon began to buckle (Figure 18.1). In a 2011 BBC interview, Sir George Martin recounted his first revisit to the AIR Studios in the wake of Hurricane Hugo: finding the keys of the piano coated in green mold he realized that the electronics used for recording and editing were also certain to have been damaged beyond repair. The days of AIR Studios as a state-of-the-art recording facility were over.

Although short-lived, the decade-long run of AIR Studios as an incubator for several of the 1980s' most iconic pop artists elevated its status among music fans worldwide from a remote recording complex to a sacred place, one worthy of preservation, reverence, and even pilgrimage.[1] Within the compound, musicians lived, worked, and partied. Between 1979 and 1989, artists recorded more than seventy-five albums there, many of them chart-toppers, including *Ghost in the Machine* and *Synchronicity* (The Police, 1981 and 1982), *Tug of War* (Paul McCartney and Stevie Wonder, 1981), *Rio* (Duran Duran, 1982), *Too Low for Zero* (Elton John, 1982), *Brothers in Arms* (Dire Straits, 1984–85), and *Steel Wheels* (Rolling Stones, 1989). Dozens of other bands and musicians also recorded at AIR Studios.[2]

The music produced at AIR Studios was intended for a global market well beyond the confines of Montserrat, but the experiences of music-making relied heavily on local connections. Iconic pop figures intermingled freely with island residents, building relationships and contributing to the local economy by patronizing businesses, recruiting local talent as back-up musicians for recording sessions, and even inviting extras to participate in their music videos. As a result, there remain many first-hand accounts among Montserratians of their involvement in legendary recording sessions, dinners, and parties at AIR Studios. Their stories fondly recount a carefree time of creativity and prosperity, before disasters upended the landscape, economy, and society of the island. For Montserratians and foreigners alike, the music produced at AIR Studios is widely appreciated for its global influence in shaping the tastes and experiences of the music video generation. Almost 35 years after its closure, the site continues to be appreciated as a tangible connection to both the pop icons of the 1980s and innovations in digital recording technology that were pioneered there. Such connections, many stakeholders argue, make the buildings worth preserving as a heritage site whose global status might attract tourists to the island and thereby contribute to local revitalization efforts.

CONTEMPORARY ARCHAEOLOGY AND POPULAR MUSIC

What does this sad story have to do with archaeology? Are our various interventions at AIR Studios too far outside-the-box to be considered a form of archaeological practice? In what follows, we argue for the potential of archaeology in documenting the past and future affordances of a contemporary site of popular music production. Between 2010 and 2019, we conducted periodic documentation of the AIR Studios complex. Here, we have integrated archaeological information from surveys of the property, targeted excavation, documentary sources, and oral historical accounts (many of them online) to chart the processes of maintenance and ruination that compete for primacy in the nostalgic memories and narrative space of AIR Studios. Our findings illustrate the role of a contemporary archaeological intervention within the context of ongoing heritage preservation initiatives. In discussing the future of AIR Studios, we reflect on how visions of preservation and commemoration have changed over time, in reaction to shifting volcanic and economic circumstances, but also in response to the exposure that our publication of the initial work in 2010 garnered.[3]

Contemporary archaeology, at the time we began our work in 2010, was still gaining traction, and was certainly uncharted with respect to the study of sites associated with popular music production. Since then, contemporary archaeological practice and theory have become considerably more mainstream, as shown by the proliferation of scholarship involving sites of the recent past.[4] We identify contemporary archaeology as an archaeological practice that involves critical engagements with the material and social phenomena of late modern societies, particularly during the period of living memory and into the present.[5] Our study of AIR Studios focused on the material remains of a 1980s music-making enterprise and, in so doing, intersected with one of the core foci of contemporary archaeology—the interrogation of global processes (in our case, the global music industry) through their local expressions (such as a particular setting of music production).

The number of contemporary archaeological studies focused on sites of popular music production, consumption, and related heritage sites has also been increasing in recent years. When we first investigated AIR Studios a decade ago, there were few archaeologists researching contemporary sites associated with popular music experiences. Since then, some have joined conversations among urban geographers and heritage practitioners in recognizing the significant, and often highly emotional, connections people maintain between popular music and associated experiences, memories, places, and material culture.[6] Recent projects by archaeologists in Berlin, Detroit, Dublin, and London have illustrated how the relationships between archaeology and popular music survive in a wide variety of acoustic, material, personal, and place-based venues. Of particular importance in these studies is the role of archaeology in examining the tensions between music as an ephemeral product and stakeholder desires to preserve the remains of the setting in which creative expressions were produced.[7] Scholarship on the contemporary archaeology of popular music is expanding, but still remains a topic well outside the mainstream. However, this outsider status, we would argue, is at the same time well suited to attract broad interest among non-professional audiences in archaeological contributions.

ARCHAEOLOGY AT AIR STUDIOS

The AIR Studios complex was designed by Sir George Martin to be a secluded retreat, invisible from the main road and located at some distance from the distractions of the capital at Plymouth. Visitors passed through a pair of iron gates, before proceeding up a narrow dirt road and turning off into a semi-circular driveway. While the compound was modest in size (Figure 18.2), it spared no expense in its amenities and recording technology. The main house included two stories of entertaining space (living room, kitchen, bar, dining area, game room), and half a dozen guest bedrooms, storage areas, and workrooms. Across an interior courtyard attached to the back of the main house were the production offices of the studio. A narrow covered walkway separated the bar on the ground floor from the expansive swimming pool and patio area, affording sweeping views down to the Caribbean Sea, where musicians, technicians, and visitors lounged during brainstorming sessions and between recording takes. At the far end of the covered walkway was the recording studio itself, with two large rooms separated by a wall containing a large window: one used by producers and engineers for recording and editing, the other a space for the musicians to perform.

Our investigations at AIR Studios included three visits, with permission of its owner, in 2010, 2012, and 2019.[8] The complex is located immediately above and to the north of the Belham River valley. At the time of our first visit, the situation was dangerous: a major volcanic dome collapse on 11 February 2010 had inundated the valley with pyroclastic debris and mudflows,[9] and scientists from the Montserrat Volcano Observatory were warning that additional major eruptions might further extend the area of devastation. Another volcanic event had the real potential to destroy AIR Studios altogether, and with the site thus at risk we approached it as if its loss was imminent, employing a full suite of archaeological techniques—photo-documentation, mapping, survey, excavation, surface collection of diagnostic portable objects, and video recording.

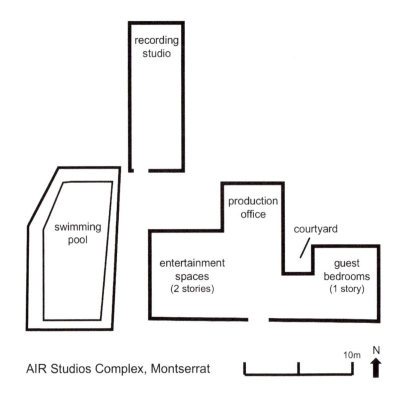

Figure 18.2. Sketch map of the AIR Studios complex. *Drawn by Krysta Ryzewski.*

When we first encountered it, the complex still retained many traces of the daily activities taking place there when it was hurriedly abandoned in the hours before Hurricane Hugo. Cans of food remained in cupboards, reel-to-reel tapes were piled in the recording studio, guitar cases stacked in closets, and personal items stowed away in guest bedrooms. The infrastructure of the buildings remained relatively stable and intact, while regular ash-falls had helped suppress the encroachment of vegetation. These were the circumstances in which we documented the various areas of the compound.

THE MAIN HOUSE AND SWIMMING POOL

The main house served as the entertainment and lodging space for visiting musicians and their crews of technicians, producers, and companions. The central space of the main house was a multi-purpose room that served jointly as a lounging, dining, and practice space. Its open-plan design was unified by hardwood floors, accented by a stone fireplace, and brightened by windows on three sides. It was in this space that up to two dozen diners would often gather around a long table to enjoy elaborate buffet dinners featuring local Montserratian delicacies such as goat water (a stew of goat meat, breadfruit, vegetables, and spices) and mountain chicken (*Leptodactylus fallax,* a large frog). The dinners frequently lasted late into the evening, and occasionally guests became rowdy. One former staff member recalled being witness to an epic post-dinner food fight during Elton John's visit in 1981–82, during which his entourage spilled such great quantities of Remy Martin cognac onto the floor that it stripped it of its varnish.[10] No sign of wear and tear from these episodes was visible on the floor in 2010, but a small hole half a meter wide had punctured the roof, allowing enough moisture into the interior space to introduce decay to its flooring and walls.

In between the multi-purpose room and the poolside patio was a square bar room. In its southwest corner stood an L-shaped bamboo and wicker bar, but by the time of our survey the only remaining indication of its former location were traces of the two tiers of mirrored shelving that stood behind it—the bar itself having been salvaged for use elsewhere on the island. Nearby, sliding glass doors opened onto the covered walkway that led to an irregularly-shaped patio and in-ground pool. Locals recall that the swimming pool was the main social attraction for visitors and musicians alike during their leisure time, at all hours of the day and night. Flanked by a water slide at one end and a spring-loaded diving board at the other, the pool was intended to be an active space of enjoyment. Sometimes, in between takes, musicians would gather for brainstorming conversations on the diving board. Photographs from the 1980s depict such luminaries as Phil Collins, Sting, and Sir George Martin in such unconventional board meetings (Figure 18.1).

THE RECORDING STUDIO

At the end of the covered walkway stood the entrance to the recording studio itself. In 2010 the door hung precariously on one hinge, but access to the interior was otherwise unfettered. This space originally housed a Sony 24-track digital tape machine and its Neve recording console, one of only three in existence at the time. The Neve was reputed for its unparalleled sound quality and editing capabilities, and it was highly sought after by AIR Studios musicians. Fans of The Police will recognize the Neve console in the 1984 video for *Every Little Thing She Does is Magic,* in which Sting enthusiastically dances on top of it. Many of the recording artists, including Dire Straits, suggested that it produced a sound that was distinct to AIR Studios Montserrat. Their 1985 *Brothers in Arms* album, recorded entirely at AIR Studios, is in fact credited for initiating the shift to the digital age and, by extension, transforming the technological practices of the recording industry.[11] A recipient of a Grammy award for Best Engineered Album, *Brothers in Arms* is an acoustic artifact of the Neve and the early digital acoustic innovations in AIR Studios.[12]

Entering the dark and windowless studio rooms, we discovered stacks of undisturbed documents, tapes, reels, and other portable equipment in the editing room (Figure 18.3), but all of the major recording equipment was removed from AIR Studios prior to or immediately after Hurricane Hugo. What remained in the editing room for us to document in 2010 were dozens of manuals, notebooks, and other paperwork used by the sound engineers and producers. Along its northern wall, a large picture window separated it from the performance space of the musicians. By 2010, that space contained few traces of the recording process, except for electrical boxes on the walls, along with amplifier and electric instrument ports. But the stone-faced walls, with an alcove for the drummer, and other distinctive features of the room that are clearly recognizable in 1980s images and videos (such as the 1989 recording of *Mixed Emotions* by the Rolling Stones) remained intact.

Figure 18.3. View into the recording studio from the editing room in 2010 (left) and 2012 (right). The Neve recording console would have been positioned in the foreground against the window. *Photographs by John Cherry and Krysta Ryzewski.*

THE PRODUCTION OFFICE

A small square extension to the main house served as the business office for AIR Studios, accessible from the courtyard between it and the recording studio. When we first surveyed the property, this one-room office was flooded with six inches of water. Reams of paperwork, blank studio invoice forms, recording logs, journals, mail, computer parts, and electronics manuals covered the countertops and lined the drawers. Adjoining this workspace was a large storage area. Shelving covered its walls, and on the shelves remained reel-to-reel tapes, microphone stands, headphones, an empty guitar case, and boxes of other equipment parts.[13] The office contained portable items that the caretakers of the property and scavengers alike had deemed to be of lesser value; but, to us, they provided a glimpse into how the studio functioned as a business operation and technological innovator.

THE COURTYARD

Nestled between the production office and main house was a U-shaped grass courtyard. Along its east side ran a corridor, leading to three guest rooms, bordered by a decorative pavement of four extant one-meter-wide concrete squares. These panels, evidently, were added gradually over time, and musicians and support crew inscribed their names, drawings, or handprints into the wet concrete, creating what they intended to be a permanent record of their time at AIR Studios. By the time of our work in 2010, the so-called graffiti sidewalk had become the source of local lore on Montserrat. Ash and vegetation had long since made them invisible, but, with the assistance of the local caretaker, we relocated and carefully excavated the four portions of the sidewalk that still survived, other segments having previously been removed.[14] Careful troweling revealed the inscriptions of the Climax Blues Band, the first group to record at AIR Studios in 1979, alongside numerous other nicknames of less famous band members and sound engineers whose contributions to the albums AIR Studios created are often under-recognized (Figure 18.4).

Figure 18.4. Luke Pecoraro excavating a portion of the courtyard sidewalk in 2010. *Photograph by John Cherry.*

STILL STANDING . . . BARELY

Don't you know I'm still standing better than I ever did
Looking like a true survivor, feeling like a little kid
I'm still standing after all this time
Picking up the pieces of my life without you on my mind
I'm still standing, yeah yeah
(Elton John, "I'm Still Standing," recorded at AIR Studios in 1982)

AIR Studios did not meet a sudden and catastrophic end at the hands of a subsequent volcanic eruption, as we had feared might happen. In fact, the February 2010 dome collapse would be the last major volcanic event of the decade (although the volcano remains active). We decided to revisit AIR Studios in June 2012. Six months earlier Sir George Martin, who was optimistic that the eruptions were ending, organized a clean-up of the complex and took steps to secure the property from trespassing tourists and scrappers. In their efforts to make it ready for an intended refurbishment, Martin's crew discarded all of the portable objects and debris that we had documented two years earlier. Their work, unfortunately, did not involve any maintenance to the buildings, which then showed signs of advancing decay—especially in the main roof of the house, where the minor damage we noted before had grown into a gaping hole, causing the wooden floors of the living room to buckle and rot, with similar conditions in the guest rooms. In 2012 AIR Studios was a hollowed-out, decaying shell of the complex that we had surveyed just two years earlier. There were no portable materials and few undamaged architectural features left to illustrate the experience of living and working at AIR Studios in its 1980s heyday. Such absences were doubtless intended by Martin to be just temporary, and he held out hope of restoring the studio complex and converting it into a museum or tourist site; but any such future plans stalled with his death in 2016.

By the time of our next evaluation of the studio in April 2019, the complex had fallen into complete ruin as a consequence of both neglect and fading local interest in its maintenance. The holes in the roof of the main house led to its total collapse, leaving the interior open to the elements. Without significant ash-falls in recent years, tropical vegetation had totally engulfed the courtyard and lawns surrounding the property. Wasp nests lined the covered walkway to the recording studio, hindering access to its interior, which had succumbed to rot from its compromised roofing. The thick vegetation blanketing the site now made it difficult even to envision the layout of the original complex and the courtyard locations where we had excavated almost a decade before. There is no question

Figure 18.5. Interior of Hilltop Coffee House, Montserrat 2019: albums recorded at AIR Studios and tape reels salvaged from the site hang on the wall, while the chair of a guitarist is suspended overhead. *Photograph by Miriam Rothenberg.*

whose construction in the new capital at Little Bay Martin helped finance in the mid-2000s. In its lobby hang bronze casts of the handprints impressed into the missing portions of sidewalk that we excavated: visitors can measure their own hands against those of Paul McCartney, Mick Jagger, or Phil Collins, among others. Nearby, patrons of the popular Soca Cabana at Little Bay can belly up to the former AIR Studios bar, now rebranded as the *Bar of the Stars,* with plaques above each stool bearing the name of a famous musician who recorded at AIR Studios. Elsewhere, long-term resident David Lea has been salvaging memorabilia and furnishings from AIR Studios since its closure: the walls of his Hilltop Coffee House are lined with the covers of albums recorded at AIR Studios and artifacts from the studio, while the chair of a guitarist from the recording studio hangs from the ceiling (Figure 18.5).

SAVING AIR STUDIOS

This coming and going
Is driving me nuts
This to-ing and fro-ing
Is hurting my guts
You're not the only one
With mixed emotions
(Rolling Stones, "Mixed Emotions," recorded at AIR Studios in 1989)

Numerous proposals have emerged since the late 1990s to restore AIR Studios for the benefits of future economic development, tourism, and local history. Although these plans shared a desire to recognize the unique role of Montserrat in global pop music history, they differ considerably in their focus on local or foreign audiences, economic sustainability, and recognition of the threats posed by ongoing volcanic activity. Government planners, tourism consultants, and local residents devised redevelopment plans for the island that incorporated AIR Studios as a must-see attraction.[16] For instance, in the Montserrat Tourism Master Plan 2015–2025,[17] there was

that the standing remains of AIR Studios will not survive much longer in their current state of neglect.

That is not to say, however, that AIR Studios will be lost. The decay of the structures is tempered by the widely-scattered remains of the AIR Studios experience, both material and musical. In fact, many of the most treasured materials of the AIR Studios experience have been removed and are curated both locally and internationally. Prior to Hurricane Hugo, for example, Sir George Martin removed the Neve recording console and sold it to another recording studio in Los Angeles. From there, the Neve traveled around North America and today resides in the care of the Subterranean Sound Studios in Toronto.[15] On Montserrat itself, remnants of AIR Studios are prominent public fixtures in the Montserrat Cultural Centre, envisioned the establishment of a Music Heritage Centre at the site of AIR Studios by 2019. The exhibits of musical memorabilia and studio restorations would cater to tourists whom these consultants anticipated were drawn to the site by their nostalgia for 1980s pop music and a desire to connect with the rock stars who recorded there.

The estimate of half a million East Caribbean dollars for the repair and restoration of the buildings, however, was well in excess of available government funding, and enthusiasm for such a scheme began to wane. Thus another comprehensive report, Montserrat Tourism Strategy, 2019–2022 acknowledged AIR Studios as "a perfect example of a co-working space that facilitated work carried out by the creative class," but went on to conclude that, rather than investing government money in its revitalization, Montserrat needed to "broaden its horizon and attract other members of the creative class."[18] An even more somber view appeared soon thereafter in the Economic Growth Strategy and Delivery Plan for Montserrat by the Mott Macdonald Consultancy. Its report cautioned against committing resources to AIR Studios, concluding only that its investment potential "as a music industry development built on past traditions [is] unlikely but perhaps conceivable."[19]

Yet despite the absence of official support for converting AIR Studios into a government-sponsored heritage and tourism site, there still remains an active and passionate grassroots base—both locally and abroad—committed to preserving the studio and its history. As recently as August 2019 local blogger Craig Brewin proposed developing an AIR Studios Musical Heritage Tour. Inspired by multi-sited music heritage tours, such as The Beatles Story and the British Music Experience in Liverpool, Brewin imagined a branded tour where local guides might take cruise ship passengers and day trippers to various sites around the island associated with AIR Studios and its artists—the Cultural Centre, Hill Top Coffee House, Olveston House (the island residence of Sir George Martin), the former home of Montserratian calypso superstar Arrow, a Hollywood-style walk of fame in Little Bay, and the gates leading up to AIR Studios (but not the now-dangerous complex itself), all topped off with a drink at the Bar of the Stars.[20] Brewin's idea neatly

sidesteps the expensive consultancy and feasibility studies proposed in earlier plans and instead enlists established local resources and accessible sites. In recent months it has gained momentum among followers of the AIR Studios Montserrat—Rock Music page on Facebook, moderated by Yve Robinson, a former employee of the studio. Meanwhile, visitors continue to make (unsanctioned) pilgrimages to the rock 'n' roll shrine, publicly broadcasting their experiences in conspicuous venues that include international media outlets.[21]

Our own publication on AIR Studios became unexpectedly bound up in imaginations of the future of the studio, well outside the discipline of contemporary archaeology.[22] Perhaps because it was the first academic publication to focus on AIR Studios, it attracted considerable attention, especially on the open-access academic research website on which it was also posted. Readers included music history fans, journalists, recording artists, filmmakers, and local residents with past connections to the studio. By highlighting the decay of the studio and its uncertain future as a physical site, as well as its important musical heritage, this publication seems to have been a conversation-starter that inspired a flurry of renewed interest in documenting the site and its stories. For example, American journalist and former AIR Studios musician Brian Sallerson conducted interviews and research for a book on the history of the studio,[23] while in 2021 Australian filmmakers Cody Greenwood and Gracie Otto released a documentary on the legacy of the studio called Under the Volcano (like Sallerson, Greenwood has a personal connection to the studio: her mother, the artist and author Frané Lessac, was a frequent visitor to the studios during the 1980s when she lived on the island).

It will be especially interesting to us, as archaeologists, to observe how these documentary portrayals and future grassroots heritage initiatives featuring AIR Studios will conceive of the space as dynamic even in its post-music-production afterlife. As our archaeological surveys demonstrated, despite the fact that the site was quickly vacated in 1989 and many remnants of the periods survived in situ through 2011, the complex is continuously changing as a result of human and natural interventions. Even as a decaying building complex, it was not and is not a static, abandoned space—a ruin frozen in time. This archaeologically documented reality poses distinct challenges to preservationists who variously yearn to refurbish the studio to its 1980s heyday, curate it as a ruin, or reminisce about a ten-year period of the much longer existence of the property. Such challenges echo Paul Graves-Brown's (2009) advice to archaeologists about exercising caution when monumentalizing music as if it, too, is a physical thing fixed to a particular place or point in time. Like the music made at AIR Studios, we suggest that the studio complex is best understood archaeologically, as a fluid cultural landscape. AIR Studios is still standing in its original location; but it is also dispersed across Montserrat and much farther afield. What remains of AIR Studios is, in some measure, in the eyes and ears of the beholder. To save AIR Studios requires reorienting focus away from the site itself; coming to terms with a certain degree of loss; and recognizing that the most significant physical traces of AIR Studios have now diffused well beyond their place of origin, much like the pop music that was produced there years ago.

NOTES

1   Cherry et al. 2013.
2   See the appendix in Cherry et al. 2013 for a full discography.
3   Cherry et al. 2013.
4   Graves-Brown et al. 2013, Harrison and Schofield 2010, McAtackney and Ryzewski 2017.
5   McAtackney and Ryzewski 2017, 4.
6   Arjona 2017, Darvill 2014, Lashua et al. 2010 , Parkman 2014, Roberts 2014, Ryzewski 2017.
7   Graves-Brown 2009.
8   Cherry et al. 2013, Cherry and Ryzewski 2020, 156–58.
9   Cherry et al. 2013, fig. 12.1.
10 Martyn 2019.
11 Runtagh 2019.
12 Wheeler 2019.
13 Cherry et al. 2013, figures 12.4 and 12.5.
14 Cherry et al. 2013, fig. 12.6.
15 Wheeler 2019.
16 Graves-Gabbadon 2016.
17 Tourism Planning Associates 2016, 20, 55, 88, 112.
18 Tourism Intelligence International 2017, 98.
19 Tourism Intelligence International 2017, 57.
20 Brewin 2019.
21 Galloway 2015, Scheussler 2016.
22 Cherry et al. 2013.
23 Sallerson 2022, https://www.sallerson.com (accessed 13 February 2023).

BIBLIOGRAPHY

Arjona, Jamie M. (2017), Homesick Blues: Excavating Crooked Intimacies in Late Nineteenth- and Early Twentieth-Century Jook Joints, *Historical Archaeology* 51(1), 43–59.

Brewin, Craig (4 August 2019), "Coming soon? The AIR Studios Musical Heritage Tour," https://livinginmontserrat.wordpress.com/2019/08/04/coming-soon-the-air-studios-musical-heritage-tour/?fbclid=IwAR1V4BdauWpyYb8uhNsJfIHGLfZqiWNYZoj50B8Qt81fgm02yUZaL3jHhAQ.

Cherry, John F. and Krysta Ryzewski (2020), *An Archaeological History of Montserrat in the West Indies*, Oxford (Oxbow Books).

Cherry, John F., Krysta Ryzewski, and Luke Pecoraro (2013), "'A Kind of Sacred Place': The Rock and Roll Ruins of AIR Studios, Montserrat," in: Mary C. Beaudry and Travis G. Parno, eds., *Archaeologies of Mobility and Movement*, New York (Springer), 181–98.

Darvill, Timothy (2014), Rock and Soul: Humanizing Heritage, Memorializing Music, and Producing Places, *World Archaeology* 46(3), 462–76.

Davison, Phil (12 August 1997), "Under the Volcano: How a Rock Music Legend was Turned to Dust," https://www.independent.co.uk/news/under-the-volcano-how-a-rock-music-legend-was-turned-to-dust-1245023.html.

Fottrell, Stephen (9 March 2016), "Sir George Martin's Caribbean Legacy: AIR Studios Montserrat," https://www.bbc.com/news/entertainment-arts-35761728.

Galloway, Gloria (2 February 2015), "A Rock 'n' Roll Pilgrimage to Montserrat," https://www.theglobeandmail.com/life/travel/destinations/a-rock-n-roll-pilgrimage-to-montserrat/article22745580/.

Graves-Brown, Paul (2009), Nowhere Man: Urban Life and the Virtualization of Popular Music, *Popular Music History* 4(2), 220–41.

Graves-Brown, Paul, Rodney Harrison, and Angela Piccini, eds. (2013), *The Oxford Handbook of the Archaeology of the Contemporary World*, Oxford (Oxford University Press).

Graves-Brown, Paul and John Schofield (2011), The Filth and the Fury: 6 Denmark Street (London) and the Sex Pistols, *Antiquity* 85(330), 1385–1401.

Graves-Gabbadon, Sarah (2016), "Six Reasons Why You Should Visit Montserrat," https://www.caribjournal.com/2016/01/01/six-reasons-why-you-should-visit-montserrat/.

Harrison, Rodney and John Schofield (2010), *After Modernity: Archaeological Approaches to the Contemporary Past*. Oxford (Oxford University Press).

Lashua, Brett, Sara Cohen, and John Schofield (2010), Popular Music, Mapping and the Characterization of Liverpool, *Popular Music History* 4(2), 126–44.

Martin, Sir George (25 April 2011), "Sir George Martin Talks about Montserrat and AIR Studios (originally aired on BBC2)," https://www.youtube.com/watch?v=77BhKRaJpBA.

Martyn, Shona (31 May 2019), "Rocketman and Me: My Caribbean Life with Elton John," https://www.smh.com.au/entertainment/music/rocketman-and-me-my-caribbean-life-with-elton-john-20190531-p51t3k.html.

McAtackney, Laura, and Krysta Ryzewski, eds. (2017), *Contemporary Archaeology and the City: Creativity, Ruination and Political Action*, Oxford (Oxford University Press).

Mott MacDonald (December 2017), "Economic Growth Strategy and Delivery Plan for Montserrat," http://www.gov.ms/wp-content/uploads/2012/06/Growth-Strategy-Delivery-Plan-2017-DRAFT-.pdf.

Parkman, E. Breck (2014), A Hippie Discography: Vinyl Records from a Sixties Commune, *World Archaeology* 46(3), 431–47.

Roberts, Les (2014), Marketing Musicscapes, or the Political Economy of Contagious Music, *Tourist Studies* 14(1), 10–29.

Runtagh, Jordan (1 July 2019), "The Summer of '85: Relive the Eleven Biggest Musical Moments," https://www.rollingstone.com/music/music-features/summer-1985-madonna-michael-jackson-back-to-future-movie-853250/.

Ryzewski, Krysta (2017), "Making Music in Detroit: Archaeology, Popular Music, and Post-industrial Heritage," in: Laura McAtackney and Krysta Ryzewski, eds., *Contemporary Archaeology and the City: Creativity, Ruination and Political Action*, Oxford (Oxford University Press), 69–90.

Sallerson, Bryan (2022), *Island Music: The History of AIR Studios Montserrat*, Independently published by the author.

Scheussler, Ryan (28 January 2016), "George Martin's AIR Studio is a Symbol of Montserrat's Lost Era as a Pop Music Hub," https://www.theguardian.com/world/2016/jan/28/george-martin-air-studio-montserrat-paul-mccartney-stevie-wonder.

Tourism Intelligence International (2017), "Montserrat Tourism Strategy, 2019–2022, Prepared for the Government of Montserrat," http://www.gov.ms/wp-content/uploads/2019/03/Montserrat-Tourism-Strategy-DRAFT.pdf.

Tourism Planning Associates (29 April 2016), "Montserrat Tourism Master Plan, 2015–2025, Final Report Submitted to Government of Montserrat," http://www.gov.ms/wp-content/uploads/2018/11/MONTSERRAT-TOURISM-MASTER-PLAN.pdf.

Wheeler, Brad (26 July 2019), "Every Little Thing It Does Is Magic: A Revered Sound Board and Its Toronto Fate," https://www.theglobeandmail.com/arts/music/article-every-little-thing-it-does-is-magic-a-revered-sound-board-and-its/Toronto-fate.

RADICAL STRATIGRAPHY

EXCAVATING A CENTURY OF LOS ANGELES GRAFFITI

SUSAN A. PHILLIPS

This thought-piece about graffiti as radical stratigraphy is in two parts. The first is a section on theory and history that links archaeology and cultural anthropology. Part two introduces some sites and examples, providing a demonstration of method and analysis within my case studies of urban Los Angeles (another, very different project associated with graffiti in Los Angeles is discussed by Maite Zubiaurre and Filomena Cruz in Chapter 7 of this volume).

PART 1: HISTORY AND THEORY

When German philosopher Walter Benjamin toured Pompeii and Herculaneum, he was struck by their isolation. The presence of Neapolitan guards added to the unpleasantness, he said. His 1931 broadcast on *Radio Berlin* hints at things missing. Benjamin first dangles the labyrinth: unnavigable but for a ball of string. He then tempts the audience with the lost Samnite city destroyed by a previous earthquake and by subsequent rebuilding that meant progress for Roman Pompeii. He ends with the apocalyptic biblical writing of a Christian or Jew in the sand, Sodom and Gomorrah, and so points to someone outside of Roman ideal types. Benjamin's short piece amplifies one of the key lessons of Pompeii: that preservation is embedded in destruction. He conjures people, writing, and places that are suggestions and definitive statements alike.

Graffiti offers a similar history of things missing, that same tension between what we can know and what we cannot. Graffiti is perspective-shifting because it opens up new realms of understanding. But it also represents a partial telling based on incomplete contexts and absent authors.

I have often wondered whether my history of graffiti in Los Angeles might be considered a kind of archaeology. Phrased in slightly different terms, I have wondered what

Figure 17.1. "Nouveau Lascaux," the storm drain tunnel bull, 1969. Photograph taken in 2015. *Photograph by the author.*

kind of archaeology graffiti might help to inform. As a cultural anthropologist, my interest has been in how graffiti builds from deep relativism and cultural context, from connections to individuals, and from sitedness in place and time. Graffiti as a phenomenon crosscuts conceptions prehistory and history, ancient and modern. The role of graffiti through time has shifted radically, which is why scholars are hesitant to draw too many neat comparisons between graffiti in ancient and modern worlds. In literate societies with little or no paper, people scratched, carved, and etched on public, private, and religious surfaces with abandon—and impunity. Graffiti was an accepted part of literacy, a wide swath of individuals wrote it, and it played a different role in society than it does today.[1]

The study of graffiti has long been linked to archaeology. Even the word itself is Pompeii-derived. Graffiti denoted scratchings found on the walls of Pompeii, while dipinti indicated paintings.[2] It is a cliché to link graffiti to Pompeii as I am doing here—always, always Pompeii and then, God forbid, rock art (Figure 17.1). Whenever graffiti makes an entrance into scholarly endeavors, these things beg to be brought up. My desire is to make them more than facile comparisons. Pompeii and Herculaneum are immense case studies, which demonstrate how graffiti is a key to human-centered interpretations.

My own research on Los Angeles graffiti started almost thirty years ago, when I was a graduate student at UCLA studying gang graffiti. It took me nearly ten years before I began to see older writing. I needed to look in different places, underneath things, in an upside-down way. I learned to search at a smaller scale, to seek out works in pencil, or charcoal, chalk, and the other media that were pre–spray-can. I became interested in the way that the infrastructure of the city had become the custodian of a history I began to find everywhere.

For the past century, an alternative written record has been tied to the underbelly of Los Angeles. The infrastructure of railroads, bridges, storm drain tunnels, harbors, and rivers houses a vernacular history inscribed mostly on concrete with rocks, chalk, charcoal, pencil, and sometimes railroad tar. As the urban landscape of Los Angeles developed, groups as diverse as hobos, children, gay men, container ship sailors, and blue-collar workers have used graffiti to write themselves into the infrastructure of the city.[3] As illicit material representation, graffiti cements the tie between landscape, cultural memory, and social life. Early on, I began to blend archaeological and ethnographic theories, methods, and subsequent interpretation. Archaeology has always given me a sense of grounding. The kind of archaeology that I do is less than actual excavation, but more than just a metaphor.

A point of theoretical transfer between archaeology and cultural anthropology, the analysis of graffiti provides fodder for the archaeological turn within anthropology, and for continued attention to the excavation of the present and recent past.[4] Alfredo González-Ruibal (2008) argues that, if we avoid the archaeology of more recent events, we in turn neglect the social, political, and environmental fallout of excess and its negative impacts on the lives of people. He asserts (2008, 251) that archaeological projects do not necessarily hinge on the production of new narratives, but rather that we need a new way of seeing: "facing the devastation and pain brought about by failed modernities, more than an explanation what we need is a kind of revelation—another way of seeing." I offer graffiti as one potential pathway that necessitates the fusion of archaeology, urban history, and ethnography.

Destruction is a key concept for authors who treat the negative outcomes of capitalism through a material lens. These authors have landed on the idea of ruin, on deposits or traces. They often speak of palimpsest, a particular kind of jumbled layering, and about the erasure by which information is included or excluded. Anthropologist Vyjayanthi Rao (2009) sees the city itself as an archive. For Rao, the palimpsest is not benign. It is the physical manifestation of inequality: active, nefarious, and process-oriented, rather than a simplistic way of understanding how layers accumulate. Seen in this way, even if infrastructure is in continual usage and structurally sound, it is already a ruin of capitalism, whose promises have failed, and a monument to those promises (and failures) at the same time. Cultural anthropologist Anna Lowenhaupt Tsing (2015) similarly writes of the uncanny ability of mushrooms to flourish in disrupted soils. Mushrooms are the first thing to reappear after nuclear disaster; they are the first thing that people seek as they prepare for war. Like the archaeologists cited above, Tsing is also interested in what it means to make lives on the ruins of capitalism and late capitalism. Like the mushroom, graffiti flourishes in constrained, disrupted, or hostile circumstances. Its availability, immediacy, and, ultimately, its illegality make it a flexible and powerful medium and a signature of resilience.

Graffiti is rarely tapped as a primary source material within the contemporary history of cities. Ferdinand de Jong and David Murphy (2014, 2) suggest that "leaving the archive, then, we need to look for traces in the street, the gutter, the hidden alleys, all those spaces never intended to commemorate, but on which history has nevertheless made its 'impressions.'"

Figure 17.2. The exterior of the Belmont Tunnel in 1993. *Photograph by the author.*

Figure 17.3. Microphotograph of a sample of a wall of the Belmont Tunnel. *Rendered in 2017 with the assistance of Dr Tami Lasseter Clare of Portland State University.*

Seeing the city as sites of history, they write (2014, 14), "one is compelled to excavate the strata of deposits, but typically for the palimpsest such strata have intermingled to the extent that past and present are hard to disentangle."

Graffiti flattens time while simultaneously giving visual depth to flat surfaces. Graffiti renders the experience of time as cobbled together, as bricolage, as merged in a simultaneous past–present–future. Susan Buck-Morse (1991, x) writes that "if history is abandoned as a conceptual structure that deceptively transfigures the present, its cultural contents are redeemed as the source of critical knowledge that alone can place the present into question." The tie of sympathy between infrastructure and author makes graffiti into a kind of time machine, perpetually stuck in the "present" in which it was created, but also permanently fixed beyond that present and into both past and future.

Figure 17.2 shows part of the exterior of the now-destroyed graffiti hotspot Belmont Tunnel. Belmont was a wildly active spot in the late 1980s and 1990s. On the weekends, the defunct structures comprising the one and only subway tunnel in Los Angeles had become a de-facto park, crowded with graffiti writers and players of the Maya ballgame *tarasca*. Belmont housed the only *tarasca* ball court in the United States. Due to the proximity of the site to downtown Los Angeles, though, the lot that was officially considered vacant was slated for redevelopment. Community organizers attempted to fight the redevelopment and instead convert the site into a public art park that legitimized both the *tarasca* and the graffiti. But real estate won, and developers converted the site into condominium buildings. During the teardown of the site in 2003, I collected several pieces of the graffiti-heavy walls. The microphotographs of these show more than a hundred layers (Figure 17.3).

Several things interest me about this scan. First is the story of the location, whose interpretation involves a much more extensive history that necessitates broader conversations about housing inequality, immigration, lack of park space, and undervalued people or illicit activities deemed dangerous. The second thing regards stratigraphy. When archaeologists discuss strata, they generally talk about its accumulation from the bottom up, its superimposition horizontally in the earth. Archaeology also depends on processes of accumulation, which—in the terms of de Jong and Murphy (2014)—become mixed with human elements. The stratigraphy that emerges in the investigation of graffiti becomes horizontal because of the accumulation of writing on a vertical surface, while the excavation becomes vertical. The layering in this scan is temporally compressed. Seldom do archaeological sites compress layers created at such rapid-fire speed. Third, these deposits have to do with what many people think of as another kind of dirt: graffiti. In the twentieth century, people carry entrenched negative associations with what is now an illicit mode of expression. That was part of the reason why the site could not be saved. In 2003, graffiti was still considered dangerous. Today, I can see how the increasingly legitimate position of graffiti could have allowed for a different outcome for the site, especially due to the popularity of that style of graffiti work today.

Ruined, 'unimportant,' or overlooked areas where graffiti survives are critical to telling alternate Los Angeles histories. The infrastructure of the city has been a form of protection for the messages they carry. Because it can be forsaken or isolated, city infrastructure—such as the old subway tunnel at Belmont—can function as a form of commons in the absence of city-sanctioned public space.

In contemporary thinking about graffiti in the twentieth century, the local, historical traditions of graffiti that comprise most historical writing are unlike the art pieces that used to be produced at the Belmont Tunnel. They are generally unknown in scholarly and public realms and are undervalued due to their simple aesthetic. The broader public seems to know about gang writing and the colorful graffiti that emerged from the subways in 1970s New York. But older material is a rarely tapped primary source material for charting urban development and the voices of people normally excluded from the historical record. While graffiti in the moment is often a cause for public outcry, give it fifty years and it suddenly becomes interesting. Give it a hundred—or a thousand—and it becomes a rare direct link to the past. After a hundred years, the attrition of early Los Angeles graffiti is at an all-time high, but the stories are still within reach. Some writers and many of their descendants are alive. As Los Angeles rebuilds its water infrastructure surrounding the Los Angeles River, elements have begun to shift, revealing some layers beneath and destroying others. Insularity or inaccessibility protects graffiti as a material object, as in various labor contexts, or because hard-to-reach infrastructure protects messages from view.

PART 2: SITES AND EXAMPLES

The Civil War Powder Magazine. One equation in the work that I do is that the oldest infrastructure equals the oldest graffiti. If you want to find old writing, you have to go to the old places, whether these are buildings, bridges, storm drain tunnels, or city blocks. The Los Angeles 1862 Civil War–era powder magazine is one of the oldest buildings in Los Angeles, and one of just two remaining buildings of the original Drum Barracks camp. Constructed in the harbor town of Wilmington during the Civil War, the powder magazine and camp were decommissioned ten years later. Most of the writing began then. The earliest dated signature on the building is from 1862; most, however, are dated after 1874. All four sides of the 6 × 6 meter (20 × 20 foot) exterior of the building are covered with carvings through the late 1800s and beyond. A fluke in the history of the building preserved the writing on its surfaces. In 1927, the Larsen family built a grocery store around the diminutive structure, which began to serve as cold storage. The wooden exterior of the grocery sheltered the delicate plaster, stone and brick surfaces of the powder magazine for decades. At some point, the grocery store was converted into a residential dwelling until its demolition in 1982. The subsequent removal of the

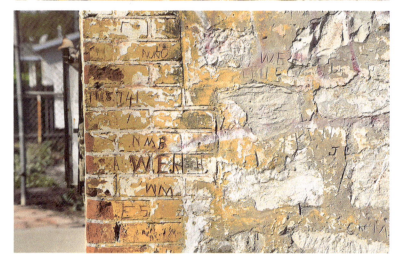

exterior building revealed the long-forgotten powder maga-zine, and the local community fought to save it—successfully, this time. The powder magazine, with signatures covering its surface, is now designated as a historic monument. Today, it is privately owned, with no public access to the location.[5]

A site like this holds the potential interest of historical archaeologists but, for the present, without the potential for excavation. The building sits on a concrete-covered corner lot at the end of a block of single-family dwellings. Functioning oil derricks are across the street. A historic map of the original Drum Barracks shows the powder magazine flanking the edge of a large parade ground and within easy sight of other Civil War structures. For now, the only possible 'excavation' is based on gathering contextual information about the location of the site, its relation to other Civil War structures (only one of which remains today), and the analysis of the writing on its surfaces. This turns out to be the work of neighborhood boys and girls, a few enlisted men, locals, and at least one hobo ("KC Kid Oct 2 1902"—the 'Kansas City Kid,' most likely).

It has been difficult to trace the names on the powder mag-azine. Many are just initials. Most are incomplete and others indecipherable. Some have been scratched or gouged out of the brick or plaster (Figure 17.5). Perpetual shade on the north side of the building has better preserved the writing there. The building is near the ocean, so the air is damp. All sides of the building are missing chunks of concrete or plaster, revealing the local stone beneath and contributing to the irreparable loss of the lettering. According to the experts of the Drum Barracks Civil War Museum, one of the oldest signatures, "WSB 1874," represents the initials of William S. Banning. William was the son of Phineas Banning, who owned most of the land in Wilmington near the harbor of Los Angeles. The elder Banning deeded land for the Drum Barracks in order to ensure that Banning's union proclivities would be represented in more confederate-leaning Southern California. Other signatures

Figure 17.4. The Civil War Powder Magazine, overview and details, 2019. *Photographs by the author.*

Figure 17.5. Details of the Civil War Powder Magazine, showing graffiti and differing levels of wear. *Photographs by the author.*

intrigue me more: "WBriggs" carved a name in cursive in the brick. One "J. Burke"(?) carved a name with the date, "1888." Several women or girls inscribed their first names, "Rhoda," "Nellie," and "Charline," but their surnames remain unintelligible: "MCCollum"(?), "Bofkiji"(?), and "HA"(?). "Victor" wrote in cursive near the bottom of one wall, including his own full name and the name of the town, "Wilmington." Another man

wrote his initials and last name, "F.R. Berg," but later wished a more complete representation and returned to add his full name, "Frank."

A 1910 photograph shows three boys staging a mock incarceration at the site—one boy is handcuffed while two others push him into the small door. The initials "CH" carved into the brick are easily visible due to their large size. Another undated picture shows a man, two children, and several sheep and cows in a lush landscape surrounded by grass. Larger-scale graffiti on the roof is illegible in that photograph, and smaller initials carved into the brick can only be seen with a loupe. The building has been through many changes. Given the current crumbling brick and caved-in roof, kegs of gunpowder are easier to imagine inside than milk, beef, or beer in cold storage. I wonder about what it meant for previous owners to interact daily with the structure; what did they think of the carvings there?

I also wonder about the neighborhood itself. When neighbors dig holes in backyards for trees, fences, or plumbing, what do they find? When the oil derricks, railroad, and container shipping infrastructure were put in across the street, what artifacts made an appearance and who, if anyone, did they tell?

The signatures on the Powder Magazine recall the deeply sited nature of graffiti, its radical condensation, and its indexical tie to absent authors. One of the graffiti marks in the bottom image of Figure 17.6 was carved at the same time as philosopher Charles Sanders Peirce's famous words on the index (1885, 181): "The index asserts nothing; it only says 'There!' It takes hold of our eyes, as it were, and forcibly directs them to a particular object, and there it stops." A medium stripped down to its barest elements, graffiti markings similarly "denote things without describing them." No matter how elaborately adorned, the most common of graffiti's stripped-down elements is the name—the tag, the moniker, the *placa*, initials, a signature. This is part of what Alessandra Russo (2006) calls "aesthetic condensation," or what Ralph Cintron (1997) terms a "condensed social narrative." What one makes of that narrative is the work of scholarship and can vary with authors and their interpretive leanings.

The King Edward Hotel. The condensed nature of graffiti requires aesthetic, spatial, and sociological unpacking. Interpretation is further complicated by layering, or palimpsest, which often provides its most immediate context. In the basement of a former downtown Los Angeles speakeasy at the 1905 King Edward Hotel, a room full of graffiti turned out to be the site of a former men's bathroom (Figure 17.6). I had been invited to the location by preservationists interested in gaining municipal historic preservation status for the building. They had noticed a great deal of graffiti in pencil and knew the marks were of value—both intrinsically and to their argument that the building deserved historic status. During my first visit to the basement, we decided to remove some 1970s wood paneling to reveal the walls beneath. It took us a while to figure out what the small room with all the graffiti even was. Like a slow dawning of consciousness, we realized that the room had been a men's bathroom. Certain patterns on the walls indicated urinals; drains in the concrete floor indicated a sink and toilet stall. Layers of paint aided our conclusion that the toilets had gravity-pull-chain tanks up high on the wall.

A doorway had provided entry on the basement side to the speakeasy, and a now-blocked stairwell had at some point provided access to the room through a storefront on the floor above. A hole in the hollow tilework sealing off the stairway allowed me to reach in and grab a vintage newspaper boasting of Bela Lugosi's *Dracula* (a stage performance), Yehudi Menuhin's performance at the Los Angeles Philharmonic for $0.25-$1.00, and the Al G. Barnes Circus, which boasted of "monster-lipped urban savages from Congo, Africa." The 1932 date of the paper provides an approximate date that access to the room was sealed from above. Dates surrounding the speakeasy and its adjoining bathroom remain ambiguous, but prohibition came early to Los Angeles. Prohibition began in 1918 and did not end until 1933. Only one of the many graffiti pieces is dated: 1922, but the date is obscured and not definitive.

Although the bathroom has writing on all four walls, most of the work is clustered by the urinals, which boast a great deal of pornographic material, blow-job fantasies, and homoerotic content. People give one another information about where and when to meet up, or how to rendezvous with a certain kind of companion.

> "I want to meet a colored man/to go 50-50/ I am white/say where I can meet you/I love big ones"
> *Response:* "See col doorman at Rose Bud"
> *Response:* "Where is the Rose Bud"

Accompanying the explicit nature of graffiti writing here are clear efforts at graffiti eradication. Because graffiti was largely written in pencil, eradication consists of rubbing off and painting over. Rubbing tended to smear rather than erase the pencil markings. The stall and sink area were at some point painted what I presume to be an anti-graphite gray, with has some further writings in pencil and crayon.

In addition to sexualized content, three drawings depict people that seem to be from the early 1900s. These include a caricatured man of Chinese descent with a queue hairstyle who seems to be speaking in characters (Figure 17.7, top), a man with a high collar, and a man with a bulbous nose. One individual in the bathroom wrote his name repeatedly: Willie Garing. His initials, signatures, hearts and boxes comprise the most miniscule graffiti that I have ever seen. Willie writes his initials, and in one instance his full name (Figure 17.7, bottom), more than thirty times on the walls adjacent to the urinals. Who was Willie Garing? What was his job? Was he a bouncer? A washroom attendant? A doorman of sorts? I found several Willie or William Garings in the United States Census. None are from Los Angeles, and only one—a German bartender from Chicago—even come close to making sense. Signatures and initials like this provide little information except for the fact of their presence. In Peirce's terms (1885), they tell us nothing.

Research about speakeasies is difficult. They are part of a hidden culture and have been deeply mythologized. The signatures and messages found here may not eliminate ambiguity, but they are fodder for generating questions. Graffiti upends conventional histories in two primary ways. First and most predictably, graffiti expands the telling of history

Figure 17.6. The former bathroom in the basement of the King Edward Hotel in 2019 with remains of stalls and graffiti, including writings about a hook-up time. *Photographs by the author.*

Figure 17.7. Graffiti on the walls of the former bathroom in the basement of the King Edward Hotel in 2019, showing caricatures (top) and the name of Willie G(aring) (bottom). *Photographs by the author.*

Figure 17.8. "Hobbie" (Pasadena, written around 1926, photograph taken in 2005). *Photograph by the author.*

by including a wider range of voices. But graffiti also necessitates an embrace of ambiguity. Graffiti often carries an imagined past and an imagined history. In all that imagining, a truly generative production of knowledge can happen that is based around a different way of thinking about the materials that human beings produce through time. It makes me want to shed new light on this subject. Literally. My greatest desire now is to use a multi-spectrum camera at the site where earlier writing was clearly painted over in an anti-graphite gray. Who do I turn to in order to ask questions about how to do this? Archaeologists. I know that if I were ever to get to use such a camera to reveal more writing, the process would simply open more questions. But that is how knowledge is produced in this field of study—from the bottom up or from the top down, in fits and starts, with dead ends and missing pieces. You learn to live with partial knowledge and, in the best cases, to make speculation generative, grounded, and empirical. The preservationists who initially invited me to the site in January 2019 argued successfully before the City of Los Angeles Planning Commission to grant the King Edward Hotel

historic preservation status in April 2020. The graffiti was one of the points in their argument that they rightfully indicated as "needing further investigation."

The Holly Street Bridge. The powder magazine and the speakeasy bathroom have a nearly absent person-centered ethnographic context. In those cases, I was able only to interact with the sites as physical places and with the writing as material traces. In this final example, I want to focus on what it means to bring a living human element into this work. I brought Christine Shedley to see her grandfather's name in chalk and charcoal on the Holly Street Bridge in Pasadena: "Hobart Gormley," "Hobbie," and "Hobbie G.," written around 1926, soon after the construction of the bridge. I had tracked Christine down through Hobart's obituary and her Facebook page. We met and talked, and eventually we went to the bridge, where his name appeared. Hobart had taken custody of Christine at a critical time in her life, and she was overcome when she saw his "Hobbie G." "Oh my goodness," she said. "Papa." She said her heart was happy to be able to see his writing, that it helped her to believe the other things he told her about his life. Of the graffiti, she said, "I never imagined that it would still be here. It is amazing for it to stand. It has been ninety years? That is almost a century, and to still be here. That is amazing. It speaks volumes to me about him. Because that is how strong he was." Since our first visit, the bridge has become where Christine goes to see her grandfather. She says she wants to visit him where he was alive, rather than to visit him where he is buried. She sometimes comes alone, or she brings her children. She reflected: "It just makes me think. It is never really over. Now my son can bring his sons to see what his great-grandpa did. The story never ends."

Many examples in the work that I do exhibit an intense connection between signature and personhood. This connection is accentuated because of the way that our society considers signatures and individuals to be connected legally. Our signatures are stand-ins for ourselves, like a second face. As a researcher, I often experience this kind of connection due to the added sensory connection to place: standing in the same locations where a person once stood, touching someone's signature that is such an intimate representation of self. That connection is a clear thread in the ethnographic work that I do with people like Christine.

CONCLUSION

Graffiti alters the way we construct knowledge. It is a way of doing history by looking at how people write about and for themselves. In my work, they are often coming from places that are in between, from people on the fringes, from elements who have been cast out. Another generalizable equation in my work has been that the most marginalized people write in the most marginalized places—under bridges, in isolated work areas, underneath the fabric of the city. That marginality protects the messages they leave behind, but also leaves those messages vulnerable to erasure. Graffiti writers often write against the system. In so doing, they create new forms of layering—a radical stratigraphy, if you will.

Ian Hodder (2012, 3) describes the entanglement between human life and materiality: "So, subversively and subtly, the focus has changed from how things make society possible to the thing itself and its multiple connections. The gaze shifts to look more closely, harder at the thing, to explore how society and things are co-entangled." According to Hodder (2012, 5), the lack of inertness of an object may be directly linked to its isolation. This implies a method akin to reanimation for understanding such objects.

In the present moment, graffiti occupies a curious space. It is the center of a massive global art movement with an accompanying, powerful art market. Graffiti is also at the center of citywide battles over spatial control. As youth usurp public and private spaces for their own purposes, they gain the enmity of the supposed arbiters of that control: the police, general citizenry, developers, business owners. As scholar and photographer I have found something different in graffiti, a unique window into social histories that might otherwise be lost from view. Most people who write graffiti do not make it into the historical record.

I like to think of the process of studying those voices more as excavation, unearthing, or uncovering rather than discovery. Uncovering is another archaeological metaphor signifying what it means to derive meaning from things that have been buried, or that are underground or submerged. Uncovering is the opposite of a colonial project in that it focuses on unseen or unnoticed images and attempts to reconnect them with the contexts and people surrounding their original production. Combining cultural anthropological and archaeological approaches informs the interpretation of overlooked materials in their specific media, locations, and social contexts.

NOTES

1   Fleming 2001.
2   Tanzer 1939.
3   Phillips 2019.
4   Dawdy 2010.
5   Seaman et al. 2008.

BIBLIOGRAPHY

Buck-Morss, Susan (1991), *The Dialectics of Seeing: Walter Benjamin and the Arcades Project,* Cambridge (Massachusetts Institute of Technology Press).

Cintron, Ralph (1997), *Angels' Town: Chero Ways, Gang Life, and Rhetorics of the Everyday*, Boston (Beacon Press).

Dawdy, Shannon Lee (2010), Clockpunk Anthropology and the Ruins of Modernity, *Current Anthropology* 51(6), 761–93.

de Jong, Ferdinand and David Murphy (2014), Archiving the Postcolonial City, *Francosphères* 3(1), DOI:10.3828/franc.2014.1.

Fleming, Juliet (2001), *Graffiti and the Writing Arts of Early Modern England*, Philadelphia (University of Pennsylvania Press).

González-Ruibal, Alfredo (2008), Time to Destroy: An Archaeology of Supermodernity, *Current Anthropology* 49(2), 247–79.

Hodder, Ian (2012), *Entangled: An Archaeology of the Relationships between Humans and Things*, Oxford (Wiley-Blackwell).

Peirce, Charles Sanders (1885), On the Algebra of Logic: A Contribution to the Philosophy of Notation, *American Journal of Mathematics* 7(2–3), 180–202.

Phillips, Susan A. (2019), *The City Beneath: A Century of Los Angeles Graffiti,* New Haven and London (Yale University Press).

Rao, Vyjayanthi (2009), Embracing Urbanism: The City as Archive, *New Literary History* 40(2), 371–83.

Russo, Alessandra (2006), A Tale of Two Bodies: On Aesthetic Condensation in the Mexican Colonial Graffiti of Actopan, 1629, *RES: Anthropology and Aesthetics* 49(1), 59–79.

Seaman, Simie, Hank Osterhoudt, Jane Osterhoudt, Susan Ogle, and Michael Sanborn (2008), *Images of America: Wilmington,* Charleston (Arcadia Publishing).

Tanzer, Helen H. (1939), *The Common People of Pompeii: A Study of the Graffiti*, Baltimore (Johns Hopkins Press).

Tsing, Anna L. (2015), *The Mushroom at the End of the World: On the Possibility of Life in Capitalist Ruins,* Princeton (Princeton University Press).

16

CHOKEHOLD ON FREEDOM

ARCHAEOLOGY, INCARCERATION, AND THE IDEOLOGY OF WHITENESS

BARRA O'DONNABHAIN

"Archaeology is not just about the past. Archaeologists use the past to contextualize and understand the present. . . . As we mourn George Floyd and the many other lives lost to systematic racism and injustice, archaeologists must continue to examine the imbalances of power in society that lead to racial violence. We believe that proper, contextual understanding of power is necessary to overcome and heal from the problems we face today. . . . The challenges of the present call for scholars of history and culture to address the impact of structural inequalities then and now."

The quote above is taken from the response of the Society for American Archaeology to the killing of George Floyd, published on their website on 2 June 2020. George Floyd was killed by police during an arrest in Minneapolis on 25 May 2020, and his death is yet another example of the vulnerability of Americans of color when it comes to dealings with the criminal justice system in the United States. This chapter seeks, in a small way, to address the challenges to archaeology as a discipline—contained in the statement of the Society for American Archaeology—by looking at one problematic aspect of the criminal justice system in the United States: incarceration.

Due to its emergence as a democratic constitutional republic (at least for some) at the time when all people in Europe were ruled by despotic monarchies with intolerant state religions, the national self-image that emerged in the United States is one of a bastion of freedom and democracy.[1] The concept of liberty plays a central role in American nationalism. It promotes an exceptionalist perspective where the country represents the high point in the evolution of freedom, while the rest of the world can only look on in envy and struggle to catch up. Yet today the Unites States has the dubious distinction of being the country that imprisons more of its own citizens than any other on the planet. Over the past fifty years, the number of people incarcerated in American prisons has ballooned from about 200,000 in 1972 to just under 1.5 million in 2018.[2]

The prison population has a marked bias toward ethnic minorities, particularly African Americans and Hispanics. In 2018 the Bureau of Justice Statistics of the Department of Justice reported that the incarceration rate for black men was 5.8 times that of white men, while the imprisonment rate of black women was 1.8 times that of white women.[3] Having held steady for decades at about 200,000 people incarcerated at any one time, the prison population began to climb after Richard Nixon formally declared a war on drugs in 1969, five years after the signing of the Civil Rights Act. The prison population doubled in the eleven years after 1969 and then doubled again under the presidency of Ronald Reagan (1980–88). The increase has not just been a feature of Republican administrations, as the system of mass incarceration gained further impetus under President Clinton (1993–2001). This was particularly so after the passage of the Violent Crime Control and Law Enforcement Act in 1994. This law, the main sponsor of which was Senator Joe Biden, created incentives for states to build more prisons and increase sentences.

So instead of a bastion of freedom, the rest of the world sees a system of mass incarceration that is a human rights disaster, a policy that is an affront to the concepts of republic and democracy, and a prison regime that undermines the ability of the United States to advocate internationally on behalf of the democratic ideals that are supposed to be at its core. Obviously there is an urgent need for change. Greater knowledge of the past can enlighten the present and elucidating how earlier centuries have shaped the current system is an important step in understanding how this situation has developed. The archaeology of key locations in the development of the modern incarceration regime provides a means of deepening our comprehension of the roots of current circumstances and informing debate about the aims, purposes and future of this aspect of a criminal justice system that is clearly broken. Here I will look at the history and archaeology of Spike Island, a key site in the development of what was known as the Irish System, a model that influenced penology internationally from the 1870s onward, including in the United States.

THE PENNSYLVANIA AND AUBURN SYSTEMS OF INCARCERATION

While the roots of incarceration as a mode of dealing with what is judged to be criminal behavior can be traced back to the Middle Ages, and earlier, the modern prison system is for the most part a product of the late eighteenth and early nineteenth centuries. This development is often portrayed as reflecting Enlightenment ideals with a touch of religious zeal but, in the age of revolutions in the late 1700s, power played a central role, as the maintenance of the hegemony of the propertied ruling class was the key driving force. The operation of this power was multi-scalar. Michel Foucault (1977) famously suggested that the development of prisons intended for long-term incarceration involved a shift from punishing bodies to reforming souls. This was achieved by subjecting prisoners to intrusive surveillance and regulation, what Foucault described as the "micro-physics of power."[4]

In common with many other countries, the current American prison system is primarily a product of nineteenth-century experimentation, with both home-grown reforms and outside influences producing different waves of innovation. The 1820s and 1830s were important decades of reforms that centered on a debate about the virtues of the Pennsylvania versus the Auburn systems, also known respectively as the Separate and the Silent systems. The Pennsylvania model took its name from the novel approach taken at Eastern State Penitentiary in Philadelphia. This facility opened in 1829 with a design and ethos influenced by contemporary construction campaigns in Britain and Ireland. Eastern State Penitentiary operated on the principle that solitary confinement fostered repentance while preventing contamination by contact with other prisoners. In its strictest mode of operation, a prisoner had no contact with other inmates. The alternative approach was the Auburn system, named after Auburn State Prison established in 1816 in Auburn, New York. In common with the Pennsylvania system, prisoners there were kept in solitary confinement at night, but endured forced labor in groups during the day, with strict silence imposed on such work parties. Both systems aimed at the reformation of the prisoner, but while the Pennsylvania approach took an almost monastic approach—by stressing repentance through contemplation of one's crime—the Auburn sought to inculcate personal discipline and respect for property through forced labor. As the nineteenth century progressed, the Auburn system became the dominant model of penology in the United States. This was primarily driven by economic considerations. The Pennsylvania model was seen to be too expensive (Eastern State Penitentiary had individual exercise yards for each cell), while in some states the forced labor of prisoners held in the Auburn system was monetized for profit. It was also noted that prolonged solitary confinement had a negative impact on the mental health of the prisoners. Despite these factors, while the Auburn system gradually became the more popular of the two models in the United States, the Pennsylvania approach became very influential in Europe.

Throughout the nineteenth century there was a two-way flow of influences across the Atlantic Ocean in experimentation and knowledge-sharing. This process of sharing data was formalized in the 1870s. The first annual meeting of the National Prison Association of the United States was held in New York City in 1871. Reports from this conference were made by American delegates to the first International Penitentiary Congress held in London the following year. This coincided with another wave of prison reforms that was informed by a number of emerging sciences, including anthropology, criminology, and, indirectly, archaeology. One of the leading figures in the development of anthropological criminology was the Italian scholar Cesare Lombroso (1835–1909), who is still referred to by some as the 'Father of Criminology.' Lombroso promoted a biological determinist view of criminality that drew on Social

Darwinist views of degeneration. After the unification of Italy in 1870, Lombroso and his colleagues played a significant role in creating the criminal justice system for the new state. In seeking models of best practice for the new prison system, the Italians rejected the Auburn and Pennsylvania systems and chose instead what was called the Irish System. This was preferred because data suggested that the approach was successful in lowering overall rates of crime and discouraging recidivism. Unlike one-size-fits-all regimes, such as the Pennsylvania and Auburn models, the Irish System was more individualized and encouraged good behavior through a multi-stage process where prisoners earned promotion within and between stages through compliance with the rules and through their labor. Its promotion at the International Penitentiary Congresses of the 1870s legitimized and bolstered the Irish System and resulted in it influencing prison regimes around the world.

THE IRISH SYSTEM

The Irish System emerged after an 1853 government inquiry into the state of Irish prisons. Even though Ireland had been made an integral part of the United Kingdom with the Act of Union of 1801, it retained a prison service that was independent of those operating in England, Wales, and Scotland. A network of county and city gaols was developed in the early decades of the nineteenth century throughout the entire United Kingdom; the same construction campaign that influenced the design and ethos of Eastern State Penitentiary. Unlike the situation in Philadelphia, these new gaols were not intended as places of long-term incarceration, as the Irish and British criminal justice systems were predicated on the transportation of convicted felons and repeat offenders to overseas penal colonies, principally in Australia. By the time this network of prisons was established, overseas visitors were shocked by the social conditions in Ireland and by the sharp contrast with Britain. During the seventeenth century, the Irish sociopolitical landscape had been transformed as a result of the transfer of land and wealth from the local population to a small ruling class of settlers from Britain. From the late 1600s onward, the systematically impoverished local population had come to rely on the monoculture of the recently introduced potato as their chief means of subsistence. When an airborne plant disease caused a failure of this crop, which impacted all of Western Europe in the mid-1840s, this had a catastrophic impact in Ireland due to the structural inequalities that had been imposed during the preceding two centuries.

The resulting Great Famine (1845–52) put significant pressure on the network of city and county gaols built just a few decades earlier. In a society characterized by gross inequality in the distribution of wealth and by endemic poverty, theft of any kind was punished harshly to protect the interests of those with property. Poverty was understood as a personal, class, or racial failing, rather than as a form of structural violence derived from political policies of dispossession and systematic pauperization. Starvation was not understood as a mitigating circumstance. In 1847, the response of the government in London to the famine-related overcrowding of Irish prisons was to create a convict depot to house male felons from the entire island of Ireland. In the spirit of "never waste a good crisis," this was established in a large military fortress that had been left unfinished after the defeat of Napoleon in 1815, located on Spike Island in Cork harbor on the Irish south coast (Figure 16.1). This was an ideal embarkation point for transportation overseas, and while awaiting passage to Australia, convicts could be a source of labor to complete the fortress. Legally, felons sentenced to transportation were "chattels of the Crown." This gave them a legal status akin to that of slaves, albeit on a temporary basis, and forced labor was part of the prison and transportation regimes.

Between 1790 and 1853, more than 37,000 men and women were transported from Ireland to Australia. After their release, transported criminals were not allowed to return and most sentences involved periods of unpaid servitude on arrival before the convict was given conditional freedom. Before 1840, most convicts arriving in Australia were assigned to private individuals who benefitted economically from this source of free labor. This privatization of prisoner labor was not permitted in Ireland or Britain where convicts could only be used to work on what were deemed to be projects of Imperial importance such as the construction of forts or naval bases. While the privatization of convict labor was phased out in Australia in the 1840s, the opposite happened in the United States. In 1844 the state of Louisiana privatized its penitentiary and leased out convict labor for profit. Later in the nineteenth century this process of prison privatization gained further momentum.

In the decade after convict labor was no longer available to private individuals, civilian colonists in Australia agitated against the transportation system, and the shipment of prisoners from Ireland ceased. This prompted the government inquiry into the state of prisons that led to the emergence of the Irish System. The period of forced labor in Australia could be shortened by good behavior prior to and during transportation. Reforms instituted after 1853 were designed to replace that incentive. The restructured system was run by a new Directorate of Irish Prisons that was chaired by Walter Crofton, a retired British army officer. Primarily due to his promotion of the system, it is with Crofton's name that the new model came to be associated, even though the general concept and many of the details of the progressive stages had been developed at the Norfolk Island penal colony between Australia and New Zealand by Alexander Maconochie when he served as governor there from 1840 to 1844.

What became known as Crofton's Irish System entailed male convicts spending the first six months of their sentence in solitary confinement in a new model prison in Dublin. The bulk of the sentence was then served on Spike Island where prisoners engaged in forced labor. In the months prior to release, convicts were transferred to an intermediary prison where they had more privileges. The first of this new type of prison was located on the mainland immediately south of Spike Island. The final stage of the Irish System involved conditional liberty, with the released prisoner reporting regularly to local police. Promotion within each stage, and from one stage to the next, was gained by the accumulation of marks that were calculated on a monthly basis. Demotion was also possible. The performance of each prisoner was assessed according

Figure 16.1. Spike Island in the center of the harbor of Cork on the south coast of Ireland. *Photograph by Con Brogan, National Monuments Service, Ireland.*

to three criteria: discipline, labor, and school. The status of a convict was indicated on a color-coded conduct badge sewn onto the prison uniform. This showed the number of good conduct marks needed to gain promotion to the next level, while the grades through which the prisoner had to pass (probation, third, second, first, and exemplary) were indicated by the color of the badge. The letters and numbers on badges of the exemplary class were made of brass. Progression through the various grades also came with a financial reward, rising from one penny per week in the probationary class, to seven pence per week in the exemplary class. These funds accumulated during the sentence and were disbursed as a weekly stipend after the prisoner's release. If a former convict agreed to emigrate after their discharge from prison, the funds would be made available as a lump sum. In the register kept on Spike Island during its last years as a convict depot, the vast majority of prisoners indicated their intention of emigrating to the United States upon their release.

SPIKE ISLAND

The Spike Island Convict Depot played a central role in the experimentation associated with the development of the Irish System. Innovations trialed on the island included the provision of education and training as well as separating juvenile prisoners from the adults. Children as young as twelve years of age were imprisoned at the Spike Island prison in its early years and those under sixteen were housed in dormitories in a windowless, disused ammunition store. In contravention of the prevailing philosophy in prison design, adults were housed in dormitories in buildings originally constructed as barracks (Figure 16.2), a situation that resulted from the emergency conversion of the fortress. These accommodation arrangements were seen as unsatisfactory as they allowed for what was described as "evil communication" between prisoners. This was later rectified by the construction of cell-sized metal cages in each dormitory space.

Archaeological investigations have uncovered a series of palisaded divisions constructed around these buildings. Forming a series of yards and walkways, these structures secured the accommodation of prisoners while restricting and regulating their movements. With a prison population just over 2,500 by 1850, the accommodation on the island was grossly overcrowded. The result was a calamitously high death rate. Of the nearly 1,200 prisoners who died in the thirty-six years that the prison was active (1847–83), more than 80 percent died between 1850 and 1854. The review of the entire prison system in 1853 recommended decreasing the number of prisoners on Spike Island to below one thousand, and this reduced the death rate dramatically. In about 1860, the cemetery used during the years of high mortality was covered by prison laborers under at least 6 meters (20 feet) of

Figure 16.2. Former military barracks used as prison accommodation on Spike Island, Ireland. *Photograph by the author.*

soil in order to complete the fortifications. A new cemetery was commissioned on the east side of the island and it was this burial area that was in use during the years of the implementation of the new Crofton system.

Archaeological excavations here have shown that the graves were laid out in a series of uniform rows reminiscent of a military cemetery, something that would have been dictated by the institution (Figure 16.3). Grave locations were indicated by informal head and foot markers of local field stones, but these were removed some time in the twentieth century. All investigated burials were in coffins with relatively sophisticated carpentry. The exteriors of some of these were decorated with faux finishes, usually used to make cheap pine look like more expensive wood. These would have been made by fellow prisoners and can be interpreted as assertions of individuality and self-worth in the face of an anonymizing system that declared the opposite. The majority of the excavated burials were younger adult males. It was clear that the institution made sure that these men carried their convict identity to the grave as they were buried in their prison uniforms. Among the evidence

Figure 16.3. The convict burial ground on Spike Island, Ireland, during excavations in 2018. *Photograph by the author.*

for this were brass letters that had been sewn into conduct badges (Figure 16.4). Osteological evidence for tuberculosis was found at a much higher rate than would normally be seen in early modern skeletal assemblages, and this tallied with annual reports made to the government by the prison authorities.

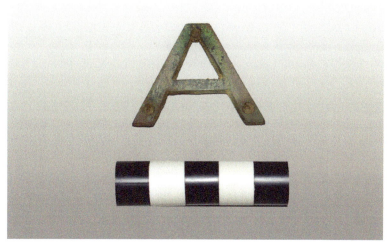

Figure 16.4. A brass letter found in a convict burial at Spike Island, Ireland. *Photograph by the author.*

One glaring aspect of those annual reports is the racialized conceptualization of the inmates. For example, at the time of the establishment of the prison, there was some debate about the value of providing education and vocational training. One contributor to this discussion argued that teaching trades would be a waste of time as the Irish working class male was only suited to being a general laborer. Later on, in explaining the high levels of mortality in the 1850s, the reports mention that the Irish were particularly susceptible to tuberculosis. This can be seen as part of a wider discourse of regarding the Irish in general, and the Irish poor in particular, as the racial *Other.* Initially used to legitimize the transfer of land and wealth, racialized understandings of the population of Ireland by the British elite informed political and social policies, particularly in dealing with the poor and the criminalized. These understandings were further legitimized by 'science.' The influential British anatomist John Beddoe (1826–1911), reported in 1870 that he had developed an index of "Nigrescence" based on the analysis of hair and eye color. Beddoe did not need to be explicit about the implications of "Nigrescence" for his readership.

When applied to Ireland, Beddoe found that there was not a perceptible pattern, but he concluded on the basis of his index that Irish 'Celts' were distinct from the Anglo-Saxons of England and more Africanoid in origin.

Despite the fact that Ireland was constitutionally integrated into the United Kingdom in 1801, aspects of the British–Irish relationship such as the dispossession of the local population, the presence of a social elite that perceived itself to be distinct in terms of race and religion, as well as the almost annual Coercion Acts involving the suspension of civil rights, indicate that the association between the two islands was one of colonial master and subject. In common with British colonialism in other parts of the world, the unequal relationship between the two islands and unequal social relations within Ireland were legitimized and sustained by narratives such as those created by Beddoe of the racial distinctiveness and inferiority of the Irish. These ideas were often articulated in terms of moral failure due to inherent flaws. Similar narratives of racial difference and inferiority were promoted by early work in physical anthropology. As archaeology emerged as a distinct discipline in the last decades of the nineteenth century, it also strove to confirm such narratives through the selective reading of data and to demonstrate that the subordinate status of the population of the island had its origins in deep time. While the conceptualization of Irish inferiority was rooted in the idea of racial difference, it also had a strong class dimension, which was in keeping with broader perceptions of the poor being 'a race apart' in Victorian society. However, within these intersecting discourses, race seems to have trumped social class as racialized otherness allowed for the suspension of norms applied to the English poor. This is exemplified by one of the responses from the government to the accommodation crisis on Spike Island which was to permit in 1848 the diversion there of a prison building that was prefabricated in London for the convict depot on Bermuda. Designed to accommodate about two hundred (mostly English) prisoners on Bermuda, the authorities decided that it could house over four hundred (Irish) men on Spike Island.

The colonial relationship is important from another perspective in that it allowed for experimentation and innovation. A range of social innovations, the national primary education system being a good example, were introduced in Ireland first and if judged a success, extended to other parts of the United Kingdom. The corollary of this, of course, was that if innovations failed, potential damage was limited to Ireland. The novel approaches taken at Spike Island and the development of Crofton's Irish System have to be understood as part of this wider process of colonialist experimentation and attendant cavalier attitudes to the lives of colonial subjects. The perceived value of this experimentation and the perception of convicts as the criminal and racial *Other* combined to permit a casual indifference to the high levels of morbidity and mortality noted at the time among the inmates at Spike Island.

By the time of the first International Penitentiary Congress in 1872, Crofton had published a number of articles about the Irish System. He was adept at self-promotion and in these publications Crofton was able to document a significant decline in the number of criminal convictions in Ireland between the 1840s and the 1860s, as well as a decline in numbers reoffending. He argued that these data demonstrated the effectiveness of his reforms to the prison system. The Presbyterian chaplain on Spike Island, Charles Bernard Gibson, tried to point out in his annual reports to government that the decline in convictions was actually related to the general improvement in social conditions after the Great Famine, as well as to the sharp decline in the population of Ireland, which halved in the eighty years between 1840 and 1920, dropping from eight million to four million, primarily due to emigration. Crofton was effective in silencing Gibson, whose later reports were suppressed and who was eventually dismissed from his post. An uncritical reading of the data and of Crofton's perhaps self-serving interpretations of these figures led to the acceptance at the international congresses of what was regarded as an effective means of reducing criminality. In turn, these meetings promoted, in the United States and elsewhere, the Irish System concepts of self-regulating prisoners, intermediate prison, and conditional release.

THE TWENTIETH CENTURY

Crofton's Irish System had a significant influence on penology in the second half of the nineteenth century and left a legacy that can still be detected today. The system had its roots in colonialism and imperialism, which promoted the concept of the superiority of one population, or a cohort of that population, over all others. In seeking legitimation, colonialism and imperialism readily co-opted emerging scientific attempts to understand human variability and anti-social behavior that were deeply flawed and racist. Crofton's claims about the impact of the approach on reducing overall levels of crime and recidivism do not stand up to scrutiny when seen in the context of the dramatic demographic changes in Ireland after the Great Famine. Crofton's system was predicated on the conceptualization of the prisoner as *Other* due to race, class, and propensity to criminality. This was reinforced by the colonial context, which permitted experimentation at the cost of human life. The result was a prison system with a stated goal of the reformation of criminals, but which was really about protecting the propertied class and had at its core a casual indifference to the mental and physical well-being of those it held. Apart from the details of the approach that were widely adopted in other jurisdictions, the racialized ethos of the model must have served to strengthen biological determinist views such as those of Lombroso, whose Italian School of Positivist Criminology promoted the system and gave it the authoritative approval of 'science.'

In terms of a genealogy of ideas, a clear link can be drawn between Lombroso's concept of the born criminal and the twentieth-century Harvard anthropologist and eugenicist Earnest Hooton, whose influential work *The American Criminal* was published in 1939. While rejecting some of Lombroso's ideas, Hooton upheld his contention of the association of biological inferiority with mental and moral weakness leading to criminality. He examined the conviction data of different racial groups in the American population (including Irish 'Celts') across a range of crimes, strengthening a link rooted in pseudo-science between arbitrary racial classifications and propensity to criminality. Hooton's work served to underpin biological explanations for criminal behavior into the twentieth century, to reinforce racial profiling as a methodology, and, again, to provide all with the imprimatur of 'science.'

A close examination of the archaeology of nineteenth-century prisons suggests that the real engines driving the development of the system were efforts to control the poor and the racial *Other* and to contain the threat—real or imagined—posed by those who have little to those who have a lot. Sprinkle in ingredients such as expediency, opportunism, trimming costs, institutional inertia, and careerism and you have a more rounded portrait of the legacy of the nineteenth century in shaping prisons today. In the United States there was the added dynamic of the privatization of prisons, where convict-leasing was used widely throughout the southern states after the Civil War. This generated significant profits for some states and the vast majority of convicts whose labor was exploited in this way were African American men.

Even by the low standards of the nineteenth century, once profit became the principal goal of prison, inmate care suffered. Convict-leasing declined in the early decades of the twentieth century and was abolished in 1941, stalling the privatization of the prison system for a few decades. In the 1980s, the Reagan administration facilitated the re-emergence of the for-profit private prison business. This is now a multi-billion dollar industry that in recent years has also diversified into the immigrant detention market. Since the 1980s, the United States has played an evangelizing role in the international spread of the privatized prison model. This toxic mix of prison and profit has led to the development of a system that is deeply imbricated in American society and its economy. A substantial number of people and agencies have a vested interest in maintaining high incarceration rates, to the extent that the industry is best described as predatory.

In a context such as this, it is almost comforting to frame the origins of the modern prison system as a mix of Enlightenment and religious ideals because doing so implies that an approach that we all tolerate is fit for purpose and is basically a force for good. Nationalistic delusions of exceptionalism provide similar cover. However, closer inspection of the development of the prison reveals that racism and class-based disdain are at the core of the system. These are not just elements skulking in the ancestry of the modern prison system, but remain as key features today, operating in plain sight and generating corporate and shareholder profits. In discussing the need for reform of the mass incarceration system in the United States—which she has convincingly labeled the New Jim Crow—Michelle Alexander (2010, 230) has written that "tinkering is for mechanics, not racial-justice advocates." Considering this from the perspective of the challenge posed by the Society for American Archaeology, quoted at the outset, can leave us feeling overwhelmed. However, I would argue that archaeology has a critical role to play if the discipline tackles the ideology of whiteness that plays a central role, not just in criminal justice systems that are not fit for purpose, but in the wider structural inequalities with which we struggle.

The example of the work of Beddoe and the application of his index of "Nigrescence" to the Irish demonstrates that whiteness is socially constructed. This was the central thesis of Noel Ignatiev's 1995 volume *How the Irish Became White.* Irish immigrants arriving in the United States in the nineteenth century, including those released from Spike Island, would have also found themselves regarded as the racial *Other* at their destination. Throughout that century, sectors of the American press followed the British lead and promoted conceptualizations of Irish 'Celts' as being fundamentally different from the English or American 'Anglo-Saxons.' Caricatures showing the similarities between the simian Irish and African American populations were commonplace (Figure 16.5). Ignatiev documented how the low social standing of Irish immigrants did not foster any sense of solidarity with their even more disadvantaged African American neighbors. Rather it fostered an intense and deadly rivalry as these two groups met along a fault-line of race. Ignatiev argued that it was the promise of white skin privilege that led the Irish in America to side with their economic exploiters and turn their backs on the African American community. This process continues today, when race

Figure 16.5. The 9 December 1876 cover of *Harper's Weekly,* a political magazine published in New York between 1857 and 1916.

is exploited to ensure that working-class people with white skin privilege vote against their own interests rather than seeing the elision of their well-being with that of their black and brown neighbors.

WHITENESS IN ARCHAEOLOGY

Our first task in interrupting such a dynamic is to acknowledge that the ideology of whiteness exists. Many of us with white skin privilege tend to think of race like we think of accents: something that other people have. Similarly, the discipline of archaeology needs to acknowledge that it has a whiteness problem and by that I do not just mean that the significant majority of people I see at the annual meetings of the Society for American Archaeology look like me; nor do I just mean that for many of us our passage through the education system has been easier because of the color of our skin; nor do I just mean that many of us live in places appropriated by Europeans where that appropriation was legitimized by myths such as *terra nullius*, Manifest Destiny, or White Man's Burden; nor do I just mean that many of us take for granted the well-functioning infrastructure and monumental architecture of cities that were built with resources siphoned out of other parts of the world through colonialism and imperialism; nor do I just mean that when sections of the media mention looting as a way of undermining legitimate protest that we need to pay attention to the materials filling our museums and other cultural institutions that were looted from around the world; nor do I just mean that many of us studied or work at prestigious universities whose wealth is founded on slavery or the colonial strip-mining of resources from other countries; nor do I just mean that many of us work at institutions that own stock in CoreCivic, the largest owners and operators of private prisons.

What I mean by saying that the discipline needs to acknowledge that it has a whiteness problem is that archaeology has played an important role in the formulation of the foundation myths of whiteness and that we archaeologists have created narratives that continue to sustain it. White chauvinism has colored much of what the discipline produces, from depictions of human evolution to narratives about the rise of civilization, to the idolatry of the Classical World. Just as American nationalism has created a teleological myth where the United States represents the high point in the evolution of freedom, archaeology has created teleological narratives where the hegemony of Europeans and their descendants is the logical outcome. So I would expand the challenge and suggest that as individual archaeologists we need to examine the hidden assumptions and unquestioned privileges that have structured our lives. We, as individual archaeologists and as a discipline, need to examine how the ideology of whiteness lurks mostly undetected and unchallenged in our envisioning of the past, seeping into the narratives we create and framing our research. Archaeology has played an inglorious role in constructing some of the myths that legitimized and sustained structural inequalities and systemic racism. It is not sufficient that the discipline simply atones for these original sins. Acknowledging past mistakes does not go far enough. We need to address the myth-making that underpinned and underpins the ideology of whiteness and its role in creating and sustaining structural inequalities and rank injustice.

NOTES

1   Only white men who owned property could vote in the decades after the American Revolution, some states even specifying "Christian men." All white men could vote by the time of the Civil War. The franchise was extended after that conflict to include all men, regardless of race, though many states effectively suppressed the African American and Native American vote by introducing literacy tests, poll taxes, and other such measures. The franchise was extended to women in 1920. Selective voter purging and other suppression tactics continue to this day, including, in some states, the permanent disenfranchisement of those with criminal convictions.
2   Carson 2020.
3   Carson 2020.
4   Foucault 1977, 26.

BIBLIOGRAPHY

Alexander, Michelle (2010), *The New Jim Crow: Mass Incarceration in the Age of Colorblindness,* New York (New Press).

Carson, E. Ann (2020), Prisoners in 2018, *Bulletin of the Bureau of Justice Statistics, United States Department of Justice, NCJ 253516,* April 2020.

Foucault, Michel (1977), *Discipline and Punish: The Birth of the Prison,* New York (Vintage, translation by Alan Sheridan of the 1975 French original).

Hooton, Earnest A. (1939), *The American Criminal: An Anthropological Study,* Cambridge (Harvard University Press).

Ignatiev, Noel (1995), *How the Irish Became White,* Abingdon (Routledge).

KITCHEN DETRITUS IN MODERN ARCHAEOLOGY

LA VERGNE LEHMANN

In the decades following the Second World War, the modern western kitchen started to develop because of a combination of improved infrastructure, such as running water and electricity coming directly into the home, along with the post-war manufacturing boom that supplied homes with a range of new kitchen appliances. In the supply of food to consumers, industrial agricultural practices led to an increase in the range and availability of produce, and food-processing technology increased the shelf life of many packaged food products. By 1960 when Vance Packard (1960) published *The Wastemakers*, kitchen-appliance manufacturers had already identified the kitchen as a room where they could increase consumption through planned obsolescence.

Since that time, changes to lifestyles, working habits, technology, food health standards, labeling, and food availability, along with increased knowledge of different cultural food options, have changed how people purchase, prepare, and consume food. The meals we consume are a combination of processed and packaged food, fresh produce or food we grow ourselves, and the processes by which we prepare that food for consumption, culminating in the activity of consumption along with the production of waste.

Waste is the consequence of our consumption-focused society. Thus, while the kitchen is the most productive room of the home, being the space where daily meals are produced and consumed, it is also the room where the most waste occurs. Kitchen consumption involves everything from the mundane in the form of the weekly grocery shopping to the purchase of a top-of-the-range cooker, and everything in between. Each has a different relationship to the type and nature of the waste that they produce. Whereas food is a transient item, which moves through the kitchen fairly quickly, the cooker is a more durable item that can last for generations. Waste is nonetheless considered to have a negative value and as a result is banished from view by sending it to landfills.[1]

THE PROBLEM OF KITCHEN WASTE

Food waste is a global problem, with over a third of food never to reach a stomach (Figure 15.1). Besides creating food insecurity, food waste also represents wasted resources, such as water, energy, and potential raw materials.[2] In Australia, food systems are highly developed and capable of producing large quantities of nutritious food. Nonetheless food waste is estimated to cost the Australian economy $20 billion each year. It also has significant environmental impacts because of wasted resources such as land, water, energy, and fuel to produce and distribute food. Finally, food waste that ends up in landfills results in the production of greenhouse gas emissions. Many of these impacts are avoidable. While not all food waste is generated in households, understanding how and why food waste is generated and disposed of at the household level will lead to improved avoidance programs. In 2019 the Australian government released the first significant step in that direction with the National Food Waste Policy and the establishment of the Fight Food Waste Cooperative Research Centre.[3]

But kitchens produce more than just food waste. Other waste includes the transient packaging materials and the more durable gadgets and infrastructure. In recent years the problem of rapidly growing landfills, the environmental impacts of poorly managed landfills, and the recognition that much of what was being thrown away still had some value has seen the emergence of waste resource recovery. This positive reappraisal of waste material and its value increasing is a direct result of the recognition of waste as a resource that can be reused or recycled (Figure 15.2). Where we once considered the process of consumption into waste a relatively linear path, that process can now result in a number of pathways where items—or the materials in those items—can be diverted back through the system several times before completing their journey. This research has sought to identify the consumption–waste pathways in the modern kitchen as they relate to the transient food and packaging waste as well as the more durable forms of kitchen waste.

Figure 15.1. Food waste at the household level is between 25 and 30 percent. Not all of it goes to landfill, with home composting and worm farms consuming some of it.

Figure 15.2. Other forms of kitchen waste found in thrift stores and other second-hand markets. These demonstrate greater durability and a different path compared to the kitchen waste process.

MODERN KITCHEN WASTE THROUGH THE LENS OF ARCHAEOLOGY

I was finishing a Masters in food studies and working in waste management when I first came across Bill Rathje's Garbage Project (also a source of inspiration for Alice Gorman and Justin St.P. Walsh, Chapter 13 in this volume; and Anthony Graesch and Timothy Hartshorn, Chapter 14 in this volume). Rathje used some real outside-the-box thinking, not only in his approach to teaching practical archaeology to his students, but also in how we can use archaeology to understand aspects of our modern world in relation to consumerism and the creation of waste.

It was in 1973 that Rathje and his students at the University of Arizona started what was to become a twenty-year research project looking into American consumer waste habits. As an archaeologist, Rathje adapted traditional archaeological methods and applied them to contemporary archaeological situations.[4] In doing this, Rathje and his students were able to increase the understanding of what was really happening in the household garbage bin. The Garbage Project was able to study consumer behaviors directly from the material realities left behind, rather than from the self-conscious self-reporting of surveys and interviews.[5]

Despite starting out as a practical exercise for archaeology students, the Garbage Project ultimately evolved into a multipurpose enterprise capable of considering such diverse interests as diet and nutrition, food waste, consumerism, socioeconomic stratification, resource management, recycling and source reduction, and the inner dynamics of landfills.[6] I initially followed up the Garbage Project with some research looking at waste audits in southeastern Australia in 2013. I had the opportunity to look at household waste audits, work through the detritus of our modern society, and gain a better understanding of food packaging waste and what it told us about our modern lifestyles.

So where does outside-the-box archaeology go from here? In looking at waste at a household level, there is a natural hierarchy in how materials flow through the household. Food waste and the packaging relating to food are relatively ephemeral. They come into the house, mostly the kitchen, and move through quickly, somewhere between weeks and months, with things like staples, milk, and bread moving through almost within days. Using contemporary archaeological methods to record the variety of kitchen and food-related waste and thus create a snapshot in time has provided a contemporary narrative about the waste we generate in the most productive room in the modern home. This can help in developing an updated understanding of the relationship that we have with the kitchen, cooking, and eating.

The main research question for this study is: What does kitchen, food, and packaging waste tell us about current kitchen and food consumption practices?

Subsidiary questions could include: How can contemporary archaeological methods be used to record modern kitchen waste and detritus? How can the evolution of a kitchen, food trend, or dietary habit be identified from kitchen waste?

The data collection for this research started with regular curbside waste and recycling collections as randomized bulk samples to ensure that no individual household could be identified. Local transfer stations that accept recyclable and landfill materials as well as material recycling facilities were sampled periodically. The data collection was later extended to other waste pathways including thrift stores, garage sales, secondhand markets, and online secondhand venues such as eBay and Gumtree.

APPLYING THE GARBAGE PROJECT APPROACH

As noted above, part of the inspiration for this research project came from the Garbage Project, developed in 1973 by archaeologist Bill Rathje at the University of Arizona. When Rathje began the Garbage Project as an opportunity for archaeology students to learn about practical archaeological methods and relate what they found to a society by looking at its rubbish, however, he would not have realized that he was starting what would become one of the longest running social science research initiatives in history. Rathje was not only interested in categorizing the contents of rubbish bins and waste sites, but also wanted to get answers to questions concerning waste decomposition, waste contribution to pollution, recycling impacts, composting, and other forms of waste diversion from landfills. The Garbage Project became a means for complementing other research into sociocultural behaviors such as alcohol use, food waste, and consumer behavior during food shortages.[7]

Using the Garbage Project rationale, this study looked at the waste generated by four regional communities in southeastern Australia. This includes direct waste intended for landfill, in the form of curbside collections, and indirect waste, in the form of waste intended for a materials recycling facility or secondary markets, in order to develop a profile of the kitchen, food, and packaging waste practices in these communities. The samples were taken from around one hundred unidentified households in each community, thereby ensuring that no household could be identified by the researcher.

The second part of the data collection was to consider other forms of kitchen waste and how they are disposed of by the household. These are the more durable consumer items such as kitchen gadgets, machines, furniture, and other kitchen ancillary items such as plates, cups, glasses, and cutlery. While some of these items can be found in traditional household waste streams, many are diverted to other places such as thrift stores and secondhand markets.

Once the nature of the item was identified, analysis of the types of products as waste items was undertaken. Each item was rated on a scale of durability, with food items rating very low and white goods and furniture rating higher. They were also analyzed for how they might have been used or consumed in the household, how much was wasted, their estimated length of stay in the kitchen, the reasons for disposal, and their overall purpose in the kitchen.

By understanding the nature of the flow of materials through the kitchen in the form of food, packaging, and other kitchen materials, it is possible to create a narrative around the way in which modern kitchens are used, but also food storage, processing, cooking and consumption practices, as well as the length of the stay of items in the kitchen. If we better understand how consumers utilize their kitchens and the food they purchase and discard, it will ultimately be possible to develop better food education programs.

WHAT DOES KITCHEN WASTE TELL US?

In trying to understand what kitchen, food, and packaging waste can tell us about contemporary Australian society, archaeological methods were applied to generate and analyze the evidence. The reasoning behind this choice is based on the idea that if archaeologists are able to understand societies that are no longer in existence, based on patterns in ancient garbage, then the same approach can be applied to a contemporary society. Items such as fragments of pottery, parts of stone tools, animal bones, and shells that are extracted from old middens are capable of providing a surprisingly detailed view of how people once lived. Modern food debris, food packaging and kitchen detritus will likewise reveal intimate details of our lives today.

It has only been in recent decades that archaeologists have broadened their study of food beyond diet to explore its role in a society and consider the connections between politics, ideologies, and economies with food production, preparation, consumption, and discard practices. Indeed the potential and challenge of food archaeology lies in the fact that many different social phenomena contribute to the foodways of any society.

There is no doubt that food has been a constant presence and preoccupation in human lives. Food procurement, preparation, and consumption are all deeply embedded in a wide variety of social relations, and in every culture great amounts of time are spent on food-related activities. Many food-related activities occur on at least a daily basis, meaning that their social importance is constantly reinforced. Archaeological interest in the sociality of food has grown dramatically in recent decades, with theoretically diverse investigations into how food practices articulate with economics, politics, ethnicity, gender, and ideology. Such studies have provided detailed and complex reconstructions of past social lives across numerous societies and periods.

Recognition of the ubiquity of food in culture, and of its associated material culture in archaeological contexts, means that there is still much more to understand about the human relationship with food, its preparation, and its consumption. This study was grounded in the sorting of quantifiable bits and pieces of kitchen waste, rather than collecting data through interviews or surveys, government documents, or industry records. Consequently, this project has endeavored to study consumer behavior directly from the materials that they leave behind, rather than from biased self-reporting.

For the archaeologists who were involved in the Garbage Project, garbage bin contents and landfills represented lodes of information that could provide valuable insights into our modern-day society. In order to rationalize the adoption of this methodology, we must pose the question, Why look at waste? The reasons identified by Rathje in the Garbage Project were:

1. The creation of waste is an unequivocal sign of human presence and there is now an uninterrupted chain of garbage that stretches back more than two million years to the first debitage (waste flake) that was struck off an early stone tool.
2. If waste can hold a key to our past, then surely it holds a key to the present.
3. Waste is not an assertion or a claim but a physical fact. Keeping in mind that it still has to be interpreted, waste can be used to either confirm or deny what other evidence may claim.

Waste essentially represents a physical reality rather than folklore or mythology. Rathje reminds us that for each individual there are two realities: the mental reality that encompasses beliefs, attitudes, and ideas; and the material reality that is the picture developed from the physical record. The study of waste has the capacity to provide evidence of what may be an alternate reality for many people as it may conflict with their mental reality.[8]

GENERAL WASTE BIN CONTENTS

The data for this study originated from a combination of traditional garbage audits across four regional communities in southeastern Australia where the opportunity to undertake a more detailed analysis of the food packaging and food waste was possible. During the same period stock was taken of kitchen-related objects found in secondhand stores and markets.

The main items of interest from the curbside garbage audits in the recycling and general waste bins are those items that appear as food or food packaging. In analyzing ten 120-liter (26-gallon) bin samples from each community streams, food packaging was divided into glass, hard plastics, soft plastics, paper and cardboard, and metals. Percentages were calculated by volume. Soft plastics were not allocated a volume in the original analysis, but have been separated for the purpose of analysis here. The following observations were made.

Non-recyclable soft plastics: The main items of packaging included bread bags, chip bags, biscuit packaging, nuts and snack packets, clear plastic inner packaging (non-identifiable), instant meals such as noodles, sauces, rice, and pasta mixes, cling wrap plastics from meat or fruit and vegetable packaging, small sauce or dressing sachets, packaging for pasta, sugar, flour, and rice.

Paper and cardboard packaging (9 percent): Tetra Pak® containers were the only beverage-related products in this stream and made up 36 percent of the overall volume. Fast food packaging made up 14 percent of the volume. Most common were processed food meals such as single meal dinners (18 percent), pizza boxes (15 percent), cereal packets (15 percent), diet meals (14 percent), with other categories including flour, sugar, cake mixes, chocolates, biscuit boxes. Very little food waste was found in these items.

Hard plastics (6.5 percent): Food-related plastics comprised 51 percent of the waste stream compared to 49 percent for beverage-related items. Thirty-five percent of food-related plastics contained some food still in the container, with 74 percent being past the best-by or use-by dates. The most common food containers were fresh fruit and vegetable packaging

(21 percent), yogurt pots (small containers 16 percent), margarine or butter containers (17 percent), salad dressing containers (9 percent), meat trays (8 percent), and containers for cream (8 percent), yogurt (large containers 7 percent), ice cream (4 percent), and sour cream (4 percent). Food products with mold growing in them were almost entirely yogurt or cream. Beverage-related items included milk bottles (57 percent), water bottles (20 percent), soft drink bottles (15 percent), and cordial bottles (8 percent).

Glass (3.6 percent): Fifty-three percent of all glass in the waste stream was for alcohol-related beverages, and 34 percent of all food-related glass in the waste stream contained some form of waste food. Sixty-nine percent of products were branded rather than supermarket home-brand products, and 61 percent of the food in glass jars was after the best-by date. Glass containers with a significant amount of food remaining in them had mold growth. The most common food items in glass jars were pasta sauces (16 percent), followed by Asian-style sauce mixes (12 percent), sandwich spreads such as vegemite or peanut butter (12 percent), jam or honey (11 percent), baby food (10 percent), salad dressings (8 percent), tomato sauce (7 percent), taco sauces (5 percent), and pickles and chutneys (4 percent).

Metal (3 percent): Forty-one percent of the volume in this stream was beverage-related and 85 percent was alcohol-related. The main food items in the stream were canned vegetables, soup, fruit, fish, or baked beans and spaghetti. Four percent of food containers had food still left in them.

From the data above the following observations were made: recyclables were presented in cleaner condition than similar items in the general waste stream. It was generally the case that empty containers were not washed out if they had been placed in the general waste. Education programs to encourage residents to rinse out items to be recycled seem to have been successful.

More than half the glass containers and a third of hard plastic containers still had some food in them. This suggests that consumers are unable, in the appropriate time frame, to use the entire contents of that container or have not stored the contents appropriately after opening. This could relate to a lack of understanding about good storage practices, purchasing an inappropriate size of product, or trying a new product and not liking it.

Assuming that all packaged food was fit for consumption at the time of purchase, then any food waste found in these audits could only be deemed avoidable. The question remains why this waste occurs. Is it poor planning, a lack of understanding about food viability time frames, or a reluctance to buy smaller volumes?

RECYCLING BIN CONTENTS

The second set of audits were for comingled recycling across the same regional communities. Recycling collections should not involve any direct food waste and if they do it is considered a contaminant. Residents are asked to rinse out containers to provide a clean stream of recycling. It is also in the recycling stream that most food packaging is found, as it most commonly contains glass, most forms of hard plastic, metals, paper, and cardboard packaging. One of the biggest issues with recycling is the level of contamination in curbside recycling. In this audit there was still 10 percent of organic compostable or food waste. The majority of this waste was found in containers that still had too much food in them to ensure that they could be successfully recycled. Food packaging makes up 85 percent of the recycled items with the combination of paper, metal, plastic, and glass.

In analyzing ten 120-liter (26-gallon) bin samples from each community the various recycling streams were divided into categories of glass, hard plastics, paper or cardboard, and metal. The following observations were made.

Paper and cardboard packaging (45 percent): Fast-food packaging made up 18 percent of the volume of food packaging; Tetra Pak® containers for beverages made up 16 percent of the volume. The majority of cardboard boxes were flattened or squashed, with the inner plastic bags removed. Most common items were frozen pre-made single-meal dinners (15 percent), cereal packets (15 percent), diet meals (9 percent), pizza boxes (8 percent), with other categories including packaging for flour, sugar, cake mixes, chocolates, and biscuit.

Glass (21 percent): Fifty-seven percent of all glass in the recycling stream was for food-related purposes and 43 percent was for alcohol-related beverages. Six percent of all food-related glass in the waste stream contained some form of waste food in the container. Seventeen percent of the food in glass jars was after the best-by date and 1 percent of glass jar containers had not been opened at all, but were past the best-by date.

The most common food items in glass jars were pasta sauces (18 percent), baby food (13 percent), jam or honey (14 percent), Asian-style sauce mixes, mostly Chinese or Indian (12 percent), sandwich spreads such as vegemite or peanut butter (10 percent), tomato sauce (8 percent), salad dressings (6 percent), taco sauces (5 percent), and pickles and chutneys (3 percent). Seventy-eight percent of products were branded rather than supermarket house brand products.

Hard plastics (12 percent): Food-related plastics were 45 percent of the waste stream, compared to 55 percent for beverage-related items. Beverage-related items included milk bottles (63 percent), soft drink bottles (18 percent), water bottles (12 percent), and cordial bottles (6 percent). Fifteen percent of food-related plastics contained some food still in the container, with 72 percent being past the best-by dates. The most common containers were for fresh fruit and vegetable packaging (24 percent), yogurt (small containers, 21 percent), margarine or butter (16 percent), meat trays (14 percent), salad dressings (9 percent), cream (9 percent), yogurt (large containers, 6 percent), sour cream (6 percent), and ice cream (2 percent). Containers with dairy products such as yogurt or cream were the mostly likely to have mold in them.

Metal (5 percent): Forty-four percent of the volume in this stream was beverage-related of which 72 percent was alcohol-related. The main food items in the stream were found in aluminum food trays, foil, and canned soup, fruit, vegetables, fish, baked beans, or spaghetti.

It is clear that residents take more care while recycling and ensuring that containers are cleaner overall. Containers such as plastic milk bottles were extremely clean. This indicates that people continue to perceive a distinct difference in the activity of recycling to that of throwing something into general waste. Anecdotal evidence also suggests that people take pride in trying to get their recycling right.

OTHER KITCHEN WASTE

One of the roles of the modern kitchen is the storage of food, gadgets, cooking receptacles, serving plates and bowls, and a variety of eating utensils. Food storage ranges from pantry storage for dried and processed foodstuffs, refrigerators for cold storage, and freezers for longer storage options. Other kitchen cupboards will contain a variety of cookware such as saucepans, roasting trays, baking trays, and casseroles. More cupboards contain gadgets used to undertake a variety of activities ranging from chopping, blending, and mixing to serving and displaying food. Still more cupboards will contain dinner plates, cutlery, cups, glasses, bowls, and a variety of other items connected with the final consumption of the food prepared in that kitchen.

But kitchens are not just for storage, they are also a room for activities, including the preparation of food for consumption. This means that apart from storage facilities, kitchens will also have areas for preparation such as bench tops. Finally, there is the myriad of devices required to actually cook the food including stoves, ovens, cooktops, microwaves, slow cookers, rice cookers, table-top grills, sandwich makers, toasters, and kettles.[9] The post-war boom in the production of consumer goods and appliances resulted in a very different space.

Not all kitchen waste ends up in a landfill or recycling facility. Some of it has a much more circuitous path before reaching its ultimate destination in landfill. Thrift stores and secondhand markets have become a significant recipient of excess kitchen materials.

Great Grilling & Great Roasting—Now There are 2 Great Ways to Knockout the Fat!

Figure 15.3. George Foreman's great success with the Lean Mean Grilling Machine was not replicated in other endorsed kitchen gadgets.

HOW DID WE LET GEORGE FOREMAN INTO OUR KITCHENS?

Perhaps the most outside-the-box aspect to this study involved the identification of electrical goods from the kitchen. These gadgets ranged from multipurpose blenders and cookers through to single-purpose items such as hot-dog makers and popcorn machines. But the one that stood out the most was the ubiquitous George Foreman Grill.

The George Foreman Grill (Figure 15.3), also known as the Lean Mean Fat Reducing Grilling Machine is a significant item in the Australian secondhand market space. It is obvious from the sheer volume that a number of kitchens have seen a George Foreman Grill. The natural response here is to question what a boxer has to do with kitchen waste? Understanding this phenomenon was, in part, about understanding why many of these gadgets lacked longevity in our kitchens. Consequently, it is a story worth understanding.

Heavyweight boxer George Edward Foreman did not create the George Foreman Grill, he was just the face of the marketing campaign. In fact, the creator had sent George a grill for him to try, presumably so that George would promote it. After some months of the grill sitting in the Foreman kitchen, George's wife, Joan, finally gave it a go. The rest is history.[10] Since that fateful day in 1994, when Joan cooked George his first hamburger—one of his favorite meals before getting into the ring—and sold George on the grill, it has been an outstanding success. More than 100 million units have been sold around the world making it one of the most lucrative endorsement contracts in history. But despite many other attempts, George was unable to replicate the success of the grill. Indeed, numerous other celebrities have endorsed similar grills, ranging from fellow boxer Evander Holyfield to Olympic track and field athlete Carl Lewis, again without the Foreman success.

The George Foreman Grill came at a time when the market was starting to open up to a whole range of kitchen gadgets including popcorn makers, hot-dog makers, waffle makers, electric woks, a wide variety of different mixers and blenders, just to name a few. These gadgets have become symbols for the consumerism that has taken hold in our society and ultimately the waste that we produce. Where previously a frying pan or a stove grill were good enough, now we had the George Foreman Grill. The irony is that George may have sold 100 million of them, but not everyone kept them.

THE INCREASINGLY EPHEMERAL KITCHEN

What sets this research project apart from other waste studies is the archaeological behavioral science element that is not normally applied to regular curbside garbage audits or the contents of the secondhand market stream. This has allowed for the development of novel methodologies for contemporary archaeology to be applied to the analysis of kitchen waste.

This research also contributes empirical evidence to the ongoing debates over the evolution of kitchen consumption and food practices in Australia by bringing in evidence from previously underutilized sources. The kitchen is often perceived as the engine room of the family home and as such the activities that occur in it are not often subject to public display.

While much of our understanding about our relationship with the modern kitchen and food comes from what we see in the media, ranging from supermarket catalogs to reality-television cooking programs and celebrity chefs, these can only tell us what might be entering the kitchen. What it cannot tell us is what is happening in the kitchen with the consumable food and kitchen hardware. While looking at what is coming out of the kitchen in the form of waste streams, it is possible to consider how those processes have occurred and what is being consumed. While this research is not designed to provide comprehensive answers to what and how we operate in the kitchen, it puts a different perspective on that relationship through the prism of kitchen waste.

NOTES

1   Thompson 2017.

2   Institution of Mechanical Engineers (2013), *Global Food: Waste Not, Want Not,* http://www.imeche.org/knowledge/themes/environment/global-food (accessed 29 February 2020).

3   Commonwealth of Australia, National Food Waste Strategy (2017), *Halving Australia's Food Waste by 2030,* https://www.environment.gov.au/system/files/resources/4683826b-5d9f-4e65-9344-a900060915b1/files/national-food-waste-strategy.pdf (accessed 29 February 2020).

4   Rathje et al. 1992.

5   Rathje and Murphy 2001.

6   Hughes 1984.

7   Jones, Timothy W. (2007), *Using Contemporary Archaeology and Applied Anthropology to Understand Food Loss in the AmericanFood System,* https://humwp.ucsc.edu/gleaningstories/pdf/jones_foodwaste.pdf (accessed 29 February 2020).

8   Wilk and Rathje 1982.

9   Freeman 2004.

10 Foreman Grill Recipes (2019), https://foremangrillrecipes.com/the-story/ (accessed 29 February 2020).

BIBLIOGRAPHY

Freeman, June (2004), *The Making of the Modern Kitchen,* Oxford and New York (Berg).

Hughes, Wilson W. (1984), The Method to Our Madness: The Garbage Project Methodology, *American Behavioural Science* 28(1), 41–50.

Packard, Vance (1960), *The Wastemakers,* New York (Ig Publishing, 1988 reprint).

Rathje, William L. and Cullen Murphy (2001), *Rubbish! The Archaeology of Garbage,* Tucson (The University of Arizona Press).

Rathje, William L., Wilson W. Hughes, D.C. Wilson, M.K. Tani, G.H. Archer, R.G. Hunt, and T.W. Jones (1992), The Archaeology of Contemporary Landfills, *American Antiquity* 57(3), 437–47.

Thompson, Michael (2017), *Rubbish Theory: The Creation and Destruction of Value,* London (Pluto Press, new edition of the 1979 original).

Wilk, Richard R. and William L. Rathje (1982), Household Archaeology, *American Behavioural Science* 25(6), 617–39.

LITTERSCAPES IN THE ANTHROPOCENE

AN ARCHAEOLOGY OF DISCARDED CIGARETTES

ANTHONY P. GRAESCH AND TIMOTHY HARTSHORN

The material legacy of the retail and consumer goods industry in the twentieth and early twenty-first centuries is owed to a remarkable proliferation of seemingly indissoluble objects through the global market. Plastic goods are proving to be especially durable, reducible in form only to increasingly smaller bits of undiagnostic plastic that dot the physiographic features of our planet.[1] Among those small finds that can still be identified with reference to form and function, discarded cigarettes may be the most numerically abundant and ubiquitous across assemblages of refuse worldwide. These artifacts constitute a potent materialization of the expansive reach of human influence: they can be found in nooks and crannies throughout the urban landscape, but are also present in virtually every physical location that has been accessed by humans, including roadsides, hiking trails, and even at the tops of ancient temples (Figure 14.1). And where humans have not traveled, other agents—wind, water, roots,

and animals—transport these artifacts, sometimes across great distances. Indeed, mass-produced cigarettes may one day prove to be among the more diagnostic markers of strata that began as litterscapes of the present and materialize the Global North's extraordinary acceleration of manufacture, throughput, and consumption that implicate an 'Anthropocene.'[2]

As materially and experientially hybrid objects that blur the boundary between comestibles and consumer goods, cigarettes have proven to be uniquely resistant to material culture obsolescence. Even after seventy years of mass production, and despite the introduction of vaping technology, the global demand for filtered cigarettes persists, with annual production still in the trillions. Owing to their chemical causticity, cigarettes also manifest the terminus of supply lines in that they cannot be easily recycled, upcycled or economically repurposed to other forms or tasks. The aggregate contribution of toxic cigarette leachate to nonpoint source pollution may supersede the

in archaeology is that even the smallest, seemingly least significant, and, in this case, more pungent forms of discarded consumer goods in the biosphere can offer insights into the complex ways that humans think about, engage with, affect, and are affected by their material environs.

This chapter situates discarded cigarettes as subjects of archaeological study of the present as well as the future past. Our goals are twofold. First, we endeavor to shine a light on small, unwanted objects that are seldom found among the collections curated by museums or afforded the status of artifact. Cigarettes, we argue, constitute an inextricable part of the human story as it concerns the emergence of new modes of capitalism and attendant forms of unbridled resource consumption and wanton discard. In this vein, we challenge and reframe a perceived triviality or quirkiness of contemporary, mass-manufactured consumer goods as subjects of archaeological study. We also show how that which appears to be a homogeneous object type is remarkably varied and worthy of the analytic sensibilities of archaeologists. As a result, our contribution is largely descriptive and classificatory, but we contend that such groundwork is always necessary prior to imagining and building deeper research programs framed on rigorous, data-robust studies of contemporary surfaces.

Our second goal is to reconsider acts of discard as constituting domains of embodied, socially meaningful, and otherwise culturally generative behavior instrumental to the reproduction and reconstruction of urban space in everyday life. We hold that discard reflects a corpus of individual and collective dispositions that routinely reinforce and subvert the structures of confinement built into post-industrial cityscapes ravaged by global capitalism. Discard is also a forum for examining the foundations of moral dispositions concerning resource use and the impacts of humans in and on local and global biomes (see also La Vergne Lehmann, Chapter 15 in this volume). We begin by briefly recapitulating and reinforcing arguments for an archaeology of contemporary surfaces before diving into the unique production details, design attributes, and experiential qualities of cigarettes that collectively lend themselves to archaeological scrutiny via recordation and classificatory

Figure 14.1. Discarded cigarettes (clockwise from top left): resting between sandstone slabs at the top of Bakong Temple (881 CE) in the ancient city of Angkor, Cambodia; congregating in the space between a stone curb and a city street in New York; deteriorating among colonizing plant life at the margin of a New England road; and migrating into a Connecticut storm drain.

object itself as an indelible mark on the stratigraphic record. Daily, millions of used cigarettes are discarded outside of trash receptacles. Most are regarded as little more than insignificant bits of litter, if they are seen at all. But a recurring lesson methods. We conclude by highlighting some domains of research that we think can be productively pursued within an investigation of discarded cigarettes.

IN SMALL THINGS SMOKED AND DISCARDED

Since the late 1970s, much of archaeological anthropology in North America has gravitated toward the study of small finds. In part, this trend is attributable to the development and refinement of data recovery methods that allow archaeologists to do more with less. But a focus on small finds also emerged from an understanding that assemblages of lost, fragmented, and often unwanted things illuminate attitudes, dispositions, and everyday behaviors that are more difficult to glean from larger, intact, and otherwise less frequently recovered artifacts. Such an understanding is at the heart of Deetz's (1996) seminal treatment of early American lifeways, a treatise in which he compellingly advocates for the study of lost and discarded ephemera that colonial settlers and the formerly enslaved probably would not have given a second glance (such as broken pipe stems, irreparably damaged cutlery, fragments of earthenware vessels, and building hardware), but whose patterned distribution can implicate normative, everyday behaviors that are seldom and patchily documented in historical accounts.

Although surface assemblages of small, discarded ephemera in contemporary times have received comparatively less attention than the objects and features of the distant past, they nevertheless afford similar opportunities to explore questions we regularly ask of earlier archaeological records.[3] However, lest the goals of this chapter be misconstrued, we think it important to acknowledge that the archaeological study of contemporary discard(s) need not proceed from the expectation of establishing genealogical relationships with earlier archaeological records.[4] Like others before us, and like others in this volume (Smith et al., Chapter 19, and Larry Zimmerman, Chapter 21, in this volume), we see several reasons to instead situate archaeological studies of contemporary discard in the present, *for* the present, and in pursuit of various futures.[5] First, an archaeology of contemporary discard benefits immensely from opportunities to observe the embodied and social interactions in which objects participate (see also Gorman and Walsh, Chapter 19 in this volume).[6] The thoughtful melding of ethnographic and archaeological data-collection techniques can help make evident the ways that objects and materials mediate our social realities and are not merely reflections or static byproducts of complex interdependent phenomena that we label *culture*.[7] Similarly, ethnographic data help to fill significant gaps in otherwise incomplete narratives of behavioral phenomena that result from the partial and disjointed nature of the archaeological record.[8] Careful analysis of contemporary archaeological data against interviews and participant-observation data can reveal not only the context-sensitive meanings assigned to objects but also the ways that these situational meanings can shape behavior.[9]

Second, this approach acknowledges that the unique structures and processes shaping discard in the post-industrial, hyper-consumptive present are not always directly relatable to past behaviors and materialities. While insights into the circumstances by which objects come to be discarded in the present may compel a rethinking of some aspects of discard in more ancient settings, the material records of people who are still alive are arguably best suited to addressing present-day cultural phenomena.[10] At the same time, research addressing discard in the under-studied archaeological present benefits from, and elaborates on, long-established strengths of archaeology, including an inclination and substantial capacity to explore experiences that have been neglected, dismissed, and omitted from dominant narratives.[11] Such strengths afford inclusivity,[12] as the archaeological record can speak to the decisions, lifeways, and fates of those who are marginalized, dispossessed, and/or deemed unlawful (see also Larry Zimmerman, Chapter 21 in this volume).[13] Discarded cigarettes, although seemingly small and inconsequential, furnish similar opportunities to examine the interplay of myriad structural forces and urban social actors.

CIGARETTES AS ARTIFACTS

The generic physical form of a cigarette, the form that is most frequently represented in American film and television, is a lightweight, white paper tube filled with reconstituted or homogenized sheet tobacco and tipped with a cellulose acetate filter wrapped with slightly heavier, often cork-colored tipping paper. This typical cigarette measures approximately 8 centimeters (3.1 inches) in length, 8 millimeters (0.31 inches) in diameter, and weighs somewhere between 7 and 8 grams (0.25–0.28 ounces). In these features alone, the cigarette is a readily identifiable artifact, although the unique ways of interacting with this object—the ways that the cigarette is held, placed in the mouth, and incorporated into gesture—have also made it among the most cross-culturally recognizable consumer goods in recent memory.

Like other consumer goods of the twentieth and twenty-first centuries, cigarettes and the practices that surround them cannot be evaluated on the same terms as objects produced by individual craftspeople. In contrast to Melanesian exchange goods, for example, the mass-marketed cigarette does not collect the ideas, relationships, and skills of those who make, transport, and use the object.[14] Nor does it gather memories of its encounters with smokers that can be easily transmitted to future smokers. While some of the roles of cigarettes and their impacts in the co-construction of situated behaviors are certainly discernible from smoker modifications, they are also transient, given that the object is mostly destroyed in a matter of minutes.

It is in the simultaneity of use, combustion, and destruction that the individual cigarette achieves a form of material and experiential hybridity by straddling the conceptual divide of comestible and non-comestible consumer goods. On the one hand, the cigarette provides a distinctly intimate way of interacting with the material world: unlike most objects encountered in daily life, this consumer good is placed in the mouth, lit on fire, and physically taken into the body in the form of a fine-particulate, gaseous matter. The combusted matter excites taste, olfactory, and texture receptors, all the while stimulating the parasympathetic nervous system of the smoker. Similar to food, sensorial perceptions of the variable qualities of cigarettes can trigger memories, elicit nostalgia, and even serve as a basis for judgment of others. On the other hand, cigarettes are not necessary to sustain life, and while their use can be influenced by family members who also smoke, they are not at the center of nearly as many practices, beliefs, and rituals as surround the production, preparation, and eating of food. Critical to their potential for archaeological scrutiny, cigarettes are mass-produced with stylistic attributes that signal ideas and confer meanings during public-facing acts of smoking. They also persist as an altered but not fully destroyed object when eventually discarded.

It is in the empirical details—some of which are familiar but many less known—that archaeologists can imagine investigatory potential. First, cigarettes remain one of the most highly demanded of fast-moving or nondurable consumer-packaged goods on local and global scales. In the United States alone, as many as twenty-eight unique cigarette manufacturers produce over 145 brands of cigarettes available to consumers. On a continental scale, North America is home to some fifty cigarette and cigar factories, three of which are located in Mexico, seven in eastern Canada, and the other forty appearing mostly in the mid-Atlantic and southern regions of the United States.[15] But these numbers pale in comparison to global manufacturing data: as of 2013, over 640 factories—the vast majority of which are located in Asia and Europe—accounted for more than 6,200 cigarette brands and the annual production of nearly 6 trillion individual cigarettes.[16] If distributed evenly among the population of the world, this amounted to a little more than 857 cigarettes for every human on the planet in 2013, or roughly six thousand cigarettes for each of the estimated one billion smokers in 2017.[17] Acknowledging that the sheer abundance of cigarettes in global markets is a potent indicator of addiction and thus a continued cause for public health-related concerns, we argue that the persistent and interminable availability of cigarettes also affords robust data sets to archaeological studies of object use and discard.

Second, used cigarettes (cigarette butts or stubs) continue to defy popular classifications of objects or materials that constitute "garbage." The casual discard of butts at the locations where smokers conclude their smoking acts persists as normative behavior, which partly explains the wide distribution of cigarettes on sidewalks, streets, parking lots, trails, and virtually any surface on or near which humans tread. It is in this fact that archaeologists may rejoice: these artifacts often remain much closer to their primary archaeological context than nearly all other nondurable goods discarded in the twenty-first century. Indeed, most fast-moving consumer goods enter into a waste stream that dissociates objects from the spatially situated embodied acts with which they coparticipated in social life. The millions of objects aggregated in municipal landfills, for example, cannot easily be reconnected to individual or collective social behavior that unfolded in, and was shaped by, discrete physical settings. Although assemblages of cigarettes seldom remain unaffected by wind, water, and other forces for very long, an implicit tolerance of cigarette discard in most public settings permits a consideration of the relationships between discards and spatially situated behavior seldom afforded to an archaeology of the contemporary.

A third and final detail concerns the potential for cigarette preservation, and longitudinal studies of cigarette discard. An unintended outcome of the plasticization of cigarette filters is their perpetuity in the material record. Plasticized filters have been on the market since the 1950s but were not present on the vast majority of available cigarettes until as recently as the late 1970s and early 1980s. Although there are no methodical studies addressing the longevity of these artifacts, we might expect partly charred cigarette filters to be preserved indefinitely in certain depositional contexts such as arid environs. Only time will tell. In the present and immediate future, most discarded cigarettes will weather any variety of depositional and environmental conditions, but emerge in such a state that their discrete anatomical components can still be identified.

ANATOMY OF A CIGARETTE

The affordances of cigarettes to archaeological studies of contemporary behavior are also realized in both the visible and invisible (but sensorially detectable) details of cigarette anatomy. Despite broadly shared morphological attributes that make the typical cigarette easily recognizable, nearly all cigarette types or varieties have unique visual identities. Our anecdotal conversations with friends and colleagues suggest that most North Americans are aware of only a handful of cigarette brands, particularly the four most heavily advertised in the United States: Marlboro, Camel, Newport and Pall Mall. Numerous lesser-known brands can be found in both national and regional markets and, like the more popular brands, each is accompanied by a unique and remarkably durable visual identity projected on cigarette packaging. Within most cigarette brands, moreover, there is a variety of brand-specific cigarette types. For example, Altria Group, the parent company of Philip Morris USA, markets more than forty different types of Marlboro cigarettes in the United States alone. Such varieties include Marlboro Red, Marlboro Gold, Marlboro Silver, Marlboro Menthol Blue, Marlboro Menthol Gold, Marlboro Blend No. 27, and Marlboro Edge, among dozens of others (Figure 14.2, top). In southern New England markets, we identified over four hundred unique cigarette types for sale, although there may be upwards of twenty thousand types available in the larger global market (Figure 14.3).

Cigarette manufacturers often imprint unique visual identities on each of the many varieties or types of their branded cigarettes. Commercially manufactured cigarettes exhibit a degree of typological variability that is seldom observed among ancient objects. If we inspect the twenty individual cigarettes packaged as a particular type (for instance Full-Flavor Menthols) of a specific brand (for instance Marlboro), we often find that all feature a combination of morphological and stylistic attributes that differs from those observed for other types produced under the same and other brands. Marlboro Full-Flavor Menthols, for example, can be easily distinguished from other Marlboro types (for instance Marlboro Gold) as well as

a) Visible cigarette attributes

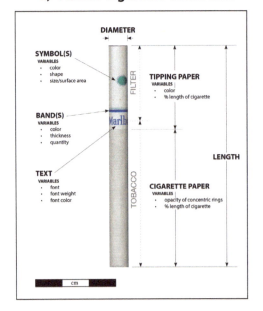

b) Marlboro-brand cigarette packages

c) Marlboro-brand cigarette varieties

Figure 14.2. Codifiable and measurable attributes of a typical cigarette (a), and packages (b) associated with the unique attribute combinations observed for each Marlboro cigarette variety (c).

menthols produced under other brands (for instance Camel Full Flavor Menthols) on the basis of several stylistic attributes, including the color of the tipping paper, icons, imprinted text, as well as the color, number, and thickness of imprinted bands. Other formal attributes that can vary include the presence or absence of a filter as well as the length (80, 100, and 120 millimeters or 3.1, 3.9, and 4.7 inches) and diameter (7–9 millimeters or 0.28–0.35 inches) of the cigarette filter and tube (Figure 14.2, bottom). We estimate that upwards of 90 percent of cigarette types sold in the United States are visually unique with respect to specific combinations of morphological and stylistic attributes. In our study alone, we documented 515 unique attribute combinations from archaeologically recovered specimens, some of which are associated with cigarette types available only in overseas markets.

Figure 14.3. A partial point-of-purchase display in southeastern Connecticut featuring thirteen cigarette brands and 117 types.

Importantly, observable variation in stylistic and morphological attribute combinations, the codifiable basis of what we define as cigarette types, corresponds to variation in distinctly experiential qualities of cigarettes. The ways that cigarette visual identity is used to signal a particular smoking experience—duration, taste, flavor, quality—can vary across brands, although there are some inter-brand stylistic regularities. Most obvious is cigarette length: longer cigarettes—100 and 120 millimeters (3.9 and 4.7 inches) varieties—often equate to longer smoking sessions. More subtly, white tipping paper on a cigarette filter almost always corresponds with light taste intensity, or filters with much smaller pores that yield less-intense taste per puff when compared to their full-flavor counterparts with cork-colored tipping paper. Similarly, green bands imprinted on tipping or cigarette paper often signal menthol-flavored tobacco. Almost as popular is the use of blue bands (and sometimes blue text) to mark medium flavor intensity. Regardless, within-brand visual identity is seemingly durable,

and brand-specific attribute combinations are readily identified by regular and long-term smokers.[18] Here, it is worth noting that, while the use of light, low, and mild in most cigarette advertising was banned by the Family Smoking Prevention and Tobacco Control Act in 2009, longstanding associations between perceived flavor profiles and stylistic features persist. Over the course of our research, for instance, we observed smokers and vendors alike repeatedly refer to Marlboro Golds by their former name Marlboro Lights, ostensibly linking brand aesthetics such as gold packaging, gold bands, and white tipping paper with milder taste.

USE WEAR

In addition to obvious visual and olfactory traces of combustion, discarded cigarettes often feature evidence of modification by their most recent users. Archaeologists often refer to the observable and oftentimes measurable ways that objects signal engagement by users as *use wear*, and changes in the morphology of the object over a lifetime of use as *use life*. While such concepts can generate insights into the technological function and formal variation of objects,[19] they have also been criticized as rendering objects as passive or inert participants in the production of social life and meaning.[20] Alternative approaches have employed object biographies or life histories to explore the meanings imbued in things, changes in these meanings over time and across actors, and the role of objects in social interaction.[21] Here, following De León (2013), we suggest a hybrid conceptual approach that considers how modifications signal aspects of interactions with and connection(s) to people. This approach considers observable alterations from original form to describe and explain changes in morphology, and to understand the ways in which such alterations reflect both user behavior and the social experiences shared by user and consumer good. The latter benefits from comparative ethnographic observation as well as documentation of various taphonomic processes.

Though brief, the interaction between a cigarette and its smoker is kinetically elaborate. The average cigarette can be

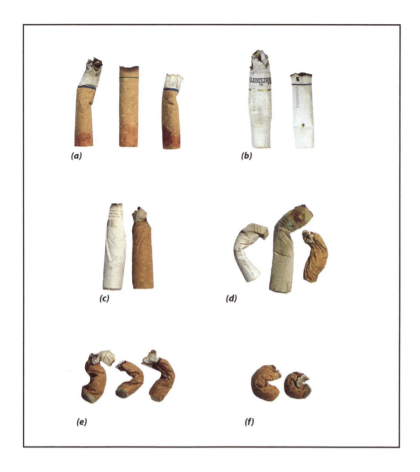

Figure 14.4. Traces of the relationship between the cigarette and its most recent smoker as materialized in observable alterations during consumption and the act of discard: Lipstick stains (a); finger pinching and light teeth impressions (b); twisted (c); twisted and stubbed (d); stubbed (e); and balled filters (f).

on cigarette filters. Even more common are teeth impressions, bite-related crimp marks, and pinching-related indentations on filters (Figure 14.4). The amount of tobacco left uncombusted in discarded cigarettes also reveals potentially meaningful variation across smoking behavior; some cigarettes are smoked down to their filters whereas others might be puffed only once or twice prior to discard. While partially smoked cigarettes may implicate aspects of the social performance, they may also be the outcome of interruptions or time pressures. Taken individually or together, these modifications to the original form of the cigarette materialize discrete details of the smoking experience.

Aspects of the interaction between cigarettes and their smokers are also evident in acts of discard. The extent to which and ways in which people extinguish and discard their cigarettes are as varied and as deeply meaningful as the ways in which cigarettes are smoked. Partially and fully smoked cigarettes can be dropped, stubbed, stamped on, ground, twisted, balled, or some combination of the above (Figure 14.4). They can also be flicked several meters from their last point of contact with a smoker. We view each and all of these discard acts, as well as the discard of smoking-related ephemera (Figure 14.5), as crucial elements of public-facing performances that may vary across time and space. As such, we argue that rigorous and consistent documentation of alterations to the original cigarette form are potentially as important to archaeological studies of patterned and idiosyncratic smoking behaviors in public spaces as the documentation of discarded cigarette types.

SOME DOMAINS OF INQUIRY

We now turn to a discussion of potential domains of inquiry that might productively be served by rigorous, data-robust archaeological studies of cigarette discard on contemporary surfaces. Our short discussion draws on ideas and data generated during a pilot study in New London, a small port-city in southeastern Connecticut. This project focused on the investigation of surfaces outside and adjacent to twenty-two drinking

smoked to tobacco depletion in only three to five minutes. In this short span of time, the cigarette is constantly handled, taken into the mouth a dozen or more times, used to gesture, and otherwise actively involved in embodied identity performances and enacted meanings. During this interaction, many cigarettes are imprinted with traces of their smoker (such as measurable amounts of DNA) and the mutually shaped smoking experience.[22] There are, however, more observable traces of the interaction. For example, choices of lipstick and lip-gloss can appear as opaque stains and semi-transparent polishes

Figure 14.5. Some cigarette packages in the United States with domestic, state-specific tax stamps affixed to transparent cellophane wrappers and indicating origin of purchase. These artifacts, among others (such as wooden and plastic tips for thin, machine-made cigars; the charred remains of roll-your-own cigarettes; empty disposable lighters) constitute assemblages that speak to localized communities of practice and performance.

Figure 14.6. Laboratory sorting of unique cigarette varieties.

establishments, but also included the comparative study of assemblages from surfaces outside a college dorm, an art park, and a major retail business. Much of the work, including thirty days of surface collection and the subsequent sorting, identification and cataloging of collected artifacts (Figure 14.6), was conducted by undergraduate student participants in a methods-intensive seminar at Connecticut College addressing the archaeology of contemporary discard. Our study revealed many potentially rewarding lines of inquiry, some of which concerned lower-order (but nonetheless critically important) phenomena relating to site formation processes whereas others concerned higher-order phenomena pertaining to the materiality of social life. Below, we focus our discussion on three interrelated domains we think germane to the larger task of theorizing discard on present-day surfaces.

TOXICITY

Cigarette discards are considerably more toxic than is generally acknowledged by consumers. The reconstituted sheet tobacco used in conventional cigarettes is sprayed with several hundred chemical additives to enhance flavor, aid nicotine delivery, and prolong shelf life.[23] Another four thousand or more chemicals are generated when the additive-laced tobacco is burned. Hundreds of these chemicals are carcinogenic when inhaled or ingested: ammonia, arsenic, benzene, butane, cadmium, carbon monoxide, cyanide, DDT, formaldehyde, lead, methanol, methoprene, polonium and tar, to name only a few.[24] Many of these chemical ingredients are used in common industrial applications, such as the production of batteries, paint, rocket fuel, household cleaners, insecticides, animal poisons, mothballs, and lighter fluid. Others, such as polonium 210, are radioactive; all are classifiable as toxic or hazardous waste owing to the fact that they are identified as carcinogenic, mutagenic, or teratogenic and thus pose long-term risks to the health of organic life.

Although the toxicity of cigarettes is widely acknowledged, the implications of this toxicity are usually referentially framed around smoking individual cigarettes and the effect(s) of inhaled chemical ingredients and combustion byproducts on the human body. That is, cigarette toxicity is regarded as a matter relating to consumption but not to discard. It follows that surface assemblages of cigarettes are rarely considered as a form of environmental pollution or a significant source of the aggregate indelible chemical impression on geological strata of the twenty-first century. Although cigarette filters are surprisingly ineffective at reducing the inhalation of chemicals and particulates to safe levels when smoking,[25] the measurable retention of heavy metals, polycyclic hydrocarbons and other toxins in the filter is still substantial and has been shown to adversely affect the mortality rates of marine invertebrates, fish, and bacteria when leached into water.[26] In effect, every used cigarette filter is a miniature, imperfect capsule of hazardous waste that, perhaps owing in part to its modest size, has evaded the same level of scrutiny and regulation applied to the discard of other consumer-available products containing toxic, reactive, and corrosive materials such as electronics, chemical cleaners, and motor oil. When tossed on the sidewalk or street, each capsule is a source of noxious leachate, or a hazardous chemical cocktail that can be transported by water runoff into soils, streams, rivers, lakes, and oceans.

Though the individual discarded cigarette might seem unimpressive, the aggregate of capsules is staggering. In New London County, for example, we collected more than 41,000 cigarettes discarded on streets, sidewalks, parking lots, and outdoor receptacles at twenty-five sites across thirty days of investigation (Figure 14.7). Controlling for first-day collections and provenience (specimens discarded in cigarette receptacles), we documented a surface discard rate of 3,229 cigarettes per week in summer months. Some of our data indicate even higher rates of deposition on certain weeks, especially those with holidays, and we imagine that cold weather adversely impacts outdoor discard during winter months. As such, we suggest a rough but somewhat conservative estimate of 168,000 cigarettes tossed on sidewalks and streets at these

Figure 14.7. An assemblage of discarded cigarettes recovered on surfaces outside a bar.

sites each year. Of course, this number grossly underestimates the total annual discard rate as a whole. To wit, if we assume that our data capture the totality of surface cigarette discard in only a modest 2 percent of public spaces in which cigarettes are regularly tossed (hospitals, courthouses, churches, restaurants, government agencies, and public parking lots), then the annual discard for New London, a small port city with only 28,000 residents (or less than 0.01 percent of the population of the United States), amounts to over 8.4 million cigarettes, or roughly 8,400 kilograms (18,500 pounds) of toxin-laden detritus.

It follows that discard can be framed as a form of destruction emergent in and from the excesses of specific forms of unfettered capitalism in the twenty-first century.[27] We acknowledge that this assertion can be made in reference to myriad social and ecological consequences of the many specific tributaries constituting the wider torrent of contemporary discard popularly labeled the 'waste stream.' So too does it speak to the broader structures of power and capital that reproduce waste and the conditions of wasting. However, we maintain that the discard of cigarettes constitutes a persistent form of background, chronic devastation—the aggregate effects of toxic leachate, stigmatization of space, affective geographies—that defies rigorous measurement and modeling for all of its complexity and sources. Given that discarded cigarette leachate is still an under-measured and altogether unregulated form of environmental pollution, no formal contaminant measurement thresholds exist; neither consumers nor cigarette manufacturers (Big Tobacco) are held accountable for their individual and collective impacts on local ecologies that result from product discard.

TAXONOMIC AMBIVALENCE

Why is much of cigarette discard impervious to the pressures or social norms and morally laden conventions applied to other forms of discard in the contemporary? Our open-ended conversations with many bar patrons suggest that much of the general public responsible for cigarette discard neither classifies butts as litter nor recognizes their toxic potential. While non-smoking residents of New London may proffer moral stances when their attention is drawn to surface assemblages of cigarette butts, an absence of public policy or municipal services concerning the creation or removal of these assemblages suggests a broader indifference. Indeed, the ways that discarded cigarettes remain a taxonomic exception to social conventions shaping acts of discard remain to be fully examined, in spite of compelling evidence to suggest that smokers who do not classify cigarette butts as litter are more than four times more likely to discard used filters on the ground.[28]

Of course, the embodied act of discard cannot be fully separated from the social meanings of performance. The communicative importance assigned by smokers to the stylistically varied acts of flicking, stubbing, and stomping may further complicate or override concerns about littering, in general, and the extent to which used cigarettes can even be regarded as trash, in particular. Nevertheless, a study of the meanings assigned to contemporary surface rejectamenta, in general, would only enhance our understanding of the semiotic and material contradictions that shape discard behaviors and, in turn, lead to particular depositional circumstances.

Consider, for example, how cigarettes, both as they are smoked and as they are tossed, occupy an ambivalent status in the conceptual schemes of everyday life and practice. These objects are readily identifiable but also stigmatized and restricted to use by adults (a taboo most recently shown by the raising of the legal age to buy tobacco products from eighteen to twenty-one). They are tangible and sensorially affective, yet experientially and materially temporary. They afford a private and intimate act of consumption even when smoking is a public-facing act. And they embody a material hybridity in that they are simultaneously organic and synthetic: paper and tobacco index a register of natural images, while cigarettes themselves are generally considered artificial products. From this latter tension emerges the contradictory but commonplace understandings of cigarettes as both compostable and non-degradable. The prevalence of cigarette refuse worldwide, as well as the general lack of systematic efforts to curb the persistent buildup of this toxic waste, indicates a widespread belief (not limited to smokers) that, if left exposed to the elements, a cigarette will eventually disintegrate. Moreover, this disintegration can be easily conceptualized in terms of biodegradation, or a breakdown of organic matter into the component parts from which organic life emerges or on which other organic life thrives. This same prevalence, however, also serves to remind people of the durability of cigarette trash. Hence, the social life of the discarded cigarette as litter and non-litter, simultaneously visible and invisible, blatant and obscured, and a materialization of both order and disorder.

THE SPACE OF DISCARD

The significance of cigarette refuse in social life extends beyond value-laden perceptions and chemical realities of toxicity and disposability. Across urban landscapes worldwide, practices of cigarette discard shape material, semiotic, and phenomenological geographies, evidencing the multi-scalar relationship between space, waste, and smoking. Recent ethnographic work on trash and dumping has highlighted the centrality of discard to experiences of space and place,[29] especially in cities, but the assemblages of cigarettes strewn across public areas throughout the globe have yet to receive sustained anthropological or geographical attention. The growing anthropological literature on tobacco has, for its part,[30] tended to emphasize public health issues of cigarette regulation, addiction, and cessation,[31] as well as tobacco production.[32] Our preliminary findings augment and intersect these bodies of work: cigarette discard, we suggest, embodies and exhibits modes of spatial production and construction fundamental to modern urban life.[33] This process of assemblage formation reflects—and, potentially, exacerbates—spatialized forms of blight and neglect reproduced under late capitalism, while also affording a creative practice of place-making at odds with structures of discipline and control.

With respect to the production of space, we note that the location of our research, New London, Connecticut, is an economically depressed post-industrial port city. Over decades, New London has been hampered by white flight to neighboring suburbs, the post–Cold War decline of naval manufacturing, a loss of retail and service-sector jobs to nearby casinos, a lack of developable land, and an excess of non-taxable property. Like many demographically similar municipalities, the city is, today, characterized by a high rate of smoking, low frequencies of street cleaning and beautification, a multitude of abandoned and neglected spaces and, in consequence, substantial concentrations of cigarette discard. Leaching toxic waste across streets and sidewalks and into sewers, such discard presents a tangible public-health threat, compounding the public-health crisis of smoking itself. Ethnoarchaeological methods and theory allow us to examine this spatialized toxicity as a material record of late capitalist violence. Yet the widespread view of New London, among outsiders and locals alike, as a seedy urban backwater suggests that these assemblages more often elicit disparaging images of localized ignorance, disease, and even danger. Put another

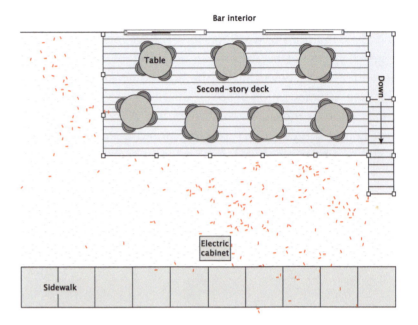

Figure 14.8. Discarded cigarettes mapped near the rear deck of a New London bar.

way, the political economic reproduction of blighted space across New London's post-industrial cityscape encourages the widespread accumulation of hazardous waste in the form of cigarette litter. This waste is socially meaningful. It opens the door to increased levels of stigmatization and neglect, which, we conjecture, might grease the wheels of inequality by keeping public services underfunded, small businesses insufficiently patronized, and residents vulnerable to illness, poverty, and exploitation.

That said, we also maintain that discard, like the practice of smoking itself, constitutes a creative form of spatial construction that informs novel and, potentially, subversive experiences of the urban landscape. It goes without saying that the ways in which smokers dispose of cigarettes actively influence assemblages of cigarette refuse. Central to our argument is an observation of the reverse: the ways in which these assemblages form actively influence patterns of disposal. The reciprocal interplay of disposal and assemblage formation, we argue, constitutes a mode of spatial construction because it prompts expressions of collective action (and reaction) that challenge the social and material constraints of the built environment. Smokers will dispose of cigarettes according to the dynamic map of discard that appears before them, often taking direct cues from the acts of others as observed or evinced at certain sites. Over the course of our research, we found as evidence of this process a prevalence of "flick zones" throughout downtown New London. These were spaces—often near curbsides, alleyways and decks—marked by the repeated discard of cigarettes as manifest in sizable assemblages (Figure 14.8). What is more, such assemblages would quickly reappear following street cleaning and our own data collection, suggesting that embodied and spatialized routines of discard persist beyond the visual index of cigarette trash itself.

Building on de Certeau (2011), we consider the continuous reconstruction of discard sites as a spatial tactic, like walking or cooking: a fleeting but meaningful opening up of space illegible to the strategic gaze of urban planning, discipline, and control. Obscured by dominant modes of spatial production—as visible in city maps, practices of governance (including the enforcement of zoning laws and regulations against littering), and the built environment itself, which is not designed to collect cigarette refuse—discard nonetheless affords creative reimaginings and expressions of space (see also Zubiaurre and Cruz, Chapter 7 in this volume). Through routine practices of discard, smokers impress on the urban landscape Lefebvrian "spaces of representation" comprising an idiosyncratic but also deeply collective geography of social life.[34] Assemblages can signify a retreat from social obligation (a place to have a smoke and 'get away from it all') or a site for spontaneous and casual interaction with other smokers, among many other possibilities. Future archaeology and ethnography of cities, especially that focused on urban space and place in everyday life, might benefit from increased attention to how smokers and non-smokers alike respond to these assemblages, which are simultaneously fleeting and durable, constructed and constructive.

SUMMARY AND FUTURE

In this chapter, we have ventured to challenge the perceived triviality of discarded cigarettes by showcasing familiar analytic concepts (corresponding morphological, stylistic, and experiential variability; use wear; spatial distribution) that otherwise warrant an archaeological gaze. Given the preponderance of cigarette discard on everyday surfaces, archaeological studies of cigarettes afford an examination of some of the nuanced and deleterious outcomes of global capitalism in a wider array of lived and depositional contexts. We have also argued that cigarette discard is, as both a social practice and a material assemblage, culturally generative: it routinely restructures the semiotics of urban space in accordance with an ethics of toxicity that renders cigarette trash a sign of poverty and danger while also obscuring the profound ecological threat of cigarette leachate. We hope that this discussion will inspire greater interdisciplinary attention to the conspicuous presence of cigarette refuse worldwide among not only archaeologists, ethnographers, and ecologists, but also planners, policymakers, and members of the general public.

NOTES

1   Jambeck et al. 2015.

2   Edgeworth 2014, Graves-Brown 2014.

3   Graves-Brown 2011, Harrison 2011, Lucas 2004.

4   Dawdy 2009, Shanks et al. 2004.

5   Buchli 2007, Dawdy 2009, Graves-Brown et al. 2013, Harrison 2011, Zimmerman and Welch 2011.

6   Graves-Brown et al. 2013, Yaneva 2013.

7   Latour 2000, 2005.

8   Chenoweth 2017, González-Ruibal 2008, Lucas 2005.

9   De León 2013, 2015, Gokee and De León 2014, Zimmerman and Welch 2011.

10 Dawdy 2009.

11 Chenoweth 2017, González-Ruibal 2008, Harrison and Schofield 2010.

12 Buchli and Lucas 2001.

13 De León 2012, 2013, Graesch et al. 2020; Zimmerman and Welch 2011.

14 Mauss 1966, Strathern 1988.

15 Cigarette Citadels (2015), *A Research Project by Stanford's Global Tobacco Prevention Research Initiative,* https://web.stanford.edu/group/tobaccoprv/cgi-bin/wp/ (accessed 29 February 2020).

16 Eriksen et al. 2015.

17 World Health Organization (2016), *Tobacco: Fact Sheet,* http://www.who.int/mediacentre/factsheets/fs339/en/ (accessed 29 February 2020).

18 Scheffels 2008.

19 Hayden 1977.

20 Gosden and Marshall 1999.

21 Gosden and Marshall 1999, Kopytoff 1986, Tringham 1995.

22 Apostolov 2012.

23 R.J. Reynolds Tobacco Company (2018), *Cigarette Ingredients: R. J. Reynolds List of Ingredients,* http://www.rjrt.com/commercial-integrity/ingredients/cigarette-ingredients/ (accessed 29 February 2020).

24 American Lung Association (2015), *What's in a Cigarette?* http://www.lung.org/stop-smoking/about-smoking/facts-figures/whats-in-a-cigarette.html; and Center for Disease Control and Prevention (2011), *Chemicals in Tobacco Smoke,* http://www.cdc.gov/tobacco/data_statistics/sgr/2010/consumer_booklet/chemicals_smoke/ (both accessed 29 February 2020).

25 Harris 2011.

26 Micevska et al. 2006, Moerman and Potts 2011, Slaughter et al. 2011.

27 González-Ruibal 2008.

28 Rath et al. 2012.

29 Ferrell 2005, Fredericks 2018, Millar 2018, Nagle 2013.

30 Kohrman and Benson 2011.

31 Nichter 2003, 2015, Nichter and Cartwright 1991, Nichter et al. 2009, Singer 2004.

32 Benson 2011, Van Willigen and Eastwood 1998.

33 Low 2016.

34 Lefebvre 1992.

BIBLIOGRAPHY

Apostolov, Aleksandar (2012), DNA Identification of Biological Traces on Cigarettes: Vices Reveal, *Biotechnology and Biotechnological Equipment* 26(3), 2994–98.

Benson, Peter (2011), *Tobacco Capitalism: Growers, Migrant Workers, and the Changing Face of a Global Industry,* Princeton (Princeton University Press).

Buchli, Victor (2007) Opinion, *Conservation Bulletin* 56, 14.

Buchli, Victor and Gavin Lucas (2001), "The Absent Present: Archaeologies of the Contemporary Past," in: Victor Buchli and Gavin Lucas, eds., *Archaeologies of the Contemporary Past,* pp. 3–18, London (Routledge).

Chenoweth, John M. (2017), Natural Graffiti and Cultural Plants: Memory, Race, and Contemporary Archaeology in Yosemite and Detroit, *American Anthropologist* 119(3), 464–77.

Dawdy, Shannon L. (2009), Millennial Archaeology: Locating the Discipline in the Age of Insecurity, *Archaeological Dialogues* 16(2), 131–42.

de Certeau, Michel (2011), *The Practice of Everyday Life*, Berkeley (University of California Press, translation by Steven Rendall of the 1984 French original).

De León, Jason (2012), Better to be Hot than Caught: Excavating the Conflicting Roles of Migrant Material Culture, *American Anthropologist* 114(3), 477–95.

—— (2013), Undocumented Migration, Use Wear, and the Materiality of Habitual Suffering in the Sonoran Desert, *Journal of Material Culture* 18(4), 321–45.

—— (2015), *The Land of Open Graves: Living and Dying on the Sonoran Desert Migrant Trail,* Oakland (University of California Press).

Deetz, James (1996), *In Small Things Forgotten: An Archaeology of Early American Life,* New York (Doubleday).

Edgeworth, Matt (2014), Archaeology of the Anthropocene: Introduction, *Journal of Contemporary Archaeology* 1(1), 73–77.

Eriksen, Michael, Judith Mackay, Neil Schluger, Farhad Islami Gomeshtapeh, and Jeffrey Drope (2015), *The Tobacco Atlas,* Atlanta (American Cancer Society, Inc., fifth edition).

Ferrell, Jeff (2005), *Empire of Scrounge: Inside the Urban Underground of Dumpster Diving, Trash Picking, and Street Scavenging,* New York (New York University Press).

Fredericks, Rosalind (2018), *Garbage Citizenship Vital Infrastructures of Labor in Dakar, Senegal,* Durham (Duke University Press).

Gokee, Cameron and Jason De León (2014), Sites of Contention: Archaeological Classification and Political Discourse in the US–Mexico Borderlands, *Journal of Contemporary Archaeology* 1(1): 133–63.

González-Ruibal, Alfredo (2008), Time to Destroy: An Archaeology of Supermodernity, *Current Anthropology* 49(2), 247–79.

Gosden, Chris and Yvonne Marshall (1999), The Cultural Biography of Objects, *World Archaeology* 31(2), 169–78.

Graesch, Anthony P., Corbin Maynard, and Avery Thomas (2020), "Discards, Emotions, and Empathy on the Margins of the Waste Stream," in: Kisha Supernant, Jane E. Baxter, Natasha Lyons, and Sonya Atalay, eds., *Archaeologies of the Heart,* pp. 141–61, Heidelberg (Springer Verlag).

Graves-Brown, Paul (2011), Archaeology: A Career in Ruins, *Archaeological Dialogues* 18(2), 168–71.

—— (2014), Archaeology of the Anthropocene: When was the Anthropocene? (and Why?), *Journal of Contemporary Archaeology* 1(1), 77–81.

Graves-Brown, Paul, Rodney Harrison, and Angela Piccini (2013), "Introduction," in: Paul Graves-Brown, Rodney Harrison, and Angela Piccini, eds., *The Oxford Handbook of the Archaeology of the Contemporary World,* pp. 1–23, Oxford (Oxford University Press).

Harris, Bradford (2011), The Intractable Cigarette 'Filter Problem,' *Tobacco Control* 20(1), 10–16.

Harrison, Rodney (2011), Surface Assemblages: Towards an Archaeology in and of the Present, *Archaeological Dialogues* 18(2), 141–61.

Harrison, Rodney and John Schofield (2010), *After Modernity: Archaeological Approaches to the Contemporary Past,* Oxford (Oxford University Press).

Haviland, William, Harald E.L. Prins, Bunny McBride, and Dana Walrath (2017), *Cultural Anthropology: The Human Challenge,* Boston (Cengage Learning).

Hayden, Brian (1977), *Lithic Use-Wear Analysis,* New York (Academic Press).

Jambeck, Jenna R., Roland Geyer, Chris Wilcox, Theodore R. Siegler, Miriam Perryman, Anthony Andrady, Ramani Narayan, and Kara Lavender Law (2015), Plastic Inputs from Land into Ocean, *Science* 347(6223), 768–71.

Kopytoff, Igor (1986), "The Cultural Biography of Things: Commoditization as Process," in: A. Appadurai, ed., *The Social Life of Things: Commodities in Cultural Perspective,* pp. 64–91, Cambridge (Cambridge University Press).

Kohrman, Matthew and Peter Benson (2011), Tobacco, *Annual Review of Anthropology* 40(1), 329–44.

Latour, Bruno (2000), "The Berliner Key," in: Paul Graves-Brown, ed., *Matter, Materiality, and Modern Culture,* pp. 10–21, New York (Routledge).

—— (2005), *Reassembling the Social: An Introduction to Actor-Network-Theory,* Oxford (Oxford University Press).

Lefebvre, Henri (1992), *The Production of Space,* Hoboken (Wiley-Backwell, translation by Donald Nicholson-Smith of the 1974 French original)

Low, Setha M. (2016), *Spatializing Culture: The Ethnography of Space and Place,* Abingdon (Routledge).

Lucas, Gavin (2004), Modern Disturbances: On the Ambiguities of Archaeology, *Modernism/modernity* 11(1), 109–20.

—— (2005), *The Archaeology of Time,* London and New York (Routledge).

Mauss, Marcel (1966), *The Gift: Forms and Functions of Exchange in Archaic Societies,* London (Cohen and West Ltd., translation by Ian Cunnison of the 1950 French original).

Micevska, Tina, Michael St.J. Warne, Fleur Pablo, and Ronald Patra (2006), Variation in, and Causes of, Toxicity of Cigarette Butts to a Cladoceran and Microtox, *Archives of Environmental Contamination and Toxicology* 50(2), 205–12.

Millar, Kathleen M. (2018), *Reclaiming the Discarded Life and Labor on Rio's Garbage Dump,* Durham (Duke University Press).

Moerman, Jessica W. and Gretchen E. Potts (2011), Analysis of Metals Leached from Smoked Cigarette Litter, *Tobacco Control* 20(1), 30–35.

Nagle, Robin (2013), *Picking Up: On the Streets and Behind the Trucks with the Sanitation Workers of New York City,* New York (Farrar, Straus and Giroux).

Nichter, Mark (2003), Smoking: What Does Culture Have to do with It? *Addiction* 98, 139–45.

Nichter, Mark and Elizabeth Cartwright (1991), Saving the Children for the Tobacco Industry, *Medical Anthropology Quarterly* 5, 236–56.

Nichter, Mark, Mimi Nichter, Siwi Padmawathi, and C.U. Thresia (2009), "Anthropological Contributions to the Development of Culturally Appropriate Tobacco Cessation Programs: A Global Health Priority," in: Robert A. Hahn and Marcia C. Inhorn, eds., *Anthropology and Public Health,* pp. 298–331, New York (Oxford University Press).

Nichter, Mimi (2015), *Lighting Up: The Rise of Social Smoking on College Campuses,* New York (New York University Press).

Rath, Jessica M., Rebecca A. Rubenstein, Laurel E. Curry, Sarah E. Shank, and Julia C. Cartwright (2002), Cigarette Litter: Smokers' Attitudes and Behaviors, *International Journal of Environmental Research and Public Health* 9(6), 2189–2203.

Shanks, Michael, David Platt, and William L. Rathje (2004), The Perfume of Garbage: Modernity and the Archaeological, *Modernism/modernity* 11(1), 61–83.

Scheffels, Janne (2008), A Difference that Makes a Difference: Young Adult Smokers' Accounts of Cigarette Brands and Package Design, *Tobacco Control* 17(2), 118–22.

Singer, Merrill (2004), "Tobacco Use in Medical Anthropological Perspective," in: Carol R. Ember and Melvin Ember, eds., *Encyclopedia of Medical Anthropology: Health and Illness in the World's Cultures,* pp. 518–28, New York (Kluwer Academic).

Slaughter, Elli, Richard M. Gersberg, Kayo Watanabe, John Rudolph, Chris Stransky, and Thomas E. Novotny (2011), Toxicity of Cigarette Butts, and Their Chemical Components, to Marine and Freshwater Fish, *Tobacco Control* 20(1), 25–29.

Strathern, Marilyn (1988), *The Gender of the Gift,* Berkeley (University of California Press).

Tringham, Ruth (1995), "Archaeological Houses, Households, Housework, and the Home," in: David N. Benjamin, ed., *The Home: Words, Interpretations, Meanings, and Environments,* pp. 79–107, Aldershot (Avenbury).

Van Willigan, John and Susan C. Eastwood (1998), *Tobacco Culture: Farming Kentucky's Burley Belt,* Lexington (University Press of Kentucky).

Yaneva, Albena (2013), "Actor-Network-Theory Approaches to the Archaeology of Contemporary Architecture," in: Paul Graves-Brown, Rodney Harrison, and Angela Piccini, eds., *The Oxford Handbook of the Archaeology of the Contemporary World,* pp. 121–34, Oxford (Oxford University Press).

Zimmerman, Larry J. and Jessica Welch (2011), Displaced and Barely Visible: Archaeology and the Material Culture of Homelessness, *Historical Archaeology* 45(1), 67–85.

ARCHAEOLOGY IN A VACUUM

OBSTACLES TO AND SOLUTIONS FOR DEVELOPING A REAL SPACE ARCHAEOLOGY

ALICE GORMAN AND JUSTIN WALSH

Outer space was occupied in human imagination long before technology enabled actual visitation to these regions. For many early commentators, planets and stars were inhabited just like Earth; however, these aliens were frequently invented to make a philosophical or satirical point, for example, in Lucian of Samosata's *True History* (second century CE) or Voltaire's *Micromegas* (1752). Galileo Galilei's observations of the near planets of the solar system with his new telescope in the 1600s was the first application of remote sensing to off-Earth landscapes. In the late 1800s, Percival Lowell's observations of "canals" on Mars raised hopes that sentient solar system neighbors would soon be in communication with Earth, or fears they would be invading it. Until the advent of space travel in the 1950s, the need for the as-yet non-existent professions of space archaeology (the study of human material culture in space) and xeno-archaeology (the study of non-terrestrial material culture) was equally balanced. As the 1960s and 1970s passed, not only were humans sent to the Moon, but deep space probes flew by all of the planets from Mercury to Neptune. The results were disappointing. Where there were solid planetary surfaces, there were no canals or pyramids hinting at civilizations beyond our world, past or contemporary. The archaeological record of the solar system was confined to human activities. And so xeno-archaeology became the realm of speculation, while space archaeology started to find a foothold within the discipline.

Space archaeology is defined as the study of "the material culture relevant to space exploration that is found on Earth and in outer space (that is, exoatmospheric material) and that is clearly the result of human behavior".[1] Human activity in space is worthy of archaeological research because it represents our attempts to live in an environment for which we are not evolutionarily adapted. The variable success of the technological and other engineering efforts to make the space environment survivable, habitable, and even comfortable for humans also has its own impacts on human behavior.

The general public, and occasionally archaeological peers, sometimes struggle with the idea that archaeologists can study activities that have happened within our lifetimes; the association of space travel with futurism only intensifies this perception. As the other projects described in this volume make clear, however, the archaeology of the contemporary world is rich with possibilities. Like our colleagues (such as Anthony Graesch and Timothy Hartshorn, Chapter 14 in this volume, and La Vergne Lehmann, Chapter 15 in this volume), we have been inspired by work such as the Tucson Garbage Project, which examined household waste and interviewed the residents of homes whose trash was sampled. William Rathje's team showed that merely interviewing people about their discard habits did not reveal their practices in the way archaeological sampling of their trash did.[2] For example, Latina mothers who participated in Rathje's investigation stated that they made all food for their babies from scratch, while their garbage demonstrated that they discarded just as much store-bought baby food as other households. The point of this example is not to criticize anyone for how they feed their children (or what they say to researchers), but to demonstrate that people often do not want to discuss their behaviors and motivations because they conflict with the identity that they want to project, or because they do not trust the investigator. Sometimes they are simply unable to articulate their motives and reasoning. Contemporary archaeology can fill that gap, as shown by Rathje and numerous other projects.[3]

That archaeologists might turn their attention to the borderlands between the present and the future was presaged as long ago as 1967, when James Deetz, in his slim volume *Invitation to Archaeology*, noted that starships may well become the subject of future research. At this time the first human landing missions to the Moon were deep in the test phase and 1961 had already seen Yuri Gagarin's successful orbit around Earth. Yet despite the growth in terrestrial sites related to rocket launches and the satellite industry, as well as off-Earth places where human material culture had come to rest, few took up this challenge. Space made a brief appearance in the modern material culture movement that emerged in the United States in the 1980s when David J. Meltzer analyzed the National Air and Space Museum in Washington, DC as a cultural artifact.[4]

A decade later, Greg Fewer (2002) proposed that a heritage listing system was needed for sites on the Moon and Mars. This suggestion came in the context of a conference session exploring intersections between archaeology and science fiction but was the first serious attempt to apply terrestrial heritage principles to the off-Earth record. But what about sites that had already been destroyed, in the absence of any recognition that space hardware could have heritage value? The first permanent human habitation in space, the Soviet/Russian Mir space station, lasted fifteen years before it was taken out of orbit in 2001. Robert Barclay and Randall Brooks (2002) lamented the fact that no thought had been given to preserving the legacy of this unique habitat. They proposed a system for heritage listing based on World Heritage principles. As they expressed it, "our space vehicles are the twentieth and twenty-first century legacy of antiquity; they are our counterpoint to Stonehenge, the Pyramids, Harrison's chronometers and the telescopes of Galileo and Newton."[5]

The first systematic archaeological study of a space site was Beth Laura O'Leary's Lunar Legacy Project (1999–2001). She identified 106 objects left behind at the Tranquility Base site of the 1969 Apollo 11 landing. However, O'Leary and her team did not investigate the sociocultural significance of that material. She later worked successfully with Lisa Westwood and Wayne Donaldson (who, at the time, was State Historic Preservation Officer for California) to list the Tranquility Base objects as state historic resources in California and New Mexico in 2010. The sites themselves could not be registered, as this might have been interpreted as a territorial claim, forbidden by the Outer Space Treaty of 1967. Their 2017 volume *The Final Mission: Preserving NASA's Apollo Sites* is the definitive text covering Apollo heritage from Earth to Moon. P.J. Capelotti (2010) identified the facies of what he termed the "Apollo culture," and created a list of sites associated with both crewed and uncrewed human interventions across the solar system, but he did so without analyzing the material culture of any particular site in detail. As Michael Schiffer (2013) concluded in his survey of space archaeology, establishing the credibility of the sub-field and addressing heritage concerns was the predominant focus of the first two decades of research.

We were also part of this process. Alice Gorman (2007, 2009a) studied the landscapes of the rocket launch sites in Australia, French Guiana, and Algeria, describing how European colonial projects were deeply entangled in the growth of the space industry. During a surface survey of the former NASA satellite tracking station of Orroral Valley in Australia, she identified cable ties as a common artifact type across the aerospace industry which had also migrated into everyday life.[6] In space, Gorman (2009b, 2015) has focused on the heritage and archaeological potential of orbital debris and the impacts of mining in off-Earth environments. Justin Walsh (2012) has studied the consequences of international law for the preservation of heritage located in space contexts, suggesting that a new treaty is needed to provide adequate protection. He also has identified new, ephemeral characteristics of space technology, and investigated the consequences of those characteristics for future archaeology of human space exploration.[7]

Research in space archaeology to date has mapped and investigated terrestrial infrastructure such as launch sites, tracking stations, and industrial complexes, as well as museum collections. Off-Earth material culture includes satellites, orbital debris, and planetary landing sites. While these studies demonstrated that space archaeology can be used to address new questions about human interactions with space, there has never been a substantive analysis of data collected from space sites. Carrying out an archaeological study of a site in space, whether in low-Earth orbit or on the surface of another planet, presents clear difficulties for researchers. For one thing, archaeologists typically need to be present at their site for data collection, usually by means of survey or

excavation. In an outer-space context, it is generally impossible to visit sites in person, due to the high costs and other technical barriers associated with space travel. An additional obstacle to archaeological studies of space sites is that most active space agencies with human missions have explicitly barred social science researchers from participating in space crews. This position was reiterated by NASA in its most recent call for new astronaut candidates in February 2020; however, the Japanese space agency JAXA dropped its requirement for a natural sciences degree in 2021.

With a new emphasis by space agencies and corporations on multi-year missions to Mars and beyond, we saw an opportunity to show the relevance of an archaeological perspective by investigating how a space crew uses material culture to help structure and maintain a society. Indeed, a 1972 report by the National Academy of Sciences, with the title "Human Factors in Long-Duration Spaceflight," specifically referred to the crew of a spacecraft as "a microsociety in a miniworld." Yet after almost fifty years since that publication, sociocultural aspects of life in space continue to be neglected in favor of physiological and psychological research. The International Space Station Archaeological Project is explicitly designed to fill this lacuna. We are extending archaeology into a new context, asking new questions, and contributing insights that have the potential to improve future mission success, in the first systematic archaeological study of a space habitat.

Space stations have come and gone over the decades, from the launch by the USSR of the Salyut 1 station in 1971 to the de-orbit of the Chinese space station Tiangong 1 in 2018. Only the International Space Station is permanently occupied. Planning for this station began in 1983, the project was announced to the public by Ronald Reagan during his State of the Union speech in 1984, and its first modules entered orbit in 1998. The International Space Station is the largest spacecraft ever built, comprising multiple modules and a habitable volume of approximately 1,000 cubic meters (35,500 cubic feet, often compared to a five-bedroom house by NASA), with a total footprint equal to an American football field. At least two astronauts have continuously inhabited it since 2 November

2000, 9:21 am (UTC); for more than seven thousand consecutive days as of early 2020.[8] The International Space Station project has involved five space agencies (NASA, Roscosmos, the European Space Agency, the Japan Aerospace Exploration Agency, and the Canadian Space Agency), twenty-five national governments, countless private contractors, and at least 253 human visitors from nineteen countries. The flight crew has varied between two and six people, representing from two to six nationalities at a time, and includes both men and women (although only thirty-eight out of 253 visitors—only 15 percent—have been women). In 2031 the station will be de-orbited, as Mir was before it. Hence there is a limited opportunity to study society and material culture on board.

Questions that are being addressed through the archaeological analysis of material culture on the International Space Station include:

- How people adapt their behaviors and tools to the specific requirements of life in space; and in particular how microgravity affects the development of the society and culture on board the space station.
- How a crew composed of people from different nations, with different languages and cultures, builds cohesion, accommodates each member, and manages conflict, in a milieu that is itself multicultural (built in different design and engineering traditions, with instruments and spaces labeled in different languages).
- The gendered use of spaces and objects within the space station.
- How the sounds, smells, views, tastes, and textures associated with life on the space station affect crewmembers, and how astronauts adapt their behavior, movements, or the station itself in order to improve those experiences.
- How spaces and time are structured to negotiate surveillance and monitoring by ground staff, and interactions with the public.

The prohibitive costs and other obstacles to fieldwork in the International Space Station necessitated the development of new methodologies to allow observation and data acquisition by re-imagining traditional archaeological practices. Our inability to visit the site has already been mentioned; we therefore have to rely on proxy methods to collect data. As there is no up or down in microgravity, we also had to develop new ways of ascribing locations of artifacts and people. Where traditional archaeologists working on Earth can rely on latitude–longitude or the Universal Transverse Mercator coordinate system to geolocate objects and installations, we have had to develop a system that is oriented along axes relative to flight direction of the space station around Earth: forward–aft, starboard–port, and zenith–nadir. We divided each module into twenty-seven sub-spaces (for instance, forward–starboard–zenith or center–port–nadir) where an item can be found. Another variable, tied–loose, indicates whether an object is floating freely or attached to a surface.

Over almost twenty years of occupation of the International Space Station, NASA has archived millions of images of everyday life and work. This is a different type of archaeological research: not waiting for the actors to leave, but recording while they are actually in the process of daily activity, albeit frozen in an image. Using these photographs, we proposed to catalog associations between crewmembers, spaces within the station, and objects/tools, to discover patterns of behavior the psychologists, sociologists, and engineers have overlooked (Figure 13.1). As with other historical and contemporary archaeology, the augmentation of material evidence with the documentary and oral records offers insights into behavior that it would be remiss to ignore. The Tucson Garbage Project demonstrated how the differences between the archaeological data and what people were willing to relate illuminated the social meanings of objects, such as the mundane baby food containers that were thrown away. Hypotheses generated by the image analysis about the role of artifacts and spaces in the constitution of the "microsociety in a miniworld" can be tested against astronaut accounts in much the same way, through the administration of anonymized questionnaires to flight and ground crew.

The International Space Station is far from the ideal of a self-sustaining habitat; it is reliant on continual supply from Earth. The objects we observe on the station are curated and

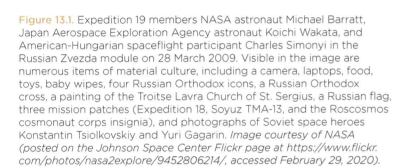

Figure 13.1. Expedition 19 members NASA astronaut Michael Barratt, Japan Aerospace Exploration Agency astronaut Koichi Wakata, and American-Hungarian spaceflight participant Charles Simonyi in the Russian Zvezda module on 28 March 2009. Visible in the image are numerous items of material culture, including a camera, laptops, food, toys, baby wipes, four Russian Orthodox icons, a Russian Orthodox cross, a painting of the Troitse Lavra Church of St. Sergius, a Russian flag, three mission patches (Expedition 18, Soyuz TMA-13, and the Roscosmos cosmonaut corps insignia), and photographs of Soviet space heroes Konstantin Tsiolkovskiy and Yuri Gagarin. *Image courtesy of NASA (posted on the Johnson Space Center Flickr page at https://www.flickr.com/photos/nasa2explore/9452806214/, accessed February 29, 2020).*

Figure 13.2. Cosmonaut Alexander Misurkin discards an electronic box on 2 February 2018 by throwing it out and away from the International Space Station. It will eventually burn up in the atmosphere: a) Misurkin holds the electronic box in front of him; b) he casts it away; c-d) the box is seen flying away. *Screen captures from video courtesy of NASA; tweeted from the official International Space Station Twitter account at https://twitter.com/Space_Station/status/959514377207476224, accessed 29 February 2020.*

managed through a complex inventory management system consisting of over 130,000 items. The crew interact with a depauperate artifact assemblage compared to Earth, determined by factors such as space qualification, flammability, size, and weight. A limited number of items come back from the station to Earth. Since the end of the Shuttle program in 2011, up to approximately 2,000 kilograms (4,400 pounds) of items are brought back on each flight of the SpaceX Dragon capsule. All other materials sent to the space station either remain there, in use or in storage, or they are placed into other supply craft that are designed to be destroyed through the re-entry process. Working from archaeological analogy, we interpret the return of items from the International Space Station as a form of discard process. Certainly, watching how some items are discarded from the station provides much food for thought

for the archaeologist. Since 2018, both Russian and American crew members performing spacewalks have been instructed to simply throw broken equipment, such as a high-gain antenna electronics box, away from the station so that it will eventually fall into the atmosphere and burn up (Figure 13.2).

To contextualize the use of these items in space properly, a crucial method is observation of items returned from the International Space Station, the practices and policies that comprise the cargo return ('de-integration') activity, and analysis of the values and meanings associated with those items.[9] In 2018, we observed two return flights of the Dragon capsule, laden with scientific samples, broken, or used equipment, and personal items of the crew. Through photography, video and interviews with participants, we documented the procedures used by NASA contractors from Leidos Corporation and Jacobs Engineering Group to maintain control and care of the objects, some of which must remain chilled to –80°C (–112°F)

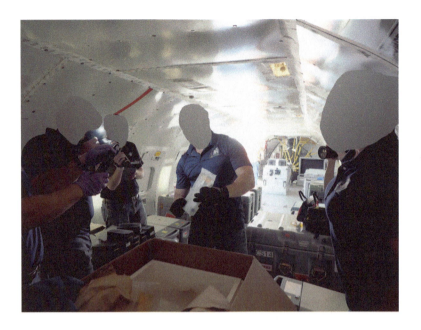

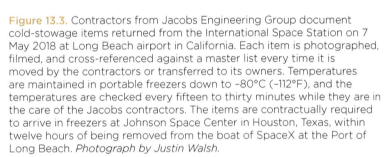

Figure 13.3. Contractors from Jacobs Engineering Group document cold-stowage items returned from the International Space Station on 7 May 2018 at Long Beach airport in California. Each item is photographed, filmed, and cross-referenced against a master list every time it is moved by the contractors or transferred to its owners. Temperatures are maintained in portable freezers down to –80°C (–112°F), and the temperatures are checked every fifteen to thirty minutes while they are in the care of the Jacobs contractors. The items are contractually required to arrive in freezers at Johnson Space Center in Houston, Texas, within twelve hours of being removed from the boat of SpaceX at the Port of Long Beach. *Photograph by Justin Walsh.*

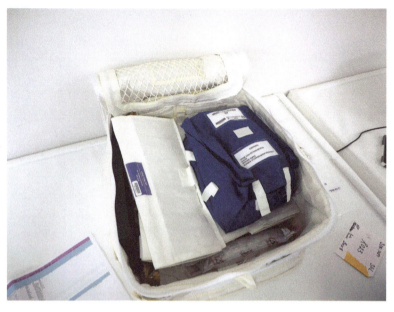

Figure 13.4. A cargo transfer bag from the International Space Station is opened at the facilities of NASA cargo management contract-holder Leidos Corporation on 19 January 2018. *Photograph by Justin Walsh.*

throughout their return from the station to California, Houston, and finally to customers.

We observed the handling of returned cargo from the International Space Station on the Dragon CRS-13 and CRS-14 capsules in January and May 2018, respectively. During the observation, we visited work locations in Houston, Texas and Long Beach, California; photographed and filmed the activities in which the returned items were documented and handled; and interviewed participants at all levels and various responsibilities relating to the cargo-return process (Figures 13.3–13.5). We gained insights into the choices made about which items to leave onboard the station, which to destroy, and which to bring back to Earth. The items designated for return typically fall into

one of three categories: scientific samples, broken equipment and equipment that needs to be studied on Earth for some reason, and personal effects of crew members. We also documented the protocols for packing, unpacking, and monitoring various kinds of items. These items include paper that is sent up for the printer on the International Space Station, scientific samples—such as blood samples of crew members, frozen at –80°C (–112°F)—and the ice cream chosen by the cold-stowage team to send to crew, usually Snickers ice cream bars, because their shape fits the bags best. We even got a personal introduction to the smell of the International Space Station when one of the cargo transfer bags was opened in front of us. Crew cannot wash thoroughly during their time on board, and they exercise for two to three hours daily. 'Locker room,' or 'gym bag,' with a touch of 'doctor's office,' goes a long way toward describing the smell of a human habitat in space.

Archaeological work on the International Space Station requires an adaptation of traditional methods. The NASA image

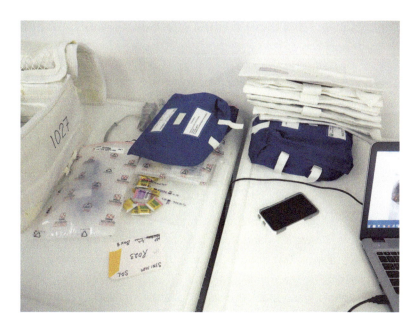

Figure 13.5. The contents of the bag shown in Figure 13.4 are arranged on a table waiting to be documented and recorded. *Photograph by Justin Walsh.*

archive provides a proxy for an actual survey of the interior spaces, but it may not be necessary to completely abandon the idea of fieldwork inside a space habitat. Astronauts have conducted an extraordinary range of physical science experiments and research aboard the station, including biological, chemical, physical, astronomical, medical, and climate research. Not all of the astronauts have significant scientific backgrounds, and if they do, they are frequently required to run experiments outside their area of expertise. More than one astronaut has mentioned to us in conversation that following instructions precisely is a key part of this process—initiative is not encouraged!

Generally speaking, crew are expected to be comfortable with any kind of work, and they therefore receive on-the-job instruction to enable them to perform successfully whatever kind of experiment is required, and to use whatever equipment is available. This seems an ideal setting to develop procedures for one or more crew members to carry out an archaeological

survey of the interior of International Space Station during a future mission. While the analysis of the NASA image archive will enable a longitudinal mapping of human–object interactions, this more fine-grained survey will document aspects of life on board that fall between the photos, or are best achieved by direct fieldwork. Among the techniques we plan to use are surface sampling in various modules for the accretion of dust, hair, skin cells, oil, dirt, food, and other materials, analogous to soil sampling through excavation; audio recording to identify levels of ambient sound and the extent to which voices and other sounds carry through the architecture of the station; photography to establish lines of sight from various positions, using the full freedom of movement afforded by microgravity; and documentation of specific public spaces such as eating areas, and, if possible, private spaces such as crew berths. In January–March 2022, we flew the Sampling Quadrangle Assemblages Research Experiment onto the International Space Station, in which the crew photographed six sample squares of approximately 1×1 meter marked on the walls in different modules over two months. The aim of the experiment was to document the movement and use of artifacts over time, thus providing information about daily life in space. This was the first archaeological fieldwork ever conducted outside Earth.[10]

The techniques described here are not the only methods that can enable archaeological study of space habitats. Other scholars are likely to conceive of different, even more creative approaches in the future. However, these methods are an important starting point for a subdiscipline that, like its subject matter, is still in its infancy. By combining the methods here, we can conduct research in an archaeological context where such work has rarely been attempted. We may even be able to identify problems and propose solutions that will improve mission success by promoting harmonious social and cultural interactions in future long-duration spaceflight. Finally, the development of this methodology for space archaeology may also be useful for researchers considering contemporary archaeology projects in other remote locations or hostile environments such as under the deep ocean, in polar regions, in war zones, or anywhere else.

As well as providing an opportunity to study a unique culture created by the permanent occupation of a space habitat, the International Space Station Archaeological Project invites us to turn the lens back on terrestrial archaeology. To date, archaeological investigations have of necessity taken place predominantly against the background of terrestrial gravity. Because it is both ubiquitous and unavoidable in this setting, the role of gravity in shaping human bodies, material cultures, and environmental interactions has largely remained unexamined in archaeology.[11] The International Space Station is the first site of human habitation where it is possible to examine adaptations to another gravitational regime through the archaeological record.

Rather than taking the International Space Station as a special case, it may be more productive to consider it as one example of three human gravity adaptations (Earth, Earth orbit, and the Moon), at the beginning of a trajectory that will likely come to include more (for example, Mars surface, Venus high atmosphere, and the variable gravity of crewed missions in deep space). Which social and material forms persist across these different gravity regimes will surely reveal as much about the nature of human existence as any investigation of our earliest ancestors.

NOTES

1   Darrin and O'Leary 2009, 5.
2   Rathje and Murphy 1992.
3   Such as Arnold et al. 2012, Bailey et al. 2009, Buchli 1999, De León 2015, and Harrison and Breithoff 2017.
4   Meltzer 1981.
5   Barclay and Brooks 2002, 181.
6   Gorman 2016.
7   Walsh 2015.
8   In contrast, the Soviet/Russian Mir station, launched in February 1986, was occupied for almost twelve years and seven months in total, and for almost ten of those years continuously.
9   Walsh et al. 2022.
10 International Space Station Archaeological Project (January 2022), *Space archaeology (for real),* https://issarchaeology.org/2022/01/ (accessed 28 February 2022).
11 Gorman 2009c.

BIBLIOGRAPHY

Arnold, Jeane. E., Anthony P. Graesch, Enzo Ragazzini, and Elinor Ochs (2012), *Life at Home in the Twenty-First Century: 32 Families Open Their Doors,* Los Angeles (Cotsen Institute of Archaeology Press).

Bailey, Greg, Cassie Newland, Anna Nilsson, and John Schofield (2009), Transit, Transition Excavating J641 VUJ, *Cambridge Archaeological Journal* 19(1), 1–27.

Barclay, Robert and Randall Brooks (2002), In Situ Preservation of Historic Spacecraft, *Journal of the British Interplanetary Society* 55, 173–81.

Buchli, Victor (1999), *An Archaeology of Socialism,* London (Bloomsbury).

Capelotti, P.J. (2010), *The Human Archaeology of Space: Lunar, Planetary and Interstellar Relics of Exploration,* Jefferson (McFarland and Company Inc.).

Darrin, Ann Garrison and Beth Laura O'Leary (2009), "Introduction," in: Ann Darrin and Beth O'Leary, eds., *The Handbook of Space Engineering, Archaeology and Heritage,* pp. 1–15, Boca Raton (CRC Press).

De León, Jason (2015), *The Land of Open Graves: Living and Dying on the Migrant Trail,* Oakland (University of California Press).

Deetz, James (1967), *Invitation to Archaeology,* Garden City (Natural History Press).

Fewer, Greg (2002), "Towards an LSMR and MSMR (Lunar and Martian Sites and Monuments Records): Recording the Planetary Spacecraft Landing Sites as Archaeological Monuments of the Future," in: Miles Russell, ed., *Digging Holes in Popular Culture: Archaeology and Science Fiction,* pp. 112–72, Oxford (Oxbow Books).

Gorman, Alice C. (2007), La terre et l'espace: Rockets, Prisons, Protests and Heritage in Australia and French Guiana, *Archaeologies* 3(2), 153–68.

—— (2009a), "Beyond the Space Race: The Significance of Space Sites in a New Global Context," in: Angela Piccini and Cornelius Holtorf, eds., *Contemporary Archaeologies: Excavating Now,* pp. 161–80, Bern (Peter Lang).

—— (2009b), "Heritage of Earth Orbit: Orbital Debris—Its Mitigation and Cultural Heritage," in: Ann Garrison Darrin and Beth L. O'Leary, eds., *Handbook of Space Engineering, Archaeology and Heritage,* pp. 381–97, Boca Raton (CRC Press).

—— (2009c), The Gravity of Archaeology, *Archaeologies* 5(2), 344-59.

—— (2015), "Robot Avatars: The Material Culture of Human Activity in Earth Orbit," in Beth L. O'Leary and P. J. Capelotti, eds., *Archaeology and Heritage of the Human Movement into Space,* pp. 29–47, Heidelberg (Springer Verlag).

—— (2016), "Tracking Cable Ties: Contemporary Archaeology at a NASA Satellite Tracking Station," in: Ursula K. Frederick and Anne Clarke, eds., *That Was Then, This Is Now: Contemporary Archaeology and Material Cultures in Australia,* pp. 101–17, Newcastle-upon-Tyne (Cambridge Scholars Publishing).

Harrison, Rodney and Esther Breithoff (2017), Archaeologies of the Contemporary World, *Annual Review of Anthropology* 46, 203–21.

Meltzer, David J. (1981), "Ideology and Material Culture," in: Richard A. Gould and Michael B. Schiffer, eds., *Modern Material Culture: The Archeology of Us,* pp. 113–25, New York (Academic Press, Inc.).

Rathje, William L. and Cullen Murphy (1992), *Rubbish! The Archaeology of Garbage,* New York (Harper Collins).

Schiffer, Michael B. (2013), *The Archaeology of Science: Studying the Creation of Useful Knowledge,* Heidelberg (Springer Verlag).

Walsh, Justin (2012), Protection of Humanity's Cultural and Historic Heritage in Space, *Space Policy* 28(4), 234–43.

—— (2015), "Purposeful Ephemera: The Implications of Self-Destructing Space Technology for the Future Practice of Archaeology," in: Beth L. O'Leary and P.J. Capelotti, eds., *Archaeology and Heritage of the Human Movement into Space,* pp. 75–90. Heidelberg (Springer Verlag).

Walsh, Justin, Alice Gorman, and Paola Castaño (2022), Postorbital Discard and Chain of Custody: The Processing of Artifacts Returning to Earth from the International Space Station. *Acta Astronautica* 195, 513–31.

Westwood, Lisa, Beth L. O'Leary, and Milford Wayne Donaldson (2017), *The Final Mission: Preserving NASA's Apollo Sites,* Gainesville (University Press of Florida).

WAR NEAR AT HOME

AN ARCHAEOLOGY OF CONFLICT

ALFREDO GONZÁLEZ-RUIBAL

DOING CONFLICT ARCHAEOLOGY

I hate violence and aggression. I abhor conflict. Since I was a child these are things that terrify me. Perhaps this is why I am so fascinated by them, the reason I made them into the subject of my research. I cannot imagine hurting anybody, let alone killing, and therefore mass violence as experienced in war is both intriguing and disturbing for me. As an archaeologist, I am interested in how war shapes people, things, and landscapes. How it makes everyday spaces into killing fields and places of fear. How a neighborhood, a campus, or a building becomes part of a topography of terror. War scenarios are not only game boards for military action, flat and neutral spaces, like military maps lead one to think. Landscapes and things are inextricably enmeshed with conflict and shape the sensorial experiences of soldiers and civilians, contribute to trauma and horror, become allies or foes.[1] Think of the rubble of Stalingrad, or the mud of the western front, or the jungles of Vietnam. These are not the neutral backdrops where history is played out, but essential actors. The same happens with things: objects (napalm or simply bullets) provoke unimaginable damage, but they can also be soothing (a crucifix brought to the trenches, a lock of hair from the woman one loves). Artifacts and places are the material traces of the tragedy. They tell powerful stories that archaeologists can reveal.

Since 2006 I have been studying the Spanish Civil War (1936–39) from an archaeological point of view, trying to tell stories from things and revealing something about the specificity of this conflict through its material remains.[2] The conflict started as a coup d'état on 18 July 1936 staged by a group of right-wing officers against the democratic regime of the Second Spanish Republic (1931–39). The coup failed and a war ensued, which was eventually won by the rebels, known as Nationalists in the English-speaking world.[3] A dictatorship was then established that lasted until the death of Francisco Franco in 1975. Outside Spain, this conflict does not mean much to many people today, particularly younger generations. But at the time, the situation was completely different, because the Spanish Civil War was much more than an internal conflict. It was followed globally with both concern and enthusiasm from the United States to Russia. What was happening in Spain was seen as a critical struggle between dictatorship and democracy, fascism and anti-fascism. The war was not just followed by foreigners, but actually fought by foreigners as well: at least eighty thousand troops from fascist Italy, thousands of soldiers and advisors from Nazi Germany and the Soviet Union, and fifty thousand volunteers who came to fight for the Republic, many of them from the United States as part of the Lincoln Battalion.[4] The world later discovered that the Spanish conflict was the first chapter of the Second World War. It was so in many ways: it was the first industrialized war in the west where civilians were systematically targeted (around half of the 500,000 mortal victims were non-combatants); it was the first conflict in which systematic aerial bombings of civilian settlements were carried out; it was the testing ground of new weapons and tactics, including combined arms warfare, heavy bombers, and tanks.

I live in a city—Madrid—that experienced violence in all its intensity: it was part of the frontline for almost the entire duration of the conflict. It suffered bombing and mass killings of civilians in the rearguard and it saw military action unrivaled in intensity since the end of the First World War. Madrid was only occupied by the Nationalists after it surrendered on 28 March 1939. They had arrived on 7 November 1936. It was the longest modern siege until Leningrad during the Second World War. Today, few of the millions of tourists that visit the city every year are aware of its traumatic history. And not just the tourists: most Madrilenians go about their business without noticing the traces of shrapnel and bullet impacts on the façades, ignorant of the basements that were used to detain, torture, and kill people. Perhaps the same basements where their offices are located today.

The past is remote, but at the same time very present. Traces of the war are everywhere, but one has to be able to see them, interpret them. This is the task of archaeology after all: how many people drive past a prehistoric mound without knowing it? This is one of the reasons why I decided to do archaeology of the Spanish Civil War, to look for the traces of violence, excavate them (literally or metaphorically), expose them, and tell their stories. But there are more reasons: the history of the war and the postwar period, and particularly the political violence against civilians was systematically distorted by the dictatorship. There were many myths that had to be deconstructed, and archaeology, with its potential to produce tangible, often incontrovertible, evidence, looked like an ideal discipline to do it. There are more personal reasons, as well. Unlike most archaeologists working on the topic in Spain, I did not decide to excavate the war because my grandparents had been murdered by the Nationalists and buried in an unmarked grave.[5] My relatives sided with the victors and fared well after the war. My grandfather, in particular, made a fortune as a building contractor during the postwar years. Yet this does not mean that my relatives did not suffer during the conflict. Far from it. Two of my grandfather's brothers, who were living in Madrid in July 1936, were murdered by revolutionaries in the outskirts of the city and my grandfather himself only survived because he had to leave Madrid shortly before the coup.

The area where I conducted archaeological research in Madrid between 2016 and 2018, University City, is located midway between the former home of my granduncles and the place where they were shot. They were kidnapped in front of their wives and children, taken by truck to one of the many improvised centers of detention and from there to an execution place, probably following the road leaving Madrid through University City. The same road that I used to go to college for several years. The banal scenario of my everyday life was marked by a violence that was at the same time brutal and intimate. Yet I only realized this much later. In our excavations in Madrid, my team and I discovered a forgotten landscape shaped by war in many ways, not all of them evident. And also the fragments of the war itself and the world that it destroyed.

LANDSCAPE

One of the places that we studied on the university campus and the one that yielded the more interesting results was the subsector of the university hospital, which incorporated a large hospice inaugurated in 1896. Known as the Asylum of Santa Cristina, it was endowed by wealthy families and served the poor, abandoned women, orphans, and the elderly. Ironically, a space that had been used for looking after people ended up becoming a killing field. The premises (mostly large rectangular pavilions with dormitories and refectories) were occupied by the Nationalists during the Battle of Madrid (7–23 November 1936) and remained in their hands until the end of the war. By then, the entire place looked more like a lunar landscape than anything else. Virtually all buildings had been razed to the ground and the surface was pockmarked with thousands of artillery and mine craters and crisscrossed by trenches. I said virtually all buildings, because one at least remained reasonably untouched. Thanks to its location away from enemy enfilades, the structure was spared the worst of the devastating effects of mortars, cannons, and machine guns. Photographs of the period show the brick pavilion, built in the 1910s, with some damage from mortar and bullet fire but otherwise in a usable condition: even the roof did not collapse.

Today, however, there are no traces of it or of any other building of the hospice. Only the university hospital survives, thoroughly reconstructed after the conflict, on the nearby hilltop. The only pavilion still standing was demolished, its building materials reused in the reconstruction of the hospital, and the battlefield covered under tons of rubble and dirt, landscaped and transformed into a garden. There is nothing that remembers the war today: neither ruins nor memorials. It would be impossible to tell that this was a battlefield eighty years ago, indeed one of the most iconic of the Spanish Civil War. This is particularly striking, considering that the Republicans surrendered in this exact spot to the Nationalists, and that the war ended, to all effects, in the very same place where we conducted our excavations.

We decided to find whatever could remain of the pavilion that survived the war. It was used as a base by the Nationalists and we thought that it could yield some relevant materials. What we found greatly surpassed our expectations. Although the building had been razed down to its foundations, these still existed and were well preserved. As it turned out, it was the foundations that were the most interesting, not the superstructure. This makes sense: in a very exposed position such as this, regularly under mortar and sniper fire, the above ground was extremely dangerous. Soldiers spent most of their time in underground shelters. But where were these? In the war-time photographs of the area they are nowhere to be seen. The best photograph of the pavilion, however, shows a tunnel entering the foundations of the building. Yet based on textual and visual evidence from the period alone, it is impossible to know what was going on underground. We found out.

Our excavations exposed a large part of the pavilion and a laundry room nearby. Both had been largely modified during the conflict. The war-time photograph of the main building turned out to be misleading. The apparently untouched space had actually been transformed into something else: a real war machine. Three bomb shelters were hewn into the foundations, two in the pavilion and one in the laundry room, to provide protection for the soldiers stationed in the subsector; a communication trench was dug that gave access to the rearguard; the drainage system had been used to dispose of the garbage and the materials that we found inside, including many nails from the beams and furniture of the asylum that had been burned as fuel. We also found two accesses to mining tunnels (Figure 12.1).

This subsector of the frontline was characterized by mine warfare, a modality of combat that had developed during the First World War and that consisted in setting up loads of explosives underneath the enemy lines. A single explosion could kill or bury alive up to seventy soldiers and the mine threat spread an atmosphere of psychosis. The Republicans had the upper hand in this kind of warfare, whereas the Nationalists mostly limited themselves to setting up countermines and destroying the mining tunnels of their enemies. The transformation of the hospice into a battlefield had at the same time an architectural

Figure 12.1. Excavation in 2018 of the shaft giving access to a Nationalist mining tunnel under one of the buildings of the Asylum of Santa Cristina, Madrid, Spain. *Photograph by Álvaro Minguito.*

Figure 12.2. Crater left by a mine set up during the last months of the war on the university campus frontline in Madrid. *Photograph by Álvaro Minguito.*

and a geological dimension, as the subsurface was deeply changed by trenches, mines, mining tunnels, shelters, dugouts, and craters. A huge volume of soil was displaced during and after the war, and the entire stratigraphy of the site, to a depth of four or five meters in places, was thoroughly disturbed. This is most obvious in a huge crater left by a mine that can still be seen (Figure 12.2). Yet the transformation was not only architectural and geological. It was also biological. Photographs from the beginning and the end of the war show the total disappearance of the organic topsoil and the vegetation, whereas archaeology reveals the proliferation of rats and mice in this very favorable new ecosystem.

THINGS

If the structures are eloquent, the objects that we found were not less so. I would like to introduce a few that have particularly powerful stories to tell.

A CHAMBER POT

A chamber pot is not the first thing one associates with modern war. Yet relieving oneself is of great concern in the frontline. The context in which the chamber pot appeared speaks eloquently about the nature of the violence in this battlefield. It appeared in an underground shelter, next to an entrance to one of the mining tunnels mentioned above (Figure 12.1). It is not difficult to imagine the enormous tension experienced by soldiers having to go underground, to fight the enemy in the worst possible scenario, with machetes and pistols, in the dark, under the threat of being buried alive or poisoned by toxic gases. It is not difficult to imagine, either, how relieved they were when they returned to the surface. In both cases, a chamber pot was essential. And it informs us about the sensorial experience of mining warfare: the stale air, the darkness and dampness, the gritty texture of the tunnel and the acrid smells: trinitrotoluene, gunpowder, sweat, urine, and alcohol.

A BRACELET

As said at the beginning, battles do not develop in empty space. This is true even for the Sahara and the Arctic, but it is more so in the middle of a city of a million people. Thus, in our work we found not just the remnants of war, but also of civilian life shattered by war. In the case of Spain, the fragments of antebellum life are particularly poignant, because what came after the conflict was a darker, more oppressive world; a world in which universal suffrage as had existed only a few years before, or women's rights, or religious freedom looked like an impossible dream. During the survey of the campus we found a bracelet, an elegant art deco jewel of copper alloy with a green glass cabochon (Figure 12.3). The University of Madrid opened its new campus during the Republican period. Its modernist design was in tune with the aspirations of a modern society that were essential to the Republican program. Part of this modernization was the enrolment of women in higher education. Whereas in 1910 there were only thirty-three female university students, in 1936, the number had risen to 2,588.[6] Did the bracelet belong to a student? It is likely. Perhaps one studying pharmacology: the college was nearby and many women were enrolled there at the time. The jewel itself, with its modern design, is a metaphor of the universe of possibilities that was opening to many women. With the dictatorship, the dreams of emancipation were shattered, and the patriarchal order was reinstated with a vengeance. The leader of the female section of the Spanish Fascist Party, Pilar Primo de Rivera, recommended women: "You must not to become a girl congested by books, a girl who cannot speak about anything else . . . . you must not be an intellectual." The lost bracelet attests to a broken dream of equality and social justice.

TWO WEDDING RINGS

The excavation of the laundry room yielded many notable finds, including several elements of dress and insignia, which were perhaps lost by soldiers who used the laundry room as a washing area (the concrete basins were still there). Among

Figure 12.3. An art deco bracelet, perhaps lost by a student of the University of Madrid before the war. *Photograph by the author.*

the lost items were two wedding rings. One was made of gold, the other of silver. Silver rings were typical of the lower classes, who could not afford the more expensive gold rings. The gold ring had a date inscribed into it: 1926. Considering that the mean marriage age for males in Spain in the 1920s was 28, the owner of the ring was probably in his late thirties or early forties. Maybe it belonged to an officer, as middle-aged privates were uncommon on the Nationalist side. This would be consistent also with the expensive material, as officers came from middle-class families. The rings indirectly tell us about a group of invisible actors in the war: the women waiting for their husbands in the rearguard, always under the fear of losing them with all the terrible implications that being a widow in Spain in the 1930s implied, as they depended on their husbands economically. Were the owners of the rings killed in this extremely dangerous frontline? Or did they manage to return safely? In which circumstances did they lose the rings? Did they make widows themselves?

A SWASTIKA

The soldiers who defended the subsector of the hospice belonged to the Nationalist side, whose ideology was aligned with that of the fascist powers. The Nationalists believed in a strong leadership (a *caudillo*, similar to the Italian *duce* and the German *Führer*), decried democracy, and supported ultra-nationalist and conservative ideas. Not surprisingly, both Axis powers provided wide support to the rebels, including weapons and munition that turn up regularly in former battlefields. In our excavations at University City we found something else related to the Nazis: a swastika. It was not a proper insignia or an official item. The tiny cross was made by cutting a piece of tin sheet and can therefore be considered a form of trench art.[7] There was some debate as to who was responsible for its making. Some argued that it could have been worn by a Basque soldier. The Basques, fighting for the Republican Army, stormed this position in 1937. They wore swastikas (called *laburu*, a traditional symbol in Basque with no relation to fascism) in their berets. Yet the insignia was very different from those in use among Republicans, and it appeared well inside the Nationalist position, which the Basques never reached. The makeshift symbol was doubtless made by one of the soldiers stationed at the hospice. There is nothing extraordinary about it. The Nazis, after all, were their allies, swastikas appeared in some of their equipment, and Nazi flags were a common sight in the news. The insignia is a powerful reminder of who was backing the rebellion against the Republic. The context of discovery is also interesting. It appeared in a shaft of the drainage system, amid a heap of rat bones. Sometimes the archaeological record is a form of poetic justice.

TWO PORCELAIN CUPS

Much of the material remains that we found during our excavations at the campus belonged to the hospice. This does not mean that the artifacts had no relation to the war. Many of the abandoned objects were reused, mostly crockery. It seems that the pavilion that we excavated was a refectory before the war. This would explain the large amount of different

Figure 12.4. Fragment of a porcelain tea cup decorated with scenes of playing children, found amid war debris at the Asylum of Santa Cristina, Madrid, Spain. *Photograph by the author.*

dishes and glassware that we found during the excavation. Two objects stand out: fragments of two delicate tea cups in porcelain. There is no doubt that they predate the war. One is as thin as paper and has a beautiful representation of three ladies in classical costume. It might be a representation of the judgment of Paris, when he was asked to decide which of the three goddesses—Aphrodite, Athena, and Hera—was the most handsome. The other piece is very different: the decoration shows children playing games, painted in a cartoonish way and dressed in the typical attire of bourgeois children (Figure 12.4). The porcelain cups were almost certainly gifts of rich Madrilenian families to the asylum. Both items speak volumes of high-class values and worldviews in early twentieth-century Spain. They speak at the same time of huge social inequalities (illiterate, half-starving orphans living only a few blocks away from extremely wealthy families) and of a high bourgeoisie that was dramatically detached from the real social conditions of the country. Both phenomena had much to do with the three decades of social unrest that preceded the Civil War. The porcelain tea cups surely impressed the inmates, who could hardly imagine the existence of such refinement. What did they make of such gifts? How did these shape their political imagination? One of the most vicious killers of the Spanish Civil War, Felipe Sandoval, was an orphan who spent part of his childhood in a hospice in Madrid and then worked as a young man for a wealthy family. The hardness of the orphanage and its contrast with the life of the high bourgeoisie were crucial in his becoming an anarchist leader and a mass murderer. The porcelain cups of the asylum were likely reused by the rugged Nationalist legionnaires who occupied the position. For many, the cups and dishes were also their first contact with bourgeois material life and probably also the last time in their life that they experienced this.

A CALTROP

The Spanish Civil War, as pointed out at the beginning, is widely known among historians for the technological innovations that were first tested there, from blood transfusions to dive bombers. Archaeological remains tell another story: a story of very old technologies mobilized for the war effort, including Iron Age hillforts reused as military positions, mid-nineteenth-century cannons taken from museums and pressed back into service, and weapons that were millennia old. Among the latter was the caltrop. This is a simple and very ancient military technology: a piece of iron with four sharp points that always has one of them pointing upwards. They were used from Roman times onward to hamper the advance of horses or infantry. The nail could damage the hoof of a horse and perforate the foot of a soldier. During our survey of the campus we found one of these caltrops, called *abrojo* (thistle) in Spanish. Only

the iron ball survived: the nails had disappeared, but their location in the piece can easily be discerned. The caltrop appeared in the short strip of no-man's land that separated the Republicans from the Nationalists in this part of the campus. The Republicans occupied the School of Medicine, the Nationalists the hospital and hospice. Again, institutions of life and care mobilized for the purpose of killing and destruction. We know that many assaults were launched from one side or the other during the war. Combat was a close-quarters affair and horrifying: soldiers employed grenades, bayonets, knives, shovels, and rifle butts to maim, crush bones, and break open skulls. A savage war, a return to the brutal and straightforward fighting methods of the Middle Ages, of which the caltrops were but another expression.

A BOTTLE OF CIDER AND A MORTAR GRENADE

Modern war brings together disparate objects. This is what art critics call 'parataxis,' the juxtaposition of things that have little or nothing in common but whose friction produces something new, often disturbingly so. Parataxis has been a typical resource of contemporary art since the 1910s. In contemporary archaeology, and particularly the archaeology of modern conflict, we find such parataxes all the time, whether we look for them or not. It is in the nature of the contemporary era and its conflicts. A parataxis is what we discovered in one of the bomb shelters that we dug at the Asylum of Santa Cristina. Lying on the occupation floor we found several complete bottles of cider, lamb bones, and many unused cartridges, shell casings, and two unexploded grenades belonging to an 81-mm Stokes-Brandt mortar (Figure 12.5). It is a strange combination that tells something about the Spanish Civil War and, more specifically, about its end.

The stratigraphic unit was formed during the last days of the conflict. We know this because it is a level of abandonment that was immediately sealed with tons of rubble and war debris. We also know it because the layer was covered by a very thin layer of silt of the kind that is typically deposited by rain, and we know that for three days after the surrender

Figure 12.5. The end of the Spanish Civil War in one stratigraphic unit: abandoned mortar grenades, ammunition, and bottles of cider. *Photograph by Álvaro Minguito.*

of Madrid on 28 March 1939 there was rain, following a long drought. One of the bottles was still filled with rain water. But why bottles of cider and mortar grenades? What we see is the materialization of the end of the war. It is victory for the defenders of the Asylum, who suffered enormously. It is celebration. Soldiers are given bottles of cider (a surrogate for champagne) and a lamb stew. They drink, eat, laugh, and sing and then throw everything into the bomb shelter, which they will never have to use again. In a burst of enthusiasm, they also throw grenades and ammunition into the structure, which they are ordered to seal immediately thereafter. No more violence, no more killing. Not at least, in the battlefield. Not at least of Nationalists. Among the vanquished Republicans, there is little reason for joy. In Madrid alone, almost four thousand people would be executed by the new regime in the postwar period.

CONCLUSIONS

Modern conflict changes landscapes and objects deeply and therefore shapes the experience of violence of both civilians and soldiers. Archaeology, with its focus on the materiality of the past, is an ideal discipline to explore this transformation, which is at the same time physical, sensorial, and psychological. In this chapter I have explored a battlefield of the Spanish Civil War in Madrid from an archaeological perspective. I have shown how the war, between 1936 and 1939, radically altered the landscape, transforming a space of care and education into a killing field, but also a machine for killing. This modification of the landscape had geological and biological dimensions of lasting consequences: today, the hill where we conducted our surveys and excavations is almost in its entirety an artificial structure, the result of war and postwar activities. The experience of war is shaped by architecture, topography, and geology and the manifold ways in which they are destroyed or rearranged. But it is also determined by the artifacts that people use. Many of the objects to which I have resorted to illustrate the conflict are not directly related to violence or the military: a chamber pot, a wedding ring, or a bottle of cider. My intention has been to demonstrate two things: on the one hand, that in a war every artifact is touched deeply by violence, even if violence does not alter its materiality: ordinary objects, such as a chamber pot, take a tragic meaning in the context of a war. This is also true of prewar artifacts that appear in the battlefield: it is impossible to look at such innocent objects such as a tea cup or an art deco bracelet without knowing what happened afterwards. On the other hand, I have tried to emphasize the poetry of things. Sometimes a simple object can reveal something true and profound about a historic situation. And it is my argument that this revelation is, perhaps, the main task of the archaeologist.

NOTES

1   Saunders and Cornish 2017.
2   González-Ruibal 2020.
3   Thomas 2001.
4   Hochschild 2016.
5   Ferrándiz 2013.
6   Guil Bozal and Flecha García 2015, 132.
7   Saunders 2003.

BIBLIOGRAPHY

Ferrándiz, Francisco (2013), Exhuming the Defeated: Civil War Mass Graves in 21st Century Spain. *American Ethnologist* 40(1), 38–54.

González-Ruibal, Alfredo (2020), *The Archaeology of the Spanish Civil War,* Abingdon (Routledge).

Guil Bozal, Ana and Consuelo Flecha García (2015), Universitarias en España: De los inicios a la actualidad, *Revista Historia de la Educación Latinoamericana* 17(24), 125–48.

Hochschild, Adam (2016), *Spain in Our Hearts: Americans in the Spanish Civil War, 1936–39,* Boston (Houghton Mifflin Harcourt).

Saunders, Nicholas J. (2003), *Trench Art: Materialities and Memories of War,* Oxford (Berg).

Saunders, Nicholas J. and Paul Cornish, eds. (2017), *Modern Conflict and the Senses,* Abingdon (Routledge).

Thomas, Hugh (2001), *The Spanish Civil War,* New York (Random House, third, revised and enlarged edition of the 1965 original).

STORIES THAT CHANGE THINGS

REFLECTIONS ON THE MATERIALITY OF LIVING MEMORY

BONNIE J. CLARK AND IAN KUIJT

As archaeologists who study the recent past, we have recognized similar challenges and striking commonalities while working with very different human communities, in very different social and geographical settings. A primary one is how to use material objects and oral histories in ways that incorporate the voice of living communities. One strategy we both employ in speaking about our work (whether as friends or as colleagues) is to frame the past and present through stories, both of the people we talk to and of the objects that exemplify these stories.

We speak from a thin temporality: both of us work on sites abandoned between fifty and seventy-five years ago. On some level enough time has passed that these sites can be viewed from a traditionally archaeological standpoint; the material remains on the ground are subjected to the suite of site-formation processes taught in every introductory archaeology class: decay, collapse, and deposition. And yet on other levels some of our

work deals with living human communities who inhabited these spaces, participated in daily life, and created memories of the past. Some of these memories have been repeated, retold, and perhaps in some cases, sharpened in the retelling. Others have been quiet, or even repressed, but slumbering. In our efforts to understand these places, we each work with people who now live in new locations but who remember their time living at these sites, and on some level both idealize and are nostalgic about the worlds they left behind, while at the same time recognizing the hardships they experienced when living there. We have both been deeply focused on understanding human communities through oral history, archaeology, historical research, and above all else first-person narratives of the past. As storytellers embedded in living communities, privileged by being able to help record and narrate the past, to an extent we have been entrusted as temporary custodians of local knowledge. It is that local knowledge we share with our readers.

Figure 11.1. The mantlepiece with objects in the main room of the McHale house, 2015. Inishbofin, County Galway, Ireland. *Photograph by Ian Kuijt.*

OBJECTS IN PLACE: WHEN THE LIGHTS WERE TURNED UP, IRELAND 1950S

"When we got the reflector, it was like we went from a 50 to a 100 watt light bulb."
(Noel Gavin, 2010 interview, speaking about his family purchasing a reflector for a kerosene lamp in the 1950s)

Ian's story begins with this simple statement that Noel Gavin made to him years ago. In the 1940s and 1950s around thirty people lived on the remote island of Inishark, some eleven kilometers (seven miles) off the western coast of Ireland. When the island was evacuated on 20 October 1960 only twenty-five people still lived in the two- or three-room stone houses there. While Noel Gavin was growing up on Inishark, daily life for islanders was shaped by the sun and the weather. Bounded in space, living on an island, fishing, farming, and daily tasks were shaped by location and setting. With no electricity, gas, or telephones, light inside the houses was provided by the dim light of peat fires in hearths and the soft glow of kerosene lamps on the mantlepieces (Figure 11.1). With no more than one or two small windows, the spaces inside of these buildings are typically poorly lit. Kerosene lamps function with the burning of a cotton wick surrounded by a glass globe to protect people and other objects, so that the lamp could be set on a table or mantelpiece, or hung on a wall. The wick absorbs the kerosene and as the oil burns off light is produced, often with a low crackling and the production of soot. When set correctly the kerosene produces a clear, dull yellow flame. During the winter, with less than eight hours of sunlight, often with grey clouds, flat-wick kerosene lamps provided the only illumination for people working and living in their houses. At least one kerosene lamp was normally kept on the mantlepiece with a collection of functional objects such as matches, a clock, items for cooking, and family items such as family photographs and letters.

It was into this historical and emotional context that in 2011 Noel Gavin returned to Inishark for the first time in more than fifty years. Born in 1942, Noel Gavin left Inishark when he was eighteen years old, moving to the mainland and then to

When we ask people about their past, to consider the world they lived in and the things they used, we are repeatedly startled and surprised by their answers. The foundation of all oral history is, of course, conversation between people interested in other worlds and people: to reveal and collect stories of a world gone by and on the edge of being forgotten. Our work requires us to consider how objects exist in space and place. Given voice by survivors, simple and mundane objects reveal aspects often overlooked by researchers. These narratives unravel the meaning of objects to the people who used and displayed them. They also provide insight to researchers into personal history and heritage that are hidden. In this spirit we present human stories entwined with two humble, mundane objects that are now provided sound and context through the words of the living about their past.

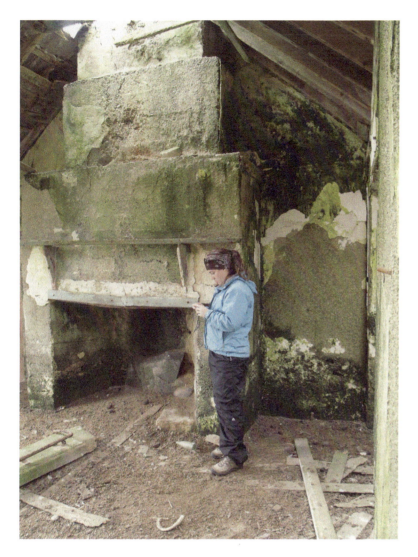

Figure 11.2. Main room fireplace with mantelpiece, Gavin-Lacey house, 2010, Inishark, County Galway, Ireland. *Photograph by Ian Kuijt.*

Figure 11.3. Kerosene lamp, with its glass chimney removed to show the home-made reflector that would have reflected light, 2014. Inishbofin, County Galway, Ireland. *Photograph by Ian Kuijt.*

England where he soon lived in a world of plumbing, running water, and above all else, electricity. On a fine summer day in 2011, Ian brought Noel back to the house that he had lived in a long time ago to talk about life on a remote island before the 1960s. This visit was organized with Kieran Concannon, an Irish filmmaker, with the aim of recording some of the stories and memories some of these people had before they pass on (Figure 11.2). As with each of the islanders brought back to Inishark, Noel wanted to go home, to go to the house that he grew up in, and that he left forty-eight years previously. So Ian walked with Noel from the broken pier up along the pathways between empty stone houses, and to the Gavin-Lacey house.

Walking into his old home, now empty of furniture, with no windows or doors, but still roofed, Noel was flooded with memories and recollections, many of which were painful. While now inside a stone shell, he remembered where family members slept, where items of furniture were placed, and the smell of his mother's bread. A few of these memories brought forth a smile, a perspective on the past, and a slight grin. One of these was when he walked over to the mantelpiece, a simple light-blue plank of wood above the fire place, held in place by two wooden braces. While lighting up a cigarette, he talked about the objects they used to keep on the mantelpiece above the fire. These included a range of functional objects, such as matches and tools, as well as religious icons and pictures. He also said that this was where they kept a kerosene lamp, and asked us if we knew what this was.

He started telling us how important kerosene lamps were, as they were the only source of light in the house, often running in the winter for hours at a time. Pointing to the mantelpiece in the empty room he gestured to where the lamp used to be positioned. Then, as an afterthought, he recalled the time when his mother acquired a simple reflector for the kerosene lamp. This simple piece of folded shiny metal, now commonly available, was designed to be placed behind the lamp so that it reflected light in a specific direction (Figure 11.3). As a child he and his siblings marveled at the new technology and how it changed their world. Searching for a way to explain the impact of this new reflector to us he drew upon a now familiar commodity and stated that "when we got the reflectors it was like we went from a 50- to a 100-watt light bulb." He appeared surprised at his own statement, chuckling at the effectiveness of the phrase, and with a smile he shook his head in wonder. To Noel this small piece of shiny metal, something most anthropological archaeologists would easily overlook, was an object that lit up his past and cast light on a time and place that is now disappearing into the shadows.

PEOPLE OUT OF PLACE: BATTLING THE MESS HALL FLIES, AMACHE, COLORADO 1940S

"This is exactly where I want to take a picture."
(Masako Hashioka Kanazawa, pointing to a map of Amache.)

Bonnie's story happened the day she met Masako Kanazawa at Amache, Colorado, in 2012. Amache was an involuntary community of more than seven thousand people, living within guarded barbed wire fences during the Second World War. The center was built on the plan of military forts, and the families were forced to live in flimsy structures in an institutional setting. Today the frame buildings are gone, but most of the foundations on which they sat, some of the landscaping created beside them, and many objects lost or dumped out of buildings remain. Like many who travel back to the place where they were incarcerated with their families during the Second World War, Masako came with a clue: a photograph saved for nearly seventy years (Figure 11.4). In the black-and-white snapshot, she stands between her mother and father in front of the mess hall in their block. It was to this locale that she requested the archaeology crews guide her to have her picture taken.

Mess halls were part of the institutional regime at Amache, the daily grind that made this place feel a lot less like home. Among former incarcerees of the camp, memories about the food in the camps are lively, filled with recollections of items unfamiliar to pre-war palates, like cottage cheese or beef tongue. Queuing up for meals with two hundred other people was another annoyance. The waiting was made only a little bit more pleasant by mess hall gardens crafted by residents not just in mess hall 9E, where the Hashioka family lived, but in most of the blocks at Amache (Figure 11.5).

Despite their institutional flavor, mess halls were a critical node in the social life of the camp. They provided face-to-face contact for people who often hailed from the same towns or neighborhoods.[1] Images of mess halls during holidays show how they were lovingly decorated. Like their counterparts

Figure 11.4. Historic photograph of Genichi, Masako, and Nobu Hashioka (left to right) in front of the mess hall 9E at Amache, Colorado, taken between 1942 and 1945. *Photograph courtesy of Masako Hashioka Kanazawa.*

outside of the barbed wire, the Japanese American kids of Amache were obsessed with the swing bands of the day. As reflected in saved invitations and dance cards (Figure 11.6), those dances were often held in a mess hall, temporarily transformed by music and crepe paper into a venue for the latest swing tunes.

Figure 11.5. Amache residents begin to line up for a meal along the garden of trees and stone gracing an unidentified mess hall. This still was captured from a 16 mm movie made at Amache. *Photograph courtesy of the Amache Preservation Society, Tsukuda Collection, Granada, Colorado.*

The foundations of the mess halls are the largest in each block, so they are pretty easy to spot. As we walked up to the location of mess hall 9E that day, both Masako and I were delighted to see that the limestone garden wall evident in her photograph was still visible, decaying certainly, but obviously present. That made it easy for Masako to pose in exactly the right spot for her desired picture. While there, she pointed out the one-room quarters of the family in barrack 9E-12F, which stood adjacent to the mess hall, where her father worked.

On the day she shared this photograph and in a later conversation, Masako talked about the work of her father as the chief cook for the mess hall in their block. Looking at the photograph one will notice the hat and the apron he was wearing. Like the majority of the men who lived in his block, Genichi Hashioka had primarily been a farmer before camp. But he had also worked as a cook for a time and he took his role as chief cook for his block very seriously. Along with overseeing a group of female cooks, he was responsible for the even distribution of food, something difficult in a time of rationing and food shortage. He was committed to food safety and as Masako recalled, mess hall 9E was immaculate.

Figure 11.6. Invitation to a mess hall dance from an Amache scrapbook. *Image courtesy of the Amache Preservation Society, Akaki Collection.*

After Masako's visit, Bonnie noticed something in Genichi's right hand in the photograph: a flyswatter. She flashed back to an until-then unidentifiable piece of bent wire her crews had documented during an intensive pedestrian survey that summer. Of course, that is what they had found, the wire handle to a decaying flyswatter. How much more quotidian an artifact can you ask for? It might seem inconsequential, but for Genichi Hashioka, a flyswatter was a tool wielded in his long days managing a mess hall. And because of a story shared with archaeologists, a flyswatter becomes a sign of care for a community confined.

DISCUSSION AND REFLECTION

If wisdom sits in places, as argued by Keith Basso (1996), then we can equally argue that memory and objects are deeply interconnected, existing within a web of human history, of stories and memories that are changing and situational, and often unrecognized by archaeologists trained in, and focused on, the description and quantification of the past. The two stories we present, while focused on very different geographical locations and historical moments, exemplify light shed on the often overlooked ways in which personal history is linked to the material world. This is something that the philosophers of New Materialism would lead us to expect, and yet, as pointed out by Bjørnar Olsen (2010), as a discipline we have not yet really grappled with the linkages between personal history and objects. Things matter in part because they have matter. Their physicality pushes the past into the present as materials for archaeologists to find.[2] We have been trained to draw, quantify and describe the objects and places that we encounter. We photograph them, develop catalogs and charts, and think in terms of where they were produced and what they tell us about the economics of the past.

Yet when archaeology is embedded in communities connected to place, these same materials matter in a different way. They can spur the memory of those who left the objects behind or heard stories of those places.[3] In some cases, what is spurred are the kind of memories that often are not spoken aloud, because they live primarily in the body.[4] Features like mantelpieces and stone walls once existed in a living world of people, objects, and ongoing experience. The physicality of objects affected lives in the past and, through engaged archaeology today, continues to live on. As archaeologists of the living past, we are increasingly drawn to the personal narratives of the people we work with, and not just as a means of understanding disappearing worlds, for stories and memories of place and objects create a rich tapestry of a more humane history.

Our intention with this chapter is not to create a cautionary tale for those archaeologists who do not have access to the stories of things. Rather it is to challenge all of us to imagine the importance and value of the mundane, the simple and often overlooked. To envision how people, places, and things interacted in the material and immaterial worlds of the past we encounter. The past and stories may seem to be gone, but of course they are not, for their matter continues and continues to matter.

ACKNOWLEDGMENTS

We are deeply thankful for the opportunity to tell two of the stories shared with us by members of the communities that we work with. Bonnie would like to thank Mrs. Kanazawa for her forthrightness about what was not right with the first two versions of her story. As always, the result is far better for the conversation, which involved not just the two of them, but other Amacheans who confirmed or challenged Masako's memories. Bonnie is indebted to every community member who has contributed to understanding this tragic American story better. Ian would like to thank the many people who have shared their stories and history related to island life on Inishbofin, Inishturk, and Inishark. Noel Gavin had an extraordinary ability to capture the poetics of place and time, speaking of personal history and at the same time a collective experience. The richness of islander stories, and the willingness to share these stories, provides a glimpse into a rich and disappearing past.

NOTES

1   Kamp-Whittaker and Clark 2019.
2   Olsen 2010.
3   Clark 2017.
4   Bergson 1998.

BIBLIOGRAPHY

Basso, Keith (1996), *Wisdom Sits in Places: Landscape and Language among the Western Apache,* Albuquerque (University of New Mexico Press).

Bergson, Henri (1998), *Creative Evolution,* Mineola (Dover, translation by Arthur Mitchell of the 1907 French original).

Clark, Bonnie J. (2017), "Cultivating Community: The Archaeology of Japanese American Confinement at Amache," in: Fernando Armstrong-Fumero and Julio Hoil Gutierrez, eds., *Legacies of Space and Intangible Heritage: Archaeology, Ethnohistory, and the Politics of Cultural Continuity in the Americas,* pp. 79–96, Boulder (University Press of Colorado).

Kamp-Whittaker, April and Bonnie J. Clark (2019), "Social Networks and the Development of Neighborhood Identities in Amache, a WWII Japanese American Internment Camp," in: David Pacifico and Lisa Truex, eds., *Excavating Neighborhoods: A Cross-Cultural Exploration,* Archeological Papers of the American Anthropological Association 30, pp. 148–58, Arlington (Archaeology Division of the American Anthropological Association).

Olsen, Bjørnar (2010), *In Defense of Things: Archaeology and the Ontology of Objects,* Lanham (Altamira Press).

THE BAKKEN HUNDREDS

WILLIAM CARAHER AND BRET WEBER

The Bakken Hundreds describe seven seasons of archaeological fieldwork (2012–18) in the Bakken oil patch of North Dakota.[1] The North Dakota Man Camp Project focused on workforce housing through archaeological documentation and authorized interviews. Here, the co-authors alternate 100-word statements from project notebooks, interviews, and publications, loosely following Lauren Berlant and Kathleen Stewart's (2019) composition style in *The Hundreds*. Our assemblage reveals the material and social conditions of the Bakken by emphasizing the frenetic, dreamlike precarity of boom times. For entries with specific dates, we included the West Texas Intermediate Crude oil price per barrel as a rough indicator of Bakken prosperity.

PUBLICATION

Bret Weber, Julia Geigle, and Carenlee Barkdull (2014), Rural North Dakota's Oil Boom and Its Impact on Social Services, *Social Work* 59(1), p. 62.

Over the last five years, North Dakota has experienced an oil boom based on high oil prices and hydraulic fracturing technologies. This has brought economic expansion and population growth to rural communities that had previously experienced decades of depopulation and economic struggle. Although the state has enjoyed many benefits—especially in juxtaposition to a sluggish national economy—the boom has also meant . . . dramatic impacts on largely rural social service systems. In the midst of a rapidly changing situation, available information tends to swing between euphoria over economic success and hysteria about rising crime and shifting cultures.

INTERVIEW

Camp 65: Riker Brown, camp owner, 21 August 2013 ($106.42).

RB: Right. So we went with the RVs and actually, this is like a family park. We have kids on bikes and dogs. We promote families, dogs, kids. So it's temporary housing but some of these people bring their families for the summer and they'll go back for the winter, but they'll stay here.

Bret Weber (BW): Mom and the kids are here when school's out?

RB: Right.

NOTEBOOK WILLIAM CARAHER

Camp 40: camp manager, 31 July 2015 ($47.12).

The owner was interested in transitioning the RV park to a more permanent mobile home park. This involved fixing significant code violations—especially the water and sewage pipes being in the same trench—and installing a $500,000 septic system. Camp makes no money. Despite the optimism, the camp appears rather rough with abandoned RVs, lots of abandoned equipment, and a run-down playground. Some trash. Owner noted the difficulties in keeping the camp clean. Thinking of installing wind breaks, trees, and snow fences.

INTERVIEW

Camp 75: Diane Skillman, camp resident, 4 October 2014 ($89.74).

DS: Well, I think everybody keeps a bit of water running just to keep it from freezing. Although, they did freeze up there at the other end.

BW: Is that the water tank over there?

DS: No, that's the poop tank [laughs].

BW: Oh, so where do you get your water from then . . . it's ground water?

DS: Yeah, he has a well and everybody is pumped into that, and then he's got, well last year that froze.

PUBLICATION

William Caraher and Bret Weber (2017), *The Bakken: An Archaeology of an Industrial Landscape,* Fargo, ND (North Dakota State University Press), p. 41.

To enter Stanley proper, turn left from old US 2 onto Main Street. About a half mile south, Main Street passes beneath the Highline, which is carried on a deck-girder concrete bridge dating to the 1930s. It is listed on the National Register of Historic Places, reflecting the importance of rail to this part of the state. Today, Amtrak's Empire Builder continues to serve Stanley from a small, modern railway station on the east side of Main Street. Farther south on Main Street is the Two Way Inn and Bar, which offers a delicious patty melt in authentic surroundings for the oil patch.

INTERVIEW

Camp 14: William Nelson, camp resident and 'fisherman,' 11 August 2012 ($85.38).

WN: I'm a consultant and my specialty is fishing. When they lose things in holes, I fish it out. It's not everybody's favorite but . . . people on rigs don't want to see me coming but when they need me, then there it is.

INTERVIEW

Camp 14: Don Ashton, owner of the land under the camp, 28 October 2016 ($48.70).

DA: Well, I bought the land in '85. I've been living here since '81. All the investors come out of South Dakota, Rapid City, to see if I wanted to do kind of trailers . . . they said they were gonna put in water and sewer for 'em, and that never happened . . . . They had big dreams and everything. I gave them a longer term lease, cause they said, oh they wanted long, you know, maybe do it a motel or a hotel, so they figured maybe ten acres or so . . . . Then I found out they were trying to sell this ten acres out from underneath me and I got pissed off and took them to court.

INTERVIEW

Camp 77: Juan Gonzales, camp resident, 2 May 2015 ($59.15).

JG: It's not easy, you know, living out here, but, I mean it is a good way—me, for example, I'm young, I started out at a young year, it's a good way so I can get a good start at life and then, invest in a home where I'm going to be able to live and move on later as soon as everything calms down here. I think a lot of people are taking advantage of it and making the best of all this stuff and they're gonna—whoever's taking good advantage of it is gonna be making—is gonna have a good future.

NOTEBOOK WILLIAM CARAHER

Camp 29: Indoor RV Park, 10 August 2014 ($97.65).

The indoor RV park seems filled with a large number of RVs not in the garages or bays, but ringing the outside of the garages forming a camp around the electrical masts. Unlike our last visit in the winter, there is some evidence for cooking and even socializing outside of the garages with tables, lawn chairs, and coolers set around the garage doors. More distinctly, there are propane tanks and gas canisters, which are not permitted in the bays, set outside around the garages with chains securing them. It is clear that the spaces inside of the

bays are also used as living areas as well with pallets and chairs set up inside.

PHOTOGRAPH

Camp 77: Abandoned mudroom, William Caraher, 6 March 2015 ($49.61).

INTERVIEW

Outside the camper of Isaac and Carol Douglas, 10 February 2013 ($95.72).

BW: You're headed for church, yes? Which church will you be attending?

ID: First Assembly in Watford City—and it's an awesome church—and people have been real nice, and I mean I go to the grocery stores and they're real friendly, and the laundry and we made blankets, 750 blankets the church did. The four churches joined together for the abused children in this part of the world, so it was real neat.

BW: Are the people in the church mostly locals, or mostly oil folk?

ID: A little bit of everybody.

INTERVIEW

Camp 10: David Donaldson, camp resident, 11 July 2015 ($52.74).

DD: I heard there used to be a lot of meth out here, but you know, nothing that I ever really had a problem with, so. But yeah, you know, just a million different personalities and people living with their kids and family, and a lot of drinking and fighting, just, I've seen pretty much everything you can possibly think of out here, that just random stuff. You come home and everybody's just got chairs set up around your camper having a fire outside your camper, and you can't get any sleep and, blowing flames out of their mouth with alcohol in front of the little kid.

INTERVIEW

Gene Veeder, executive director, Jobs Development Authority McKenzie County, 11 August 2014 ($97.65).

GV: Your law enforcement and your sheriff's department are all transporting so it's pretty hard for them to, if they have to go to even Bismarck, you know, it's an all-day trip and their entire trip is spent transporting prisoners so it's way more costly than we originally thought.

BW: What's the local police force, the size?

GV: We have city and county. We have gone from six sheriff deputies to nineteen. Police force went from two to nine. We've always got openings of course too.

INTERVIEW

Camp 40: Donny Bringwatt, camp resident who just arrived from Texas, 16 January 2016 ($29.42).

BW: Right. So when the work starts what will the work cycle be? How many days on, how many days off?

DB: [inaudible]

BW: I don't know what that means.

DB: It means you start in the mornings, and you work till, however many hours a day you can work . . . seven days a week.

BW: Yeah.

DB: We're here to work, we're not here to, you know.

BW: . . . well right now, you're not working, so you're cooking a ham, what else do you do when you . . . ?

DB: [inaudible] [laughs] I'm just cookin' a ham, I'm gonna eat it [laughs]. Play dominos, play poker.

INTERVIEW

Camp 28: Will Oldman and his roomate, 9 February 2013 ($93.13).

WO: As long as you don't go to the strip clubs from what I hear [laughs] I've heard some pretty horrible stories about some strip club, I think it was in Watford, closed it down because guys were getting raped in the bathroom, viscously I mean.

Roommate: Crime has gone up almost 100 percent around here, compared to what it ever was, just a quiet town where you could leave your keys in your door open, keys in your car and stuff like that, nowadays you can't do that and uh not only that but the women that are here fear for their lives.

(Authors' note: There is no, and there has never in recent memory been, a strip club in Watford City.)

NOTEBOOK WILLIAM CARAHER

Description of the material outside two units in Camp 11, 10 August 2012 ($92.87).

Massive built deck, grill, plants, fence, dog run. stone, satellite tv, ramp leading to deck, potted plants, hanging plants, plywood around the base of a planted tree. Scrap wood underneath various garden features, propane tanks, table set on cinderblocks, outdoor bed, tarp, pallets, trashcan. Pallet deck, kids' toys, wading pool, small table, camp chairs (some kids sized), potted plants, plywood, small fence between unit and road, toy truck, strange tubs, propane tanks, water jugs, grill, cooler, satellite TV.

INTERVIEW

Camp 11: Angela and Bob Williams, 13 December 2014 ($57.81).

AW: Lots of insulation. That, you'll find a ton throughout the park. Any insulation, any wood. If you can get their hands on it they'll take it. So many people skirting and mudrooms are built from recycled materials. You know, it's just used over and over and over.

BW: It's like "well I'm moving if you want it, and make a little modifications," you know.

AW: If it's coveted, everyone wants a mudroom. If you leave behind a mudroom.

BW: But now they knock the mudrooms down, they don't give people opportunity to take them anymore.

PUBLICATION

William Caraher, Bret Weber, Kostis Kourelis, and Richard Rothaus (2017), The North Dakota Man Camp Project: The Archaeology of Home in the Bakken Oil Fields, *Historical Archaeology* 51, p. 271.

Our approach to documenting workforce housing drew on recent directions in archaeology and architectural history. First, archaeology of the contemporary world informed our work, and particularly this subfield's interest in sites of short-term or ephemeral occupation. Zimmerman's (2010) archaeology of homelessness, the archaeology of contemporary protest sites, photographic documentation of graffiti, and the archaeology of tourism collectively demonstrate how archaeological approaches to contemporary sites of contingency have the potential to inform issues of immediate social and political concern.[2]

DOCUMENT

Camp 11: Mudroom Guidelines, 10 August 2012 ($92.87).

1. Mudrooms require plans be submitted to Park Management.
2. Mudrooms smaller than 5×10 may be made and will require no deposit.
3. Any Mudrooms larger than 5×10 will require an additional $300 clean-up deposit.
4. Maximum Mudroom size is 20×8.
5. Maximum height of Mudroom is no higher than the RV.
6. No Mudroom additions may fully enclose the trailer (may not extend over the top).
7. RV must be able to be removed from lots without obstructions (no part of any mudroom may extend behind or in front of RV).

INTERVIEW

Camp 11: Barb Bendle, 10 August 2012 ($92.87).

BB: Mudrooms yeah. We do check them out and make sure they meet the fire code and that they're not built shoddily, so that if the wind comes up 80 mph, it's not going to blow away. That's what we do. Right. So it's safe for people. So it's not blowing down and hitting the next trailer or anything. My husband looks at their plot plans that we have them draw. Little plan telling us what they want to do and then we usually okay it because you know, we want them to have a little piece of land [trying to light a lighter for a cigarette in the wind].

MW: Well, during the wintertime if we are lucky we burn them.

BW: Who . . . Does the county allow you to do that?

MW: They did let you burn, when you know, when you can, with the snow, and (when) the wind's not gonna affect it, and the land around it.

ILLUSTRATION

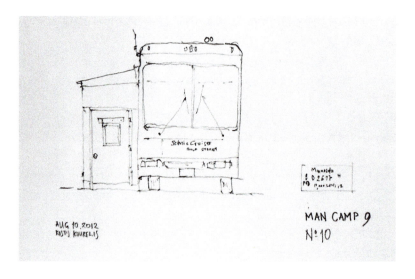

Camp 9, Unit 10, Kostis Kourelis, 10 August 2012 ($92.87).

PHOTOGRAPH

Battery Tank Explosion near Alexander, ND, William Caraher, 7 March 2015 ($49.61).

INTERVIEW

RV Graveyard: Roy Harrison and Garfield Washington, 11 July 2015 ($52.74).

BW: So you're bringing trailers when people abandon them?

RH: Yeah, when people abandon their vehicles and what not. . . . We had other things we were doing, but this was the most cost-effective way. We were taking an excavator and we were crushing them and cycling the metal and the wood out and putting them in different dumpsters and just having them hauled off that way, just picking them all up at once and just shoving them in a dumpster and trashing it.

NOTEBOOK BRET WEBER

First trip to the Bakken, 31 January 2012 ($99.56).

We drove west out of town on Highway 23, went south on 22, and then looped back west (probably on 73), then north eventually turning east again on Highway 23. We seemed to pass a number of smaller, ad hoc 'man camp' areas with various vehicles and RVs. The main thing that we witnessed was the night sky illuminated by dozens of flares—15–20 foot flames that burst straight into the air to burn off the natural gas that wells produce.

PHOTOGRAPH

McKenzie County, ND, memorial set up to Brendan Wegner, who died in a well blow-out 14 September 2011 ($87.96), photograph by William Caraher, 1 August 2015 ($47.12).

INTERVIEW

Camp 4: Clark Brewsman, camp resident, 9 February 2013 ($95.72).

CB: The longest I ever worked was fifty-seven hours, with a two-hour nap. You don't want to do it, but when the oil's coming out of the ground it won't stop and it needs to be tended to.

INTERVIEW

Camp 16: Sally Burnick, camp resident, 28 October 2016 ($48.70).

SB: When the oil, when the oil tanked up there, and the oil went away, I lost my job, his overtime got cut, so our primary home, we couldn't afford the big mortgage on it any more, so that got foreclosed on, and we had another little rental house that we sold at a huge loss.

BW: So, how much stuff did you bring with you?

SB: We got rid of a lot of our stuff, like almost, we had a 3,000 square foot house, we got rid of almost all the furniture, almost all the artwork. . . . Most of our stuff is in a storage shed packed into our horse trailer, um, we kept a couch, TV, entertainment center, DVDs, you know, knick knacks we were really fond of, family heirlooms. . . . Everything else went, so we're down to what's in the horse trailer, our storage shed, our boat, and our camper [laughs].

INTERVIEW

Camp 8: Mark, 9 August 2012 ($92.87).

M: They guaranteed sixty hours a week and holiday pay.

BW: You've been here a month, have you ever worked sixty hours a week?

M: No. I've only worked one week so far. One full week. I can't stay much longer because I'm going broke. When I show up every morning, they give me two hours for showing up. And this week, so far, I have six hours. So I can't make it. I'm buying my own food and paying rent and trying to pay bills at home. . . . I'm getting the hell out of North Dakota.

PHOTOGRAPH

Camp 11: William Caraher, 25 August 2013 ($97.26).

INTERVIEW

Camp 10: Claudia Nielsen, camp resident, 10 August 2012 ($92.87).

CN: He's from San Antonio, Texas. I met him while I was bartending, of course, I wasn't drinking but I was working. What else do you do out here besides work and drink? So we just hung out a couple times and actually he proposed to me after about a week so, it happened really really fast. But when you know, you know. We're both out of six-year marriages and I have actually, my kids are in Helena, Montana. Yeah he's a very successful man so it's going really well. He was in a man camp actually so he's enjoying the freedom of sharing my camper with me now.

INTERVIEW

Camp 65: Riker Brown, camp owner near Watford City, 2 August 2015 ($41.80).

BW: Are you seeing changes in the people who are living here now from a couple years ago?
RB: I'd say a lot of change. A lot more families, a lot more couples.
BW: More permanent?
RB: More permanent. Or there's, like the guys been out here so the next time he can bring his wife out, he's kind of got it figured out, he's got it like, he's got an RV park, so then they bring, or have their wives come on out. Yeah. But first it was way more, you know, single guys, three guys living in a trailer, you know, but now, we're seeing way more families.

INTERVIEW

Camp 6: Sue Christiansen, camp resident, 9 August 2012 ($93.36).

SC: Like the living conditions are terrible here. Like people are shitting behind, in the trees, past the trees right there. There's flies everywhere … We're like brothers, like a family, brothers and sisters out here, like a family. We're close, tight-knit family. Like all my men, like I owned, I own a construction company called Christiansen Construction so we were working, we were all contracted in Idaho but a bunch of us just got together. My husband and his boss decided to uh come up here by themselves in the winter last year. It was terrible in the winter too. Terrible fricking conditions.

PUBLICATION

William Caraher (2016), "The Archaeology of Man Camps: Contingency, Periphery, and Late Capitalism," in: William Caraher and Kyle Conway, eds., *The Bakken Goes Boom: Oil and the Changing Geographies of Western North Dakota,* Grand Forks, ND (The Digital Press at the University of North Dakota), p. 190.

Charley Hailey's exhaustive study of the camp as an architectural form both locates this within the history of vernacular architecture, the rise of leisure activities, and the emergence of substantial, mobile populations displaced by war, natural disasters, or economic need.[3] Like the midcentury tourists who towed their RVs to parks of the American West, the lack of infrastructure associated with camps, their contingent residents, and their temporary status have marked these spaces as peripheral no matter where they emerge. . . . The use of "blue tarp," modular housing units, shipping pallets, and other mobile, readily available, and ad hoc approaches has produced a common form of temporary settlement suitable to accommodate diverse situations and populations around the world.[4]

INTERVIEW

Camp10: Richard Scrum, camp owner in Wheelock, ND, 10 August 2012 ($92.87).

RS: Well I had to put in power and water and sewer. The campers had full hookups here. It took me a while. I did it all by cash. I don't use credit so I did everything in cash. Anything you do is really expensive out here. They want, for example, my well is bad here. They messed it up, the previous owners messed it up one night and I uh put $6,000 into fixing it and didn't get it fixed yet. They said I have to put another $10,000 into just drilling a new well. I haven't done it. I just put in a holding tank and I haul my water from Ray. It's uh, there's no city services here. The power's the only city service and gas, I guess, we do have natural gas which is nice. But as far as water and sewer, you're on your own.

PUBLICATION

William Caraher, Bret Weber, and Richard Rothaus (2016), Lessons from the Bakken Oil Patch, *Journal of Contemporary Archaeology* 3(2), p. 200.

With the collapse of oil prices in 2014, our work in the Bakken has come to focus increasingly on various forms of abandonment, as the number of temporary workers in the Bakken declined concurrently with the oil-rig count. Numerous coffee-makers in an abandoned RV revealed signs of methamphetamine use, trashed trailers smeared with human feces showed frustration and anger, and squatters' occupying empty rooms at defunct crew camps reflect a shifting reality.

INTERVIEW

Camp 17: Shana Berritt, newcomer and camp resident, 28 October 2016 ($49.72).

SB: Um, don't count on the oil field.
BW: Don't count on an oil field?
SB: Don't count on it, um, when it's good it's great, but when it tanks, it affects an entire community, if you haven't been smart about it, you haven't squirreled any money away, you're going to be in trouble when it all drops off [laughs] we learned the hard way, um, you know, my dad has seen the oil field rise and fall a couple times, and he kinda tried to warn us, but, you know, we said the oil field is so big, it's going to last forever [laughs].

NOTES

1   The North Dakota Man Camp project began in 2012 and sought to document the social, architecture, and archaeological conditions at workforce housing sites in the Bakken Oil Patch of Western North Dakota. The project is directed by the archaeologists and historians William Caraher and Richard Rothaus and the social worker and historian Bret Weber, and over its seven-year history included collaborations with architectural historian and archaeologist Kostis Kourelis, visual artists John Holmgren, Kyle Cassidy, and Ryan Stander, and colleagues in social work and history. The project team documented over fifty workforce using textual descriptions, photography, video, and over one hundred hours of unstructured interviews with residents. These sites ranged in character from informal and illegal squats in tree lines near construction sites, which we called Type 3 camps, to large RV parks or Type 2 camps and state-of-the-art camps provided by global logistics companies, which were Type 1 camps in our typology. The main phase of the project concluded in 2018, but low-level fieldwork is ongoing with periodic visits to Western North Dakota continuing on an irregular basis. The 2008–18 Bakken oil boom was the third such boom in Western North Dakota, with earlier booms occurring in the 1950s and late 1970s and early 1980s (Conway 2020). The improvement in horizontal drilling and hydraulic fracturing technology in the early twenty-first century and the high price of oil (which we included in this chapter) encouraged oil companies to return to the Bakken and Three Forks formation. By April 2014, the thousands of Bakken oil wells were producing over a million barrels of oil per day from sites concentrated mainly in Mountrail, Williams, and McKenzie Counties. The rapid rate of exploration and drilling, along with the increase in production, drew tens of thousands of workers to the region, not only to work in the oil industry directly but also to work in construction and service industries necessary to support the growing population. As had happened in previous booms, the increase in population outpaced housing, and a wide range of temporary housing situations filled the gap (Caraher et al. 2020).
Our original goal was to document and analyze workforce housing conditions and to produce a dataset that could inform historical and policy studies in the future. Our work in the Bakken, however, revealed more than just creative adaptions to the precarious employment, inadequate housing, and extreme weather. As this chapter attempts to communicate, fieldwork in the Bakken was also deeply affecting. The fieldwork team encountered diverse attitudes and situations that reflected the struggles, hopes, and experiences of workers in the aftermath of the Great Recession and the sub-prime mortgage crisis and the tireless efforts to negotiate the promises of middle-class life against contingencies of the global extractive economy. While our other publications provide a more scholarly view of our work in the Bakken (Weber et al. 2014, Caraher 2016, Caraher et al. 2016, Caraher et al. 2017, Caraher and Weber 2017, Caraher et al. 2020, Rothaus et al. 2021), this chapter seeks to offer an affective view of our experiences in this landscape and serve as a reminder that archaeology, especially of the contemporary world (Gonzalez-Ruibal 2019), is as much about our critical, reflective engagement with the contemporary situation as the material context for the present.

2   Schofield and Anderton 2000, Graves-Brown and Schofield 2011, Kiddey and Schofield 2011, 2014.

3   Hailey 2009.

4   Hailey 2009, 377–83.

BIBLIOGRAPHY

Berlant, Lauren and Kathleen Stewart (2019), *The Hundreds,* Durham (Duke University Press).

Caraher, William (2016*),* "The Archaeology of Man Camps: Contingency, Periphery, and Late Capitalism," in: William Caraher and Kyle Conway, eds., *The Bakken Goes Boom: Oil and the Changing Geographies of Western North Dakota*. Grand Forks (The Digital Press at the University of North Dakota), 181–96.

Caraher, William and Bret Weber (2017), *The Bakken: An Archaeology of an Industrial Landscape,* Fargo (North Dakota State University Press).

Caraher, William, Bret Weber, Kostis Kourelis, and Richard Rothaus (2017), The North Dakota Man Camp Project: The Archaeology of Home in the Bakken Oil Fields, *Historical Archaeology* 51(2), 267–87.

Caraher, William, Bret Weber, and Richard Rothaus (2016), Lessons from the Bakken Oil Patch, *Journal of Contemporary Archaeology* 3(2), 195–204.

—— (2020), *Making Home in the Bakken Oil Patch in K. Conway, Sixty Years of Boom and Bust: The Impact of Oil in North Dakota, 1958-2018.* Grand Forks (The Digital Press at the University of North Dakota), 287–308.

González-Ruibal, Alfredo (2019), *An Archaeology of the Contemporary Era,* London (Routledge).

Graves-Brown, Paul and John Schofield (2011), The Filth and the Fury: 6 Denmark Street (London) and the Sex Pistols, *Antiquity* 85(330), 1385–1401.

Hailey, Charlie (2009), *Camps: A Guide to 21st Century Space.* Cambridge (Massachusetts Institute of Technology Press).

Kiddey, Rachael and John Schofield (2011), Embrace the Margins: Adventures in Archaeology and Homelessness, *Public Archaeology* 10(1), 4–22.

—— (2014),Turbo Island, Bristol: Excavating a Contemporary Homeless Place, *Post-Medieval Archaeology* 48(1), 133–50.

Rothaus, Richard, William R. Caraher, Bret Weber, and Kostis Kourelis (2021), "Wheelock, North Dakota: 'Ghost-Towns,' Man Camps, and Hyperabundance in an Oil Boom," in: Rebecca M. Seifried and Deborah E. Brown Stewart, eds., *Deserted Villages: Perspectives from the Eastern Mediterranean,* Grand Forks (The Digital Press at the University of North Dakota), pp. 389--428.

Schofield, John and Mike Anderton (2000), The Queer Archaeology of Green Gate: Interpreting Contested Space at Greenham Common Airbase, *World Archaeology* 32(2), 236–51.

Weber, Bret, Julia Geigle, and Carenlee Barkdull (2014), Rural North Dakota's Oil Boom and Its Impact on Social Services, *Social Work* 59(1), 62–72.

Zimmerman, Larry (2010), Activism and Creating a Translational Archaeology of Homelessness. *World Archaeology* 42(3): 443–54

A LOSS OF AN ABSENCE

REINHARD BERNBECK

TRANSITIONS

On 30 July 2013, students excavating at the Tempelhof Airfield in Berlin found a small metal object (Figure 9.1). Like many of the other things recovered that day, this one was put in a bucket and taken to a nearby workroom. There a student carefully cleaned the unremarkable artifact, following the guidelines of the State Historical Preservation Office for handling materials made from metal. This involved brushing it cautiously without any use of water. The artifact was then temporarily stored with other metal objects in a bag placed in one of the large grey metal storage shelves. On 26 August of the same year, another student seated at a rickety table in the unattractive, yellow-tiled workroom bent over the same object to inspect it and enter information on its function, size, shape, weight, and color into a data table. She described it as a "flat, round object with opening mechanism & opposing lugs => locket / watch with cover?" (translated from German by the author). She described the general shape and the individual component parts with little hesitation, but the question

mark after the assignment of a function shows an uncertainty that prevented a definitive identification and led her to record two possible uses.

The somewhat mysterious find was then professionally cleaned and restored. The latch was opened cautiously, but the metal case nonetheless fell into two pieces. The function as a watch could be immediately ruled out because of the absence of any traces of clockwork. Instead, parts of the inner lid had a brown, dried-out leather-like lining, as might be expected of a locket. On 6 September 2013, excavation photographer Jessica Meyer captured the small round metal object a total of ten times from different sides and in different light conditions and on 10 October of the same year, Beatrix Nordheim made a precise pencil drawing of it. The brief descriptions of the find on the drawing and in the photo database that accompanied these documentation steps differ only insignificantly from the initial identification cited above.

Figure 9.1. Find number 1873-0225-982-1 from Tempelhof Airfield. State after a first cleaning in the summer of 2013. *Photograph courtesy of Jessica Meyer, Landesdenkmalamt Berlin.*

Figure 9.2. Oblique view of the locket in Figure 9.1, restored and opened. *Photograph courtesy of Jessica Meyer, Landesdenkmalamt Berlin.*

TRACES

Even in a roughly cleaned, unrestored state, the locket reveals decorative corrugations, regularly placed in eight groups of ridges and fine narrow grooves over the base and the lid. The decor of the lid and underside match exactly when it is closed. Due to the delicacy and exactness of the embellishment, the locket stands out from many other, somewhat cruder finds. Greenish corroded metal residues and yellowish traces of soil initially adhered to its surface, but could be carefully removed during restoration. After that, it became even clearer that the two rectangular lugs attached to the base were bent. When viewed obliquely from above, the lid proved to be seriously dented. The opening hinge was broken (Figure 9.2). On the exterior of the base there is an off-center oval mass of shimmering material, which on closer inspection can be identified as molten plastic. The inner ring of the lid is broken and bulges at one point. Only under a magnifying glass do we see that the

case has rudiments of a coating that had largely flaked off due to extremely high temperatures, but remains recognizable as a thin black varnish in a few places (Figure 9.3). Perhaps the locket was originally silver-plated, something that future analysis could clarify. The coating had flaked off on the inside and then partially melted onto the base. The inner surface is clearly different in its poison-green corroded color from the red-black exterior and the unknown brown filling material of the lid.

CHANGING CONTEXTS

Who owned this locket, and what did it contain? The context in which the object was found helps us to address these questions. It was assigned to context number 225, which the excavators were able to determine belonged to a barracks in a large Nazi-period forced labor camp of Weser Flugzeugbau GmbH (Weser Aircraft Construction Company); more precisely,

Figure 9.3. Close-up of the external base of the locket, with partly preserved black coating and molten plastic. *Photograph courtesy of Jessica Meyer, Landesdenkmalamt Berlin.*

Barracks 8 (according to the count at that time) in a camp containing a total of eighteen such buildings.[1]

Weser Aircraft took on the task of building JU 87-type dive bombers, the so-called Stukas, for the Nazi government during the Second World War. These aircraft were equipped with a device that caused a terrifying howling sound when nosediving, as a harbinger of the bombing terror that thereby set in. Weser Aircraft in Berlin produced these murderous two-seaters in Tempelhof Airfield. Because German men were drafted to the front in the Second World War, the Nazi-friendly industry and the genocidal repressive organs of the state—Gestapo, SS, and security service—had agreed to restrictive conditions under which they would exploit people from Poland and the Soviet Union as forced laborers. Without this vicious exploitation, the production sectors of the industry that were crucial to the war effort would have come to a standstill. The agreement was only possible after overcoming the initial resistance of the Gestapo and SS, who, because of racism that was even more

extreme than that of industry, did not want to let Slavic people, whom they considered "sub-humans," work in Germany.

Sketches of the forced labor camp of Weser Aircraft—about which a community initiative within the Berlin History Workshop kindly informed us—contained a layout of the barracks and information on their occupancy. As a result, we knew that one of the five partially excavated barracks in the Weser Aircraft camp held French prisoners of war (Barracks 6, according to the Nazi numeration of the buildings), two housed "Russian women" (Barracks 14 and 18), and two others "Russian men" (Barracks 7 and 8). It was only when we found a double row of underground barbed wire around Barracks 7 and 8 that it became clear to us that their occupants were male Soviet prisoners of war and not Russian civilians, as subterranean fencing was prescribed only for the former. The elongated barracks usually had a central corridor and rooms leading off to both sides. At the north end there was a washroom that was far too small for the number of people living in a barracks. Archaeological context 225, where our locket comes from, was an anteroom to the sanitary facilities of Barracks 8.

BOMBING AND ITS CONSEQUENCES

In April 1945 the Soviet army became the first military unit to reach Berlin. On 26 April 1945, they drove the Nazis out of Tempelhof Airfield. So why did the locket remain on site rather than being taken by the liberated owner? The reason is simple: in early 1944, more than a year before the end of the Second World War, the Royal Air Force and the United States Air Force carried out intensive bombing of German cities, including Berlin. Incendiary bombs were primarily used in order to set fire to the roofs of apartment buildings. Such a bomb hit the forced labor camp, likely in late February 1944. Almost all of the wooden barracks that were still standing at the time were destroyed in the course of this raid (Figure 9.4). The bomb fell right next to the barracks from which the locket came. On the aerial photograph a black hole is visible; it is the bomb crater. A halo of lighter rays around it consists of sandy substrate hurled out to the surface by the impact. Otherwise the area all around is burned black. In the distance along the street opposite the camp, the surface is white with the remains of snow. Two nearby barracks have visibly destroyed roofs.

Where the forced laborers from Barracks 8 were at the time of the bombing remains unknown. If the attack took place during the day, they were probably at work. For the nighttime there were rudimentary, zigzag-shaped air-raid shelters nearby where they could shelter for a modicum of safety. However, it is obvious that in that cold snowy winter the people living in the barracks lost all their possessions. The destruction leads us to take a closer look at the archaeological circumstances surrounding the context of the locket.

The story of the place did not end in 1945; the area where the forced labor camp had stood also had a post-war history. The Red Army occupied the field in late April 1945 and remained there until the summer of the same year, after which the occupation was turned over to the United States Air Force, which soon redesigned the field. We have little archaeological evidence of when and how the American military destroyed the material remnants of the former forced labor camps, in some instances leveling and filling in spots with the use of big excavators and erecting sports fields in their place. In any case, the barracks that were still standing were torn down, ruins of an old airport terminal from the 1920s were removed, and reservoirs for fire-fighting purposes left from the war were converted into swimming pools and rubbish pits.

The war of the Allies against the Nazis was over, the Nuremberg trials had resulted in death or imprisonment for a few of the important Nazi personalities, and the "normal Nazi citizens" took up their posts once again in administrations, courts, universities, factories, schools, shops, and kindergardens; in West Germany mostly as if there had never been a Holocaust. Meanwhile, the Cold War cast its first shadows. Less than five years after the end of the Second World War, the next test of strength came in the form of the Berlin Airlift, when the Soviet Union tried to bring West Berlin to its knees through a complete blockade. The Tempelhof Airfield played a central role as the location for makeshift landing strips for

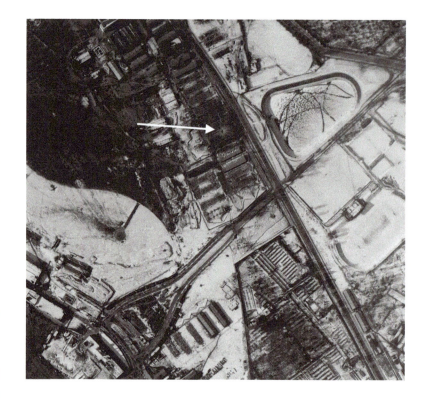

Figure 9.4. Aerial photograph of the Weser Aircraft forced labor camp after an incendiary bombing raid; the white arrow marks the bomb crater next to Barracks 8. *Photograph taken by the Royal Air Force, 20 February 1944.*

the supply planes of the western Allies: France, Great Britain, and the United States. It thereby mutated from a factory of weapons of war to a bulwark of freedom against the Soviet Union under Stalin. In the process, grass grew—literally—over the former barracks.

A THING AS GUARANTOR

A locket is a very special item because it has a referential character. It usually marks a person who is not present by means of a picture or a lock of hair. Lockets of this type are commonly worn on a chain, often around the neck, but in any case on the body. This allows opening, viewing, and reminding oneself of another person at any time. The interior of a locket is a material synecdoche, the metal case its protection.

From within the small container, an *Other* is brought to mind. In our case, it remains unclear whether this person was a child, spouse, parent, or friend. Evoking presence by opening the locket is a process that brings the past into the present. At the time when one of the male prisoners in Barracks 8 opened the lid and looked at the contents, he was not only far away but also temporally separated from the person, or persons, he remembered. Such a presentification of a relation with an *Other* attains fictitious qualities even just a few days after separation, as conditions of life for those connected via the locket developed in diverging fashions, and in the case of the find at Tempelhof Airfield we can be sure that this development was torturous, distressing, cruel. The battles of the early months of the extermination campaign against the Soviet Union ended mostly in victory for the Wehrmacht. By the summer of 1941, the Nazis had captured hundreds of thousands of Soviet prisoners of war. They were deliberately consigned to a likely death by being confined in the open air, surrounded by barbed wire and watchtowers, without any care for food, drink, hygiene, or a roof over their heads. Well over half of the five million Soviet prisoners of war died miserably in these ordeals.

Because we know that the owner of the locket who ended up in a Berlin forced labor camp was a member of the Red Army, he is likely to have experienced first the brutality of war and then a first phase of unimaginable conditions of inhuman captivity. In the perverse logic of life under the Nazis, we can say that the deportation to forced labor was a potentially life-saving 'stroke of luck' for those affected.

However, that misses the mark. Aleida Assmann (1999, 157) quotes psychiatrist Ernst Simmel, who, in his research on trauma related to the First World War, wrote: "The flash of terror produces a photographically accurate impression" (translation by the author). Extraordinarily cruel moments drill themselves deeply into memory. They fundamentally change the *Self* who has to live through them and with that all the relationships such a person may have had and or may have in the future. It is well known from interviews with survivors of the Holocaust and the "Russian camps" of the Second World War that such deep traumata never disappear and can re-emerge at any point.[2]

An object such as the locket is then not just a souvenir, but, in the case of a separation in a previous face-to-face relationship to someone, an illusion, the core of which lies in the falsehood of the immutability of personal relationships. The gaze that fell onto the locket when it was opened in the forced labor camp at Tempelhof Airfield was likely that of a person whose recent trauma had shaken and changed him to the core. And yet the sight of those unknown contents kept within the metal case by the prisoner of war may have comforted him in the face of a present full of desperation. This evocative object combined previous happy experiences with hopes of being able to restore and even re-live them in the future.

It is precisely the distorting power of unchangeability residing in things that imposes itself on the remembering and the remembered person. The 'social life of things' has a temporal rhythm that is much too slow for a synchronization with the life circumstances of people. The continuity of an object suggests interpersonal stability and bridges the painful unavailability of an *Other;* it deceives the viewer into believing in the unchangeability of a relationship. The locket is a materialization of a space-time gap between two people, but when the gaze falls on it, it produces the illusion of there being only a spatial difference.

A LOSS OF AN ABSENCE

Today the locket is, unfortunately, empty. We have no idea who the person was about whom the object reminded. We can only make guesses in terms of a cardinal direction (east), a language (Russian), a gender of the owner of the item (man), and a social position (better off, because of its high quality). No age, no facial features of the person who was remembered gaze at us to give us vague hints about its owner, although the two parts of the object laid next to each other almost seem to look back at the viewer (Figure 9.5). Silently, the broken locket avers that the prisoner for whom the case was likely a treasure will remain completely unknown to us. The piece of metal and leathery material is a bridge between two human shores, both of which have disappeared into the fog of time.

More tragically, an air raid caused the owner to lose this keepsake. The objectified presence of the absence of a subject was thereby turned into a double absence, of both person and object. The emotional bridge to one another was destroyed when the Western Allies together with the Red Army defeated the Nazis. The archaeological presence of this object leads not only to the question of who was remembered by means of a picture, a lock of hair, or in some other materialized way, but also how and whether the prisoner of war, whose few possessions went up in flames in the winter of 1943–44 on the northern edge of the Tempelhof Airfield, grieved about his loss.

Figure 9.5. The open locket, with leathery brown cover inside its lid and green corrosion on its base. *Photograph courtesy of Jessica Meyer, Landesdenkmalamt Berlin.*

DISCOVERING A LOSS

The archaeological discovery of the locket is much more than an excavated find of personal property. It is a trace, a piece of evidence of the inhumane politico-military turmoil of the twentieth century and the attempt to deal with these conditions on an individual scale. It is a vestige of the endeavors of the Allies at devastation as a way to stop the terror of the Nazi regime. And it is a trace of losing a memory.

Three stages of despair are reified here. The locket is a reminder of the separation of people that takes place through war. It offers a glimpse into the desperation that accompanied the building of weapons in a foreign context under life-threatening conditions, weapons that potentially targeted one's own relatives and friends. And the discovery of the locket evokes the pain at the loss of a memento.

The object bridges the time between deposit and excavation for us, but not for the former owner. The deception attributed to the thing, as it suppresses the changeability of subjective history, also applies to our archaeological interpretation. A real understanding of what the personal item meant for its owner is impossible, not only because it has been burned, lost, and become ambivalent without its interior contents, but also because a real recognition, an 'understanding' of the terrorizing human conditions it survived must remain impossible for us.

CODA

And yet the blackened metal housing embodies the core of an alternative way of conceiving history, which Walter Benjamin (2003, 390; emphasis in original) formulated in his second thesis on history: "The past carries with it a secret index by which it is referred to redemption. Doesn't a breath of the air that pervaded earlier days caress us as well? In the voices we hear, isn't there an echo of now silent ones? . . . If so, then there is a secret agreement between past generations and the present one. Then our coming was expected on earth. Then, like every generation that preceded us, we have been endowed with a *weak* messianic power, a power on which the past has a claim."

The locket is one of those indices but it must be understood in a darker sense than Benjamin suggests. It is a materialization of "missed opportunities to intervene on behalf of the oppressed during the Nazi regime".[3] In this sense, every twisted rusty nail, every brick fragment from Tempelhof Airfield and the tens of thousands of sites of Nazi repression and annihilation is to be read as a guarantor in the present that the shameful silence, the anxious unwillingness to intervene, the selfish failure to defend the persecuted will not be forgotten.

NOTES

1   Bernbeck 2017, 243–47.
2   Caruth 1995.
3   Santner 2005, 89.

BIBLIOGRAPHY

Assmann, Aleida (1999), *Erinnerungsräume: Formen und Wandlungen des kulturellen Gedächtnisses,* Munich (C.H. Beck).

Benjamin, Walter (2003), "On the Concept of History," in: Howard Eiland and Michael W. Jennings, eds., *Walter Benjamin: Selected Writings, Volume 4,* pp. 389–400, Cambridge (Belknap Press, translation by Edmund Jephcott of the 1940 original).

Bernbeck, Reinhard (2017), *Materielle Spuren des nationalsozialistischen Terrors,* Bielefeld (Transcript).

Caruth, Cathy (1995), *Trauma: Explorations in Memory,* Baltimore (Johns Hopkins University Press).

Santner, Eric L. (2005), "Miracles Happen: Benjamin, Rosenzweig, Freud, and the Matter of the Neighbor," in: Slavoj Zizek, Eric L. Santner, and Kenneth Reinhard, eds., *The Neighbor: Three Inquiries in Political Theology*, pp. 76–133, Chicago (University of Chicago Press).

ARCHAEOGAMING IS *X*

JOHN AYCOCK AND KATIE BIITTNER

Humans play games. This was true thousands of years ago, as dice from Mesopotamia and the Indus Valley attest,[1] and it is still true today. Throughout much of human history, these games involved physical, tangible artifacts such as cards, dice, counters, pawns, and boards. In the more recent past, in only the brief span of a human lifetime, we have seen a shift from these physical games to virtual ones: video games. Video games, along with their associated video game culture, have gradually become part of mainstream culture since the 1970s. This acceptance can be attributed to many things, but the technological changes that facilitated the widespread access to video games, including the expansion from computer and console-based games to game apps that can accompany us everywhere we take our smart phones, are of particular interest to those of us who study the past. As a ubiquitous and truly global phenomenon, the creation, dissemination, adoption, and use of video games are interesting and relevant topics for both academic and non-academic researchers.

What do video games have to do with archaeology? For archaeology, everything. A strong trend in archaeological method and theory today is a shift towards archaeologies of the contemporary. These take many forms, from space archaeology (Alice Gorman and Justin Walsh, Chapter 13, this volume) to homelessness (Larry Zimmerman, Chapter 21, this volume), but most are centered around challenging the traditional temporal boundaries of what the past is. What this volume makes very clear is that archaeology that does not embrace the modern as well as the ancient consigns itself to a perpetual curiosity in the public mind, interesting but never completely relevant to modern life.

This might sound as though we are simply making a case for contemporary archaeology, and in fact that would not be incorrect, but we can be even more precise in our argument and in our answer to the "what is the past" question. For us, the answer lies in the realm of archaeogaming.

What is archaeogaming? Reinhard (2018, 2) defines archaeogaming as "the archaeology both in and of digital games." As an area of study, the scope of archaeogaming includes work as diverse as how archaeology is depicted in video games,[2] the ethics of archaeological research in video games,[3] and creating video games as a form of archaeological communication.[4] A project that uses gaming technology for academic archaeological research is briefly discussed by David Fredrick, Rhodora Vennarucci, and William Loder in Chapter 23 in this volume. Taken together, this means that the focus of archaeogaming can be as diverse as the researchers themselves, but they all share the common element of video games. And while many archaeologists play games,[5] those who study video games, 'archaeogamers,' seek to apply the lens of archaeology, the theoretical frameworks and methodologies that serve as the foundation of our discipline, to our analysis and interpretation of these digital games. There is, however, no comprehensive nor unified theory of archaeogaming, nor are there set methods. Archaeogaming, in many ways, is in its infancy and still developing. Much of the initial and emerging research is still asking the important "what if" questions: what if we treated a video game as an archaeological site? Could we survey and document a virtual landscape in a video game the same ways we would for a site or region in the real world?[6] We will examine only one aspect of archaeogaming, however, namely the study of the implementation of videogames: the study of digital artifacts. Our reason for this focus is to illustrate that archaeogaming allows us to challenge not just our understanding of what the past is, but also of what 'material culture' is.

"BUT THEY ARE DIGITAL ARTIFACTS" ARCHAEOGAMING IS COMPUTER SCIENCE

While it might be easy to look at games in general and see the broader historical shifts in the kinds of games played over time, archaeogamers focus specifically on video games, treating them as digital artifacts. Traditional dirt or 'meat-space' archaeologists are fundamentally interested in artifacts or material culture (the stuff made, used, and modified by humans), but examining *digital* artifacts requires a shift in thinking.

The challenges that digital artifacts present for archaeologists are two-fold. First, understanding the technology used in a digital artifact is a specialty unto itself that falls into the area of computer science (Figure 8.1). Just as archaeologists train for years to learn their profession, computer scientists train similarly to learn theirs, and few people should be expected to be expert in both. At present we see very little archaeological research that delves into digital artifacts in any substantive way, which, given the knowledge required to understand them, is wholly unsurprising. Second, there is certainly no shortage of digital artifacts to study, and herein lies the problem of scale. We can learn from studying single digital artifacts, which presents challenges enough, but how do we choose a single artifact from all those that are available? The obvious answer is to not choose at all but rather to study digital artifacts *en masse*. However, the body of digital artifacts is not static. Untold numbers of new digital artifacts were created as this passage was written, yet more still when this passage is read. The only way to make meaningful progress studying digital artifacts is by harnessing the computers themselves, constructing tools—yet more digital artifacts—to ask and answer questions. The people who create such tools are computer scientists.

It might seem at this point that the circle is complete, and it is not one that has need of real archaeologists, but this is misleading. Ultimately the computers driving our videogames are both technology and tool, and archaeology has been considering the human relationship with those for much longer than computer science has been a discipline. Archaeology has a vital role to play in the study of these digital artifacts alongside computer science.

Additionally, archaeology already has examples of incorporating the incorporeal. Since the 1980s there has been much study on ideology, symbolic thought, and the evolution of the human brain, all broadly framed as cognitive archaeology. Adjacent to cognitive archaeology are discussions of what materiality is and what it means, which challenge not only static conceptions of materials and their properties but seek to acknowledge our definitions of the materiality of objects as relational and constantly in flux.[7] Questioning materiality leads to considerations of that which is not captured in physical form: the intangible. In archaeology we see this in a focus

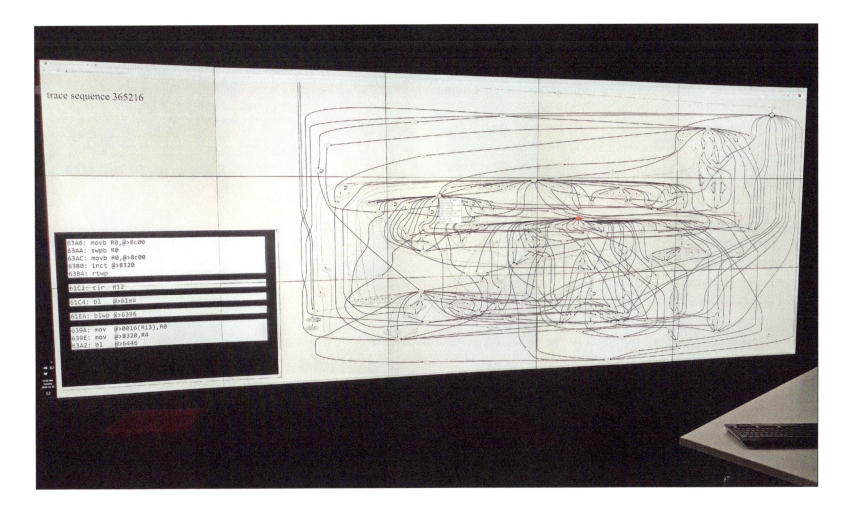

```
trace sequence 365216




63A6: movb R0,@>8c00
63AA: swpb R0
63AC: movb R0,@>8c00
63B0: inct @>8320
63B4: rtwp

61C2: clr  R12

61C4: bl   @>61ea

61EA: blwp @>6396

639A: mov  @>0016(R13),R0
639E: mov  @>8320,R4
63A2: bl   @>6446
```

Figure 8.1. Using a wall-sized visualization tool for the analysis of the computer code of a game; the keyboard in the lower right corner can serve as scale.

"A VIDEOGAME IS A TEXT"
ARCHAEOGAMING IS HISTORY

on intangible cultural heritage. The safeguarding of intangible cultural heritage, including its identification, documentation, and revitalization, has been centered as the responsibility of archaeologists, particularly those working in and on post-colonial and decolonizing contexts.[8] By explicitly including computer science, archaeogaming not only allows us to question the materiality of the archaeological record but gives us the tools to undertake robust and meaningful investigations into our digital heritage.

Clearly, archaeogaming challenges many traditional disciplinary boundaries, and this is perhaps most the case when we turn to considering videogame-as-text. Text is the province of history according to some definitions, leaving material artifacts to archaeology,[9] but in fact the question of how a game is a text and what discipline should be studying it is much more complicated.

The field of game studies adopts a broad, humanities-driven view of what a text is. As Fernández-Vara (2015, 5) puts it, "what *text* means extends to other artifacts . . . from literal text, such as . . . historical documents, to non-written or even non-verbal text." In other words, a game is a text, and if literary theory is the hammer, then everything is a nail. Computer scientists would take a much narrower outlook, by contrast, one perhaps more in keeping with the field of history. In computing, text implies literal human-readable text; a text file contains plain, no-frills text (often encoded using a standard method such as ASCII), and the source code for a program is typically just text written in an artificial yet human-understandable programming language. Since all the permissible activity in what humans experience as a videogame is defined—intentionally or otherwise, in the case of glitches—by the code run on the computer, one could argue that treating a videogame as a text is a superficial artifice. The focus should instead be on the code, the text underlying the game.

Even this perspective has numerous problems; let us start with the text of the source code of a game, what the game programmer(s) directly created. Seeing the actual source code of a game is a rarity. For older games, it may already be lost, and for games both old and new, source code may exist, but remain inaccessible for legal or other reasons. For the sake of argument, however, assume that the source code text is available. Is this what a videogame player experiences as 'the game'? Not exactly, although there is a strong relationship between the two. For programmers, the days are long past when they would write code in a binary form that the computer could understand; instead, programmers use higher-level, more human-readable, more textual programming languages. These, in turn, are translated by software tools in a toolchain—compilers, assemblers, linkers—into the binary code of the game that the computer can run. By way of analogy, the programmer is a puppeteer, a skilled performer who pulls strings knowing their effect, but the puppet we see is the actual game. So by studying the source code, do we see the text underlying the game? When available, source code is certainly an important piece of the puzzle, but the translation process into a text the computer can understand may introduce complications.

The other extreme is where we have no source code, and our sole information must come from the binary ones and

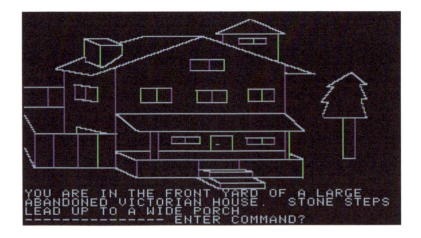

Figure 8.2. Reverse engineering can reveal much about the development of a game, as was the case for the 1980 Apple II game *Mystery House*.

zeros of the digital artifact itself. It might be difficult to still see this as a text, but insofar as a text is really just a set of symbols arranged in a particular way, the binary is indeed a text, just not one that is easily read by humans. Making sense of this requires reverse engineering the binary, a specialized skill within computer science, one often employed in computer security where, for instance, it is helpful to know if an unknown piece of binary code is malicious or not. Binary reverse engineering is a laborious process, although not impossible, and allows us to archaeologically understand the technical means through which videogames were made (Figure 8.2).[10] Archaeology already has a deep relationship with reverse engineering, as Moshenska (2016) observed, just not the reverse engineering of digital artifacts, yet.

Where reverse engineering struggles, in terms of what we can learn, is in all the information that is lost. The translation process from source code to binary code mentioned above discards everything that the computer does not need, which unfortunately includes much of what would be useful to interpret the digital artifact. For example, programmers will often select variable names in their code that convey meaning about how the variable was to be used, as well as how the programmer conceptualized their task, and what programming practices they used. We also lose comments in the source code that were intended to document the code for other programmers or for that same programmer at a later date, at times capturing choices the programmer made and did not make. In reverse engineering digital artifacts, we must additionally be mindful that the translation toolchain may have altered the text intended by the programmer, or inserted text that the programmer never intended to include.

The game studies view of game-as-text does offer one notable advantage, in that it permits a connection to the notion of paratext. Genette (1997) distinguished between the main text of a literary work and the text that accompanies the main text, which he called paratext. In terms of a book, paratext would include the table of contents and the preface, and also external material like author interviews. This has been adopted and applied to videogames,[11] although here again digital artifacts create complications, because the underlying assumption of paratext is that it can be seen, but we can have paratext in digital artifacts that the programmer did not intend to include, as mentioned, or included text that was not meant to be seen.[12] In any event, paratext does have a clear connection to something very important in archaeology: context.

Our ability to interpret any material culture comes down to its context, the material surrounding the artifact (the matrix), the physical location of the artifact within the matrix, and the association of the artifact with other material culture. But how context is defined for virtual or digital artifacts is never straightforward and ultimately comes down to the archaeologist and the theoretical foundations that inform their practice. Reinhard (2018), for example, treats the game as an archaeological site. This approach establishes the code as a digital artifact within the context of the game-as-site. We, on the other hand, chose to situate the code-as-digital-artifact using technological organization as its context.[13] Using technological organization as context engages us in a larger discussion of the implementation, use, and 'discard' of the game, or its *chaîne opératoire.* Because games are not created, nor used, nor discarded separate from the broader technological culture of gaming, the matrix of games is the

paratext: all of the surrounding materials about the game that are created by its designers, reviewers, publishers, and players, including walkthroughs, print ads, posters, letters to the editor, and game reviews.

Technological organization as context also permits an examination of individual and of cultural choices around game design. The individual choices or decisions made during coding, as with any technological production, reflect those that an individual has learned as a member of a group. These choices, manifest in the end product or the artifact, can tell us not just about the individual maker, but also their social groups and associated technological traditions. The code in a game is the product of the decisions made by its programmer, but those decisions made are the product of the broader understanding of the programmer in terms of how games should be coded, and what players expect of a game. It also informs us as to the constraints experienced by the programmer that influence choices, like storage, memory, cost, and labor. By understanding the dynamics of technological behavior—the interrelations of economic, social, functional, environmental, and behavioral variables of social structure manifest as, and in, material culture—we can emphasize the individual behind the tool and not just the tool itself.

This, then, is one of the goals of archaeogaming as we have outlined here: to study digital games with the purpose of understanding not just the technologies that produced them but the people, the agents, behind the game. Archaeogaming can therefore be seen as an agency-based approach.

"YOU CAN JUST ASK THEM" ARCHAEOGAMING IS ETHNOGRAPHY

A common refrain is that the creator(s) of a game can simply be asked about what they did, an advantage shared by other archaeologies of the contemporary. Interviews are potentially valuable because of their ability to capture both technique and technological thought from the perspective of the individual maker, resulting in detailed technological descriptions. The outcomes of creator interviews can read like how-to or step-by-step instruction guides for the technology, though ideally they should also contain the context in which this knowledge was obtained and produced. Game developer culture, programming culture, and the video game industry influence how creators talk about the work they do. Ethnographic work that captures both the technology and the context of technological knowledge and production is therefore crucial.

We need not limit ourselves to game creators. Other means of conducting ethnoarchaeology of games include focusing on real-world players and the games they play. This approach allows for a greater consideration of how meaning is created in contemporary gaming culture, reminding us that games serve as cultural landscapes themselves, and more generally that games and play are entangled within the broader context of culture. Insofar as gameplay stems from the game code, one could also argue that studying how players experience the game—the game the code produces—is valuable. In fact, Newman (2012) makes the case that preserving how games were played and experienced is more important than preserving the games themselves.

What these other approaches highlight is that creator interviews are only one tool in the toolkit of ethnoarchaeologists. Certainly interviews are valuable, but are not as enlightening about technical aspects of game creation as might seem to be the case. In general, recollections of past events may contain errors, exaggerations, and exclusions.[14] Expecting the flawless recall of technical minutiae from decades prior is unrealistic in the extreme. This is, of course, assuming that the people to ask are alive, locatable, and willing to participate; assumptions that in our experience do not always hold true. These are not the only hurdles. The culture of the game industry can prevent significant or sustained access to the individuals behind the game; this limits the access of archaeogamers and ethnoarchaeologists to insider perspectives and knowledge.[15] Sexism and a distrust of academia can contribute to a hostile environment for researchers and research.[16] Ultimately, and unfortunately, we may be left with only the artifact itself.

INSERT COINS TO CONTINUE

Here we have focused on only a single aspect of archaeogaming, the implementation of videogames. Already, it is apparent that there are many challenges in this one aspect alone, challenges that are mainly associated with the immaterial record we seek to study and understand. Sufficient expertise in computer science is required, including a specialized skill set that allows for the development of tools for the analysis of digital artifacts; this means that archaeogaming requires collaboration between computer scientists and archaeologists with a shared interest in developing an interdisciplinary research program. In our experience this is not actually a challenge or a limitation, but in line with the long tradition of archaeologists collaborating with experts from outside of our discipline. The greater challenge lies in reimagining what it is that archaeologists do and how we do it.

Archaeogaming is, and is not, an area of study that fits comfortably within archaeology, and that is not a bad thing. Challenging traditional definitions of the past and material culture allows for positive, transformative (decolonizing, democratizing) growth in our discipline. Here we are forced to consider artifacts from the recent past which, despite their relative newness, are already difficult to understand. The additional immateriality of these artifacts, these culturally important digital artifacts, makes archaeogaming a bellwether for archaeology as it grapples with the explosion of digital cultural artifacts. Fortunately, archaeology is nothing if not adaptable and historically willing to include other disciplines, which portends well for its interdisciplinary future.

NOTES

1 Dales 1968.

2 Meyers Emery and Reinhard 2015.

3 Dennis 2016.

4 Copplestone 2017.

5   Mol et al. 2016.

6   Reinhard 2018.

7   Ingold 2007.

8   Keitumetse 2006.

9   Halsall 1997.

10   Aycock and Biittner 2019.

11   Fernández-Vara 2015.

12   Aycock and Finn 2019.

13   Aycock and Biittner 2019.

14   Ritchie 2015.

15   O'Donnell 2014.

16   Chess and Shaw 2015.

BIBLIOGRAPHY

Aycock, John and Katie Biittner (2019), Inspecting the Foundation of *Mystery House*, *Journal of Contemporary Archaeology* 6(2), 183–205.

Aycock, John and Patrick Finn (2019), Uncivil Engineering: A Textual Divide in Game Studies, *Game Studies* 19(3), http://gamestudies.org/1903/articles/aycockfinn.

Chess, Shira and Adrienne Shaw (2015), A Conspiracy of Fishes, or, How We Learned to Stop Worrying About #GamerGate and Embrace Hegemonic Masculinity, *Journal of Broadcasting and Electronic Media* 59(1), 208–20.

Copplestone, Tara Jane (2017), "Designing and Developing a Playful Past in Video Games," in: Angus A.A. Mol, Csilla E. Ariese-Vandemeulebroucke, Krijn H.J. Boom, and Aris Politopoulos, eds., *The Interactive Past: Archaeology, Heritage and Video Games*, Leiden (Sidestone Press), pp. 85–97.

Dales, George F. (1968), Of Dice and Men, *Journal of the American Oriental Society* 88(1), 14–23.

Dennis, L. Meghan (2016), Archaeogaming, Ethics, and Participatory Standards, *Society for American Archaeology: Archaeological Record* 16(5), 29–33.

Fernández-Vara, Clara (2015), *Introduction to Game Analysis*, New York (Routledge).

Genette, Gérard (1997), *Paratexts: Thresholds of Interpretation*, (English translation by Jane E. Lewin of the 1987 French original), Cambridge (Cambridge University Press).

Halsall, Guy (1997), "Archaeology and Historiography," in: Michael Bentley, ed., *Companion to Historiography*, London (Routledge), pp. 805–27.

Ingold, Tim (2007), Materials against Materiality, *Archaeological Dialogues* 14(1), 1–16.

Keitumetse, Susan (2006), UNESCO Convention on Intangible Heritage: Practical Implications for Heritage Management Approaches in Africa, *South African Archaeological Bulletin* 61(184), 166–71.

Meyers Emery, Kathryn and Andrew Reinhard (2015), Trading Shovels for Controllers: A Brief Exploration of the Portrayal of Archaeology in Video Games, *Public Archaeology* 14(2), 137–49.

Mol, Angus, Csilla Ariese-Vandemeulebroucke, Krijn Boom, Aris Politopoulos, and Vincent Vandemeulebroucke (2016), Video Games in Archaeology: Enjoyable but Trival?, *Society for American Archaeology: Archaeological Record* 16(5), 11–15.

Moshenska, Gabriel (2016), Reverse Engineering and the Archaeology of the Modern World, *Forum Kritische Archäologie* 5, 16–28.

Newman, James (2012), *Best Before: Videogames, Supersession and Obsolescence*, London (Routledge).

O'Donnell, Casey (2014), *Developer's Dilemma: The Secret World of Videogame Creators*, Cambridge (Massachusetts Institute of Technology Press).

Reinhard, Andrew (2018), *Archaeogaming: An Introduction to Archaeology in and of Video Games*, New York (Berghahn).

Ritchie, Donald A. (2015), *Doing Oral History* (third, revised edition), Oxford (Oxford University Press).

PART I

HUMANS AND OBJECTS

THE WALL THAT GIVES/EL MURO QUE DA

TRASH IN A BOX

MAITE ZUBIAURRE AND FILOMENA CRUZ

In Chapter 1 in this volume, "Beyond Archaeology: Disarticulation and Its Consequences," Doug Bailey describes the following performance:

In a session with the title "Entangling Ancient Art" at the 2019 meetings of the Theoretical Archaeology Group in Syracuse, New York, I placed a painstakingly reconstructed and conserved ancient ceramic amphora into a reinforced plastic shipping bag and pounded the bag (and the amphora inside it) with a 10-pound lump hammer. Seven or eight whacks and the amphora was a pile of newly created sherds and dust. Part performance piece, more an illustration of the potentials one can explore by disarticulating an object from its archaeological status, the aim of the destruction was to investigate what an art/archaeology might enable. When they left the session, many members of the audience took one of the newly liberated sherds with them; I asked each sherd adopter to take their fragment on their travels, to work, on holiday, and then to report back with photographs and comments which could be posted on social media.

Though the pleasure to destroy is deeply ingrained in human nature, so is the pleasure to construct and to repair. According to Elizabeth Spelman (2002, 1), "the human being is a repairing animal . . . . *Homo sapiens* is also *Homo reparans*" and archaeological restoration and conservation are further proof of it. In fact, and somewhat ironically, by playfully "disarticulating an object from its archaeological status," Bailey further emphasizes the 'repairing' nature and goals of archaeological inquiry. Certainly, archaeology (and even more so archaeology outside-the-box), and the impetus to retrieve and to 'repair' is at the crux as well of my own performance, *The Wall that Gives/El muro que da*.

Since its inception in 2015, I too pick up 'sherds' (litter and small pieces of trash) from the floor, and "report back with photographs" posted on social media. Only this time, these photographs portray a 'repaired' and thus embellished version of the collected sherds, for I use pictures of debris and of garbage bins and dumpsters to make what I—or rather Filomena Cruz, my artistic alter ego—calls 'trash-collages.' This term coined by Filomena Cruz probably needs some explanation. First of all, its point of departure is 'small trash,' of the kind that routinely soils the pavement. Both my scholarly work and Filomena Cruz's art make a point of looking at urban refuse at its early stages, when it is still tiny and unassuming, and has yet to grow, leave town, and accumulate elsewhere. Trash as litter and as city-bound miniature is what intrigues us,[1] much more so than the monumentality of piled up garbage or the gigantism of faraway landfills. Thus what you will find in my art are flowers made of tiny pieces of scrap metal as part of Filomena Cruz's *Flora Inmortalis* series (Figure 7.1); beach trash turned into anthropomorphic creatures—Filomena Cruz calls this particular series *The Immortals*, as plastic never dies (Figure 7.2)—Martians made of bottle caps folded in half (Figure 7.3); dumpsters and garbage bins, empty or overflowing, brand new or rusty and covered in graffiti; and one particular trash can, so intensively blue and plasticky that it looks like a toy, showing up again and again in many of the art pieces (Figure 7.4).

Filomena Cruz is foremost a collagist, and a photographer only because she likes to cut and paste her own pictures of urban debris and use them as the prime material of her collages. Her working tools are quite straightforward: a phone with a camera, a color printer, a scanner, a pair of scissors, a glue stick, acrylic paints, and a rich supply in trash and goods retrieved from thrift stores. She is particularly fond of the whimsical variety of frames and platters one can find in second-hand shops, and often integrates them into her art, as the photographs in Figures 1–4 show. But mostly, Filomena Cruz's trash-collages are pasted on 10 × 10 centimeter (4 × 4 inch) tiles that then find refuge in an 18 × 18 centimeter (7 × 7 inch) niche carved into a wall in Venice, California (Figure 7.5). In the pages that follow, I will tell the story of *The Wall that Gives/El muro que da*, which is the story of an artistic performance, but also of a community spontaneously engaging in anonymous

Figure 7.1. *Flora Inmortalis*, Filomena Cruz, Venice, California (scrap metal, tiles, and a thrift store platter).

Figure 7.2. Two beach trash creatures from the series *The Immortals*, Filomena Cruz, Venice, California (made with trash from the beach).

Figure 7.4. *Trashscape (Venice Beach on a Thrift Store Platter)*, Filomena Cruz, Venice, California.

Figure 7.3. *Marsling and Mannequin: Impossible Love*, Filomena Cruz, Venice, California (a discarded bottle cap folded in half, the inner pocket of a suit found in a dumpster, and a thrift store mannequin, all on a tile).

Figure 7.5. *The Wall that Gives/El muro que da*, Filomena Cruz, Venice, California.

bartering and gift-giving and receiving practices. More importantly, it is a philosophical and anthropological reflection upon contemporary urban refuse as an empathy and solidarity-forging 'archaeological' artifact, and of what it means to be 'disposable' (be it an object or a living being) in the era of savage capitalism.

In 2015 I intervened a wall on Pacific Avenue (between Breeze Avenue and Brooks Court) in Venice, California, and created *The Wall that Gives/El muro que da*. It is a 27.5 ×1.7 meter (90 × 5.5 foot) gray wall with a small 18 × 18 centimeter (7 × 7 inch) niche in it, in the fashion of the niches inhabited by saints or the Virgin of Guadalupe one finds on the streets of Mexico and in the Latino neighborhoods of Los Angeles. The concept that informs my intervention is very simple and straightforward: if walls and borders separate, create or enhance rifts, and institutionalize violence, this particular wall I decided to transform from a hostile chronotopos into a 'friendly' one, one that unites, tears down barriers, and creates a sense of community and solidarity. Thus, for the last eight years, the wall says in bold letters "The Wall that Gives/ El muro que da," or in some of its iterations, "El muro que da/ The Wall that Gives" (Figure 7.6).

Every day I leave a 10 × 10 centimeter (4 × 4 inch) tile with one of my trash-collages pasted on it in that niche, and every day, somebody takes the tile and very often leaves something in return (Figure 7.7). These are only some of the many presents that the niche has housed so far: two bananas; a tightly folded black T-shirt; playing cards; a lollypop; an orange with the inscription in Spanish, "hecho en Venice;" five dollars under a stone (this has happened twice); quarters, nickels, and pennies; a miniature cactus on a clay pot with "love" written on it; a box with cough drops; cigarettes; a kiwifruit; a bag of nuts; a candy bar; a beer can; an apple; flowers; a cigarette case with marijuana leaves; a dreamcatcher; and a bag with a roll of toilet paper and a small bottle of hand sanitizer, an extremely generous gift in times of a pandemic.

I usually do not take any of these presents, but leave them for somebody else to enjoy, and with only one exception that I will discuss later, I do not know who takes and gives when

walking on the narrow sidewalk along *The Wall that Gives/El muro que da*. One day, though, I received the following email (Filomena Cruz's g-mail address <filomenecruz@gmail.com> is printed on the back of the tile):

> Hi there! This is out of the blue but I wanted to tell you thank you for something. You don't know me & I don't know you, but one day I was walking home down the street and wasn't having the best of days and came upon a hole in the wall. I saw your piece of fine art that captured my attention and it was the one that had trash cans on the beach with many colors in it on the tile piece [Figure 7.4]. I picked it out from the hole and thought "what is this?" Little did I know that, as my mind wandered into the art piece, I found myself no longer bothered by my 'bad' day. Your art had taken my mind off of something negative and turned it into a positive. How could trash cans be so awesomely artsy and cool?! I felt a bit hesitant to take it home with me, but I did. In return I left $5.00 under a rock in the hole that hopefully someone walking by in need would find it. Again, thank you. Keep up the beautiful work you do. It makes a difference. Best, Kyle.

It is important to note that *The Wall that Gives/El muro que da* has gone through many iterations, of which this article offers only some examples. The collaged tile-giving ritual remains steady, but the wall changes all the time. As happens with refreshingly free and 'unprotected' walls, they become urban canvasses where art is short-lived, and where muralists and graffiti artists fight their ephemeral fights (the graffiti in Los Angeles is briefly discussed by Susan Phillips in Chapter 17 of this volume). Armed with spray cans and taking advantage of the darkness and solitude of the night, the latter hurriedly tag and 'bomb' the wall and its murals. Interestingly, since I intervened the wall in 2015 and practiced a tile-collage–giving niche in it, tags on the wall have diminished but not disappeared by any measure. Also, taggers have become more respectful, at least for a while. When they spray their tags on a pristine wall they make sure at first to paint around or between the letters that read "The Wall that Gives/El muro que da."

Figure 7.6. Different iterations of *The Wall that Gives/El muro que da*, Filomena Cruz, Venice, California.

Figure 7.7. *The Wall that Gives/El muro que da*, Filomena Cruz, Venice, California (presents of Venice locals).

With time, however, graffiti artists become bolder: rival gangs compete in aggressive tagging, which often results in the erasing and mutilating of the letters. And I do not mind, for as I like to say, "A wall that gives is a wall that lives," and vice versa, and there is no life without constant transformation: Muralists and graffiti artists are both welcomed.

THE WALL THAT GIVES/EL MURO QUE DA

At its inception, *The Wall that Gives/El muro que da* only gave away tiles with Filomena Cruz's trash-collages on them, but very soon the whole wall became a gift, in the sense that I gladly agreed to 'give' it to local muralists who approached me and asked me if they could cover it with their art. Art is free, and I will never impose a style or a theme, but there is one requisite, namely, that artists write "The Wall that Gives/El muro que da" into their murals. That is precisely what Venice muralist Jules Muck did (Figure 7.8), when she decided to intervene the wall with the help of a group of young men who were struggling with addiction. The wall thus became the site of an art therapy session, but it was not the first time that the renowned Venice artist had embellished it with her art. When I moved to Venice in 2010, the long wall on Pacific Avenue that stretches from Brooks Court to Breeze Avenue was the canvas to her extensive mural[2] "Venice Rebirth Wall: A Mural dedicated to the People of Venice, CA," a then "ongoing mural project . . . that celebrated Venice residents with huge black and white portraits on multicolored backgrounds."

As expected, the mural never stayed 'quiet.' The loud voices and colors of graffiti would continuously change its appearance, and sometimes leave an invasive imprint on cheeks and foreheads. Most of the time, however, graffiti would remain at the fringes, and 'politely' fill out the spaces between the faces, in the same way it remains polite now for a while, and respects the letters that read "The Wall that Gives/El muro que da." One day, however, a neighbor woke me up with the horrifying news that somebody had taken advantage of the dark of the

Figure 7.9. *The Wall that Gives/El muro que da*, Filomena Cruz, Venice, California, with an unfinished "Black Lives Matter" mural created by the Mural Team of Santa Monica High School, 2020.

night to savagely disfigure the faces of the mural by spraying thick, black swastikas on them: hatred and antisemitism had destroyed Muck's mural.

For a couple of years, the wall was just a gray surface, routinely restored back to its dull monotony by a municipal employee in charge of covering up graffiti. As mentioned above, once I started my intervention, the wall has kept evolving, always in unexpected ways: first, local muralists unknown to me approached me and I gave them permission to embellish the wall with their ephemeral creations; then Jules Muck came with her artists-in-recovery team; then students from Santa Monica High School put up a mural that the Covid-19 pandemic left unfinished (Figure 7.9). I still call *The Wall that Gives/El muro que da* a wall, but more and more I think of it as a powerful mirror that, not unlike trash, reflects reality and showcases the imprint human emotions and behaviors leave on it.

When the pandemic struck, a mural could not move beyond its first stages and, for the first time, graffiti did not intervene the wall. But the wall kept 'doing' and reacting, this time by offering gifts on various instances that Covid-19 had made invaluable and scarce: toilet paper, hand sanitizer, and

Figure 7.10. *Trashscape during the Pandemic*, Series *The Immortals*, Filomena Cruz, Venice, California.

masks. Filomena Cruz's trash-collages, on the other hand, also engaged with the global health crisis: the anthropomorphized trash creatures that repeatedly appear in her tiles—the Martian made from a bottle cap bent folded in half; the discarded plastic mesh (yet another 'immortal' found on the beach)—served the purpose of promoting safe physical distancing and the use of masks (Figures 7.10 and 7.11). *The Wall that Gives/El muro que da* did not remain silent or aloof either when police savagely killed George Floyd. The backdrop to many recent

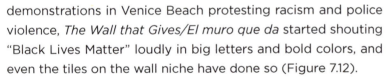

Figure 7.11. *Six Feet Apart (Pandemic)*, Filomena Cruz, Venice, California.

Figure 7.12. *The Yellow Dumpster*, with "Black Lives Matter" written on it, Filomena Cruz, Venice, California.

demonstrations in Venice Beach protesting racism and police violence, *The Wall that Gives/El muro que da* started shouting "Black Lives Matter" loudly in big letters and bold colors, and even the tiles on the wall niche have done so (Figure 7.12).

Finally, in June 2020, poet and teaching artist Natalie Patterson and artist and muralist Allison Kunath, founders of *A Love Language Project,*[3] which "aims to amplify black voices and encourage meaningful conversation around the liberation of black lives . . . by transforming boarded up store fronts and walls into protest messages in Los Angeles," accepted the gift of *The Wall that Gives/El muro que da*, and graced it with the following words from bell hooks (Gloria Jean Watkins): "For me, forgiveness and compassion are always linked: how do we hold people accountable for wrongdoing and yet at the same

time remain in touch with their humanity enough to believe in their capacity to be transformed?" (Figure 7.13).

The words of African-American writer, feminist, and activist bell hooks imprinted on *The Wall that Gives/El muro que da* are particularly fitting, because "transformation" and the "capacity to be transformed" are what define the nature not only of the wall but also of the artifacts and materials that inspire Filomena Cruz's tile art and trash-collages. First of all, transformation happens through dialogue, and the collages printed on tiles left in the niche constantly entertain a vivid visual conversation with what other artists write or paint on *The Wall that Gives/El muro que da.* For one, Filomena Cruz made sure that bell hook's quote be part of one of her collages, and that it be yet another gift of the wall (Figure 7.14).

Figure 7.13. Intervention of *The Wall that Gives/El muro que da* by *A Love Language Project*.

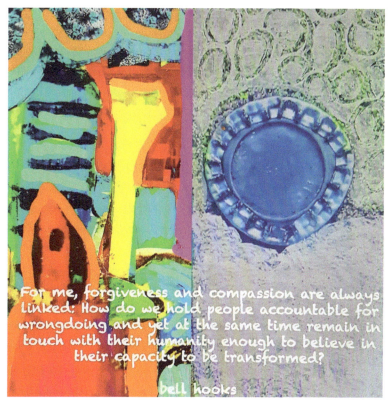

Figure 7.14. *The Raising Trash*, with a quote of bell hooks (Gloria Jean Watkins), Filomena Cruz, Venice, California.

I did something similar when I first wrote "Black Lives Matter" on the wall and then replicated the message in my tiles. In fact, the wall–tile dialog is a recurrent phenomenon that started right after I initiated my wall installation. Anonymous art was quick to engage with the wall and its tile-giving niche. During the first week, somebody painted a scary clown close to the niche, and the next day, yet another artist had corrected the clown's sinister rictus, and used blue ink to turn it into a smile (Figure 7.15). Filomena Cruz added her voice to the visual dialogue by taking a picture of the clown, and integrating it into one of her collages. 'Her' clown was gone in a couple of hours, whereas the intervened original remained on the wall for roughly three weeks.

Figure 7.15. *Clown Integrated*, Filomena Cruz, Venice, California.

TALKING TRASH

It is important to note that the intense and longstanding visual dialogue and art happening on the grainy surface of a wall in Venice, California has its origin in the very simple spatial strategy of 'elevating' and 'exhibiting' trash. As I have extensively argued in my recent book *Talking Trash: Cultural Uses of Waste*,[4] and in my adaptation and translation of it into Spanish, *Basura: Usos culturales de los desechos*,[5] what intrigues me is not the monumentality of landfills, but the smallness of urban refuse, and what I like to call the 'invisible pervasiveness' of litter. Cigarette butts, crumpled receipts, dirty Kleenex, lately also masks and latex gloves—cast-offs of the Covid-19 pandemic—soil the pavement and often serendipitously mix with dried leaves and small branches, the detritus of nature. Litter is everywhere, but it is also chronically invisible. Passersby surely see the dirt, and complain about it when it becomes too much, but they pay little or no attention to the distinctiveness of discarded artifacts. William Rathje, the founder of 'Garbology' as a new branch of archaeology,[6] certainly saw the archaeological and anthropological relevance of trash. But whereas his choice and method were to dig deep into the stratified accumulation of landfills, I decided to pay close attention to litter that remains on the surface, with one goal in mind, namely, to replace horizontal invisibility with vertical resignification. In other words, I was intrigued by what happens when one picks up trash from the streets, rescues it from oblivion and disdain through art, and proudly displays it on a wall.

As you may have noticed, the central image on Filomena Cruz's tile in Figure 7.14 is a flattened bottle cap. I found it on the pavement, took a picture of it, and made it play the role of the sun or the moon in my collages. In other words, I 'elevate' trash, both literally and figuratively, let it go up on a wall, and up into the skies, and by doing so, I restore its lost value and make it desirable again. Desire is important here, because trash is precisely that what one does not want or desire any more. The renewal of desire has the ability to 'untrash' the discarded. More importantly though, the process of 'untrashing' and desiring again forces us to think hard about why it is that we 'trash' and discard in the first place; why we do so with such impulsive eagerness; and why is it that we are so skilled at discarding not only 'things' but also the living. As I teach my students, slowing one's pace and carefully canvassing the ground for the discarded not only activates the intellect, it directly appeals to our emotions. Being able suddenly to 'see' (and thus desire) trash is an emotive act that can quickly evolve into an ethical imperative. When we train ourselves to really 'see' and reflect upon discarded objects, we are learning not to ignore the criminal easiness with which our contemporary urban world discards and tosses out human beings.[7]

The motivation behind creating *The Wall that Gives/El muro que da* was, and is, trash. It was born out of the pressing need to elevate and 'detrash' the discarded by making collages with pictures of litter and trash containers. I do not do archaeological excavations *sensu strictu*, but I certainly search for material remnants and castoffs. I restore and conserve them via art, and I also curate them and exhibit them in a niche—trash in a box—on my wall. More than as an artist, Filomena Cruz sees herself as an archaeologist of the contemporary, a restaurateur, and a curator, but also as a facilitator of dialogue, solidarity, and community engagement. In fact, the simple operation of 'verticalizing' trash and exhibiting it in a tightly fitting niche, as if it were a precious jewel in its jewelry box or a museum piece, has changed the way Venice locals interact with the wall. For one, they notice it, instead of ignoring it, and they expect something from it. It elicits reactions and triggers desire, sometimes satisfied (when the tile is still in its niche, ready to be taken), sometimes not (I only leave a tile per day, and it rarely lasts more than four hours). It also invites play (for to see if the tile is still in its niche turns into a game).

Indeed, play and playfulness, and the freedom that comes with them, are very important components of my urban intervention and are closely tied to the imperative of avoiding any type of surveillance. In stark and deliberate contrast to the escalation of control and surveillance that is the landmark of the border between Mexico and the United States, and the wall along it under President Donald Trump, *The Wall that Gives/ El muro que da* operates without supervision. To this day, I do not know the names of the passersby who take the tiles and leave presents in return, and I doubt very much that locals know the true identity that hides behind the pseudonym of Filomena Cruz. Furthermore, of the many people, presumably, who have retrieved collaged tiles from the wall, I have only 'caught' one tile-taker *in flagrante delicto*, . . . on several occasions! This is a funny story, but also a very meaningful one, as it eloquently speaks to the rich versatility of the wall and its penchant for the unexpected. Here it goes. Two years ago, I was casually looking through the kitchen window while washing the dishes, when I saw the tourist double-decker bus that routinely drives down Pacific Avenue abruptly stop in front of my house. The automatic doors opened, and a man rushed out, quickly grabbed the tile from the wall, and jumped back on the bus. I witnessed the same occurrence a number of times, and on one occasion I was able to rush out of my home and talk to the recidivist tile lover. He happened to be the driver and tourist guide, and when I asked him if *The Wall that Gives/El muro que da* and its tiles had now become a new tourist attraction, he responded: "That too, but mostly I am using your tiles to retile my bathroom."

In his concise but perceptive volume *Callous Objects: Design against the Homeless*, Robert Rosenberger (2017) reflects upon the "non-innocence of technology," in Donna Haraway's words,[8] and refers to the public-space bench as a "straightforward example of a low-tech device,"[9] that "just like any technology, is multistable."[10] Its "dominant stability," the author contends, is "the purpose for which it was designed, manufactured, purchased, and installed in a public area: it provides a space to sit."[11] The "alternate stability" of a public-space bench, however, is "its potential use as a bed, and in particular its pervasive use for just this purpose by unhoused people."[12] And here is where society and technology turn urban furniture into "callous objects" that promote hostility instead of hospitality. As Rosenberger explains, it is not uncommon—in fact, it is increasingly frequent—to find public-space benches fitted with design features that discourage and prohibit their use as beds. Popular options include vertical partitions that separate each sitting space and armrests that similarly divide up the surface of the bench. The websites of bench manufacturers rarely advertise the fact that these designs are specifically intended to discourage sleeping, although on occasion such partitions and armrests are referred to as "antiloitering" features.[13]

Benches are hospitable artifacts that have evolved into hostile ones, no longer willing to offer a place to rest to the destitute. Their "alternate stability" (to function as beds) has been obliterated, and what prevails instead in contemporary urban benches is their "dominant stability" (that is, to provide a space to sit, but never to lie down). If we apply Rosenberger's categorization to walls, then the immediate implication would be that the "dominant stability" of walls as low-tech devices is to separate and divide. Unlike benches, walls are hostile from the get-go, and it is difficult to imagine friendlier "alternative stabilities" for them. As I have shown in this chapter, the purpose of my intervened wall is precisely to become an empathy-driven generator and repository of alternative uses or "stabilities" that fight hostility with hospitality and community-building solidarity.

The Wall that Gives/El muro que da does not reject the castoff, quite the contrary, it carefully rescues and treasures what people deem disposable. Lovingly displayed on a niche, 'trash' (as *pars pro toto* for all creatures discarded) regains visibility and desirability, and its uses (and those of the wall that treasures and 'elevates' it) multiply. For one, the wall relinquishes its opaque surface, and becomes a mirror that reflects contemporary developments, such as the Covid-19 pandemic and the massive protests against racism and police violence. Moreover, it reflects not only historical events but emotions and positive reactions. After retrieving the tile from its protective niche or box, locals reciprocate with toilet paper and hand sanitizers; with a colorful painted stone that reads "Value People of Color" on one side, and "We Stand Together" on the other; and with a miniature cactus with "Love" written on its tiny clay pot.

THE MATTRESS THAT GIVES

Since I intervened the wall, it has intensified its role as a free canvas to numerous Venice street muralists whose pieces creatively clash and compete with graffiti and tagging. Artists request my wall for their art, be it murals or, lately, poetry and words promoting social and racial justice, and journalists and filmmakers have portrayed it in its various iterations and meanings. *The Wall that Gives/El muro que da* has even served as art therapy to struggling addicts under the artistic guidance of renowned Venice muralist Jules Muck, and has provided a steady supply of tiles to a double-decker tourist bus driver who is remodeling his bathroom. More recently, I got a call from a young muralist whose brother is planning a big surprise and wants to use the wall to propose marriage to his girlfriend. Finally, and this happened just a week ago, a mattress showed up miraculously, leaning against *The Wall That Gives/El muro que da*, and roughly two hours into my discovery, Filomena Cruz made it into *The Mattress that Gives* (Figure 7.16).

If there is an artifact pregnant with life (and death), that artifact is a used mattress. We are born on it, spend one third of our lives in it, make love on it, give birth on it, and die on it. And, "we jump on it and crawl on it. We cuddle on it and kick on it. We pinch on it and caress on it. We bite, lick, and turn. And

Figure 7.16. *The Mattress that Gives*, artistic intervention, Filomena Cruz, Venice, California.

mostly: we dream and FLY on it," my friend Verónica Grossi aptly added. One could certainly argue that no human-made object is more human, and more drenched in and burdened with our organic and emotive existence than a mattress. Like the litter Filomena Cruz anthropomorphizes, photographs, collages, and pastes onto tiles, this discarded mattress too had relinquished horizontality (as its "dominant stability") in favor of verticality (as its "alternate stability"). It is now a sizable piece of humanity-laden trash standing tall and crying out to the world, "why are you throwing me out?" Its anguished question is no different from the question posed by the 'small' trash portrayed on the tiles, only more vociferous because it comes from a far bigger creature.

In sum, *The Mattress that Gives*, yet another unwanted artifact, adds redundancy to *The Wall that Gives/El muro que da* and its niched collection of urban refuse, but more importantly, it further confirms that walls do not need to be hardened by hostility. Humanized by the art of giving, they too can be mattress-soft and hospitable.

NOTES

1   Bennett 2010, Stewart 1993, Thill 2015.
2   https://www.behance.net/gallery/2025099/Venice-Rebirth-Wall
     (accessed 31 August 2020).
3   https://www.alovelanguageproject.com (accessed 31 August 2020).
4   Zubiaurre 2019.
5   Zubiaurre 2021.
6   Rathje and Murphy 2001.
7   Bauman 2003.
8   Rosenberger 2017, xii.
9   Rosenberger 2017, 1.
10   Rosenberger 2017, 7.
11   Rosenberger 2017, 7.
12   Rosenberger 2017, 7.
13   Rosenberger 2017, 11.

BIBLIOGRAPHY

Bauman, Zygmunt (2003), *Wasted Lives: Modernity and Its Outcasts,* London (Polity).

Bennett, Jane (2010), *Vibrant Matter: A Political Ecology of Things,* Durham and London (Duke University Press).

Rathje, William and Cullen Murphy (2001), *Rubbish! The Archaeology of Garbage,* Tucson (University of Arizona Press).

Rosenberger, Robert (2017), *Callous Objects: Designs against the Homeless,* Minneapolis (University of Minnesota Press).

Spelman, Elizabeth V. (2002), *Repair: The Impulse to Restore in a Fragile World,* Boston (Beacon Press).

Stewart, Susan (1993), *On Longing: Narratives of the Miniature, the Gigantic, the Souvenir, the Collection,* Durham and London (Duke University Press).

Thill, Brian (2015), *Waste,* New York (Bloomsbury).

Zubiaurre, Maite (2019), *Talking Trash: Cultural Uses of Waste,* Nashville (Vanderbilt University Press).

——— (2021) *Basura: Usos culturales de los desechos*, Madrid (Cátedra). [In Spanish]

6

PORTRAITS OF ANCIENT LINEN

GAIL ROTHSCHILD

FRAGMENT OF ANCIENT LINEN, 2012

The inspiration for this painting is a 10 centimeter (4 inch) square snippet of linen on display in the Egyptian Wing at the Metropolitan Museum of Art (New York) and described as a "sample of cloth from the burial chamber of Pharaoh Unis c. 2353–2323 BCE." My intention with the *Portraits of Ancient Linen* project is to elevate the humblest of ancient objects into portrait-worthy subjects. As this small piece of reddish cloth grew in my imagination, I was reminded of the glowing rectangles in Mark Rothko's painting *Red and Brown* (1957). The square format in painting only became prevalent in the latter half of the twentieth century. The square also stands for the museum vitrine in which the decay of the textile is arrested and in which it is preserved and displayed. A newly woven piece of linen may seem static as warp and weft threads are held in the tension of a Cartesian grid, but over the course of 4,300 years even the strongest fibers pull apart. I paint the process of unraveling as alive and dynamic. In this early painting in the series, I was less concerned with exploring the actual stitches than with creating a roiling field through active black brushstrokes covered with layer upon layer of red, brown, and ocher glazes.

LOIN CLOTH OF THE ARCHITECT KHA (I), 2013

When I came upon the image of bleached linen triangles in a book on ancient Egyptian textiles, the first thing that came to mind was a pyramid. So, when I learned that they were loincloths belonging to Kha, the chief architect of Pharaoh Amenhotep III (c. 1390–1353 BCE), I was hooked. As I painted this portrait of ancient underwear, with the suggestion of the vulnerable body parts it protected 3,300 years ago, I pondered the life of this quotidian piece of linen—that outlasted its owner by millennia—and was now displayed in a state-of-the-art museum. What would Kha say? What would his wife, Merit, say? On the website of Museo Egizio in Turin, Italy— where all fifty of the architect's loincloths are housed—I saw the variety of shapes

Figure 6.1. *Fragment of Ancient Linen*, 2012. Acrylic on canvas, 152.5 × 152.5 cm. (60 × 60 inches). *Photograph by Sam Monaco.*

Figure 6.2. *Loin Cloth of the Architect Kha (I)*, 2013. Acrylic on linen, 172.8 × 185.5 cm. (68 × 73 inches). *Photograph by Sam Monaco.*

and imagined a series of large paintings. This is the first of three paintings and one drawing that I have completed so far. There is a pending collaboration that would include exhibiting the loincloths alongside my portraits of them.

DEAD SEA SCROLL LINEN (III), 2014

While only some of the linen fragments dating from the early Roman Period and discovered at Qumran Cave in Nahal Qidron, in the Judea Desert, were actual wrappings for sacred texts, all of these much-decayed textiles suggest texts to me. Each time I looked at the unraveling cloth, I seemed to find new and evocative images of faces and dragons combining to

form new narratives. Leonardo da Vinci (*Treatise on Painting*, Chapter 163) maintained that artists should "look upon an old wall covered with dirt, or the odd appearance of some streaked stones, [where] you may discover several things like landscapes, battles, clouds, uncommon attitudes, humorous faces, draperies, etc. Out of this confused mass of objects, the mind will be furnished with an abundance of designs and subjects perfectly new." Fragments like this one offer a perfect opportunity for the contemplation Leonardo recommended. One elderly gentleman spent a long evening in my studio chuckling over "the chicken" in this painting. I will only admit to a vague suggestion of the Uffington White Horse from the chalk hills of Oxfordshire, England, meets the Serpent Mound of Chillicothe, Ohio. This is one of the first paintings where I used the intense

Figure 6.4. *Fayum Neolithic Linen*, 2014. Acrylic on linen 134.8 × 167.8 cm. (53 × 66 inches). *Photograph by Sam Monaco.*

FAYUM NEOLITHIC LINEN, 2014

Six years after painting this image, I finally got to see this iconic little scrap of linen—the oldest from ancient Egypt—in the wonderfully odd Petrie Museum in London. I had first seen a photograph of it in Elizabeth Barber's (1991) book *Prehistoric Textiles,* and this is the image that inspired my *Portraits of Ancient Linen* series. Represented at nearly the monumental scale of 1950s abstract expressionist painting, the frayed linen appears as a map-like landscape. Each mark of paint both makes and unmakes an image of fabric. The painting functions as a meeting of nature and culture. Through an arduous process the flax plant is transformed into the architectural grid of textile. Over millennia this fragmentary fabric is returning to its biological origins, what looks like a coastline decays and unravels with time. This painting is testament to the paradox, what is interwoven will ultimately unravel, and that which grows will inevitably decay.

Figure 6.3. *Dead Sea Scroll Linen (III)*, 2014. Acrylic on linen, 185.5 × 147.5 cm. (73 × 58 inches). *Photograph by Sam Monaco.*

shadows formed by the raking light of museum exhibitions. This increases the physicality and tactility of the painting. I loaded the brush with thicker paint and allowed the mark to suggest an equivalence with the thread represented.

TEMPLE SCROLL WRAPPER (V), 2015

I was drawn to the apparent simplicity of the plain weave in this fragment of linen from Qumran Cave 1 in Palestine, which dates from between the first century BCE and the first century CE. As with many of these earlier paintings, my whole relationship to the object was through photographs. I had to imagine the scale of an approximately 23 × 33 centimeter (9 × 13 inch) fragment as the computer screen is such a great equalizer. The fabric is cut along three sides, rolled and over-sewn with a single thread; the fourth edge has a corded starting border in twining technique, followed by a woven strip and an open unwoven space. It was found folded into a pad and was probably used as packing material for discarded scrolls. The archipelago of holes across the rectangular piece interested me as did the twined edge that looked like a field of anthropomorphic dancing grasses. I painted in a very traditional technique on a colored ground and overpainted the surface lines with many layers of glazes. The irony is never lost on me that I am representing the ravages of time on organic material using the most contemporary of acrylic paints colored with synthetic pigments.

GOAT BOY, 2018

I had been tempted to work from figurative tapestry-weaves, but had resisted for years in lieu of letting the object and its decay be the subject of the painting. But when I was invited to create a series of paintings inspired by the Rose Choron collection of Late Antique textiles to be exhibited along with the original artifacts themselves, I dove right in. My first reaction was how modern they looked. The strong black outline was a huge leap from the softly rendered form of Roman classical imagery. The shepherd's face seemed to have the cubist simultaneity of frontal and profile views. The strong outline of his leg looked straight out of the work of Henri Matisse. No surprise, I learned, because Matisse, along with many other twentieth-century artists, collected and was inspired by these tiny, colorful, and well-preserved wool tapestries of the first millennium. As I studied the jewel-like roundel, I wondered about the weaver who made it. To what extent did he or she work from a cartoon and how much was improvised. Most importantly, I wonder how a weaver nearly two thousand years ago could have anticipated Pac-Man?

Figure 6.6. *Goat Boy*, 2018. Acrylic on canvas, 168 × 109.5 cm. (66 × 43 inches). *Photograph by Sam Monaco.*

Figure 6.7. *Medusa*, 2018. Acrylic on canvas, 103 × 116 cm. (40.5 × 45.5 inches). *Photograph by Sam Monaco.*

MEDUSA, 2018

The fragment of textile from the Rose Choron collection that inspired this painting was so tiny that I was able to balloon each stitch into a really huge scale. The unraveling of the tightly packed weft stitches form tunnels from which emerge the actively unwinding warp stitches. The magnification allowed me to represent the muscularity of the threads. As they became more and more active, I imagined the living snakes of Medusa's hair. The tiny lips seemed parted in the silent scream of the famous painting by Edvard Munch. *Medusa* currently resides with an art historian, one of many different scholars who have generously balanced my creative fantasies with facts. I am pleased to report that so far she has not turned to stone.

Figure 6.8. *Head of a Dancer*, 2019. Acrylic on canvas, 170 × 109.5 cm. (67 × 43 inches). *Photograph by Sam Monaco.*

HEAD OF A DANCER, 2019

A ballet choreographer friend instigated the search for an image of a dancer. When I found Head of a Dancer on the website of Musée du Louvre in Paris, France, I did not yet know how famous this fragment was. I was drawn to the juxtaposition of the modern-seeming dark outline on the arm and gesturing hand with the careful classical rendering of the face and shoulder muscle. My challenge was to recreate on a two-dimensional canvas surface the three-dimensionality of a tapestry fragment with all the ridges and furrows formed by the dense rows of weft stitches. This landscape of tightly packed weft yarns forms the representation of the dancer's face, where different colors of wool fool the eye into seeing a rounded form. Very meta. Since the Renaissance, artists have painted the ruins of ancient civilizations. Claude Lorrain, Giovanni Piranesi, and William Turner all depicted crumbling architecture to point to the vulnerability of even the most permanent stone monuments. I reference this long-standing tradition of painting the ruins of the past, but with an important difference. Textiles were never meant to last through the ages. When I paint a portrait of an ancient linen, I am celebrating the wonder that something so old, so fragile, and so close to our own bodies actually did survive.

FIGURE IN ARCADE (II), 2019

This is one of a suite of five paintings titled *The Arcade Project*. The series is named for Walter Benjamin's (1986) study of nineteenth-century Parisian architecture and urbanity. The inspiration is a magnificent piece of domestic tapestry I first laid eyes on in the Institute for the Study of the Ancient World at New York University. It blew my mind. I could not take my eyes off the bright color and the subtle, very unclassical outlining. The Matisse-like zigzags on the garments of the figure, depicted in wool tapestry-weave, represent the sheen of luxurious imported silk. I wonder whether the arcade niches might stand for a kind of Memory Theater. Egypt in the mid-first

millennium was in the throes of a creative intermingling of Hellenic and Persian, Christian and Pagan imagery. By presenting small domestic figures at heroic scale, these paintings blow up the demotion of textiles as 'lowly women's work' and 'mere craft.' Avidly collected in the late nineteenth and early twentieth centuries, Late Antique textiles are slowly re-emerging from several generations of neglect. I hope that the Brooklyn Museum (New York) will once again exhibit this treasure of its collection, perhaps with *The Arcade Project* alongside it.

HEAD CLOTH OF TUTANKHAMUN (VI), 2020

No, there were not six head cloths found in the embalming cache associated with the New Kingdom pharaoh Tutankhamun (c. 1336–1327 BCE). But since I first saw this delicate and evocative child's head cloth (40 × 53 cm.; 15.8 × 20.9 inches) in Gallery 122 at the Metropolitan Museum of Art, I have been inspired to create ten different paintings and drawings. The subject, dyed with indigo, is quite small and may have belonged to Tutankhamun when he was a child. Whether it was worn by Tutankhamun or not, examples of dyed linen from ancient Egypt are extremely rare, making this a very precious object. This most recent portrait is by far the largest and was instigated by an invitation to present at a conference called *The Colour Blue in Ancient Egypt and Sudan.* The overall shape of the head cloth suggests to me a vessel, like one of the small round boats so common in the ancient Near East that may also have

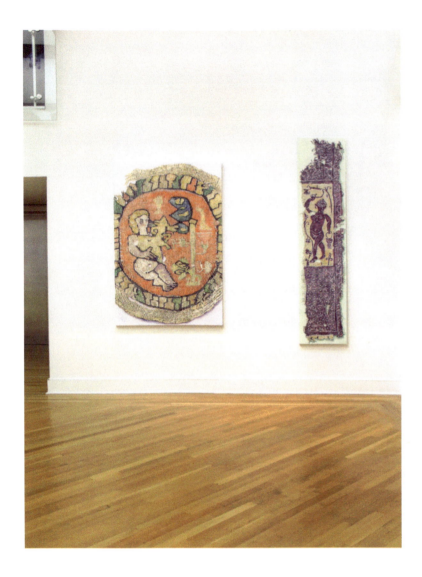

Figure 6.11. Installation view of *Goat Boy* and *Caryatid* at the Godwin-Ternbach Museum of Queens College, City University of New York. *Photograph by Sam Monaco.*

Figure 6.12. Installation view of *Medusa* at the Godwin-Ternbach Museum of Queens College, City University of New York. *Photograph by Sam Monaco.*

evidence of attempts to stop the inevitable decay of time. My painting speaks of its—and our—fragility, materiality and transience. I often think about the *Portraits of Ancient Linen* in the tradition of vanitas paintings, reminders of our mortality.

INSTALLATION VIEWS AT THE GODWIN-TERNBACH MUSEUM OF QUEENS COLLEGE, 2018–19

At the Godwin-Ternbach Museum (Queens College, City University of New York) I was given the opportunity over the course of a year to look closely and repeatedly at actual textiles from their newly acquired Rose Choron collection. Under a magnifying glass, what had first looked to me like embroidery I learned was the miniature high-wire act of supplemental weft technique. It demanded from me a response of delicate calligraphic brushwork. I looked at the clavus that had once decorated a tunic in first millennium CE Egypt and imagined the Dionysian hermaphrodite hefting a sickle to harvest grapes

navigated the River Nile.[1] The unraveling indigo-dyed threads become for me the waters of this great river. Flax, unlike cotton, is not easy to make into thread but cloth that is made from it is very strong and resists decay. In the dry desert of Egypt, linen has a particularly long life. But time and permanence are relative things. This object shows layers of repair over the ages, magnified to architectural scale. In the column-like painting that developed, the little dancing figure became Caryatid. Over the course of a year's interaction with students, art historians, and textile conservators, I created five paintings that were exhibited alongside the objects that inspired them. The subjects of all these paintings are archaeological fragments of textile from the first millennium CE that have a long history: created to decorate the tunics of the upper class, forgotten and then repurposed in burials; unearthed in the nineteenth century and cut out of the garments so that they could easily be sold as colorful knick-knacks; they have only recently been elevated, catalogued, conserved and displayed as artifacts. This project paved the way for other such collaborations, including the current series of nine paintings created for the 2022 exhibition at the Bode Museum (Berlin). The inspiration may be ancient, but these large acrylic paintings on unframed canvases—a very contemporary look—are displayed on the white-painted walls of a present-day art museum. I was gratified to discover that my paintings offered visitors to the museum access to the original textiles with which I had fallen in love.

NOTE

1   Casson 1995, 11–22, 340–60.

BIBLIOGRAPHY

Barber, Elizabeth W. (1991), *Prehistoric Textiles: The Development of Cloth in the Neolithic and Bronze Ages, with Special Reference to the Aegean*, Princeton (Princeton University Press).

Benjamin, Walter (1986), *Reflections: Essays, Aphorisms, Autobiographical Writings*, Schocken (New York, translations by Edmund Jephcott, edited by Peter Demetz).

Casson, Lionel (1995), *Ships and Seamanship in the Ancient World*, Baltimore and London (Johns Hopkins University Press, updated edition of the 1971 original).

ABANDONED PLACES AND *NO MAN'S LAND*

HENK VAN RENSBERGEN

THE DENTIST'S CHAIR (DETROIT)

Gaining access to Broderick Tower in downtown Detroit was not easy. Although the city center was relatively abandoned, there were too many folks in the streets to fumble random doors. However, I was lucky as there were some workmen busy on the ground floor and I managed to slip unseen into a side entrance. The high-rises from the 1920s are tall and narrow, almost claustrophobic. The first few floors were not very interesting, but the higher levels used to house offices of optometrists and dentists. It seemed that one day they simply left, without tidying up or even worrying about their archives. I leafed through the patient files, looking for Dutch names, as there used to be a large Flemish community in Detroit. Several members of the community indeed appeared to have been patients of this dentist. Who knows how many of these once sat and suffered in the now dilapidated chair of which I took this picture.[1]

Figure 5.1. The Dentist's Chair (Detroit).

Figure 5.2. Biblioteca (Italy).

Figure 5.3. Dome Houses (Florida).

BIBLIOTECA (ITALY)

A magic castle in northern Italy. Earthquakes, rain, and wind caused parts of its roof and ceilings to collapse. A building with a chunk chewed away resembles an old-fashioned peep-box, or the set of a soap opera, which allows cameras to move freely between different rooms through the openings in the walls and ceilings. At a single glance you can see the wallpaper of three floors. This tells a story about the people who once lived here. These impressions are the puzzle pieces with which I try to create an image of what this place once looked like. Meanwhile it is another puzzle to make my way safely around this building with its blocked corridors and collapsed staircases. It makes me completely forget the hectic world outside.

DOME HOUSES (FLORIDA)

These remarkable concrete dome houses once stood on the private beach of an island owned by a millionaire. Now everything has transformed into a mangrove forest, the beach has been washed away by numerous hurricanes, and the houses are halfway submerged in the ocean. I spent a night on this island, in a little tent, in order to capture this image in the cold light of the morning twilight, well before the sun rose above the horizon. This place has lost none of its magic.

STP 671 (FRANCE)

A beach with dogs. No owners, in their stead the remains of concrete bunkers (called *Stützpunkten* or Stp. in German). This beach in Picardy, in northern France, has appeared like this for millennia. If we could watch history in a time lapse, we would see rolling waves for minutes, with the sea advancing and receding with the rhythm of the tides. Suddenly

Figure 5.4. STP 671 (France).

pedestrians would appear on the beach, walking their dogs. Then the war comes and the bunkers appear. After the war the bunkers remain and the pedestrians return with their dogs. As humanity comes to an end the bunkers will still be there. In my imaginary future world of *No Man's Land* the dogs keep walking on the beach, maybe out of habit? They do not have any reason to be there and their offspring, which have never even known humans, even less.

MADAME DELVAUX

I created the series *No Man's Land* in an effort to create an imaginary world in which humanity has gone extinct and animals inhabit our now empty buildings.[2] This was not meant to be a scholarly thought experiment, but rather an artistic enterprise. I did, however, manipulate my images to make them as realistic as possible. The animals somehow acquired human properties when placed inside the buildings. I gave them human names to amplify the anthropomorphic character of my narrative even more, while Madame Delvaux adds a fair amount of Belgian surrealism to it.

INNOCENTIUS

In reality, Innocentius was a little pig at a farm in the village. Pigs are precious to behold: they are lively, inquisitive, and funny. Before taking any photographs of animals for the *No Man's Land* series, I observed the light and perspective of the interior of the building in which the animal was to be placed. I captured at least a thousand images of pigs, of which less than a handful proved to have all the properties necessary to be used in the ruins of this church. Once placed inside, the pig suddenly acquired the stance of a philosopher wondering what in God's name humans have done to the world.[3]

Figure 5.5. Madame Delvaux.

Figure 5.6. Innocentius.

NOTES

1   van Rensbergen 2019; see also http://www.henkvanrensbergen.com
     (accessed 29 February 2020).
2   van Rensbergen 2017.
3   Farrier 2020.

BIBLIOGRAPHY

Farrier, David (2020), *Footprints: In Search of Future Fossils,* New
     York (Farrar, Straus and Giroux).
van Rensbergen, Henk (2017), *No Man's Land,* Tielt (Uitgeverij
     Lannoo Groep, with a preface by Desmond Morris).
—— (2019), *Abandoned Places,* Tielt (Uitgeverij Lannoo Groep,
     revised and expanded version of the 2016 original).

ALL OBJECTS HAVE BEEN CONTEMPORARY

AN ARCHAEOLOGY OF US

ENRICO FERRARIS

I (the pharaoh) said to her: "Why have you stopped rowing?"
She said to me: "Because the pendant of new turquoise fell into the water."
I said to her: "Row! I shall replace it for you!"
She said to me: "I prefer my thing to one like it."
(From *Papyrus Westcar, P. Berlin 3033,* translated by Miriam Lichtheim, 1973, p. 217.)

In 2014, while my colleagues and I were doing research for the current permanent exhibition in Museo Egizio (Turin, Italy), I was genuinely inspired by the following reflection by Egyptologist Sergio Donadoni about the nature of museums: "A museum that rethinks itself thereby merely pays homage to its nature and function. The objects that constitute it and that gain a well-defined quality and significance from the fact of being preserved in it, compared to those that are still in use or forgotten and dispersed, are arranged to converse with the visitor according to often implicit programs, which the museum suggests, or allows. It is thus well within the order of things that the maturation and variation of cultural experience in the flow of time compel one to rethink the hierarchy of values and meaning of what apparently constitutes an immutable heritage. . . . the meaning of a structure of this kind is constantly renewable, even if materially it stays the same. Its growth is not a mere matter of quantity; it is also a result of the new significance it acquires over time."[1] Donadoni highlights that the scientific and cultural objectives of a collection and its organization change with the development of society over time. Hence, every temporary or permanent exhibition project necessarily becomes part of a broader historical and hermeneutic perspective.

In March 2019, we opened a temporary exhibition with the title "Invisible Archaeology," which can be considered, in many ways, a critical step in that conversation with visitors.

Figure 4.1. "Invisible Archaeology." Overview of the section "Archaeology," with two wall projections of archaeological photographs and three-dimensional photogrammetric models.

Figure 4.2. "Invisible Archaeology." Top: Overview of the section "Testing." Bottom: Detail of the showcase with pigments and binders used by ancient Egyptian artisans.

It emphasized the growing collaboration between Egyptology and the natural sciences in the study of archaeological collections and showed how Museo Egizio increasingly employs archaeometry as a method to interrogate objects. Indeed, through the use of cutting-edge technologies and instruments of analysis, we can now extract information that has always been present in the artifacts, but was always invisible to the naked eye and beyond our ability to contemplate, measure, and understand. The clues about the life of an object—from production to abandonment, rediscovery, recontextualization, and conservation in museums—are condensed into the materials that they are made out of. Therefore, through the materiality of the objects, we can discern elements of the unique biography of each.[2]

Moreover, these data not only structure the language that enables objects to speak to us about their biographies but also gives us a key to investigating their material nature. On this also depends our ability to preserve them, so that, after

traversing centuries to reach us, they can be returned to the current of time and continue their journey into the generations to come. The exhibition path was conceived as a journey to the invisible and back. It was divided into three sections, each dedicated to a specific moment in the life of an artifact.

In the first section, "Archaeology," two wall projections showed how photographic techniques have evolved into photogrammetry employed to document archaeological contexts (Figure 4.1). The second section, "Testing," welcomed visitors

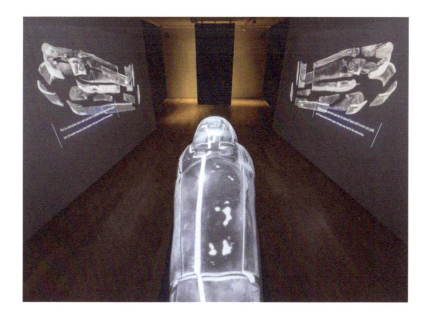

Figure 4.3. "Invisible Archaeology." Overview of the section "Conservation," in which digital images and three-dimensional models were projected on the walls as well as on a printed copy of the outer coffin of Butehamon.

with modern examples of raw minerals, binders and pigments that were commonly used by ancient Egyptian painters (Figure 4.2). These materials provided an introduction into the chemistry behind pictorial layers as well as the value of multispectral imaging techniques—including infra-red, ultra-violet, and visible induced luminescence photography, next to macro X-ray fluorescence scanning—to unveil otherwise invisible details of the work of artisans. Digital unwrappings of human and animal mummies complete this area. The third section, "Conservation," presented three case studies about conservation activities related to mural paintings, papyri, and textiles. The end of the exhibition explored the conflicts deriving from the digital and material perception of objects. The projection on the real-size, three-dimensional print of the outer coffin of the royal scribe Butehamon (around 1000 BCE) showed the invisible phases of its construction, from its carpentry to its decorative design (Figure 4.3). The understanding of ancient

artifacts through the investigation of their materials provided visitors with a more authentic experience of the finds themselves, emancipating them from a patinated and stereotyped representation of the culture and history of ancient Egypt, which traditionally reduces its depth and richness into a gallery of clichés.

A GALLERY OF BIOGRAPHIES

Because biographies of objects, materiality, and archaeometry belong to a conceptual framework that is not easy to engage our visitors with, we looked for an effective and creative way to confront them with these key concepts. Ultimately we chose to display, right at the entrance of the exhibition, a gallery of everyday objects imbued with memories of their owners, who were mostly my colleagues at Museo Egizio and me. This display aimed to provide visitors with examples of biographies that they could experience in their own daily life (a similar avenue was chosen by Hans Barnard in Chapter 2 of this volume). A text panel in the room summarized these concepts:

> Each object, whether ancient or contemporary, has its own unique and unrepeatable biography not ending with the age or civilization from which it originated. It continues to silently record fragments of new memories, as the object passes through time and the changes of history.
>
> By recounting how they have been used, altered, abandoned, forgotten, rediscovered, and then handed down, perhaps rescuing them from new oblivion, objects resist time and bear witness to our lives and those of the people who lived before us. Whether they are artistic creations or everyday things, ancient finds or items from our childhood, objects act as a bridge connecting those who produced them with those who observe them and question them today.
>
> In an attempt to make the world and the people who created these objects more evident, a museum fulfills its fundamental task of continuously refining that contact between people and experiences of every age.

To study objects and grasp the information they preserve (the materials and techniques used to produce them, the damage they have suffered, the repairs and alterations they have undergone in time), a museum uses its most profound and refined form of listening: research.

Each object had a label with a short autobiography—and therefore written in the first person—creating a parallel between ancient and present objects, both displayed in museum environments and illustrating the disruptive idea that, to misquote Maurizio Nannucci, "all objects have been contemporary."[3]

Audio cassette: "I keep the sounds of a trip to Mongolia, but the recorder has gone out of production, and I no longer have a way to play them. Will I be a silent witness forever?"

Baseball: "I bear letters and one date on me, in memory of a relevant event, but I no longer remember their meaning. What a scatterbrain!"

Box of watercolors: "Roland Batchelor still lives in his watercolors. I embody experience myself: I have suspended his colors in time and jealously keep them with me."

Camera: "I traveled from Treviglio to the North Pole with Federica's grandfather. In 2011 I was given to her for her doctorate, so marking another milestone."

Candy holder: "I was always kept in the living room. I used to contain colorful candy, and I carry a childhood memory with me. When you open me, you can still catch the faint scent of confectionery."

Class photograph. [Discussed in some more detail below.]

Coin scales: "I am 270 years old, I come from Nuremberg, and I have always been accurate. I have been handed down from one generation to another, finally reaching Turin, in the hands of Paola's son."

Coins: "You have to accept facts, dear cents; it goes round in circles! Just as happened to us 10-lira coins, you too ceased to be legal tender!"

Disposable camera: "I was forgotten in a drawer for twenty years. I contain a film never developed, and I am the last record of moments effaced by time."

George Orwell's Nineteen Eighty-Four: [Discussed in some more detail below.]

Hand drill: "In the '30s, you could not do without me; today, I'm not even sure you know how to use me."

Hand-held videogames: "We always made our presence felt. Our sounds echoed through homes and chased away our thoughts. We traveled in rainforests and cosmic spaces. We are insuperable."

Ink blotter: "My identity has been lost over time. Can anyone tell me what I was for?"

iPhone: "A place in the firmament was reserved for the Greek heroes. I won mine on the display because I fell in action during a meeting for this exhibition."

Lamp: "I was a beautiful glass bell, but nobody wanted me any more. Virginia's father found me in a flea market and turned me into a lamp, making me shine again."

Manual pantograph: "Nobody recognizes me any more. Yet once what I did was indispensable: I could make what was originally small appear bigger."

Oil lamp: "I risked being thrown away when electric light replaced oil lamps, but I was not forgotten. A total restyling in the '50s made me a lampshade."

Paintbrush: "I was Piera's companion for four years at the art academy. Now worn out by long work, her father gave me a new span of life with some riveted copper foil."

Penknife: "I come from the Italicus Premana factory. I am multi-purpose, and I was used during military service. I have some famous cousins in Switzerland—do you happen to know them?"

Pink Floyd vinyl cover: "Today, you can find me in museums. My value is now higher than before. 'The time is gone, the song is over, thought I'd something more to say' ("Time," Pink Floyd)."

Pocketwatch. [Discussed in some more detail below.]

Saucepan: "I used to cook eggs for Paola's grandmother in times of war or plenty. My work for Paola is the same, but I also cooked dishes for her dolls."

Scans of camera plates: "On bright days, I took beautiful photos of the North Pole, and during the trip, I met many people, pictured on me as a souvenir."

Slide rule: "Few remember what I am; the knowledge has been lost over time. Those who find the key to deciphering my riddle will discover that I am the forerunner of pocket calculators."

Statuette of Baby Jesus from Prague: "I fell and broke when Silvia gave birth after some complications. What a fright it gave us! Fortunately, everything was fixed and me too."

T28 telephone: "I look around and realize how far my great-grandchildren have gone! Everything changes quickly, but despite my age, I'm still going strong!"

Tabletop videogame. [Discussed in some more detail below.]

Toy car made out of condensed milk tins. [Discussed in some more detail below.]

Toy car: "Every single dent in me has its story. For example, I can tell you about when Enrico, still a child, tried to sit on me and drive me around!"

Trowel: "The companion of an archaeologist, carved on me is my date of purchase and nickname. I bear rust marks, due to contact with the damp soils of Cumae."

Vase. [Discussed in some more detail below.]

Vintage radio: "I've always been pretty, but today they look at me to recover the lost taste of the past. For this reason, I was bought in a flea market as a designer object!"

Viola. [Discussed in some more detail below.]

Walkman and Madonna audio cassette: "So many years have gone by, yet I still cannot live without you!"

OBJECTS THAT PRESERVE, LOSE, OR PASS ON A BOND

The gallery was divided into three main groups marking the entanglements and transformations that objects compile over time as they would new pages of their biography.[4] The division is based on some critical features shared by the objects to survive the passage of time. First, the capacity to create bonds with people, locations, other objects, and even ideas; second, the adaptation to the cultural and technological progress of societies; and third, the possibility of embodying new meanings as a mirror of changes in societies over time.

Pocketwatch (Figure 4.4): "I was made into a keepsake by scoring numbers and dates on me. For reasons I do not know, someone effaced them, stealing some of my identity!"

A pocketwatch peeps out of its square showcase. As often happens with family possessions, its story has, so far, only been transmitted in an oral way, from my mother to me, finding only now a written form in this chapter. In 1936 my grandfather was nineteen years old and already at loggerheads with the local fascist party. His parents, to prevent the situation from getting worse, believed it was safer for him to leave their small town of Conselve in Veneto and go to Turin, in Piedmont, where two of his sisters already lived. He took his bicycle and pedaled about 400 kilometers (250 miles) to Turin, where he lived during the war as a partisan, and, after that, as a worker at the Michelin car tire factory. He had always been partial to mechanics, and before and during the war he carried out small repairs of pocket- and wristwatches. That was how he met my grandmother, but that is another story. Due to the war, however, it could happen that those leaving a watch to be repaired never returned to retrieve it, and when my grandfather passed away in 1971, he still had in a drawer of his workbench a few watches including the one now on display.

So far for the oral tradition, let us now give the word to materiality. The mechanism of the watch still works perfectly and provides us with a reliable terminus ante quem. The technician who overhauled it informed me that it has a specific box for the spring that was used until around the 1930s. Typology perhaps allows us to narrow the chronology further. There is no brand name indicated on the dial or the case. Nevertheless, its general aspect is quite similar to some models from renowned brands—Zenith, Perseo, Fulgor—dating to around the 1930s of which it could be a cheaper sub-brand or a copy.

The investigation of materiality outlines the birth of an object, but also following the events uniquely marking its life. The back of the case, for example, has a cover inside of which there are engravings made by hand. A date (27/09/1939) seems to confirm the chronology conjectured so far while two other numbers (10-47), written a little above, by the same hand, could be another temporal indication or additional information

the meaning of which remains unclear. Other inscriptions are less legible and require closer observation. Right at the center of the case, traces of scraping probably indicate the removal of information, perhaps the name of the owner, a reference to the occasion for which the watch was bought, a motto, or possibly a dedication.

An object originating from serial production has thus become the unique witness of a micro-story made of oral and material sources and entangled with those who owned it, who repaired it, who inherited it, and even those who enter into a dialogue with it today through the exhibition. Nonetheless, this is fragile information that human actions can easily imprint in the materiality of the object, or remove accidentally or voluntarily, or even allow to disappear in the flow of time.

Class photograph (Figure 4.5): "Letizia's grandmother thought she looked ugly in this photo and cut out her face. One of the little boys in the photo must have thought differently since he later married her!"

In some objects, the documental function is so prevalent that materiality and information overlap. Specific data can thus be surgically removed unless a delicate weaving of materiality and orality restores them. Such is the case of this picture depicting a third-grade class (1932–33), which included the grandmother of Letizia Merlo (the coordinator of events at Museo Egizio), who kindly made this object available for the exhibition. She told me that at the time the image was captured, her grandmother thought she was ugly and cut out her image from the photograph. A removal which, from the comments of visitors, I learned was less idiosyncratic than I thought.

Another spot in the picture that we can precisely localize is the second row from the bottom, second seat from the left. It depicts a child who had no specific relevance at that time. However, that spot acquired a new layer of meaning many years later, when that child married Letizia's grandmother.

Figure 4.4. A pocket watch (probably 1930s); the rear cover of the watch has engravings and scrapings inside.

Figure 4.5. A photograph of a third-grade class (1932–33), with the cut made by Letizia's grandmother.

OBJECTS THAT CHANGE TO ADAPT TO THE PASSAGE OF TIME

Viola (Figure 4.6): "I was born in Milan in 1760. I changed my appearance more than once to interpret the changing world better. I met many artists and with them, I played the feelings of their generation."

This group starts with a viola belonging to the family of my father since the end of the nineteenth century. It passed from my great-uncle to my grandmother, then to my father, and finally to me. Although it lacks a label of the luthier, specialists attribute this musical instrument—on a technical and stylistic basis—to a workshop possibly connected with the famous Paolo Antonio Testore (Milan, around 1690–1767). The viola on display thus belongs to the so-called classical period of the history of violin making—from the sixteenth to the eighteenth century—which includes the instruments of famous luthiers such as Nicola Amati (1596–1684), Antonio Stradivari (1644–1737), Giuseppe Guarneri del Gesù (1698–1744), and Giovan

Figure 4.6. An eighteenth-century viola; the detail below shows the sound post as seen through one of the *f*-shaped sound holes.

Battista Guadagnini (1711–86). As other historical string instruments, the viola witnessed at least two distinct amendments related to developments in western music; both of them left traces in the materiality of the instrument that only the trained eye of a luthier can easily distinguish.

The first set of modifications took place in particular during the development of Romanticism (late eighteenth to mid-twentieth century) when a new musical language asked for more powerful sounds and pronounced virtuosity compared to the previous repertoire. Soundboards were modified to improve the power and brilliance of the sound. Metal strings replaced strings made of gut, but the increased tension in which this resulted required adaptation of the neck and fingerboard of the instrument.[5] Since the beginning of the twentieth century, studies have focused on rediscovering the practices and construction techniques of historical instruments, related to the issue of reviving the music of the past in its contemporary technical and musical context, as a requirement for an authentic cultural experience.[6] The viola was modified again to remove the changes made during the Romantic period. However, the attempts aiming to restore the original design of the instrument suffered from the limited knowledge of the construction techniques in the past and the lack of access to the original materials.

The viola is an excellent example of the complex network of connections that, through time, an object can create. For 250 years, the owners of the viola guaranteed, through use and maintenance, the perpetuation of function, identity, and—within limits—materiality. The viola itself is a living document on the history of violin making, and cultural history in general, and catalyzes oral and material testimonies—stories, photographs, audio recordings—of specific family memories. The identity of objects does not always go through transformations impressed by time. The reuse of objects can, for example, compromise their original function and appearance, adding in turn new layers of meaning and broader entanglements to their biographies. Moreover, this opportunity of adaptation marks the break between the first and second life of an object, a further conceptual tool in the biographical framework. Two other objects, among those exhibited in this group, can help to clarify this argument.

Vase (Figure 4.7): "I was the case of an SMI mod. 912 artillery shell in World War I, then I was given a new identity as a flower vase! Life's little ironies!"

Figure 4.7. A flower vase made from an artillery case.

The first object is an artillery shell dating to the First World War that was later reworked and decorated with embossed floral motifs to be used as a vase for flowers. It is a representative example of the rather widespread practice of reusing, for domestic purposes, war materials— bayonets, helmets, mess tins, parachutes—found by Italian farmers in their fields during and after the war.

Figure 4.8. A toy car made out of a tin for condensed milk.

Figure 4.9. The 2013 Penguin edition of George Orwell's *Nineteen Eighty-Four*. Left: new. Right: worn.

Toy car (Figure 4.8): "As a condensed milk tin, I was no longer useful. They might have thrown me away, but someone realized I could be something new: I was turned into a toy!"

The second object has its function and original appearance wholly removed. It is a toy, a model of a Citroën 2 CV made by reusing the material of a can of condensed milk. The primary object is gone; nevertheless, the original labels are still mostly visible and provide the information necessary to identify it. In this example visitors are confronted with the fundamental role of materiality in understanding an object, but also with the need to have the correct tool—in this case the ability to read and understand sentences written in the Latin alphabet—to decipher those data.

OBJECTS THAT BECOME ARTIFACTS

The last group of objects continues the analysis of the multiple lives of objects by focusing on a different property, no longer the change of appearance and function, but rather the shift in meaning over time. The study and interpretation of an object also depend on the culture and interests of a society and the way these change over time, unfolding a series of narratives that grow progressively wider, as the last two examples of this review may help to show.

George Orwell's Nineteen Eighty-Four (Figure 4.9): "The cover of George Orwell's *1984*, becomes less censored with wear (u/L-boyontheting on Reddit 2016)."

First published in 1949, *Nineteen Eighty-Four* is one of the most influential novels of the twentieth century. The title and some of its concepts, such as Big Brother, Newspeak, and the Thought Police entered mainstream culture, often as bywords for modern social and political abuse. In the United States the book saw sales spikes on the Amazon bestseller list in 2013 (an increase of more than 10,000 percent) after Edward Snowden revealed the extent of the surveillance program of the National Security Agency and in 2017 (an increase of more than 9,500 percent) in reaction to the spread of so-called post-truth strategies in social media, science, and politics. In 2013 Penguin released a particularly bold cover design. It was unusual because the title and the name of the author were debossed, then masked—but not entirely erased—by black foiling. David Pearson, the graphic designer behind this idea, intended the censorship of the book to reflect the theme of the novel: a dystopia set in a totalitarian state where "the past was erased, the erasure was forgotten, the lie became truth."[7]

Three years later,[8] a Reddit user posted two images of the cover: one "as new," the other "after a few months of being carried around in a backpack." On the latter, the black foiling had faded, showing with great clarity both the title of the book and the name of the author. The Redditor titled the thread: "The cover of George Orwell's, *1984*, becomes *less censored* with wear," alluding to the resilience of truth and giving voice to a widespread feeling about the current political situation. The images of the book and its specific message started to circulate on the worldwide web, and obtained broad consensus and recognition, completing the objectification of the textuality initiated by Pearson.

I was fascinated by this story and I asked the Redditor to loan his worn book as an example of the new meaning that an object can embody through sociocultural changes. As its display in Museo Egizio showed, it is no longer a material medium but a brand new object, with a particular biography and agency, allowing for further contextualization to be activated.

Tabletop videogame (Figure 4.10): "I was a great star of the 1980s, but then my fame faded. Few of us remain, and perhaps this is why the collectors and museums want me!"

To complete the narrative that started—I admit rather autobiographically—with the pocketwatch of my grandfather and continued with the viola of my father, I will next examine an object belonging to me. It is a tabletop videogame called "Puck Monster," a clone of the most famous arcade game Puck-Man (later renamed Pac Man), which was distributed by Gakken around 1982. My mother gave me this game shortly after its release when I was about seven years old. Home-based

Figure 4.10. Tabletop videogame "Puck Monster."

videogame history had started only a decade before, at the end of 1972, with the release of the Magnavox Odyssey and its ping-pong game. A few months later, Atari released that game as the famous coin-operated "Pong," followed in 1975 by a dedicated, and still celebrated console version. Within a few years, the market was invaded by hand-held and tabletop videogames, while the frantic race to develop new consoles reached saturation as early as 1982. Due also to the growing competition of the first home computers—Commodore, Apple, Amstrad, Spectrum—in the same year, the market of home-based videogames collapsed. Games like my Puck Monster not only suffered a drastic devaluation, but, in a short time, went out of fashion and ended up in attics or were thrown away. Five years later, the market flourished again with Nintendo and Sega, giving way to the course of events that made home-gaming one of the most relevant industries today, both economically and for its worldwide impact on pop culture.

The compelling history of videogames, so inextricably linked to technology, marketing and corporate culture, is told in articles, essays, documentaries, films, conferences, exhibitions, private collections, and even in dedicated museums. The latter (virtual and real), in particular, collect the first witnesses of the videogame history and display the milestones that, as in Darwinian evolution, outline the branching of new families and sub-families, enabling analysis of internal and external factors of influence. Therefore it is not surprising that other specimens of my Puck Monster are on display in museum collections such as the South West Retro Computing Archive at Plymouth University, together with other tabletop videogames of the same period. The historical contextualization superimposes a new socio-cultural meaning—derivative and collective—to the original and individual significance of an object. The market also reflects the additional value proportional to the growing interest in these items, In 1982 my mother spent the equivalent of around $20, but today the price of an original boxed Puck Monster can exceed $300. My Puck Monster is still just a videogame—it is, by the way, still working and I played a bunch of games right before putting it in the showcase—at the same time, however, it is now also a cultural item.

teenagers—one of whom was often chosen to read the labels aloud to the others—were particularly entertained, perhaps because of the short texts, which were written following the old 140 characters Twitter rule, combined with the use of the catchy first person, mimicking instant messaging.

Adults, on the other hand, were moved by objects that they remembered from when they were younger, providing the more mature generations an opportunity to tell younger visitors about objects unfamiliar to them. This dialogue happened not only between grandparents and grandchildren, as expected, but also between parents and children, showing the speed with which oblivion envelops objects and the value that they carry. Apart from some funny parents, who started inventing fantastic tales around the objects displayed just to amuse their little kids, I remember, in particular, an American dad, probably of my age, in front of the showcase with the Puck Monster. The man pointed at the videogame and addressed his son, who was around eight years old:

"Hey, do you know what this is?"

"No!"

"Really? Can't you guess what it could be?"

"No! What's it for?"

"It's a game. I had one just like this one."

"A game?!"

"Yes, I used to play that all the time when I was your age!"

"Really? And how did it work?"

"Well, listen, . . ."

CONCLUSION

The image of "objects . . . arranged to converse with the visitor," as proposed by Donadoni (1989, 3), came again to mind when we started to notice the reactions of visitors entering the gallery. Some of them were initially disoriented because they did not find immediate visual references to ancient Egypt. Nevertheless, in a few seconds, they took refuge in the most familiar and reassuring object available, usually the vinyl cover of Pink Floyd's *Dark Side of the Moon.* Groups of

NOTES

1   Donadoni 1989, 3–4, translation by Federico Poole.

2   Harding 2016, Hoskins 1998, 2006, Kopytof 1986.

3   Nannucci 2012, Meyer 2013.

4   Hodder 2012.

5   Stowell 2004, 35.

6   Hindemith 1952.

7   Orwell 1949, 75.

8   https://imgur.com/a/lqN9t (accessed 29 February 2020).

BIBLIOGRAPHY

Donadoni, Sergio (1989), "Presentazione," in: Anna Maria Donadoni Roveri, ed., *Dal Museo al Museo: Passato e Futuro del Museo Egizio di Torino*, pp. 3–5, Turin (Allemandi). [In Italian]

Harding, Anthony (2016), Introduction: Biographies of Things, *Distant Worlds Journal* 1, 5–10.

Hindemith, Paul (1952), *Johann Sebastian Bach: Heritage and Obligation*, Oxford (Oxford University Press).

Hodder, Ian (2012), *Entangled: An Archaeology of the Relationships between Humans and Things,* Chichester (John Wiley and Sons, Inc.).

Hoskins, Janet (1998), *Biographical Objects: How Things Tell the Stories of People's Lives*, London (Taylor and Francis, Inc.).

Hoskins, Janet (2006), "Agency, Biography and Objects," in: Christopher Tilley, Webb Keane, Susanne Küchler, Patricia Spyer, and Mike Rowlands, eds., *Handbook of Material Culture*, pp. 74–84, London (Sage Publications Ltd.).

Kopytoff, Igor (1986), "The Cultural Biography of Things: Commoditization as Process," in: Arjun Appadurai, ed., *The Social Life of Things: Commodities in Cultural Perspective,* pp. 64–91, Cambridge (Cambridge University Press).

Lichtheim, Miriam (1973), *Ancient Egyptian Literature: A Book of Readings: Volume I: The Old and Middle Kingdoms,* Berkeley (University of California Press).

Meyer, Richard (2013), *What Was Contemporary Art?* Cambridge (Massachusetts Institute of Technology Press).

Nannucci, Maurizio (2012), *There Is Another Way of Looking at Things*, Milan (Silvana Editoriale).

Orwell, George (1949), *Nineteen Eighty-Four,* London and New York (Secker and Warburg).

Stowell, Robin (2004), *The Early Violin and Viola: A Practical Guide*, Cambridge (Cambridge University Press).

A FIRST EXERCISE IN AUTOVOCALITY

THE ARCHAEOLOGY OF MY STUDY

HANS BARNARD

"What's the good of Mercator's North Poles and Equators,
Tropics, Zones, and Meridian Lines?"
So the Bellman would cry: and the crew would reply
"They are merely conventional signs!"
(Lewis Carroll, the third stanza of Fit the Second in *The Hunting of the Snark: An Agony in Eight Fits*, 1876)

Archaeology can be defined as the study of human development, behavior, and history as inferred from material remains. The discipline is solidly based upon and almost entirely dependent on objects. This is facilitated by the fact that objects created and used by humans intricately and inevitably complement functionality with meaning. This implies that a careful study of objects can reveal a myriad of information about their human producers and users.[1] Since the mid-twentieth century it has become clear that in different persons the same object can provoke very different emotional and intellectual responses, a phenomenon identified as 'multivocality.' Here I propose the term 'autovocality' to mean the narrative of the author prompted by one or more objects. Usually these objects predate the narrative, or both develop concurrently. In this chapter I will briefly explore the less common event in which the narrative gives rise to the objects, rather than the other way around, and finish with a case study with which I have personal experience.

Narratives about fictional places and cultures occur early in the written record, usually to serve as background for religious or literary stories—including the genre of science fiction—but at times to introduce and explore matters of philosophy or politics. Illustrious examples of the latter include Atlantis (Plato, c. 380 BCE in *Timaeus* 24e–25a and briefly in *Critias*), Utopia,[2] Lilliput and Brobdingnag,[3] and Flatland.[4] The intention behind such narratives may also be solely artistic or remain enigmatic, as is the case with, for instance, the *Voynich*

Manuscript (anonymous, early fifteenth century), the *Rohonc Codex (Rohonci kódex,* anonymous, eighteenth century), the *Codex Seraphinianus*,[5] and the *Book from the Sky (Tianshu).*[6] The above narratives did obviously not originate from objects, nor did they give rise to any.

During the second half of the 1970s two major developments fundamentally changed the Hollywood film industry. Up until the release of *Jaws* (Steven Spielberg, working for Universal Pictures, 1975) and the first, or rather the third, installment of the *Star Wars* ennealogy (George Lucas, 1977–2019), films aimed to emulate written literature, with multi-layered story lines and complex, developing characters. *Jaws* and *Star Wars* showed that it was commercially much more successful to produce summer blockbusters without intricate narratives, but instead driven by spectacle and special effects. Around the same time it was recognized that the revenue of a movie could be dramatically increased by the sale of objects copied from the props used to tell the story. In other words, by the sale of objects created after and uniquely based upon the narrative of the movie. Among the most successful examples are the *Lord of the Rings* films (2001–2003), a greatly simplified version of the 1954–55 literary trilogy by J.R.R. Tolkien, and the quite disparate series of *Harry Potter* films (2001–11), based on the rather unsophisticated 1997–2007 heptalogy by J.K. Rowling. It is noteworthy that this franchise model did not result from the books, in which the imagery was created within the imagination of individual readers, while it did blossom up around numerous comic strips, graphic novels, computer games, and television series.

From an archaeological point of view it is noteworthy that the link between objects and narratives is thus not unidirectional, but can also flow from a narrative into the creation of one or more objects. Apart from the well-known commercial examples above, there are several examples of artists who have created imaginary countries or cultures to function as a framework for their work, including the mythical world in which Richard Wagner placed most of his operas, the imaginary Fook Island where most of the works of South African artist Walter Battiss allegedly originated, the artifacts from a nameless island with a capital named Onomatopoeia created by Scottish artist Charles Avery,[7] and in a way also the poems that J.M.W. Turner wrote to complement or name some of his paintings.

AN EXERCISE IN AUTOVOCALITY

Growing up as the son of the general medical practitioner in a small village on a rural island in the north of the Netherlands, I spent my youth surrounded by children of fishermen and sheep farmers. Our different backgrounds and my innate curiosity resulted in a significant cultural and intellectual divide by the time that I started traveling to the mainland to pursue my secondary education in 1971. The large amounts of new and thought-provoking information presented to me there were partly processed during the daily boring trips on the ferry, together with some of my peers. Our mindset was the same as that of the crew in the epigraph at the head of this chapter, and our strategy was to conceive viable alternatives for all the facts and principles that we had to learn. Over the years this hobby developed into the culture of an imaginary country, the Kayenian Empire, consisting of thirteen previously independent territories around an internal sea. Soon after the obvious maps and alphabets were completed we proceeded with creating objects to make our fantasy world into a real one.[8] These objects related to many aspects of daily life, but often focused on arithmetic,[9] music, and board games. Some of these are introduced and presented here.

When developed from scratch the obvious base for a numeral system would be either a prime number, such as 11 or 13—in which the relations between common and decimal fractions are less ambiguous—or instead a number with many dividers, such as 12. Throughout history, however, there are precious few examples of the former and only slightly more of the latter. In the Western world we are familiar with a dozen (12) and a gross ($12^2 = 144$), albeit increasingly less, and we measure time in increments of 12 and 24 hours. Each hour is divided into 60 minutes and each minute into 60 seconds, a remnant of the sexagesimal (base-60) system used by the Sumerians

$$1 + 2 + 3 = 1 \times 2 \times 3 = 10 \ (= 6)$$

$$10^2 = 100 \ (= 36)$$

$$1^2 \times 2^2 \times 3^2 = 1^3 + 2^3 + 3^3 = 100 \ (= 36)$$

```
                    1

               2         3

          4    5    10

       11   12   13   14

     15   20   21   22   23

   24   25   30   31   32   33

 34   35   40   41   42   43   44

45   50   51   52   53   54   55   100
```

Table 3.1. Selected properties of the base-6 numeral system.

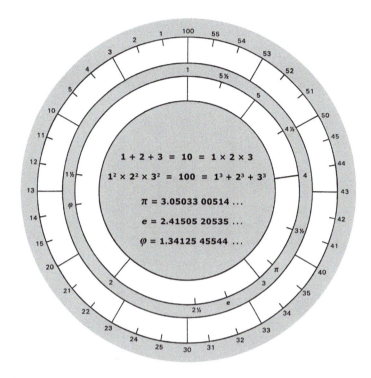

Figure 3.1. Graphic representation of the base-6 numeral system (outer circle), with its logarithms (inner circle) and some major properties (center). Note that the circle is divided into 36 (written 100) equal parts, which can be grouped into 2, 3, 4, 6, 9, 12, and 18 larger segments of 18, 12, 9, 6, 4, 3, and 2 units each.

around three millennia ago in modern-day Iraq. Similarly, a full circle is usually divided into 6 × 60 = 360°, with each degree divided into 60 minutes and each minute into 60 seconds.

Worldwide, most numeral systems are based on the number ten—neither prime nor a number with many dividers—most likely because of human anatomy. A common variant of this is the vigesimal (base-20) system, most notably the Mayan numeral system used throughout ancient Mesoamerica. Remnants of a similar system can be found in several European languages, in American English most famously in the Gettysburg Address (Abraham Lincoln, November 1863): "Four score and seven years ago...", meaning 4×20 + 7. This may sound old-fashioned in English, but is commonplace in contemporary French, in which 87 is *quatre-vingt sept.* In the United Kingdom prices are sometimes quoted in guineas, originally the equivalent of 21 shillings (currently 105 pence), to be paid by the buyer, but received by the seller in pounds, originally the equivalent of 20 shillings (currently 100 pence). This leaves a commission of 1 shilling, or 5 pence, to the pound (about 4.76 percent) for the broker. Similarly, the *vingtième* was a universal income tax of one in 20 (5 percent) intermittently levied by the Ancien Régime, the French government until the French Revolution in 1789.

The disadvantage of a smaller base is that successive numbers quickly grow awkwardly large. In the binary (base-2) system used in digital electronics the equivalent of 100 has seven digits (1100100). Conversely, the disadvantage of a larger base is that more tables of addition and multiplication need to be memorized, as well as more symbols to represent the different numerals. The numeral system used in the Kayenian Empire is base-6, a seximal or senary system, in

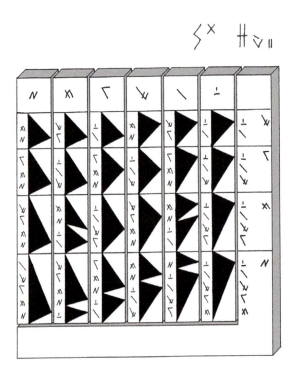

Calculation fingers

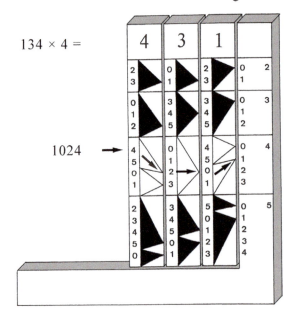

Figure 3.2. The principle behind calculation fingers (*aytshoo lee*), which greatly simplify the multiplication of large numbers. At the top the full set is shown, at the bottom an example (134 × 4) in transcription.

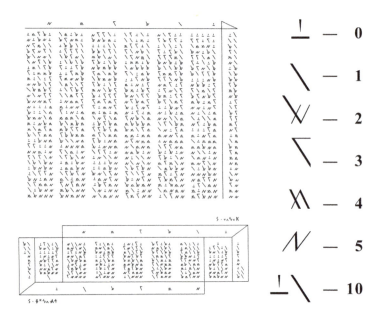

Table 3.2. Logarithms (top) and sines (bottom) in base-6. The numerals used in the Kayenian Empire are presented on the right (note that the direction of writing numerals is right to left).

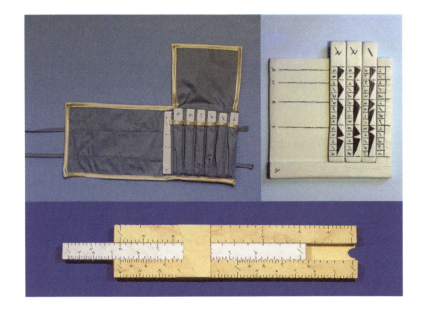

Figure 3.3. Top left: Set of Kayenian, base-6 calculation fingers (*aytshoo lee*). Top right: Calculation fingers in use, showing the table of 122. Bottom: A Kayenian base-6 logarithmic slide rule.

which the units can be counted on the fingers of one hand, and multiples of 6 on the fingers of the other hand. The number of symbols and tables to be memorized is small and the tables of multiplication are highly regular (all prime numbers above 3 end in either 1 or 5). Successive numbers remain eminently manageable: 100 is written 244 ($2 \times 6^2 + 4 \times 6 + 4$) and 1,000 as 4344 ($4 \times 6^3 + 3 \times 6^2 + 4 \times 6 + 4$). More importantly, both 6 (written 10) and 36 (written 100) have properties that make them ideally suitable for daily use as the base of a numeral system (Table 3.1). The best known and most frequently occurring transcendental number π (pi) is written 3.05033 . . . (Figure 3.1),[10] with a zero appearing twice early in the sequence,[11] allowing it to be broken off relatively accurately, while log π = 0.35000 (rounded).[12]

Despite these and other significant advantages it is not realistic to expect the very well-established decimal system to be replaced by any other system, despite the quixotic efforts of dozenal (base-12) societies in both Great Britain and the United States. Many superior inventions have suffered a similar fate simply because they arrived too late. Noteworthy examples include the Betamax video recording system, produced between 1975 and 2016, the Jankó and Dvorak keyboards, proposed in 1882 and 1936 respectively, and the many chess variants designed to prevent the game losing its appeal because of over-analysis, including those suggested by world champions José Raúl Capablanca in the 1920s and Robert (Bobby) Fisher in the 1990s.

Between 1977 and 1993 I created many tables exploring the intricacies of the base-6 numeral system, ranging from prime numbers and factorials to compound interest and trigonometric functions (Table 3.1), mostly with the help of a Brother 738SR pocket calculator (one of the first with a liquid crystal display). At the same time I adapted the inventions of John Napier of Merchiston (1550–1617) and Nicolas Bion (1652–1733),[13] among others, into true Kayenian calculating devices. These included various abacuses that assist addition, but also calculation fingers (or *aytshoo lee*, as they are refered to by their actual users) that simplify multiplication (Figure 3.2), and logarithmic slide rules that enable estimation of the result of complex calculations (Figure 3.3).

Among the many intersections between mathematics and the arts is music, and certainly musical tuning systems.[14] At its most simple, a musical tone is a column of air vibrating at a fixed frequency for a short or longer period of time. The frequency or pitch is controlled by a musical instrument and measured in cycles per second or Hertz (Hz). Two tones with the same frequency are said to sound in unison and may be difficult or impossible to distinguish. When one of these tones is slowly raised, the two tones become more or less easy to tell apart, sounding either dissonant or consonant, until one reaches double the frequency of the other. Now the two tones appear to sound in unison again and are said to be each other's octave (for instance C–C1), the most consonant of intervals. The second most consonant interval, the fifth (for instance C–G), sounds when the frequency of the rising tone reaches 3/2 (= 1.5) times the frequency of the first, stable tone. The most consonant interval after that, the fourth (for instance C–F), sounds when the frequency of the rising tone reaches 4/3 (= 1.33333 . . .) times the frequency of the first. The same tone can also be reached by not raising the second tone by a fourth, but rather by lowering it by a fifth. Other agreeable intervals are likewise associated with relatively simple fractions (for instance 5/4 = major third and 6/5 = minor third), a phenomenon already noted by Pythagoras around 500 BCE.

After starting at the same base frequency it is obvious that a stack of octaves (frequency × 2) will never again meet a stack of fifths (frequency × 3/2), resulting in an infinite number of tones within an octave, after all fifths are transposed down into a single octave (Table 3.3).

Stack of octaves (× 2) :	C-C1-C2-C3-C4-C5- . . .
Stack of fifths (× 3/2) :	C-G1-D2-A2-E3-B3- . . .

Table 3.3. The generation of a musical scale out of a single base frequency (C).

This is not an issue for instruments with variable pitch, such as the human voice, violins, and trombones. It does, however, pose a major problem for the construction of instruments that can only produce discrete intervals, including all fretted and keyboard instruments.

In Renaissance Europe this issue was resolved, primarily by Gioseffo Zarlino (1517–90), Simon Stevin (1548–1620), and Marin Mersenne (1588–1648), by not using the exact factor 3/2 (= 1.5) to find the frequency of the fifth, but rather the approximated factor $2^{7/12}$ (= 1.49830 . . .). This results in twelve intervals within the octave, each a distance of frequency × $2^{1/12}$ (= 1.05946 . . .) apart. Now every interval except the octave is a little off, but the fifths and fourths are accurate enough to remain acceptable to the average human ear. However, major and minor thirds, the next most important harmonic and melodic intervals, are relatively far off. Over the course of the centuries these errors have nevertheless become widely accepted.

Many solutions other than such a 12-tone equal temperament tuning system have been suggested. Among these are a 24-tone equal temperament (quarter-tone) system,

Tone	Ratio			Logarithmic		Frequency	
	Fractions	Exponential	Decimal	Cents	0–1900	/K·sec.*)	Hz
1	1/1	$2^0 \cdot 3^0 \cdot 5^0$	1	0	0	512	276.48
2	128/125	$2^7 \cdot 3^0 \cdot 5^{-3}$	1.024	41.06	65.01	524.29	283.12
3	16/15	$2^4 \cdot 3^{-1} \cdot 5^{-1}$	1.066667	111.74	176.92	546.13	294.91
4	9/8	$2^{-3} \cdot 3^2 \cdot 5^0$	1.125	203.91	322.86	576	311.04
5	75/64	$2^{-6} \cdot 3^1 \cdot 5^2$	1.171875	274.58	434.75	600	324
6	6/5	$2^1 \cdot 3^1 \cdot 5^{-1}$	1.2	315.65	499.78	614.40	331.78
7	5/4	$2^{-2} \cdot 3^0 \cdot 5^1$	1.25	386.31	611.66	640	345.60
8	32/25	$2^5 \cdot 3^0 \cdot 5^{-2}$	1.28	427.37	676.67	655.36	353.89
9	4/3	$2^2 \cdot 3^{-1} \cdot 5^0$	1.333333	498.05	788.58	682.67	368.64
10	512/375	$2^9 \cdot 3^{-1} \cdot 5^{-3}$	1.365333	539.11	853.59	699.05	377.49
11	64/45	$2^6 \cdot 3^{-2} \cdot 5^{-1}$	1.422222	609.78	965.49	728.18	393.22
12	3/2	$2^{-1} \cdot 3^1 \cdot 5^0$	1.5	701.96	1111.44	768	414.72
13	25/16	$2^{-4} \cdot 3^0 \cdot 5^2$	1.5625	772.63	1223.33	800	432
14	8/5	$2^3 \cdot 3^0 \cdot 5^{-1}$	1.6	813.69	1288.34	819.20	442.37
15	5/3	$2^0 \cdot 3^{-1} \cdot 5^1$	1.666667	884.36	1400.24	853.33	460.80
16	128/75	$2^7 \cdot 3^{-1} \cdot 5^{-2}$	1.706667	925.42	1465.25	873.81	471.86
17	16/9	$2^4 \cdot 3^{-2} \cdot 5^0$	1.777778	996.09	1577.14	910.22	491.52
18	15/8	$2^{-3} \cdot 3^1 \cdot 5^1$	1.875	1088.27	1723.09	960	518.40
19'	125/64	$2^{-6} \cdot 3^0 \cdot 5^3$	1.953125	1158.94	1834.99	1000	540
1'	2/1	$2^1 \cdot 3^0 \cdot 5^0$	2	1200	1900	1024	552.96

*) One K·sec. (Kayenian second) = 1.85 second; one second = 0.54 K·sec.

Table 3.4. Overview of the 19-tone musical tuning system used in the Kayenian Empire. The logarithmic scales allow easy comparison with a division of the octave in 1,200 or 1,900 equal parts.

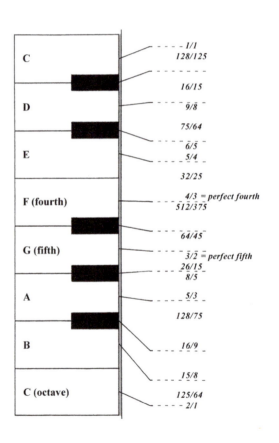

Figure 3.4. Comparison between the Kayenian 19-tone (just intonated) musical tuning system (right) and the 12-tone equal temperament keyboard (left).

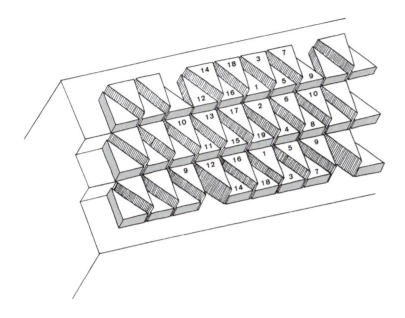

Figure 3.5. Schematic representation of the Kayenian 19-tone (just intonated) musical keyboard. Note the repeating keys at the top and the bottom, connected below the keyboard, as well as the opening between tones 9 and 12.

Figure 3.6. *Pluiging* (left) and *streemo* (right), two fretted instruments from the Kayenian Empire. Note the interrupted placement of the frets on the *pluiging*. The first and third string of the *streemo* are tuned in unison and the second string one octave higher, allowing the frets to continue across the fingerboard. These strings are used to support the melody, which is played on the fretless fourth string (tuned a fifth above the first and third strings).

advocated by Alois Hába (1893–1973), Mildred Couper (1887–1974), and Ivan Wyschnegradsky (1893–1979), among others. This does not, however, result in a significantly better approximation of the problematic intervals. Better is the 31-tone equal temperament system proposed by Christiaan Huygens (1629–95) and Adrian Fokker (1887–1972), and many existing musical works have been adapted for this. Even better, albeit technically challenging, solutions include the 53-tone equal temperament system recommended by Nikolaus Mercator (1620–87) and Robert Bosanquet (1841–1912), and the 96-tone equal temperament system promoted by Julian Carillo (1875–1965).

Others, including many outside Western classical music, firmly reject the idea of equal temperament and instead endorse a system of just intonation,[15] in which some intervals remain perfect and others very disagreeable. Among the main proponents of this approach are Harry Partch

(1901–74) and Ervin Wilson (1928–2016), among many others. In the Kayenian Empire most music is performed in a 19-tone tuning system characterized by just intonation (Table 3.4, Figure 3.4). Like alternative numeral systems, any such alternative tuning system seems destined to remain on the fringes of well-established, mainstream musical practices. Despite this sobering insight I continued to develop Kayenian musical scales and a dedicated keyboard (Figure 3.5). I also built a few instruments able to produce the music implicated by the narrative (Figure 3.6).

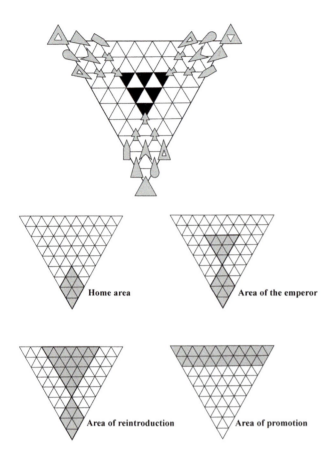

Figure 3.7. Kayenian chess board with the pieces in their starting position (top), and the four areas into which the board is divided for the player at the bottom (middle and bottom; the black triangles in the center of the board have been omitted for clarity).

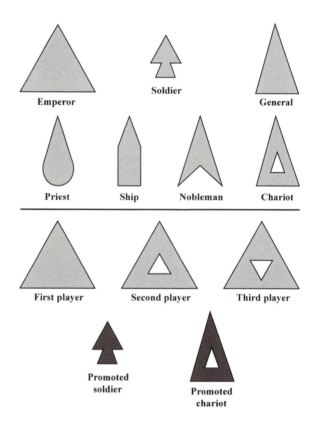

Figure 3.8. Kayenian chess pieces (top). The emperors of the three players are often distinguished by different triangles cut out of the center (middle). The reverse of soldiers and chariots are in a different color to indicate the promoted status of the piece (bottom).

A final example of objects based on the narrative of the Kayenian Empire are the alternative chess sets that I created. The game of chess is relatively old and has been considered a model for the world since medieval times. This reached its pinnacle during the Cold War and the so-called Match of the Century (Reykjavik, 1972) between Bobby Fischer (1943–2008) and Boris Spassky (born 1937). The modern international game and its associated material developed out of a series of predecessors that also gave rise to many local varieties, especially in East Asia. Many additional variants

were invented for numerous reasons, ranging from whimsical to artistic or idealistic.[16]

The chess variant popular in the Kayenian Empire is played by three players using a triangular board on which the pieces are placed on the intersections of lines (Figure 3.7, top). At the beginning of the game each player controls nine pieces: an emperor, three soldiers and a general, a priest, a ship, a nobleman, and a chariot (Figure 3.8). The aim of the game is to capture the emperors of the other players. The pieces are reminiscent of the Bauhaus chess set, designed by Josef Hartwig

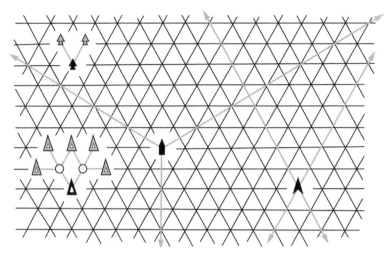

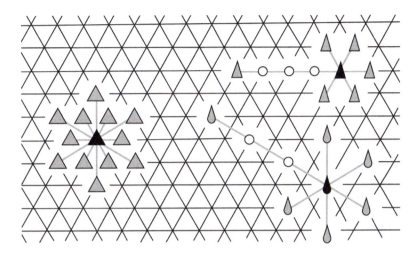

Figure 3.9. Kayenian chess moves: emperor (left), general (top right) and priest (bottom right). Open circles indicate positions occupied by other pieces.

Figure 3.10. Kayenian chess moves: soldier (top left), chariot (bottom left), ship (middle) and nobleman (bottom right). A chariot always moves two positions forward, whether the first is occupied or not. Promoted soldiers move as generals and promoted chariots as priests, but without the ability to jump. A ship that is moved to a corner of the board can reappear at its center as the only possible next move.

Figure 3.11. Kayenian chess games made of textile and leather (left) and pyro-engraved wood (right).

(1880–1956), and the only indication toward the player that controls them is the direction in which they point. Similar to *shogi* (Japanese chess), a captured piece can be placed back

on the board, within a dedicated area that is different for each player (Figure 3.7, bottom left), and positioned to show that it is now controlled by the player that captured it.

Three pieces can jump over occupied positions, generals and priests unlimited (Figure 3.9), chariots only over a single position (Figure 3.10). Soldiers and chariots can only move forward. During their first move within the last two files of the board (Figure 3.7, bottom right) they are promoted and subsequently move as a general or a priest, respectively, but without the privilege to jump. To indicate its new status the piece is turned over, displaying a different colored back (Figure 3.8, bottom). Two final noteworthy elements are that emperors can only move within a limited section of the board and that a ship that is moved into one of the corners of the board can, as its next move, reappear at the center of the board. While developing these rules I fashioned several Kayenian chess-sets, out of various materials (Figure 3.11), again creating objects based on a narrative.

This chapter is not the first public presentation of the Kayenian Empire. In November 1981 the Friends of the Kayenian

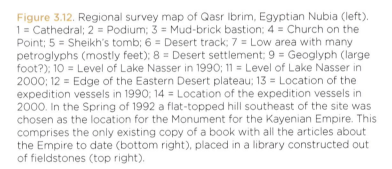

Figure 3.12. Regional survey map of Qasr Ibrim, Egyptian Nubia (left). 1 = Cathedral; 2 = Podium; 3 = Mud-brick bastion; 4 = Church on the Point; 5 = Sheikh's tomb; 6 = Desert track; 7 = Low area with many petroglyphs (mostly feet); 8 = Desert settlement; 9 = Geoglyph (large foot?); 10 = Level of Lake Nasser in 1990; 11 = Level of Lake Nasser in 2000; 12 = Edge of the Eastern Desert plateau; 13 = Location of the expedition vessels in 1990; 14 = Location of the expedition vessels in 2000. In the Spring of 1992 a flat-topped hill southeast of the site was chosen as the location for the Monument for the Kayenian Empire. This comprises the only existing copy of a book with all the articles about the Empire to date (bottom right), placed in a library constructed out of fieldstones (top right).

Figure 3.13. Scale model of a Kayenian living room, presented to the office of the *Nederlands Tijdschrift voor Geneeskunde* (Dutch Journal of Medicine) in March 1993. Note the monograph on the Kayenian Empire stored in its base.

Empire (VvK) foundation was established and in both February 1982 and November 1986 the imaginary country and its creators appeared on Dutch national television, on NCRV's *Showroom* and VPRO's *Jonge Helden,* respectively. From December 1983 until February 1984 the Empire was one of the countries that contributed to the exhibition *Imaginary Countries* in the Lijnbaanscentrum, Rotterdam. Shortly thereafter it was one of the founding members of the Association for Geofiction (GvG), established to provide a platform for creators of imaginary countries and cultures. Apart from the publications published by its creators, the Kayenian Empire featured in many journals and newspapers, including *de Volkskrant* (23 December

1983) and *NRC-Handelsblad* (7 June 1985). At the end of 1991 I collected copies of all these publications into a single bound volume, comprising seventy-five pages, and took this with me to the archaeological project in Qasr Ibrim on the Eastern shore of Lake Nasser in the Egyptian Nubian Desert (Figure 3.12, left). One Friday I walked into the desert beyond the archaeological remains, climbed one of the many flat-topped hills, and placed the book, supported and protected by rocks, in a natural niche (Figure 3.12, right). This Monument for the Kayenian Empire must be considered one of the least accessible libraries in the world.[17] It also constitutes a future archaeological find from an imaginary culture, in a way rendering it tangible.[18]

My move to Egypt in 1994 and my increasing involvement with archaeology—and the international travel associated with that discipline—brought me into contact with many alternatives to the small island in the Netherlands that I grew up on, greatly decreasing the need to devise my own. One of my last major projects was the construction of a scale model of a Kayenian living room as a farewell gift for the office of the *Nederlands Tijdschrift voor Geneeskunde* (Dutch Journal of Medicine), one of the oldest medical journals in the world, where I had worked as an intern between September 1992 and March 1993.[19] This was accompanied by a small volume containing the twenty articles that I had published as a series in *Fantas,* the journal of the Association for Geofiction, as an overview of Kayenian culture (Figure 3.13). Archaeology thus ended my involvement in the creation of the Kayenian Empire and I switched from creating objects based on a narrative to creating a narrative based on objects. I was left with an extensive experience in creative thinking, research, and publication, and obviously a small collection of unique objects.

ACKNOWLEDGMENTS

I would like to express my sincere thanks to my colleague Ruth Tringham, for encouraging me to get back in touch with my past, and to my friend Jan Kok and my brother W. (Pip) Barnard, for their inspiration. Thanks are furthermore due to Peter Biehl, Ran Boytner, Kym Faull, Efrain Kristal, and Steve Rosen for their support, and to Willeke Wendrich for her unwavering encouragement.

NOTES

1   de Muijnck 2013.

2   More 1551.

3   Swift 1735.

4   Abbott 1884.

5   Serafini 1981, 2006.

6   Xu 1987–91.

7   Of note here are also the instructional videos on world-building—creating fictional worlds to learn more about the world that we actually live in—by Edgar Grunewald, uploaded onto YouTube since February 2014 under the alias Artifexian; his series of podcasts, made together with Bill McGrath; and his TEDx presentation at the University of Strathclyde, https://www.youtube.com/watch?v=554d1lpkbLg (accessed November 3, 2022).

8   Middleton 2015, Ryan et al. 2006, Hobbs and Williams 2022, Manguel and Guadalupi 2000, Middleton 2015, Ryan et al. 2006, Sprague de Camp 1971.

9   Oberhaus 2019, 71–92.

10 In the Kayenian Empire, almost invariably the fraction 1351/305 is used, which is 355/113 in base-10. This is sufficiently accurate for all practical purposes.

11 In base-10 the first zero only occurs as the thirty-second digit after the initial 3.

12 In base-10 log π = 0.49715 (rounded) or, less accurately, 0.5.

13 Bion 1723.

14 Oberhaus 2019, 135–53.

15 Partch 1974.

16 List and Schaffner 2005, Parlett 2018, 276–308, Pritchard and Beasley 2007.

17 http://www.barnard.nl/keiolonie/monument.html (accessed 29 February 2020).

18 Farrier 2020.

19 Barnard and Overbeke 1993.

BIBLIOGRAPHY

Abbott, Edwin A. (1884), *Flatland: A Romance of Many Dimensions,* London (Seelley & Co.).

Anonymous (eighteenth century), *Rohonci kódex (The Rohonc Codex)*, Library of the Hungarian Academy of Sciences, K 114 (formerly Magyar Codex 12°1; G. Batthyány 1838), MF 1173/II (microfilm); http://real-ms.mtak.hu/80/.

——— (early fifteenth century), *The Voynich Manuscript,* Beinecke Rare Book and Manuscript Library, Yale University, MS 408 (H.P. Kraus 1969); https://brbl-dl.library.yale.edu/vufind/Record/3519597; https://archive.org/details/TheVoynichManuscript/.

Barnard, Hans and A. John P.M. Overbeke (1993), Dubbelpublikatie van Oorspronkelijke Stukken in en uit het *Nederlands Tijdschrift voor Geneeskunde*, [Duplicate Publication of Original Manuscripts in and from the *Nederlands Tijdschrift voor Geneeskunde*],

Nederlands Tijdschrift voor Geneeskunde 137, 593–97. [in Dutch with an English abstract]

Bion, Nicolas (1723), *The Construction and Principal Uses of Mathematical Instruments,* London (J. Richardson, translated and supplemented edition by Edmund Stone of the 1709 French original).

de Muijnck, Wim (2013), The Meaning of Lives and the Meaning of Things, *Journal of Happiness Studies* 14, 1291–1307, DOI:10.1007/s10902-012-9382-y.

Farrier, David (2020), *Footprints: In Search of Future Fossils,* New York (Farrar, Straus and Giroux).

Hobbs, Harry and George Williams (2022), *Micronations and the Search for Sovereignty*, Cambridge (Cambridge University Press).

List, Larry and Ingrid Schaffner (2005), *The Imagery of Chess Revisited,* New York (George Braziller Publishers).

Manguel, Alberto and Gianni Guadalupi (2000), *The Dictionary of Imaginary Places: The Newly Updated and Expanded Classic*, San Diego (Harcourt Inc., expanded edition of the 1980 original).

Middleton, Nick (2015), *An Atlas of Countries That Don't Exist: A Compendium of Fifty Unrecognized and Largely Unnoticed States,* London (Macmillan).

More, Thomas (1551), *A Little, True Book, both Beneficial and Enjoyable, about How Things Should Be in the New Island Utopia,* London (Abraham Veal, translation by Ralph Robinson of the 1516 Latin original).

Oberhaus, Daniel (2019), *Extraterrestrial Languages,* Cambridge (Massachusetts Institute of Technology Press).

Partch, Harry (1974), *Genesis of a Music: An Account of a Creative Work, Its Roots, and Its Fulfillments,* New York (Da Capo Press, second, enlarged edition).

Parlett, David (2018), *History of Board Games: The Updated Version of the Oxford History of Board Games,* Brattleboro (Echo Point Books and Media).

Pritchard, David B. and John D. Beasley (2007), *The Classified Encyclopedia of Chess Variants,* Harpenden, Hertfordshire (John Beasley, second, revised edition).

Ryan, John, George Dunford, and Simon Sellars (2006), *Micronations: The Lonely Planet Guide to Home-Made Nations,* Footscray, Australia (Lonely Planet Publications).

Serafini, Luigi (1981), *Codex Seraphinianus,* Milan (Franco Maria Ricci, first edition in two volumes).

—— (2006), *Codex Seraphinianus,* Milan (Rizzoli, third, augmented edition of the 1981 original).

Sprague de Camp, Lyon (1971), *Lost Continents: The Atlantis Theme in History, Science and Literature*, Mineola (Dover Publications, reprint of the 1954 original).

Swift, Jonathan (1735), *Travels into Several Remote Nations of the World: In Four Parts: By Lemuel Gulliver, First a Surgeon, and Then a Captain of Several Ships,* Dublin (George Faulkner, second, revised edition of the 1726 anonymous original).

Xu, Bing (1987–1991), *A Book from the Sky (Tianshu),* Hanying, Caiyu (Xu Bing).

2

A SECOND EXERCISE IN AUTOVOCALITY

THE ARCHAEOLOGY OF MY LIVING

HANS BARNARD

Organic form, in an organic medium. My steps slowed, and stopped. I stared. The sickness came over me. It seemed one of the wonders of the world. The noisy traffic on Piccadilly went silent, and I was the still center of the universe. A tingling in the palms of the hands, a loosening in the solar plexus. I looked and my tongue seemed to be moving over carved ivory, cool and smooth. Don't ask. I haven't a clue. (David Esterly 2012, p. 44)

Archaeology can be defined as the study of human development, behavior, and history as inferred from material remains. The discipline is solidly based upon and almost entirely dependent on objects. This is facilitated by the fact that objects created and used by humans intricately and inevitably complement functionality with meaning.[1] This implies that a careful study of objects can reveal a myriad of information about their human producers and users. Since the mid-twentieth century it has become clear that in different persons the same object can provoke very different emotional and intellectual responses, a phenomenon identified as 'multivocality.' Here I propose the term 'autovocality' to mean the narrative of the author prompted by one or more objects. In this chapter I will first briefly elaborate on the intimate connections between humans and objects and then explore the narratives associated with a few objects that are of specific importance to me.

Using the game of chess as a model for the world, Swiss linguist Ferdinand de Saussure (1959, 110) wrote: "Take a knight, for instance. By itself is it an element in the game? Certainly not, for by its material make-up—outside its square and the other conditions of the game—it means nothing to the player; it becomes a real, concrete element only when endowed with value and wedded to it." While developing modern marketing and advertisement strategies Ernest Dichter (2002, 98) arrived at the same conclusion: "Studies . . . show . . . that products are not inanimate objects, that to separate or neglect them as objects of scientific analysis is a major oversight on the part of the social scientist." More recently, John Urry (2007, 45) voiced a similar view: "The powers of 'humans' are always augmented by various material worlds, of clothing, tools, objects, paths, buildings. . . . Human life we might say is never just human."

That this intimate relationship between humans and their material environment has considerable time-depth is noted by Raymond Tallis (2003, 234): "The extraordinary stability of tools such as hand-axes over time (1.5 million years) and over space (Europe, Africa, Asia) could not have been an accident, nor due solely to inertia. . . . When manufacturing tools, the toolmaker would be making a sign as well as an instrument, and he would want his sign to say the same things as had the tools made by his predecessors." Gregory Bateson (2000, 318) argued that this relationship is intimate to an extent that obscures the boundary between the object and its user: "Consider a blind man with a stick. Where does the blind man's self begin? At the tip of the stick? At the handle of the stick? Or at some point halfway up the stick?" An observation echoed by Kirk Woolford and Stuart Dunn (2014, 125): "Tools may extend humans' existing action and perception capabilities. Tools are treated as functional extensions of the user. . . . The boundaries between bodies, tools, and the environment are fluid and dependent upon relationships more than materials." Or in the words of Andy Clark and David Chalmers (1998, 18): "Most of us already accept that the self outstrips the boundaries of consciousness . . . these boundaries may also fall beyond the skin . . . once the hegemony of skin and skull is usurped, we may be able to see ourselves more truly as creatures of the world."

In his essay "Regrets sur ma vieille robe de chambre," French philosopher Denis Diderot (1713–84) described how his room was once chaotic and happy, but now elegant yet grim.[2] He attributed this change to his purchase of a new dressing gown. This prompted an almost subconscious effort to match the room with the gown and consequently in a number of other purchases and modifications. The final result was a complete transformation of the room, but more importantly also a fundamental change in one's mood while residing in it. Especially formidable manifestations of the phenomenon of human individuals affected by their environment are the Stendhal and Jerusalem syndromes, in which physical symptoms—including confusion, dizziness, tachycardia, fainting, or hallucinations—result from encountering objects of great artistic or religious importance.[3]

All of us have at times been deeply touched by hearing a musical phrase, often when we least expected it. Some of us will likely have had a similar experience when confronted with a physical work of art. As argued above, every object has a profound influence on our being in the world, albeit often without being actively perceived, and thus capable of shaping our emotions. This is most evident for works of art, which are usually created specifically to tug our heartstrings. Such reactions are personal and different for each of us, so the following is necessarily an exercise in autovocality. At the same time it is meant to serve as an encouragement to take some time to look around and reflect on the emotional connections that you have with the objects that you are confronted with in your daily life (a similar avenue was chosen by Enrico Ferraris in Chapter 4 of this volume).

AN EXERCISE IN AUTOVOCALITY

The first occurrence of a visceral response to a physical work of art that I clearly remember was upon viewing the suprematist paintings by Kazimir Malevich (1879–1935) in the collection of the Stedelijk Museum, Amsterdam, one day in the 1980s. Another instance, in April 2007, was prompted by *Oath of the Horatii*. Not the painting in the Louvre, Paris, but the second, slightly adapted version completed in 1786 by Jacques-Louis David (1748–1825), with the assistance of his pupil Anne-Louis Girodet de Roussy-Trioson (1767–1824), and on display in the Toledo Museum of Art. A third time it happened when I visited the Getty Museum, Los Angeles, in the summer of 2014 and went to view *Christ's Entry into Brussels in 1889* by James Ensor (1860–1949), but was instead confronted by his *Adam and Eve Expelled from Paradise* hanging in the same room on temporary loan from the Koninklijk Museum voor Schone Kunsten, Antwerp.

Much more overwhelming and emotional, however, was my encounter with a Ptolemaic mosaic depicting a sitting dog. This happened one day in the 1990s when I saw a slide of it during a lecture presented by its excavators in Cairo, Egypt, where I was living at the time. The original was made in Alexandria in the second century BCE by combining tesserae ranging from one to four millimeters in the *opus vermiculatum* technique. The image is about 3.25 × 3.25 m. (10.5 × 10.5 feet) and seems to represent the first time that this motif occurs in an Egyptian floor mosaic. It remains unclear where the mosaic was originally located, though it is now on display in the Bibliotheca Alexandrina Antiquities Museum, Alexandria. A similar overwhelming emotional response was triggered when I entered the expiatory church of the Sagrada Familia in Barcelona, after being extracted from Egypt—with a group of undergraduate students—during the uprising in February 2011. This idiosyncratic and as yet unfinished structure was redesigned from 1883 onward by Antoni Gaudí (1852–1926) after the original architect Francisco de Paula del Villar (1828–1901) had withdrawn from the building project started in 1882. The church was consecrated and declared a minor basilica by Pope Benedict XVI in November 2010, just before its otherworldly interior touched me in a way that is difficult or impossible to put into words. For a relatively successful effort I refer to the epigraph at the head of this chapter,[4] describing a similar emotional response to a very different object.

I obviously and regrettably do not own any works by Malevich, David, or Ensor, but I hold a small collection of works of art, acquired in close collaboration with my spouse. Here I would like to tell the story of five of these. This is meant as an exercise in autovocality, but more importantly as a stimulus and inspiration for the reader to engage on a similar endeavor. I picked works of art because of their importance to me, but all of us possess objects that are of special significance to our being in the world. Doing the research for this chapter, mostly by rummaging through my personal archive, was truly inspiring and brought back many distant memories, partly also by serendipitously coming across entirely unrelated documents.

Between 1979 and 1981 I lived in Leiden, the Netherlands, on the ninth floor of a ten-floor building that housed university students. In typical local academic tradition, each floor selected new renters when rooms became available. For this, candidates were interviewed in rapid succession by all current renters. I was the chair of one such meeting and one of our potential neighbors was Arjan Loeffen, an aspiring author and painter who studied Dutch languages and literature. He made a good first impression and after being admitted quickly became one of the central characters of our small community. Apart from his studies and his social life he was painting prolifically, at the time in a style that reminded me of the luminous paintings on black velvet from Indonesia—a former colony of the Netherlands—that I admired as a child.[5] When one of his paintings came back from an exhibition unsold I purchased it at a discounted price and it has been hanging in my successive living rooms ever since (Figure 2.1). To these its dark colors and serene image added a sense of peace and mystery.

The next two pieces we obtained when living in Egypt between 1995 and 2000. After a short period in an apartment in Zamalek—an island in the Nile in the center of Cairo—we relocated to Harraniya, west of Cairo on the road between Giza and Saqqara. We moved into one of the remarkable houses built by the influential Egyptian architect Ramses Wissa Wassef (1911–74) in the back of the art center that he founded in 1951, together with his wife Sophie Habib Gorgi (born 1922). From our bedroom balcony we had a view of the Great Pyramid, until that was blocked by the high-rises sprouting up all over the Cairo metropolitan area because of the rapid population increase in Egypt. Our house was a domed structure with rooms constructed in a rising spiral around a central stairwell, with terraces on the roof of most. Apart from the summer heat, mosquitos, dust, snakes, and power outages we lived there happily for four years, with a dial-in internet connection and daily deliveries of fresh buffalo milk.

The Wissa Wassef Art Center was established by Ramses and Sophie to prove their conviction that artistic creativity is

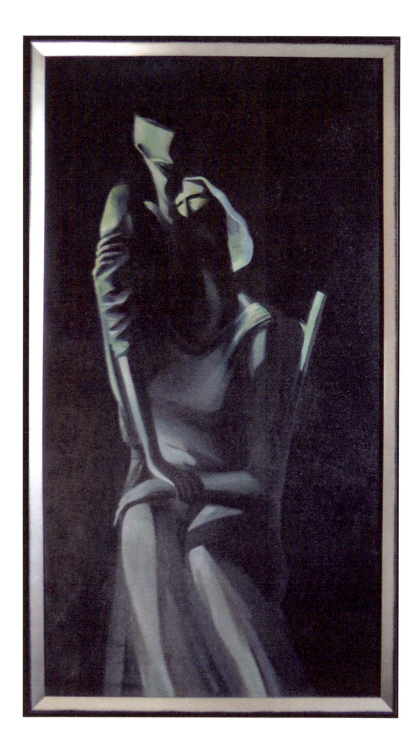

Figure 2.1. Arjan Loeffen, *Henk Loves Marleen* (c. 1980, oil on canvas, 54 × 94 cm. [21.25 × 37 inches]).

Figure 2.2. Ashour Maselhi (عاشور مصيلحي), under supervision of Sophie Habib Gorgi (Ramses Wissa Wassef Art Center), African Landscape (1994, cotton and dyed wool, 108 × 184 cm. [42.5 × 72.5 inches]).

innate in everybody and that all children are endowed with artistic potential. They started by teaching a group of children to weave wall-hangings out of wool with the imagery conceived and executed directly in the medium, without the use of a sketched design, model, or example. A second generation of weavers, working in both wool and cotton, is now supervised by Suzanne and Yoanna, the daughters of Ramses and Sophie. Others are working to produce pottery or dye the yarns needed by the weavers. Several times we came home to find the trunks of the palm trees within the compound covered with yarns freshly dyed in various colors and hung out to dry. At other times the air was thick with acrid smoke from the pottery kiln. While living in Harraniya we saved to purchase one of the wall-hangings produced by a weaver of the first generation who was inspired by a television documentary on wildlife in Africa (Figure 2.2). We chose this one among many depictions of life in Egypt as wild animals, especially raccoons, have always been a major theme in our household. The idiosyncratic perspective furthermore reminded us of ancient Egyptian art. We also bought, or were given by the family, a work in cotton, several pieces of pottery, and a watercolor painted by Sophie.

Another painting we acquired as the indirect result of my position as a local employee at the Royal Netherlands Embassy in Cairo. Once I familiarized myself with the procedures to apply for small grants in the educational and cultural sphere, I requested funding to bring Leen Vroegindeweij (1948–2006), a painter from the Netherlands and the husband of a friend and colleague, to Cairo for an 'action painting' project. For this he would bring the necessary materials and within two weeks produce a number of paintings inspired by his experiences in Egypt. These would subsequently be exhibited, and preferably also sold, in November 1999 in the Townhouse Gallery (Figure 2.3). This cultural center was founded in 1998 by Canadian educator William Wells and Syrian author and artist Yasser Gerab in a building constructed in 1890–1900 by a Jewish merchant to house Jewish families and later also an offshoot from the nearby synagogue in Adly Street. At the time the gallery was restrained by state censorship. Accusations of being a Zionist enterprise, published by the owner of a competing gallery, made the government advise art students not to visit and security forces repeatedly searched the premises. Following the popular uprising in 2011 the gallery briefly enjoyed more freedom, but in December 2015 it was again raided by the government and all activities ceased. The following spring part of the building collapsed and the government asked for it to be demolished. A committee of neighboring businesses and private individuals, however, instead secured the permissions and funding to restore and reopen the gallery and it is now thriving, at least until the time of writing.

At the end of Leen's exhibition—together with Martin McInally and Kaare Troelsen, on the first floor, and Amina Mansour and Shady al-Noshokaty on the second—not all his paintings were sold and he invited us to pick our favorite as a reward for our initiative. We chose a happy one, partly painted with a sock instead of a brush and in places created in paint mixed with desert sand to give it a more interesting texture (Figure 2.4). It has continuously hung in our successive living rooms, and looking at it now sparks feelings of happiness mixed with sorrow. In 2006 Leen came back home sick from a holiday in Spain and died of an aggressive form of cancer within days of his return.

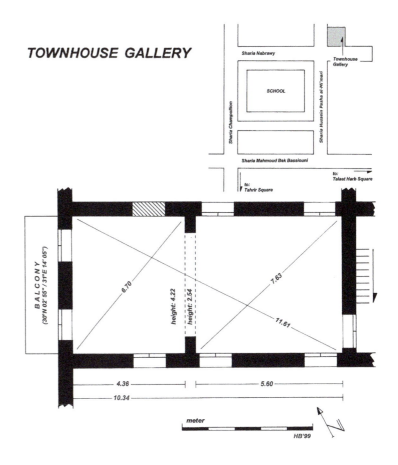

Figure 2.3. Plan of two rooms on the third floor of the Townhouse Gallery (Downtown Cairo, Egypt) prepared by the author for the 'action painting' project by Leen Vroegindeweij, sponsored by the Royal Netherlands Embassy in Cairo, November 1999.

In September 2000 we moved from Cairo to Los Angeles, where we purchased a condominium apartment in 2001, only weeks after the September 11 attacks. Ten years later, when interest rates dropped to an absolute minimum, we decided to refinance our mortgage. In the United States such actions are more or less public affairs and shortly after signing the documents we were called by one Sel Sarkin, inquiring if we were interested in taking out a life insurance. We had a few meetings with him and when we started seriously considering taking him up on his offer we decided to research his credentials. Until that moment he had appeared the archetypical

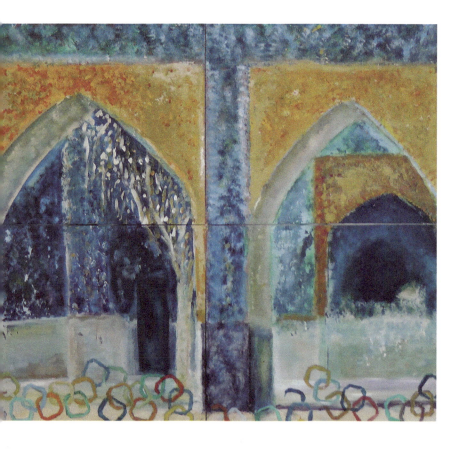

Figure 2.4. Leen Vroegindeweij, *Alhambra* (1999, acrylic on four canvas panels, 102 × 124 cm. [40 × 49 inches]).

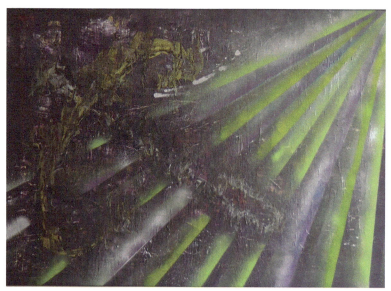

Figure 2.5. Sel Sarkin, *Untitled*, (2011, acrylic on wood, 94 × 130 cm. [37 × 51 inches]).

insurance agent, rather bland and almost boring. One website, however, showed a very different persona. Sel was shown in a leather jacket advertising his work as a painter. When we confronted him with our findings he rather self-consciously offered to create a painting inspired by his impression of us. A few weeks later we drove to his house and picked up a large, abstract painting, executed mostly in black, greens, and silver (Figure 2.5). When first encountered it was not our immediate favorite and we purchased it partly because of the associated story, partly because of the psycho-social pressure we experienced. Shortly thereafter we had to return it as the framer asked for it to be made rectangular, but ultimately it arrived in our now refinanced house. We have since moved, switched to

another financial advisor, and taken out a different insurance policy, but the painting is still displayed on our walls and has slowly grown on me.

In April 2013 we were scheduled to attend the 78th annual meeting of the Society for American Archaeology in Honolulu, Hawai'i. This is obviously a bad location for a conference. It is far and thus expensive for all participants—even from Los Angeles it is a flight of more than five hours—meaning that only those with funding could attend, excluding many students and non-academic archaeologists. Many of those who did attend brought their family and made their trip into a short holiday, leaving much of the conference unattended. We instead decided to travel a few days early and see something of Hawai'i before the scholarly part of our journey. For this we booked a room in a bed-and-breakfast run by Donald Munroe on windward O'ahu. On his business webpage Don stated that he was born in Scotland and served in the British army in the Middle East before moving to New York and Hawai'i. The reviews of his place were positive, although some warned of the erotic imagery on display. We were curious to say the least.

Upon arrival our assumption that Don had served in Afghanistan or Iraq turned out to be incorrect. He had instead been in Aden, Yemen, during the Suez crisis in 1956, worked in New York most of his life, and retired to Hawai'i with his partner Louis de Chambs. When we expressed our surprise, Dee—as Louis was invariably addressed—claimed to be able to top this, as he had been part of D-day and served in France, where he ended up collating maps for central military command. Before and after this he trained as an artist, but made a living in the fashion industry, designing accessories such as bags and belts. First these were produced in Italy, and he and Don traveled there regularly, but when the industry moved to China they went there every year instead, briefly stopping in Hawai'i more than once. They fell in love with the islands and decided to retire to one of them.

The house of Don and Dee in Kaneohe was full of memorabilia and collectibles—leaving limited space for guests and their personal effects—including many paintings and other works of art made by Dee during his long career. Most depicted attractive young men, in poses meant to be sensual rather than homoerotic, as we initially labeled them. One idiosyncratic painting was the result of a discussion that Dee had conducted with some fellow artists. They had challenged him to paint women for a change and critiqued the outcome as not showing real women, but rather men with breasts, an assessment with which we fully agreed. We could obviously not leave Dee and Hawai'i without purchasing a painting and ultimately decided on one showing a crouching young man, naked except for the ring on the second toe of his left foot (Figure 2.6), lending its name to the painting. Among artworks that I own this is my favorite painting and it is hanging above my beloved 1984 Yamaha G1 grand piano. Apart from the painting itself, I also enjoy the responses it evokes in visitors and house-guests, which are likely different from their reaction to an artistic depiction of a naked woman. I purposefully used it as a contrasting backdrop for the pictures in my 'Trachtenbuch,' a series of photographs showing me wearing different outfits.[6] This project was inspired by the book of watercolors depicting Matthäus Schwarz (1497–1574) and his

Figure 2.6. Louis de Chambs, *The Ring*, (c. 2003, oil on board, 62 × 97 cm. [24.5 × 38 inches]).

attire. Schwarz was the personal assistant of merchant and banker Jakob Fugger (1459–1525) as he became Großbürger of the Free Imperial City of Augsburg and possibly the richest man who ever lived.

This brief essay is not meant to resemble an art-historical discussion or an exhibition catalogue, but is intended to inspire the reader to think about the biography of objects of great importance to them. These need not be works of art, as all objects are able to have a profound effect on our being in the world, as briefly demonstrated at the beginning. Every object has its story and in combination with our own these determine our being in the world.[7] Recording these narratives should be considered the archaeology of one's own life; it turned into such a rewarding exercise for me that I highly recommend its implementation to others. However, as Vladimir Nabokov warns us in the first chapter of his 1972 novel *Transparent Things,* caution is warranted when doing so: "When we concentrate on a material object, whatever its situation, the very act of attention may lead to our involuntary sinking into the history of the object. Novices must learn to skim over matter if they want matter to stay at the exact level of the moment. . . . A thin veneer of immediate reality is spread over natural and artificial matter, and whoever wishes to remain in the now, on the now, should please not break its tension film. Otherwise the inexperienced miracle-worker will find himself no longer walking on water but descending upright among staring fish."

ACKNOWLEDGMENTS

I would like to express my sincere thanks to Louis de Chambs, Arjan Loeffen, Ashour Maselhi, Sel Sarkin, and Leen Vroegindeweij, as well as all the other artists that feature in this chapter. Thanks are furthermore due to Peter Biehl, Ran Boytner, Kym Faull, Efrain Kristal, Steve Rosen, Ruth Tringham, and Willeke Wendrich, as well as all the other scholars who feature in this chapter.

NOTES

1   Gosden and Marshall 1999.
2   McCracken 1988, 118–29, Tunstall and Scott 2016.
3   Innocenti et al. 2014, Witztum and Kilian 1999.
4   The author of this quote, David Esterly, passed away during the writing of this chapter. His obituary was published in *The Economist* of 29 June 2019 (p. 86).
5   By sheer coincidence much of this chapter was written on the Indonesian island of Bali.
6   http://www.barnard.nl/Trachtenbuch/ (accessed 29 February 2020).
7   Arnold et al. 2012, Iweins 2022.

BIBLIOGRAPHY

Arnold, Jeanne E., Anthony P. Graesch, Enzo Ragazzini, and Elinor Ochs (2012), *Life at Home in the Twenty-First Century: 32 Families Open Their Doors*, Los Angeles (Cotsen Institute of Archaeology Press).

Bateson, Gregory (2000), *Steps to an Ecology of Mind: Collected Essays in Anthropology, Psychiatry, Evolution, and Epistemology* (reprint of the 1972 original with a new foreword by Mary C. Bateson), Chicago (Chicago University Press).

Clark, Andy and David Chalmers (1998), The Extended Mind, *Analysis* 58(1), 7–19.

de Saussure, Ferdinand (1959), *Course in General Linguistics* (edited by Charles Bally and Albert Sechehaye, in cooperation with Albert Redilinger; English translation of the 1916 French original by Wade Baskin), New York (Philosophical Library).

Dichter, Ernest (2002), *The Strategy of Desire* (reprint of the 1960 original with a new introduction by Arthur A. Berger), New Brunswick and London (Transaction Publishers).

Gosden, Chris and Yvonne Marshall (1999), The Cultural Biography of Objects, *World Archaeology* 31(2), 169–78, DOI:10.1080/00438243.1999.9980439.

Innocenti, Claudia, Giulia Fioravanti, Raffaello Spiti, and Carlo Faravelli (2014), La sindrome di Stendhal fra psicoanalisi e neuroscienze (The Stendhal Syndrome Between Psychoanalysis and

Neuroscience), *Rivista di Psichiatria* 49(2), 61–66. [in Italian with an English abstract]

Iweins, Barbara (2022), *Katalog*, Paris (delpire & co).

McCracken, Grant (1988), *Culture and Consumption: New Approaches to the Symbolic Character of Consumer Goods and Activities,* Bloomington and Indianapolis (Indiana University Press).

Tallis, Raymond (2003), *The Hand: A Philosophical Inquiry into Human Being,* Edinburgh (Edinburgh University Press).

Tunstall, Kate and Katie Scott (2016), Denis Diderot, *Regrets on Parting with My Old Dressing Gown,* Translated by Kate Tunstall and Katie Scott, *Oxford Art Journal* 39(2), 175–84, DOI:10.1093/oxartj/kcw015.

Urry, John (2007), *Mobilities,* Cambridge and Malden (Polity Press).

Witztum, Eliezer and Moshe Kilian (1999), The 'Jerusalem Syndrome'—Fantasy and Reality: A Survey of Accounts from the 19th Century to the End of the Millennium, *Israel Journal of Psychiatry* 36(4), 260–71.

Woolford, Kirk, and Stuart Dunn (2014), "Micro Mobilities and Affordances of Past Places," in: Jim Leary, ed., *Past Mobilities: Archaeological Approaches to Movement and Mobility,* pp. 113–28, Franham and Burlington (Ashgate).

BEYOND ARCHAEOLOGY

DISARTICULATION AND ITS CONSEQUENCES

DOUG BAILEY

In a session with the title "Entangling Ancient Art" at the 2019 meetings of the Theoretical Archaeology Group in Syracuse, New York, I placed a painstakingly reconstructed and conserved ancient ceramic amphora into a reinforced plastic shipping bag and pounded the bag (and the amphora inside it) with a 10-pound (4.5 kg.) lump hammer. Seven or eight whacks and the amphora was a pile of newly created sherds and dust (Figure 1.1). Part performance piece, more an illustration of the potentials one can explore by disarticulating an object from its archaeological status, the aim of the destruction was to investigate what an art/archaeology might enable. When they left the session, many members of the audience took one of the newly liberated sherds with them; I asked each sherd adopter to take their fragment on their travels, to work, on holiday, and then to report back with photographs and comments, which could be posted on social media (also discussed by Maite Zubiaurre and Filomena Cruz in Chapter 7 of this volume).[1]

Figure 1.1. Releasing the amphora project: disarticulation (Theoretical Archaeology Group meetings, 2019, Syracuse, New York).

Much of what I had done in my presentation at the Theoretical Archaeology Group troubled several of the attendees of the session: I had intentionally broken an archaeological artifact that had been carefully and professionally reconstructed; the fragments thus created, I had distributed to individuals regardless of whether or not those people had archaeological, conservation, or other relevant skills and experience; and I had stated that I had no interest in regaining the individual sherds or in reassembling the amphora. Worse still, when asked by a sceptic what my intention was in smashing and distributing the material, I replied that I did not know that I had any intention at all, that I did not have a clear set of aims, objectives, or methods in mind, and that I did not intend to reach any academic conclusion or grand interpretation about a relevant archaeological topic.[2] I was not playing by the rules. The performance in Syracuse and its aftermath fit within the loose bounds of what I call an art/archaeology. In this chapter, I explore this concept and practice, and I offer a short comment on what art/archaeology entails (as well as what it challenges and makes possible) through a description and discussion of several recent publications, performances, and exhibitions, specifically the *Ineligible* exhibition that ran from March to June 2020 at the International Museum for Contemporary Sculpture in Santo Tirso, Portugal.[3]

ART/ARCHAEOLOGY

In two recent papers,[4] I argued that there is a fertile territory available for archaeologists to explore beyond the boundaries of archaeology as traditionally practiced. It is an uncharted domain where much of the basic premise of archaeology does not apply. It is a place where we can "let go beyond" and travel out of the reach of the existing, standard, traditional, widely practiced (and without question, excellent and professional) archaeologies of art and of artistic collaborations with archaeologists.[5] While those recent articles provide more detailed characterizations of art/archaeology, a working definition for use in this chapter runs as follows: the disarticulation of an object from its prehistoric, ancient, or historic context; the

repurposing of the resulting disarticulated fragmentary piece(s) as raw materials; and the use of those raw materials to make creative work that engages (potentially in a disruptive way) a contemporary social or political issue, debate, or challenge.[6]

The amphora-smashing event and the continued wanderings of the individual fragments that the breakage enabled, however, only do partial justice to this definition. The artifact (in this case the amphora) was disarticulated from its status as an object of the past to be preserved, conserved, guarded, stored, studied, and deployed in archaeological analysis and research. Indeed, the distribution of the fragments into the jacket pockets and lap-top bags of those session attendees who opted to participate (and a majority of those present decided to do so), made impossible any future work of that standard type. The individual sherds, thus, are the fragmentary pieces that become the raw material with which creative work is made: the latter being the image and texts, relationships and narratives, that adopters have posted on social media. Perhaps the least clear connection of the amphora project to art/archaeology, as defined above, is whether or not it engaged with a contemporary social or political issue.[7]

Here, all that I am in a position to offer is the suggestion that the smashing and distribution of fragments stimulate a discussion of the assumption that objects of the past have a particular status in our world that comes from their connection with what came before: that being of the past grants an object special value; that sharing that value are artifacts, but also antiques and other objects surviving from the past, as well as less tangible concepts that derive their essence and power from historical position (such as descent, lineage, ownership, occupation, territory, or residence), indeed perhaps even the principle of precedence as practiced in law and philosophy; and, that the ontological basis of each of these objects and senses is secure because of these connections to the past.

Put more bluntly, the question that the amphora disarticulation posed is this: what is the basis of our shared belief that the past matters, and thus that it should be preserved? Whether or not that is a political or social issue of the contemporary world that would benefit from our engagement (though, on a personal note, I suggest that it is), I would argue that the amphora-smashing project is perhaps truest to the more general element of art/archaeology (the more amorphous letting-go-beyond part) that asks us to explore new territory and untraditional practice and to make new work in ways through which we are not certain what the output, result, or end product will be (a project involving destruction in archaeological research is briefly discussed by Annelou van Gijn in Chapter 29 of this volume).

EXPLORING ART/ARCHAEOLOGY

Other examples of experiments and explorations of the shape that an art/archaeology might take are available and I have addressed them in print elsewhere. One example is my destruction through chemical dissolving of images from a set of research slides formally held in the archaeological and ethnographic archive of the university where I work.[8] Another is a series of five unconnected, multi-page-montage, article-length, publications in which I juxtaposed text and image in efforts to insert open-ended provocations about academic narrative into the table of contents of what were otherwise traditionally edited academic books, and in which I wanted to ask a range of questions about how and why we do what we do when we study the past archaeologically: about why we value differentially the surface of the human body and the surface of the earth and when that difference in perception might have emerged;[9] about how we value select categories of data (such as subsistence, or technology) as preferentially important in archaeological and historic analysis;[10] about why we promote the human-centric understanding of the passage of time;[11] and about how we justify the mismatch that separates the coarse scale of archaeological data and our analyses of it from the intimate scale of the interpretations that we offer, about agency and emotion for example.[12]

A recent monograph works through a more detailed and lengthy argument for alternative engagements with prehistoric architecture,[13] as did subsequent intentional performative disruptions of that book (itself taken to be material artifact) as a

Figure 1.2. *Breaking the Surface*: drilling and cutting the book.

component of our standard expectations of the role that should be played in academia by book writing (and by publishing, selling, reviewing, and reading) and a similarly charged challenge to the expected coherence of the monograph author's narrative. I made manifest that art/archaeological performance on the paper, ink, and binding of that book about art/archaeology when I perforated the book with a ¾-inch (19 mm.) drill bit driven by a machine-shop drill press, and in a separate set of actions, in the creation of fifty artists' copies of the book, into each of which I cut holes through the series of pages in which I had published otherwise standard renderings of archaeological data and interpretation (Figure 1.2).[14]

THE INELIGIBLE PROJECT

The aim of this chapter is not to relive those performances or repeat the arguments in those publications and, to be frank, in their non-narrative art/archaeologicability it would be difficult to repeat, here in words and printed text, the arguments originally made in image and action. In the remainder of this chapter, therefore, I report on a current project that has voyaged more deeply into the unusual terrain of an art/archaeology. From March to June 2020, the International Museum of Contemporary Sculpture in Santo Tirso Portugal hosted the exhibition "Creative (un)makings: Disruptions in Art/Archaeology."[15] A central part of this was *Ineligible*, an installation of twenty-three works created by artists and archaeologists using as raw materials the artifacts recovered during excavations that preceded the construction of the Transbay Transit Center in San Francisco, California.[16]

In San Francisco, the archaeological assessment that had taken place in advance of the building of the Transbay Center unearthed many thousands of artifacts and produced important insight into a vital period of the history of San Francisco: the mid- to late nineteenth century. William Self Associates in combination with PaleoWest of Phoenix, Arizona (the latter having acquired William Self Associates since the excavations took place) carried out the preconstruction historical assessment and digging, and had completed post-excavation analysis and produced the requisite formal reports before I took legal possession of the material. Currently, a small exhibition of some artifacts recovered is in place at the TransBay Center, and the Transbay Joint Powers Authority maintains a website providing an overview of the archaeological remains.[17] As on many archaeological projects, in their analysis of the material excavated, the PaleoWest team made standard determinations of which objects were worthy of further study, and which were surplus to requirements: the latter being objects either that had little historic or scientific value or of which multiple examples already existed in museums and archives. Those objects deemed surplus were termed 'ineligible,' in the sense that they did not fit the criteria for further analysis or public presentation. As it turned out, in an unplanned conversation with one of the PaleoWest archaeologists, I asked if I could take possession of (and legal responsibility for) the ineligible objects. Their answer was one of relief: relief from their ongoing (and ethically complicated) custodial care for these historic materials, which, though they could not formally discard, were of no scientific or cultural value.

With the help of San Francisco State University undergraduate students, with a major in anthropology,[18] I sorted through all of the ineligible materials. This process followed an art/archaeological methodology: we removed objects from the plastic and paper bags into which they had been placed on site; we discarded all labelling that provided contextual, spatial, stratigraphic, historic, or other information (this included paper labels placed in bags and Sharpie-written information on the exterior of the bags); we examined the material of manufacture (or of natural origin) for each object; we created simple new classificatory categories (such as glass bottle, metal, leather, or plastic); and finally, using those categories, we allocated each object to its new, anti-contextual, assemblage.

While this lab work was underway, I sent out an email request to eighty-two artists, archaeologists, makers, designers, and others who I had met, heard of, or long wanted to work with.[19] My request was simple and the terms of engagement brief:

In accepting the invitation to participate, contributors commit to repurpose (disassemble, take apart, grind up) the artifacts they receive, and then to use the resulting substance(s) as the raw material base(s) for making new creative work. There are no other limitations or guidelines, beyond the instruction that the work made should engage contemporary social or political issues and debates.

I worried that nobody would respond, let alone that someone would do so with a positive request for an assemblage to work with. My concerns were short-lived; positive replies arrived by return email within hours of my clicking 'send.' In the end, the response was overwhelming, and the cost of shipping materials was the main constraint that limited the number of creators I could involve.[20]

EXAMPLES

In the space that remains here, I describe two of the works created for *Ineligible* and offer comments from their makers. The first is the work of Spanish archaeologist Alfredo Gonzáles-Ruibal of the Instituto de Ciencias del Patrimonio del

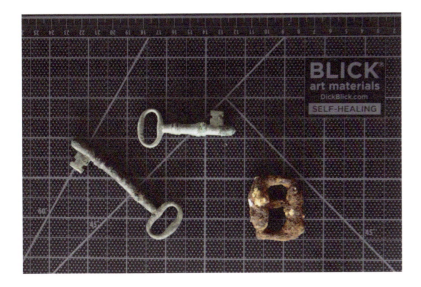

Figure 1.3. *Ineligible* project: Kit number 11.

Figure 1.4. *Ineligible* project: untitled work by Alfredo Gonzáles-Ruibal and Álvaro Minguito Palomares.

Consejo Superior de Investigaciones Científicas in Santiago de Compostela, Spain, and his colleague Álvaro Minguito Palomares; the second is work created by Portuguese photographer Valter Ventura.[21]

Gonzáles-Ruibal and Palomares received Kit number 11, an assortment of unidentified, corroded, rusted metal artifacts (Figure 1.3), and produced a short video (2 minutes and 9 seconds long) and a set of eighteen color photographs (Figure 1.4), all of which the authors made during a July 2019 visit to Cerro del Pingarrón, a small, nondescript hill 40 kilometers (25 miles) south of Madrid. In the commentary they write of their visit, Gonzáles-Ruibal and Palomares remind us that in February 1937 (during the Spanish Civil War), Republican soldiers repeatedly tried (and failed) to take Pingarrón during the Battle of Jarama; tremendous casualties resulted. With them during their 2019 visit to Pingarrón, Gonzáles-Ruibal and Palomares took two metal keys from Kit number 11, and once at the hill, Alfredo and Álvaro smashed the keys, dug a hole in the ground, and buried the fragments. As they write,[22] "Eighty-two years ago, American volunteers closed the door of their homes with similar keys and began a long journey to fight fascism.

Many never returned. Their broken bodies lay in unknown graves throughout Spain. For many years, we have excavated battlefields and exhumed victims of war and political violence. But this time we set out to inhume, to 'incavate' . . . . In contemporary war, people and things are broken into pieces, then mixed up, then swallowed by the earth."

In their performative and visual work Gonzáles-Ruibal and Palomares make a powerful statement: in contemporary war, people and things are broken into pieces, then mixed up, then swallowed by the earth. Into that, Alfredo and Álvaro mix implicit references to depositional offerings of premodern (perhaps Iron Age) cultures of objects and bodies, of funerals, and of disabled weapons and personal belongings. Unstable connections float ghost-like among long-dead American volunteers, mid-twentieth-century Spanish battlefields, late nineteenth-century (ever anonymous) San Franciscan key holders, and contemporary Iberian archaeologists. The (untitled) work that results is both intellectual and aesthetic, archaeological and artistic, historic and contemporary. Provocatively, it is none of those things and yet much more.

Figure 1.5. *Ineligible* project: Kit number 7.

When Valter Ventura opened Kit number 7, he found the fragments of a leather shoe (Figure 1.5). Ventura produced a series of differing works, all graphic: a poster that combines six hundred prints from the Cross-Domain Forensic Shoeprint Matching index with texts about the Sit-Lie Ordinance of San Francisco (a 2010 ballot measure allowing police to fine or jail people lying on sidewalks during the day); a poster that combines circular cut-outs from a historic map of San Francisco with a list of three dozen chronologically ordered events (including the 1867 street begging ban, the 1967 Summer of Love, and the first issuance of marriage licenses in the city to same-sex couples in 2004), each of which references important San Francisco political or social moments; a poster that collages newspaper clippings (with carefully selected lines of blacked out redaction) about homelessness,

aging, and gentrification in San Francisco; and, a final piece of work, ten original photographs in which Ventura reprinted tightly cropped and blurred images (from the archives of the Oakland Museum of California) of the lower legs and boots of police officers from the 1934 Bloody Thursday riots (Figure 1.6).

In his commentary, Ventura (2019) writes that images have characters both scientific and judiciary, and of how, in the works he made for *Ineligible*, he had dissected elements of the history of San Francisco "like pieces of a puzzle, and found that the city has a long tradition of counter-power, rebellion and struggle; but simultaneously [it] contains drastic asymmetries between the wealth and poverty of its inhabitants." Ventura defines what is ineligible in terms of a human footprint (footprint as archaeological, political, and social document), and he offers that his purpose is to create a tension between the notions of law and justice, between equality and solidarity, between protection and force.

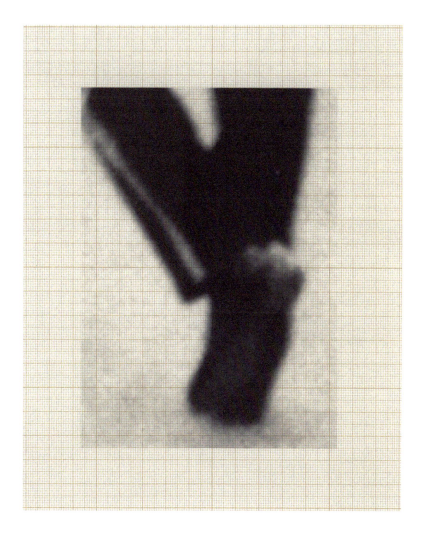

Figure 1.6. *Ineligible* project: untitled work by Valter Ventura.

CONCLUSION

The two examples of work in the *Ineligible* project briefly presented above provide a quick glimpse into the territories opened up by art/archaeology. Other works from the 2020 Santo Tirso exhibition move in similarly unregulated directions, to a variety of distances, and grapple with other social and political issues: for example, nineteenth-century displacements of native communities in North America; homelessness in twenty-first-century San Francisco; ocean pollution and plastics; and migration crises on the border between Mexico and the United States. Media and formats of works created and presented at the Santo Tirso exhibition range from still photography to video, from performance to mixed-media construction, from acoustic composition to vinyl window appliqué. Some works wander off on their own, seemingly without compass or consistent velocity; others follow individual, unplanned trajectories into expanses that broaden into an unbroken distance. Without doubt, we may never see or hear from some work that has been made, that is now being made, and that will be made in the next month or next year. I can report that some of the kits I sent out have disappeared, perhaps having found other lives in some other places.

From the *Ineligible* work created, therefore, emerge unpredicted senses of released freedoms in thought and in action, and in many ways, my attempts in this chapter (through the rhetoric of standard academic written and logical presentation) to describe the project and the work produced have failed completely to match the languages spoken by individual works or to provide any of the stimulation that face-to-face encounters provide. None of the words I offer here have the capacity or essence to represent the sequences of action and musing that swirled around the minds, hands, and materials of individual creators as they made their work. My conclusion, thus, finds its own shape from these realizations: art/archaeology is not a call for more texts and reviews, or for more written treatises about what could happen, or how new work might resonate with what has come before. Art/archaeology is the call to do, to make, to create, to explore, to experiment. *Ineligible* is one of the vibrant experiments that takes up that call.

NOTES

1   A video of the smashing is available on Vimeo, https://vimeo.com/334554728/; the Facebook page associated with this project is https://www.facebook.com/Releasing-the-Amphora-347052559341222/ (accessed 29 February 2020).

2 The reader may wonder if my writing of this chapter shows that I did have an academic intention: to publish within the established career and employment standards of my work. With full honesty, I did not intend to publish any academic article, book chapter, or other traditional report about what I gradually started to call 'the amphora project.' At the time of the amphora destruction, I had not been invited to contribute to this book, and I am writing about the amphora in my contribution only because I thought that it would be a good hook to pull the reader into a text that the editors invited me to write.

3 Bailey et al. 2020a, 2020b.

4 Bailey 2017a, 2017b.

5 Bailey 2014a.

6 A more free-ranging attempt to define art/archaeology is available through https://www.artarchaeologies.com/about (accessed 29 February 2020).

7 See Bailey (2023) for one attempt to explore a political issue.

8 Bailey 2020a, 2020b.

9 Bailey 2013.

10 Bailey 2014b.

11 Bailey 2018b.

12 Bailey and Simpkin 2015.

13 Bailey 2018a.

14 Interested readers will find online videos of both the drilling, https://vimeo.com/318865363/, and the cutting, https://vimeo.com/315603527/ (accessed 29 February 2020). A separate conversation could review the strong objections (in the end, refusal) of the publisher of the book (Oxford University Press) to introduce cuts. In reality, it would only have been presentations of cuts—provided by laying out several chapters of the book with white discs of emptiness on specially selected pages.

15 Bailey et al. 2020a, 2020b. I am indebted to Dr Sara Navarro, Dr Tania Pereira, Dr Álvaro Moreira, and the rest of the team at the museum for their willingness to experiment with art and archaeology in an open-minded and creative way.

16 Bailey 2020c.

17 https://tjpa.org/project/archaeology (accessed 29 February 2020).

18 Many thanks to students in Anthropology 699 who were the engine for *Ineligible*: Kimberly Aleman, Haley Amoroso, Miriam Cetina-Antonio, Valerie Contreras, Lexi Hamilton, John Karr, Jessica Salgado, and Dana Yong.

19 I shipped an additional twenty-five assemblages (later this term was abandoned; 'kits' took its place) to Dr Sara Navarro, a post-doctoral art/archaeologist at the Centro de Investigação e de Estudos em Belas-artes at the University of Lisbon in Portugal. Dr Navarro presented those assemblages to students in her sculpture class and invited them to make work if they desired. Many students decided to do so.

20 Important support for shipping came from the award of a Marcus Research Grant from the College of Liberal and Creative Arts at San Francisco State University; all of the members of the *Ineligible* team are grateful to this grant program and to the support that they provide to San Francisco State University.

21 Fuller details about Alfredo and Álvaro's, as well as of Valter's work, and of all the other work that was installed in the *Ineligible* exhibition in Santo Tirso are available in the catalog for the Portuguese exhibition, published by the International Museum for Contemporary Sculpture (Bailey et al. 2020a). Descriptions of and discussions about other work made, though not exhibited in Santo Tirso, are accessible at http://www.artarchaeologies.com.

22 Gonzáles-Ruibal and Palomares 2019.

BIBLIOGRAPHY

Bailey, Doug (2013), "Cutting the Earth / Cutting the Body," in: Alfredo Gonzáles-Ruibal, ed., *Reclaiming Archaeology: Beyond the Tropes of Modernity*, pp. 337–45, London (Routledge).

——— (2014a), "Art // Archaeology // Art: Letting-Go Beyond," in: Ian A. Russell and Andrew Cochrane, eds., *Art and Archaeology: Collaborations, Conversations, Criticisms*, pp. 231–50, New York (Springer-Kluwer).

——— (2014b), "Which Ruins Do We Valorize? A New Visual Calibration for the Balkan Past," in: Bjørnar Olsen and Þóra Pétursdóttir, eds., *Ruin Memories: Materiality, Aesthetics and the Archaeology of the Recent Past*, pp. 215–29, London (Routledge).

——— (2017a), Art/Archaeology: What Value Artistic-Archaeological Collaboration? *Journal of Contemporary Archaeology* 4(2): 246–56.

—— (2017b), Disarticulate—Repurpose—Disrupt: Art/Archaeology, *Cambridge Archaeological Journal* 27(4): 691–701.

—— (2018a), *Breaking the Surface: An Art/Archaeology of Prehistoric Architecture*, Oxford (Oxford University Press).

—— (2018b), "The Uexküll Calibration: Chronology and Critical Flicker Fusion Frequency," in: Stella Souvatzi, Adnan Baysal, and Emma L. Baysal, eds., *Time and History in Prehistory*, pp. 31–41, London (Routledge).

—— (2020a), "Releasing the Visual Archive: On the Ethics of Destruction," in: Þóra Pétursdóttir, Bjørnar Olsen, Mats Burström, and Caitlin DeSilvey, eds., *After Discourse: Things, Affects, Ethics*, London (Routledge), pp. 232–56.

—— (2020b), "Releasing the Archive," in: Doug Bailey, Sara Navarro, and Álvaro Moreira, eds., *Creative (un)makings: Disruptions in Art/Archaeology,* Santo Tirso (International Museum of Contemporary Sculpture), pp. 80–91.

—— (2020c), "Art/archaeology: The *Ineligible* project," in: Doug Bailey, Sara Navarro, and Álvaro Moreira, eds., *Ineligible: A Disruption of Artefacts and Artistic Practice of Art,* Santo Tirso (International Museum of Contemporary Sculpture), pp. 13–28.

—— (2023), "The Syracuse Amphora Project: On Violence Against Artifacts," in: Christopher Watts and Carl Knappett, eds. *Ancient Art Revisited: Global Perspectives from Archaeology and Art History*, pp. 112-24, New York (Routledge).

Bailey, Doug, Sara Navarro, and Álvaro Moreira, eds. (2020a), *Creative (un)makings: Disruptions in Art/Archaeology,* Santo Tirso (International Museum of Contemporary Sculpture).

—— (2020b), *Ineligible: A Disruption of Artefacts and Artistic Practice,* Santo Tirso (International Museum of Contemporary Sculpture).

Bailey, Doug and Melanie Simpkin (2015), "Eleven Minutes and Forty Seconds in the Neolithic: Underneath Archaeological Time," in: Ruth M. Van Dyke and Reinhard Bernbeck, eds., *Subjects and Narratives in Archaeology*, pp. 187–213, Boulder (University Press of Colorado).

Gonzáles-Ruibal, Alfredo and Álvaro M. Palomares (2019), Unpublished Correspondence with Doug Bailey and Sara Navarro, *Ineligible* project archive.

Ventura, Valter (2019), Unpublished correspondence with Doug Bailey and Sara Navarro, *Ineligible* project archive.

INDEX